POWERSCORE®
LSAT®
READING COMPREHENSION
BIBLE

A Comprehensive System for Attacking the
Reading Comprehension Section of the LSAT

POWERSCORE

BY BARBRI

Published by
PowerScore LLC
12222 Merit Drive
Suite 1340
Dallas, TX 75251

Authors: David M. Killoran and Jon M. Denning

Special thanks to: Steven G. Stein

Printed in the United States of America
12 15 20 22

ISBN: 978-0-99129-926-3

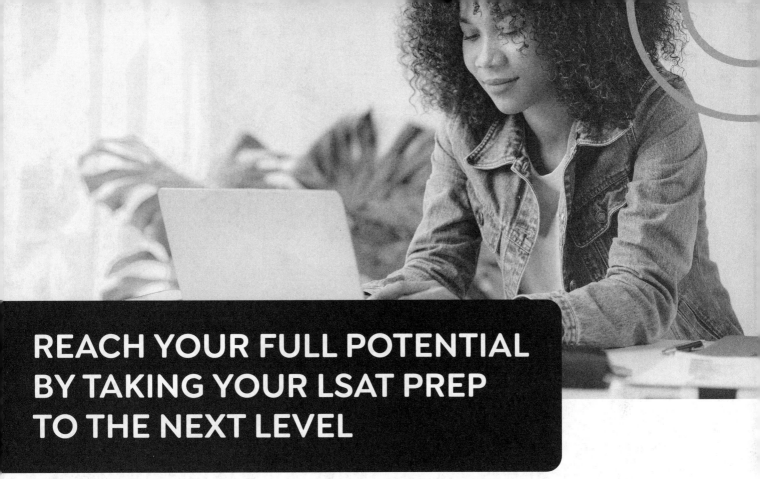

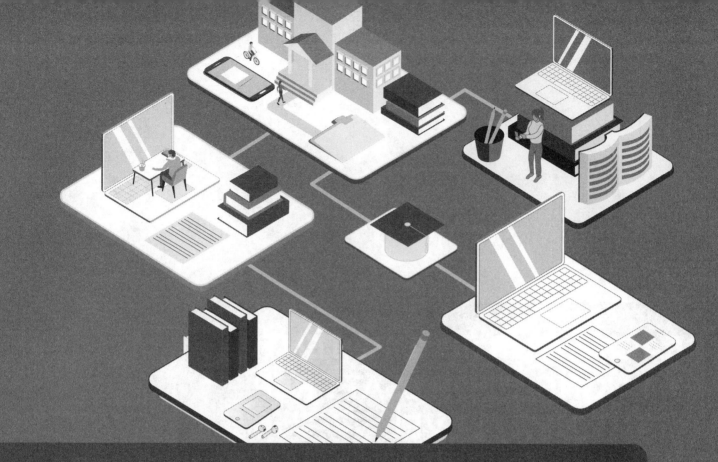

IT'S YOUR LEGAL EDUCATION JOURNEY. WE'RE YOUR TRUSTED GUIDE.

Get the most out of every step with help from BARBRI Global.

From the hard work of getting accepted and excelling in law school to walking into your bar exam fully confident in your preparation, you want to be sure you're always putting your best foot forward on your journey to a bright legal future. To stay on track, you'll want to take advantage of all the proven assistance BARBRI Global offers with a complete set of tools designed to help you to achieve your legal dreams.

 Get pre-law guidance and assistance with PowerScore and Law Preview

 West Academic arms you with casebooks, textbooks and online study aids throughout your law school tenure

 BARBRI Bar Prep is the global leader, and gives you the confidence and training you need to master the bar exam

Our mission is to make legal professionals better. To make your journey better. And it starts here, with BARBRI Global.

TAKE THE FIRST STEP TOWARD THE TOP OF THE CLASS

The Law Preview Law School Prep Course is the ultimate course for law school success. With Law Preview, you'll create a 1L game plan that gets you ahead of the competition and allows you to enter law school with the skills and confidence you need to succeed—starting on day one.

Through a series of lectures from the nation's top law professors, you'll navigate core 1L material, learn exam-taking strategies, build academic skills, and more—all in an interactive, engaging format—and all before your first day of law school.

- 48 hours of in-depth learning
- Seven top law professors
- One chance to excel

"I received all As my first semester and am ranked #1 in my class. Law Preview gave me the right mindset entering law school, and I feel the class was a big part of my success. Not only did it help me succeed grades-wise, but the class also gave me a sense of excitement to start law school."

Sean C.,
University of Houston Law Center

ENROLL TODAY!

lawpreview.com

CONTENTS

CHAPTER ONE: INTRODUCTION

CHAPTER TWO: THE BASICS OF READING COMPREHENSION

CHAPTER THREE: WHAT TO READ FOR—VIEWSTAMP

CHAPTER FOUR: PASSAGE ELEMENTS AND FORMATIONS

CHAPTER FIVE: TRACKING INFORMATION

CHAPTER SIX: THE QUESTIONS AND ANSWERS

CHAPTER SEVEN: PUTTING IT ALL TOGETHER

CHAPTER EIGHT: COMPARATIVE READING PASSAGES

CHAPTER NINE: COMMON PASSAGE THEMES

CHAPTER TEN: SECTION STRATEGY AND MANAGEMENT

READING COMPREHENSION PASSAGE RECHALLENGE

APPENDIX

GLOSSARY

About PowerScore

PowerScore is one of the world's most respected test preparation companies. Founded in 1997, PowerScore offers LSAT, GMAT, GRE, SAT, and ACT preparation classes in over 150 locations in the U.S. and abroad. Preparation options include In Person courses, Accelerated courses, Live Online courses, and On Demand courses, as well as both In Person and Live Online private tutoring. For more information, please visit our website at powerscore.com or call us at (800) 545-1750.

For supplemental information about this book, visit the *Reading Comprehension Bible* website at powerscore.com/rcbible.

About the Authors

Dave Killoran, a graduate of Duke University, is an expert in test preparation with over 25 years of teaching experience and a 99th percentile score on an LSAC-administered LSAT. In addition to having written PowerScore's legendary LSAT Bible Series, and many other popular publications, Dave has overseen the preparation of thousands of students and founded two national LSAT preparation companies. Find him on Twitter at http://twitter.com/DaveKilloran or on the PowerScore LSAT Forum at http://forum.powerscore.com.

Jon Denning, a graduate of the Georgia Institute of Technology, oversees product creation and instructor training for all of the exam services PowerScore offers. He is also a Senior Instructor with 99th percentile scores on the LSAT, GMAT, GRE, SAT, and ACT, and for the past 15 years has assisted thousands of students in the college, graduate, and law school admissions processes.

Chapter One:
Introduction

Chapter One: Introduction

Introduction

Welcome to the *PowerScore LSAT Reading Comprehension Bible*! We congratulate you on your savvy purchase—you now own the most advanced book ever published for LSAT Reading Comprehension. The purpose of this book is to provide you with a powerful and comprehensive system for attacking the Reading Comprehension section of the Law School Admission Test (LSAT). By carefully studying and correctly applying the techniques we employ, we are certain that you will increase your Reading Comprehension score.

In an effort to clearly explain the fundamental principles of the Reading Comprehension section, this book contains substantial discussions of how to deconstruct the passages as you read, how to identify and attack the questions, and how to successfully avoid the traps set by the test makers. In doing so, we recommend techniques and approaches that have been tested in our live LSAT preparation classes, through individual tutoring, and on the LSAT itself. We feel the use of real Reading Comprehension passages is essential to your success on the LSAT, and no LSAT passage in this book has been modified from its original form.

In order to effectively and efficiently apply our methods, we strongly recommend that you:

- Carefully read and re-read each of the concept discussions;

- Look at the explanation for the correct answer choice as well as the explanations for the incorrect answer choices once you have finished each question or example;

- Closely examine each problem and determine which elements led to the correct answer, and then study the analyses provided in the book and check them against your own work;

- Track every question that you miss or that you struggle with, and record each instance of difficulty in a performance tracker (see the Study Plans referenced on page 6 for more information).

By doing so, you will greatly increase your chances of quickly recognizing and reacting to key RC elements and ultimately maximizing your score.

If you are looking to further improve your LSAT score, we also recommend that you pick up a copy of the renowned PowerScore LSAT Logical Reasoning Bible and LSAT Logic Games Bible. The Logical Reasoning Bible contains our system for attacking the Logical Reasoning section of the LSAT, and the Logic Games Bible explains our methodology for attacking the Analytical Reasoning section. Both books are available through our website at powerscore.com.

This book also contains a variety of drills and exercises that supplement the discussion of techniques and question analyses. The drills help strengthen specific skills that are critical for LSAT excellence; for this reason they are as important as the LSAT questions themselves. In the answer keys to these drills we will often introduce and discuss important LSAT points, so we strongly advise you to read through all of the explanations even if you answered the problem correctly.

The last chapter of this book is an extensive analysis of overall section strategy and time management. The preceding chapters also address timing and how to go faster, but if you struggle with time management you can read the final chapter at any point in your studies (and if you cannot finish the entire book prior to your test, be sure to at least read the last chapter before the LSAT). That chapter also contains a number of targeted exercises to help you identify and remedy any specific issues still giving you trouble, so again feel free to refer to it as needed if difficulties arise.

At the end of this book there is also a complete quick-reference answer key for all of the questions, including a unique reverse lookup that lists all passages and passage sets used in this book sorted by the LSAT administration date and PrepTest number. This is helpful if you are trying to schedule practice tests and wish to avoid any overlap.

How LSAT Studying is Different From "Regular" Studying

Studying for the LSAT is different from studying for a history or chemistry test. In those disciplines, when you learn a fact or formula there is often a direct and immediate increase in your score on the exam. However, the LSAT is not a fact-based test; it is a test of reasoning processes, so the correlation between learning an idea and seeing an instantaneous score improvement is not as strong.

In a sense, it is like learning to drive a car: even after you learn the rules of the road and the mechanics of the vehicle, the first several times you attempt to drive you are probably not a good driver at all. Nothing feels familiar or comes easily, and you are more likely a menace on the road than anything else (we certainly were!). But with time and proper practice—and a healthy dose of patience—you eventually reach a state of comfort, possibly even expertise, so that now getting behind the wheel is entirely natural and intuitive. Learning to routinely beat the LSAT is no different!

Many of the tools we talk about in this book are fundamental to the LSAT, but they take time to integrate into how you approach the test, so at first they may seem slow and unwieldy. It will get better! For the time being, focus more on learning the ideas, and less on how they impact your practice tests results. Once you have completed most of the book, you should shift into a practice testing mode that will allow you to work with the techniques and to make them second nature. This practice will cement the ideas and provide the greatest scoring impact.

A Note About Timing

As will be discussed in more detail later, time pressure is one of the defining challenges of taking the LSAT. Thus, when studying LSAT questions, there can be an overwhelming urge to focus on the clock. But for now you must resist that impulse. When you are first learning new concepts, take your time to understand what is being said and focus on the mechanics of how to apply the techniques presented. Don't worry about your pace! Once you have internalized the concepts and methodology, then you can start slowly working on timing as an element of your approach. The old adage about learning to walk before you can run applies perfectly to LSAT preparation, so concentrate more on how key strategies and ideas work than on your initial speed.

Additional Resources

This book has been carefully designed to explain the concepts behind the Reading Comprehension section, and we are confident you will increase your score by thoroughly studying and correctly applying the system explained herein. Because new LSATs are administered regularly, we always strive to present the most accurate, up-to-date, and helpful information available. Consequently, *Reading Comprehension Bible* students have access to a variety of resources to help with their preparation:

1. **The *Reading Comprehension Bible* book site**. This free online resource area offers:

   - Book supplements including additional reading and relevant videos.

   - All updates to the current edition.

   - *LSAT Bible* study plans based on how much time you have available to prepare, and in conjunction with the other LSAT Bibles.

   - An LSAT Prep Mentality guide that outlines critical components for establishing an ideal mindset.

   The exclusive *LSAT Reading Comprehension Bible* online area can be accessed at:

    powerscore.com/lsatprep

Once there, create an account and then use the code on the inside front cover of this book to gain access.

2. **The PowerScore LSAT Discussion Forum**, where you can talk to the authors of this book and ask questions about the material:

 forum.powerscore.com

Forum users ask about all aspects of the LSAT, including test mentality, the best study plans, how to solve certain types of questions, and how to go faster on the LSAT.

Staffed regularly by our LSAT instructors, the Forum offers thousands of searchable answers to student inquiries, including many detailed explanations of individual LSAT questions, and additional concept and strategy discussions.

3. And please connect with us directly via **Twitter** and **our PodCast**:

 @DaveKilloran

 @JonMDenning

 powerscore.com/lsat/podcast

We frequently post about the LSAT and developments with the test, and provide breaking news on test days and score releases.

We are happy to assist you in your LSAT preparation as much as possible, and we look forward to hearing from you!

Now that we've discussed some of the prep resources available to you, let's talk about the LSAT itself.

A Brief Overview of the LSAT ▬▬▬▬

The Law School Admission Test is a standardized exam administered multiple times each year and often required for admission to American Bar Association-approved law schools. According to LSAC, the producers of the test, the LSAT is designed "to measure skills that are considered essential for success in law school: the reading and comprehension of complex texts with accuracy and insight; the organization and management of information and the ability to draw reasonable inferences from it; the ability to think critically; and the analysis and evaluation of the reasoning and arguments of others."

The LSAT consists of the following four multiple-choice sections:

1 Section of Logical Reasoning	short prompts, 24-26 total questions per section
1 Section of Reading Comprehension	3 long reading passages, 2 short comparative reading passages, 26-28 total questions
1 Section of Analytical Reasoning	4 logic games, 22-24 total questions
1 Experimental Section	one of the above three section types

You are given 35 minutes to complete each section. The experimental section is unscored and is not returned to the test taker. An optional break of 10 minutes is given between the 2nd and 3rd sections.

The Logical Reasoning Section

The Logical Reasoning Section is composed of approximately 24 to 26 short prompts. Every short argument is followed by a question such as: "Which one of the following weakens the argument?" "Which one of the following parallels the argument?" or "Which one of the following must be true according to the argument?"

The key to this section is time management and an understanding of the reasoning types and question types that frequently appear.

The Analytical Reasoning Section

This section, also known as Logic Games, is probably the most difficult for students taking the LSAT for the first time. The section consists of four games or puzzles, each followed by a series of five to eight questions. The questions are designed to test your ability to evaluate a set of relationships and to make inferences about those relationships.

To perform well on this section you must understand the types of games that frequently appear and develop the ability to properly diagram the rules and make inferences.

The Reading Comprehension Section

This section is composed of three long, single reading passages, each approximately 450 words in length, and a paired set of two shorter comparative reading passages. The passage topics are drawn from a variety of subjects, and each passage is followed by a series of five to eight questions that ask you to determine viewpoints in the passage, analyze organizational traits, evaluate specific sections of the passage, or compare facets of two different passages.

The Experimental Section

Each LSAT contains one undesignated experimental section which does not count towards your score. The experimental can be any of the three section types previously described, and the purpose of the section is to test and evaluate questions that will be used on *future* LSATs. By pretesting questions before their use in a scored section, the experimental section helps the makers of the test determine the test scale.

LSAT Writing

For many years the writing section was administered before the LSAT, and then later after the LSAT. Now known as "LSAT Writing," the section is administered separately from the test.

A 35-minute writing section is administered separately from the LSAT, using secure online proctoring software. LSAT Writing is not scored, but law schools will have access to a candidate's three most recent samples.

In LSAT Writing, you are asked to write a short essay that defends one of two possible courses of action. There is no correct or incorrect answer, and your goal is to write the most coherent essay possible. Essays are typed, and you have access to basic word processing tools such as spell check, and cut, copy, and paste.

The LSAT Scoring Scale

Each administered LSAT contains approximately 75 scored questions, and each LSAT score is based on the total number of questions a test taker correctly answers, a total known as the raw score. After the raw score is determined, a unique Score Conversion Chart is used for each LSAT to convert the raw score into a scaled LSAT score. Since June 1991, the LSAT has utilized a 120 to 180 scoring scale, with 120 being the lowest possible score and 180 being the highest possible score. Notably, this 120 to 180 scale is just a renumbered version of the 200 to 800 scale most test takers are familiar with from the SAT and GMAT. Just drop the "1" and add a "0" to the 120 and 180.

Although the number of questions per test is relatively constant, the overall logical difficulty of each test varies. This is not surprising since the test is made by humans, and there is no precise way to completely predetermine logical difficulty. To account for variances in test "toughness," the test makers adjust the Scoring Conversion Chart for each LSAT in order to make similar LSAT scores from different tests mean the same thing. For example, the LSAT given in June may be logically more difficult than the LSAT given in December, but by making the June LSAT scale "looser" than the December scale, a 160 on each test would represent the same level of performance. The looser scale would translate into needing to answer fewer questions correctly to achieve that 160 (and thus also allowing more questions to be missed). Perhaps, to achieve a 160 on the "harder" June LSAT would require answering only 54 questions correctly (meaning one could miss 21 questions on a 75 question test). For the "easier" December LSAT, to achieve a 160 perhaps one would have to answer 56 questions correctly (allowing only 19 questions missed on a 75 question test).

This scale adjustment, known as equating, is extremely important to law school admissions offices around the country. Imagine the difficulties that would be posed by unequated tests: admissions officers would have to not only examine individual LSAT scores, but also take into account which LSAT each score came from. This would present an information nightmare.

The LSAT Percentile Table

Since the LSAT has 61 possible scores, why didn't the test makers change the scale to 0 to 60? Probably for merciful reasons. How would you tell your friends that you scored a 3 on the LSAT? 123 sounds so much better.

It is important not to lose sight of what LSAT scaled scores actually represent. The 120 to 180 test scale contains 61 different possible scores. Each score places a student in a certain relative position compared to other test takers. These relative positions are represented through a percentile that correlates to each score. The percentile indicates where the test taker ranks in the overall pool of test takers. For example, a score of 166 represents the 92nd percentile, meaning a student with a score of 166 scored better than 92 percent of the people who have taken the test in the last three years. The percentile is critical since it is a true indicator of your positioning relative to other test takers, and thus law school applicants.

Charting out the entire percentage table yields a rough "bell curve." The number of test takers in the 120s and 170s is very low (only 2.4% of all test takers receive a score in the 170s), and most test takers are bunched in the middle, comprising the "top" of the bell. In fact, approximately 40% of all test takers score between 145 and 155 inclusive, and about 65% of all test takers score between 140 and 160 inclusive.

There is no penalty for answering incorrectly on the LSAT. Therefore, you should guess on any questions you cannot complete.

The median score on the LSAT scale is approximately 153. The median, or middle score, is the score at which approximately 50% of test takers have a lower score and 50% of test takers have a higher score. Typically, to achieve a score of 153, you must answer between 43 and 46 questions correctly from a total of approximately 75-76 questions. In other words, to achieve a score that is perfectly average, you can typically miss between 29 and 33 questions. To obtain a score of 170 (which is uniformly considered an excellent score), you can typically miss between 6 and 10 questions. Thus, it is important to remember that you don't have to answer every question correctly in order to receive an excellent LSAT score. There is room for error, and accordingly you should never let any single question occupy an inordinate amount of your time.

The Digital LSAT

As opposed to the traditional paper-and-pencil format used by many other tests, the LSAT is administered digitally, either remotely on your own computer, or at select, in-person locations on a provided tablet. The digital interface allows for certain advantages such as automated section timing with a visible countdown timer, and a navigation bar that shows your progress through the section and allows for the flagging of individual questions. On the next page there is a graphic showing how a typical RC passage might appear alongside one of its questions, with the most relevant parts of the interface labelled. We will talk about these elements later in the book, but as an overview they include:

- Buttons for Directions, Text Size, Line Spacing, and Screen Brightness;

- An onscreen timer that counts down from the initial allotted time to 0, and provides a warning when 5 minutes remain;

- The choice of underlining text, or highlighting using any of three colors: yellow, pink, or orange. Plus, an eraser to remove any underlining or highlighting;

- Lettered bubbles to select each answer choice, as well as an "eye" icon to grey out the answer and strike through its letter bubble;

- A flag for each question that allows you to mark selected problems for further review;

- A navigation bar across the bottom of the screen that shows the question you are currently on, which questions have been answered and which remain to be answered, as well as which questions have been flagged.

To interact with and control the on-screen content, you simply use a mouse when testing remotely, or a finger or provided stylus at a test center. However, you cannot annotate on the screen in any other fashion aside from the controls above, including freehand writing. In other words, you can't draw on problems, make notes on the screen, or otherwise mark up questions. You are limited to using the annotation tools provided by the test makers. To make any separate notes or diagrams, you must instead use separate scratch paper and a pen or pencil.

Here is a look at LSAC's digital interface, with its key features noted:

Passage Only View Option

Directions | Passage Only View

Underliner

U ✏ ✏ ✏ ✏ ◆ | Aa ‡Ξ | Time Remaining: 29:36

Highlighters   Eraser

Font Size and
Line Spacing

Countdown
Timer

Question
Flagging

For decades, there has been a deep rift between poetry and fiction in the United States, especially in academic settings; graduate writing programs in universities, for example, train students as poets or as writers of fiction, but almost never as both. Both poets and writers of fiction have tended to support this separation, in large part because the current conventional wisdom holds that poetry should be elliptical and lyrical, reflecting inner states and processes of thought or feeling, whereas character and narrative events are the stock-in-trade of fiction.

Certainly it is true that poetry and fiction are distinct genres, but why have specialized education and literary territoriality resulted from this distinction? The answer lies perhaps in a widespread attitude in U.S. culture, which often casts a suspicious eye on the generalist. Those with knowledge and expertise in multiple areas risk charges of dilettantism, as if ability in one field is diluted or compromised by accomplishment in another.

Fortunately, there are signs that the bias against writers who cross generic boundaries is diminishing; several recent writers are known and respected for their work in both genres. One important example of this trend

Scroll Bar

4. The author's attitude toward the deep rift between poetry and fiction in the U.S. can be most accurately be described as one of

(A) perplexity as to what could have led to the development of such a rift

(B) astonishment that academics have overlooked the existence of the rift

(C) ambivalence toward the effect the rift has had on U.S. literature

(D) pessimism regarding the possibility that the rift can be overcome

(E) disapproval of attitudes and presuppositions underlying the rift

Answer Choices

Answer
Markouts

Section and Passage Navigation Bar

Question Navigation

For students used to paper-and-pencil exams, the separation of the passage sets and the scratch paper can present a challenge, since your freehand notes and annotations are no longer applied directly to the passage text. This situation can initially be disconcerting, but as you practice you will find that it becomes less of a difficulty.

In your practice (especially with paper tests or prep materials), **you should use *separate* scratch paper at all times in order to prepare for the actual testing environment**, and refrain from writing notes directly on the test content itself.

LSAC provides two free, official tests online (lsac.org/lsat/prep/lawhub) that are delivered via their digital interface, and we strongly encourage you to spend as much time as possible practicing within the digital environment. Simply put, you must be extremely familiar with the platform before test day if you want to perform your best!

As we progress through this book we will further discuss aspects of the digital interface as well as diagramming strategies, so keep an eye out for those discussions. Now, with some of the basics of the LSAT out of the way, let's move on to discussing Reading Comprehension questions in detail!

Our Testing & Analytics package offers every released LSAT in digital form. It is the ideal way to prepare for this unique testing experience!

Chapter Two:
The Basics
of Reading
Comprehension

Chapter Two: The Basics of Reading Comprehension

The Reading Comprehension Section

The focus of this book is the Reading Comprehension section of the LSAT, where you will encounter four passage sets with a total of 26 to 28 questions. Since you have thirty-five minutes to complete the section, you have an *average* of eight minutes and forty-five seconds to complete each passage set. Of course, the amount of time you spend on each set will vary with the complexity of the passage(s), the difficulty of the questions, and the total number of questions presented. Thus, there will be instances where you move more quickly through a passage set (whether because it is easier or contains fewer questions) and other occasions where a passage takes longer than average to complete. So you should approach Reading Comprehension expecting to move at different speeds depending on what you encounter, and a key principle of this section is that some passages will allow you to gain time that can then be expended on other, more challenging passages. Since the time constraint is a major obstacle for nearly all students, as we progress through this book we will discuss time management as well as time-saving techniques that you can learn to successfully apply.

On average, you have 8 minutes and 45 seconds to complete each passage set. However, this time will vary per passage depending on difficulty and question counts.

In one sense, moving through the section has a "roller coaster" aspect to it, where in some places you move very quickly and in other spots you slow down considerably.

Why Reading Comprehension?

Each section of the LSAT is designed to test abilities central to the study and/or practice of law. The Logical Reasoning sections measure your skills in argumentation and logic. The Logic Games section tests your ability to understand the relationships between different variable sets and the laws which govern their interactions. Reading Comprehension, a task common to most standardized tests, provides a test of skills particularly important to both law students and attorneys: law students are required to read significant portions of dense text throughout their legal studies, and lawyers must often be ready to do the same in their normal course of business; given that the misreading of a contract or legal judgment could lead to disastrous results for a lawyer's clients (not to mention the lawyer), it should not be surprising that Reading Comprehension is an integral part of the Law School Admission Test.

The Section Directions

Let's start at the beginning. Each Reading Comprehension section is prefaced by the following directions:

> "Each set of questions in this section is based on a single passage or a pair of passages. The questions are to be answered on the basis of what is **stated** or **implied** in the passage or pair of passages. For some questions, more than one of the choices could conceivably answer the question. However, you are to choose the **best** answer; that is, choose the response that most accurately and completely answers the question."

Because these directions precede every Reading Comprehension section, you should familiarize yourself with them now. Once the LSAT begins, *never* waste time reading the directions for any section.

Let us examine these directions more closely. Consider the following sentence: "The questions are to be answered on the basis of what is **stated** or **implied** in the passage or pair of passages." Thus, the test makers indicate that you are to use the statements of the author of the passage to prove and disprove answer choices. You do not need to bring in additional information aside from the typical ideas that the average American or Canadian would be expected to believe on the basis of generally known and accepted facts. For example, you would be expected to understand the *basics* of how the weather works, or how supply and demand works, but not the specifics of either. Please note that this does not mean that the LSAT cannot set up scenarios where they discuss ideas that are extreme or outside the bounds of common knowledge, such as a passage about a difficult scientific or legal concept. The test makers can and do discuss complex or obscure ideas; in these cases, however, they give you context for the situation by providing all of the necessary additional, explanatory information.

The other part of the directions that is interesting is the discussion of the answer choices: "For some questions, more than one of the choices could conceivably answer the question. However, you are to choose the **best** answer; that is, the response that most accurately and completely answers the question." By stating up front that more than one answer choice could suffice to answer the question, the makers of the test compel you to read every single answer choice before making a selection. If you read only one or two answer choices and then decide you have the correct one, you could end up choosing an answer that has some merit but is not as good as a later option. In fact, one of the test makers' favorite tricks is to place a highly attractive wrong answer choice immediately before the correct answer in the hope that you will pick the wrong choice and then move to the next question without reading any of the other answers.

Remember, the LSAT is used for admission to US and Canadian law schools, hence the test is geared towards those cultures.

You should read all five answer choices in each question.

What's Really Being Tested?

When you consider the section directions and the nature of the passages, it becomes clear that the exam makers are really testing two basic concepts: your ability to understand what was said and your short-term memory. Neither of those tasks sounds very challenging because, after all, we work with both every single day, so how difficult could these passages be? In practice, however, the difficulty can be quite high, especially because these tasks often involve working with unfamiliar topics under intense time pressure.

In the next chapter we will discuss tools that can be used to make each task easier, but in the meantime take a moment to understand the way in which you are being tested, and how important it is for you to know what was said and to be able to remember where the author said it. Part of the process of preparing for this section is knowing what you need to do, and the earlier you lock on to the concepts that underlie this section, the easier Reading Comprehension will ultimately become for you.

The Two Passage Types

The section directions also state that "Each set of questions in this section is based on a single passage or a pair of passages." Each passage or pair of passages and its accompanying questions are collectively known as a "passage set."

Prior to June 2007, all LSAT Reading Comprehension sections consisted of four long passages, each accompanied by a series of five to eight questions. These passage types, sometimes known as Long (or Single) Passages, are still the predominant passage type on the LSAT.

Starting with the June 2007 LSAT, the test makers replaced one of the four long passage sets with a new element to the test known as Comparative Reading, wherein two passages addressing the same topic are presented, and a set of questions follows. Thus, the four passage sets in each Reading Comprehension section break down as follows:

4 Passage Sets	
3	Long passages. 5-8 questions each.
1	Comparative Reading passage of two shorter passages. 5-8 questions in total. Can appear anywhere in the section.

To locate passages written in the desired style, test makers draw from various sources, which they adapt for use in the Reading Comprehension section. Academic, scientific, and scholarly journals tend to be written in a fairly sophisticated manner, and thus routinely provide materials for the LSAT; past passage sources have included The University of California, Scientific American Library and Johns Hopkins University. Articles are also drawn from publications devoted to the arts, including recent offerings from the American Academy of Arts and Sciences and Poetry in Review Foundation. While the passages are drawn from a wide variety of sources, including newspapers, magazines, books, and journals, they tend to be written in a recognizable, academic style that generally evades simple analysis.

Long passage sets will be the focus through the first several chapters of this book, and Comparative Reading passage sets and the special considerations that follow from their unique structure will be addressed in detail in Chapter Eight. However, one important consideration is to understand that the manner of reading required to succeed on both passage types is the same, and thus our early focus will be on how to properly read and analyze any Reading Comprehension passage.

Passage Topics

Reading Comprehension passages are drawn from a wide variety of disciplines, including science, law, and humanities. Thus, you will typically encounter four passage sets with widely varying topical matter. However, even though passage subject matter differs, most sections are constructed from the same consistent set of topics, as follows:

4 Passage Sets	
1	Law-Related passage
1	Science passage
1	Humanities passage
1	Random passage, typically Humanities

So, even though the exact subject matter of each passage changes from test to test, the typical LSAT contains one Science passage, one Law-Related passage, and one Humanities passage (often with Diversity elements). The remaining passage is usually drawn from a humanities field such as history or economics, but occasionally the passage comes from science or law.

For a typical example, consider the topics from the June 2015 LSAT:

Topic	Subject Matter
Humanities/Diversity	Anthropology and Indigenous Video
Law-Related	Judicial Impartiality and Recusal
Humanities	Responses to Lying and Wrongdoing
Science	Glass Flow and Glass Manufacturing

Please note that the topic of the passage is not necessarily indicative of the level of difficulty. That is, some Science passages are easy, some are difficult. The same goes for Law-Related passages, Humanities passages, etc. In this chapter we will discuss how to attack any type of passage, and we will discuss how the underlying structure of passages can be analyzed regardless of the passage topic. Topic is examined here so that you understand the nature of what you will be reading. In some cases, knowing the topic can help you make informed decisions about the viewpoints that will be presented therein, and in many cases, students perform better on passages that contain subject matter that is familiar to them. And, although our primary analysis will focus on viewpoints and structure, later in this chapter we will examine passages from the most commonly occurring topics as a way to calibrate your test radar to the types of mechanisms and viewpoints put forth by the makers of the test.

Passage Sources and Creation

The LSAT is one of the most unique standardized tests in existence, as is clear to anyone who has ever struggled with a Logic Game, conditional or causal reasoning, or the complex prose presented in the Reading Comprehension section. One characteristic of the test that might not be quite as well known is that each LSAT contains a significant amount of content that the test makers do *not* create on their own: LSAC often relies on other, original sources for material, and then adapts that content to conform to specific LSAT standards. This is true of all five Reading Comprehension passages (the three single passages and two Comparative Reading passages), which are often heavily based on pre-existing academic articles, journal publications, text books, and even lengthy novels. On paper LSATs, the test makers go so far as to list all sources on an Acknowledgements page at the end of each test booklet, so these original sources are available for review and analysis.

The specific sources vary a great deal from test to test, and tend to represent a surprisingly disparate number of publication types and disciplines. Over one two-year period, for example, LSAC adapted material from a paper published by the Princeton University Press, an Ecology textbook, a US Fish and Wildlife Service report, a Scientific American article, and even a 2000+ page book (James P. Draper's excellent *Black Literature Criticism*). This is just a small sample of sources, taken from fewer than two years' worth of LSATs. Clearly, the test makers search far and wide for original, academically-related content as they piece together each exam.

What is perhaps most notable about the selection of sources is not the diversity of the attribution list, but rather the transformative process that takes place from the original text to the test: the test makers never create full passages from the source verbatim. Instead, they "adapt" (their word) the original work to suit the needs and requirements of the LSAT—occasionally paraphrasing the source text, but most often simply distilling a chapter/article/volume down to the roughly 450 words in each passage set. The following examples from just a single test relay the wide variety of publications, topics, and lengths of the LSAT's sources of reading materials:

- Universal Declaration of Human Rights—a largely fact-based summary of David Pitts' 2001 story about the creation of the UDHR in 1948.

- Forgery's aesthetic merits—a presentation of the viewpoint, from an outside perspective, of Alfred Lessing, in an 11-page article.

- Animal communication (Comparative Reading)—there was no source for these two passages. Interestingly, however, the Comparative Reading from the previously-administered LSAT (June 2010) was also about animal communication, specifically regarding honeybees dancing (which these paired passages also mention).

- African American transnationalism/citizenship—a summary of a short article (an excerpt of text, really) from the Organization of American Historians.

A few points to keep in mind as you consider the examples above:

- Most of the passages on each LSAT can be traced back to a pre-existing source. Starting with the source material, the process by which that material is adapted to become an LSAT passage is fairly consistent.

- The test makers are not limited to a 1:1 relationship of source to passage, either. Instead, they occasionally will create multiple passages from a single source (or on a single topic), and have even done so on closely-administered tests. It seems reasonable to conclude from this that once they find a source or topic they appreciate, they are entirely willing to then produce multiple passages related to it (and this has happened in several instances).

- Comparative Reading does not seem to follow the same patterns of sourcing/attribution as the single passages. That is, many Comparative passage sets are created solely by the test makers (no source), while others have a single source from which two passages were written—often with one reflecting the source closely and the other written by the test makers in response—and a few even give a unique source for each passage (for instance, the December 2009 test about computer modeling in climate prediction, and the power of parallel computing).

Which brings us, finally, to the crucial question, "What does all of this mean for the test taker?" That's a good question, and the answer is that understanding the test makers' practices should convey two important benefits.

First, the adaptive process the test makers utilize—distillation of lengthy and complex material into a more generalized, more viewpoint-heavy Reading Comprehension passage—is one a successful test taker must mentally follow as well: when approaching LSAT passages your emphasis should be on big picture elements (main point, tone and attitude, general structure) instead of every detail, and also on the views and viewpoints presented, both the author's and those of other people/groups. Recognizing that this is the *exact* means by which the test makers convert source text into LSAT content should serve as a clear indicator of where your focus must be if you want to perform well in Reading Comprehension on test day.

Second, because LSAC lists the sources for each test, you have the ability to actually track down and read the same text the test makers found valuable enough to repurpose. This provides a significant amount of practice material, the reading of which could be very helpful in developing comfort and familiarity with the diverse variety of publications, topics, and writing styles that you are likely to encounter on the test.

We only make the suggestion about tracking down source material for those who are truly struggling with Reading Comprehension, or who have an inordinate fascination with how the LSAT is made!

Approaching the Passages

2

Every Reading Comprehension passage set contains two separate parts: the passage(s) and the questions. When examining the two parts for the first time, students sometimes wonder about the best *general* strategy for attacking the passages: Should I read the questions first? Should I skim the passage? Should I read just the first and last sentence of each paragraph of the passage? The answer is that your basic strategy should be to:

Read the passage in its entirety and then attack the questions.

We will discuss how to systematically break down each passage shortly.

What this means is you should first read the entire passage with an eye towards capturing the main ideas, viewpoints, tone, and structure of the passage, and then proceed to the questions, answering them in order unless you encounter a question too difficult to answer. Although this may seem like a reasonable, even obvious, approach, we mention it here because there are other approaches (which we will outline later in this book) that we could reasonably attempt in certain specialized situations.

For now though, let us take a moment to discuss some of the various reading approaches that you *might* consider using, but should in general avoid:

1. **DO NOT skim the passage**, then do each question, returning to the passage as needed.

    In theory, it might seem that skimming could add a degree of efficiency, but in practice this is not the case. In fact, this approach actually reflects a fundamental misunderstanding of the nature of the Reading Comprehension section.

    Skimming might be sufficient to absorb lighter materials, such as newspaper or magazine articles, but that is because those types of passages are written with simplicity in mind. A newspaper editor wants readers to know half the story by the time they have read the headline, and magazines put the most attention-grabbing pictures on their covers; these publications are trying to draw you in, to entice you to make a purchase or form a belief. The makers of the LSAT, on the other hand, are well aware that they are dealing with a captive audience; they do not feel any pressure to entertain (as you may have noticed), and thus passages are chosen based on completely different criteria.

    For many, skimming is a natural reaction to a time-constrained test, but unfortunately the test makers are well aware of this tendency—the passages they use are chosen in part because they evade quick and simple analysis. In practice, the time "saved" on the front end by skimming a passage is more than lost on the back end. In answering the questions the skimmer invariably finds the need to go back and re-read, and is often not sufficiently familiar with the passage structure to locate relevant reference points quickly.

Note: In Chapter Ten we will discuss the limited contexts in which skimming is advisable.

2. **DO NOT read just the first and last sentence of each paragraph** of the passage and then attempt each question, returning to the passage as needed.

This type of "super-skimming" is also tempting—the prospect of breezing through the passages quickly picking up the big picture ideas is appealing, after all—but again, LSAT passages unfortunately are not constructed to allow for this technique: this shorthand and ineffective approach is based in part on the common misconception that the main idea of every paragraph appears in the first or last sentence. While this may occasionally hold true, we will see that this is far from guaranteed. After all, the makers of the LSAT are extremely sharp, and certainly familiar with these common, shortcut approaches. So naturally many passages will not follow this general rule—the test makers do not like for passages to fall victim to such a simple, formulaic analysis.

This approach is basically an even more simplistic and fruitless variation of skimming that provides neither substantive knowledge of the information in the passage nor familiarity with the structure sufficient to locate important reference points later on.

3. **DO NOT scan the questions first**, then go to the passage and read it, answering questions as you come upon relevant information.

Like the two methods discussed previously, this approach may have some initial appeal. Advocates claim that a preview of the questions gives readers more direction when approaching the passage—if they know what will be asked, perhaps they can get a sense of what to prioritize when reading the text. Then, proponents argue, students can save time and effort by focusing exclusively on the material pertinent to the questions, and skimming through any content that feels irrelevant or unhelpful.

There are several problems with this approach. For one, because there are between five and eight questions per passage, students are forced to juggle a large amount of disparate information before even starting the passage. Not only does this make retaining the details of the questions challenging, but it also detracts from one's attention when reading the passage. Second, reading the questions first often wastes valuable time, since the typical student who applies this flawed approach will read and consider the questions, read the passage, and then go back and read each question again. This re-reading takes time without yielding any real benefit.

The bottom line is that your reading approach must be maximally effective for all passages. The strategies above, although effective in some limited contexts (again, to be discussed later), do not consistently produce solid results, and thus they should *not* be part of your basic approach to each passage.

Basic Passage Strategy

Having discussed some common practices to avoid, we can now consider the proper way to attack an LSAT passage. The following is the *basic* approach to use, and in subsequent chapters we will expand on these points. So, for now, simply consider this the broad template you should use to attack each passage:

1. At the start of the section, quickly preview the four passage sets, and choose the one you feel most comfortable with from a topic standpoint. If all else is equal, choose the one with the most questions. Usually the first passage is not the most difficult one, so if you like the topic, start there!

In our experience, virtually all high-scoring LSAT takers read the passage before looking at the questions.

2. Always read the passage first. Read for an understanding of structure and detail, viewpoints and themes, and the author's tone. Underline, highlight, or make scratch paper notes as needed to help you understand what is being said (this topic will be discussed at length in Chapter Five).

3. Focus on understanding what is being said in each sentence and paragraph, which means you cannot skim or read so fast the words make little sense. At the end of each paragraph, pause briefly and consider what you have just read, and mentally distill the key points of that paragraph into a quick summary that translates the text into simpler terms. Note too how the paragraphs fit together to create the overall passage structure.

4. After reading the passage, stop for a moment and consider the entirety of the author's message and what you've been told, as well as by whom. You can be explicit in your analysis rather than worrying about "reading between the lines" at this point.

5. As you move to the questions, *generally* expect to complete them in the order given. Plan on returning to the passage when necessary to confirm your answers.

6. If you encounter a question too difficult or confusing to answer, skip it and return to it after completing the other questions in the passage set.

These are the primary steps to a proper approach to the Reading Comprehension section; each step will be discussed in greater detail shortly.

Your Focus While Reading

Have you ever reached the second, or even third paragraph of an article or reading passage and suddenly realized that you had no idea what you had just been reading? Many students have had this uncomfortable experience at some point. How are we able to read with our eyes while our minds are elsewhere? Ironically, it is our familiarity with the act of reading that has allowed many to develop the "skill" to do so without 100% focus. This approach might be fine for the morning newspaper, a favorite magazine, or an email from a friend, but these writings tend to be more simply composed and unaccompanied by difficult questions. LSAT passages, on the other hand, are chosen for their tendency to elude this type of unfocused approach. Faced with this type of reading, many people "zone out" and lose concentration. Thus, your state of mind when approaching these passages is extremely important.

Giving yourself the simple instruction, "read the passage," allows your mind too much free rein to wander as your eyes gloss over the words. Instead, you should take a more active approach, breaking down the passage as you go, creating something of a running translation, and effectively mentally outlining the passage, as we will discuss further in the coming pages.

Yes, it can be difficult to focus for long stretches of time, but you must train yourself through practice to keep your concentration at as high a level as possible. This last point is key: you must regularly practice a focused attack when you are reading to ensure an optimal performance.

LSAT reading is unlike the reading most people engage in on a day-to-day basis. For example, newspapers and magazines, and even most novels, are written with an eye towards presenting the material in the clearest and most interesting fashion possible. LSAT Reading Comprehension passages, on the other hand, are not written in this manner. They are often written in an academic style that is, at times, intentionally dense and complex.

When starting a section, keep the following mentality tips in mind:

- Channel any nervous energy into intensity.

- Enjoy reading the passages—make them into a game or learning exercise. And regularly remind yourself that you *do* enjoy it (even if it feels a bit contrived).

- If you lose focus, immediately pause, take a deep breath, refocus, and then return more intently to the task at hand.

- Read aggressively, not passively! Actively engage the material and think about the consequences of what you are reading. The passage was written for a reason, what is it?

Many passages in the Reading Comprehension section discuss conflicts between different viewpoints, and this makes the reading inherently more interesting. Getting involved in the argument will make the passage more enjoyable for you and will also allow you to focus more clearly on the material.

We will talk more on the following pages about the mentality described above, but note that each of these recommendations applies not just to the LSAT, but to your non-LSAT reading behavior as well! To fully develop and internalize this process, we strongly encourage you to become a routine daily reader of all manner of academic text—whether online or hardcopy—such as articles and content found in The Economist, National Geographic, Wired, Scientific American, The Wall Street Journal, and any other sources of reasonably dense passages. Make it a habit to scrutinize at least one or two articles daily, approaching them exactly as you would an LSAT passage, and you'll find your Reading Comprehension performance naturally improves as a result!

Finally, that last bullet is particularly critical, as it introduces a technique at the heart of any successful reading performance: Active Reading. In fact, this concept is so central to the techniques outlined in this book that we will examine it directly and at length later in the chapter (and have even included a drill to help you hone your skills), and return to it as a part of every subsequent passage discussion.

Your Attitude While Reading

Many students approach the Reading Comprehension section with some anxiety, concerned about the prospect of reading dense passages with difficult structures and unfamiliar terminology. Couple that concern with the generally dull nature of most passages and it's little wonder people's minds have a tendency to wander.

To combat this potential disinterest, maintaining the proper mindset is vital. Simply put, concerns about boredom or anxiety can quickly become self-fulfilling prophecies in Reading Comprehension. To perform well then, you must avoid a negative attitude and instead approach the passages with a positive, energetic, and enthusiastic demeanor. This upbeat mentality is something that all high-scorers embrace, and is something that you should strive to establish from the outset, as well.

How can you make the passages more interesting and turn them into a positive experience? Here are two common methods:

- Many students approach the passages as academic learning exercises and hope to find some fun new fact or interesting information (don't laugh, it happens often!). When you begin reading with the expectation that you will learn something new, the passage becomes easier to read and more engaging.

- Some students approach the passages as puzzles to solve, as if they have been challenged to navigate a maze of sorts (and this is a fairly accurate description). For certain personalities, the idea of a beatable challenge stimulates their competitive nature and makes it easier for them to focus.

The ideas above are not the only ways to make the reading more enjoyable, and you may have your own method. Regardless, the key is to look at these passages as an exercise to enjoy rather than suffer through. The truth of the matter is that if you do not try to enjoy reading the passages or get some value from them, you will be hard-pressed to perform at your best.

Note too that while strong readers obviously have many advantages on this test, becoming a more proficient reader has significant value in other contexts, as well. As you practice applying the approaches discussed in this book, keep in mind that they are applicable to reading in general, and not meant solely to help you achieve a high LSAT score (even if that is the *main* goal)!

A positive attitude is perhaps the most underrated factor in LSAT success. Virtually all high-scoring students expect to do well on the LSAT, and this mindset helps them avoid distractions during the exam and overcome any adversity they might face.

Understand the *Type* of Difficulty in the Reading Comprehension Section

There is a widespread misconception among test takers that because one's reading level is difficult to improve (having been developed over many years), one's performance on the Reading Comprehension section is also unlikely to change. But this belief reflects a common misunderstanding that LSAT Reading Comprehension passages address deep concepts that are inherently challenging, and thus initial reading ability invariably determines performance. Fortunately, this is not accurate!

First, while some of the concepts can be unusual or demanding, passage authors only have about half of a page to get their points across and are thus limited as to the degree of depth that can be reached on any subject. Therefore, with most passages, the challenge often comes from sources other than broad conceptual difficulty or a deep topical analysis. We'll talk about specific sources of difficulty in Chapter Four, but for now take comfort in the fact that you won't be outmatched by topics or discussions beyond your ability to understand. And, always keep in mind that everything you need to know to answer the questions is there in the passage.

Second, while the depth of discussion won't be beyond your capacities, the test makers do often choose subjects that lend themselves to new terms or sophisticated-sounding scientific and technical words. It is vital that you avoid intimidation as a response to words or phrases which you have never seen. Since the makers of the LSAT do not expect or require outside knowledge with regard to Reading Comprehension passage topics, unfamiliar terms or phrases will almost always be surrounded by context clues. These issues will be covered further in our discussion of reading strategy (and again as we examine Science and Technology passages in Chapter Nine); for now the key point is to understand that unfamiliar words or phrases do not necessarily make a passage more conceptually difficult, as long as you do not allow these novel terms or phrases to overwhelm you.

Because Reading Comprehension passages are relatively short, the author cannot go too deeply into the subject matter. This should reduce any intimidation factor you feel about the topic!

Any idea that you encounter that you have not seen before will be explained in the passage, which allows you to relax and seek that explanation instead of panicking over unfamiliar content.

Reading Speed and Returning to the Passage

Given that you have an average of 8 minutes and 45 seconds to read each passage and complete the questions, the amount of time that you spend reading the passage has a direct effect on your ability to comfortably complete all of the questions. At the same time, the makers of the LSAT have extraordinarily high expectations about the level of knowledge you should retain when you read a passage. Many questions will test your knowledge of small, seemingly nitpicky variations in phrasing, and reading carelessly is LSAT self-destruction. Thus, every test taker is placed at the nexus of two competing elements: the need for speed (caused by the timed element) and the need for accuracy (caused by the detailed reading requirement). How well you manage these two elements strongly determines how well you perform.

Although it may sound rather mundane, the best approach is to read each passage at the high end of your normal reading speed. If possible, you should try to step it up a notch or two, while recognizing that reading too quickly will cause you to miss much of the detailed information presented in the passage and may even force you to reread much of the text.

One fortunate thing to be aware of as you read is that you do not need to remember every single detail of the passage! Instead, you simply need to remember the basic structure of the passage so you will know where to return when answering the questions. We will cover this in more detail when we discuss passage structure.

So what's the ideal reading time? Everyone's reading speed is different, but the fastest readers tend to complete each passage in somewhere around two to two and a half minutes. Readers moving at a more deliberate pace should finish the passage in around three to three and a half minutes. Once your reading time per passage exceeds the three and a half minute mark, the likelihood of being able to complete all of the questions drops considerably. In Chapter Ten we will discuss section management and how to handle situations where time is running out, and even introduce the Speed Test designed to specifically gauge what pace is ideal for you if you are still struggling! For now however the focus centers less on target speed and more on improving your overall LSAT reading ability, in large part by teaching you what to look for when reading the passages.

Please note though that the primary aim of this book is not to make you a *faster* reader (your natural reading speed has been developed over many years and is in fact hard to increase by itself in a short period of time). Instead, as you become more adept with effective approaches to the passages, you will be able to attack the passage sets far more proficiently. The goal here is to make you a *better* reader with a greater knowledge of what to look for, and this will inevitably result in increased speed.

In seeking to increase reading speed, some students ask us about speed reading courses. In our extensive experience, speed reading techniques do not work on LSAT passages because of the way they are written and constructed. LSAT passages are written in a detailed style filled with built-in traps and formations, and speed reading techniques are not designed to detect these elements.

Unknowns and Uncertainty

One of the keys to LSAT Reading Comprehension is to accept the fact that you will not be able to know every detail of the passage. In the prior section we talked about reading speed and how this affects your information pickup and recall, and we made the point that you do not *need* to have perfect recall of the facts of the passage. But, it's also the case that it's not really *possible* to remember every detail. LSAT passages are written in a way where there is a significant amount of jumbled information and often conflicting viewpoints, as well as intentionally convoluted sentences. These sections of text can be difficult to understand, and often readers pass through with a sense that they have missed certain elements. This is okay and should not cause you alarm or undue concern! The reasons this situation is acceptable are as follows:

No reader can remember every single detail of the passage, so do not be concerned if some elements are unclear. Instead, expect that to occur, and move forward without delay. You will have time to return to review the text if needed.

1. You have the time and opportunity to return to the passage

    Every reader will return to the passage at some point while answering the questions to confirm that his or her knowledge of the text is correct. Thus, if a segment of the passage is unclear, you will have an opportunity to return to it if and when you are asked about it.

2. The rest of the passage and the questions will help teach you about difficult sections

    In the typical Reading Comprehension passage set, there is information in the remainder of the passage and even in the questions that can help shed light on challenging passage sections. In some instances, this information can help decode portions you read but did not initially understand or that you'd forgotten.

3. The segment in question may not be tested directly and is unlikely to be the central piece of the passage

    Of course, you may not be asked about the unclear section of text at all! And even if you are, it is rarely the most important part of the passage (overly-complex text may serve as nothing but a distraction).

Understanding that you won't pick up every detail releases you from the pressure of perfection. You can move more quickly through the text because you won't fear sections that aren't 100% clear to you.

If you approach the section with the realization that at times you will not be able to pick up and recall every single piece of information, this reduces the pressure and stress on you as a reader (and allows you to go faster). When you encounter a segment that is not entirely clear to you, don't panic; simply note it and then return to it if needed. As readers we are trained to attempt to fully understand and analyze every word and sentence we come across, but the LSAT is constructed in a way that at times thwarts that goal. So, do not become overly concerned if you can't figure something out on your first pass, and in fact expect that to occur at times.

Active Reading and Anticipation

As noted earlier in this chapter when discussing your focus while reading, the best readers read actively. That is, they engage the material and consider the implications of each statement as they read. They also use their involvement in the material to constantly anticipate what will occur next in the passage. This type of reading takes focus and a positive attitude, as discussed previously, but it also takes practice.

Let us take a moment to examine several short sections of text, and use them to highlight the idea of how active reading leads to anticipating what comes next:

> Governmental reforms, loosening of regulations, and the opening of markets each played a role in fueling China's economic growth over the last quarter-century.

After reading this section, one could deduce that there are a number of directions this passage could go. For example, a detailed analysis of each of the three listed factors in the economic growth could be presented, or further implications of the growth could be discussed. Let's add the next two sentences—which complete this paragraph—and see where the author takes us:

> Governmental reforms, loosening of regulations, and the opening of markets each played a role in fueling China's economic growth over the last quarter-century. Within the economy, the two most important segments are
> (5) industry and agriculture. However, industry has grown at a significantly faster pace than agriculture.

If you were reading this passage, when you reached this juncture you should have a fairly good idea of the possible directions the author can take with the *next* paragraph. Consider for a moment the information that has been presented thus far:

- Three factors were named as playing a role in China's economic growth over the last quarter-century.

- The economy is stated to have two key segments.

- One of those two segments is said to have grown at a much faster rate than the other segment.

The first part of this book is devoted to examining the theory of approaching the passages and questions, whereas the second part of the book is focused on applying those techniques and analyzing passage elements.

To aid in our discussions of passage text, we've included line references next to each passage in this book (such as the (5) next to the passage to the left) so we can quickly direct you to the relevant points in the text. On the Digital LSAT, the passages do NOT come with line references; however, they aren't needed since any specific part of the passage that is referenced is directly highlighted on screen.

Clearly, the logical direction to take at this point would be to either explain why industry has grown at a faster rate or why agriculture has grown at a slower rate, or both. There does seem to be a slightly higher likelihood that the author will focus on industry because the exact phrase used was, "industry has grown at a significantly faster pace than agriculture," and this phrasing puts the emphasis on "industry."

Let's see which direction the author chooses:

> Governmental reforms, loosening of regulations,
> and the opening of markets each played a role in fueling
> China's economic growth over the last quarter-century.
> Within the economy, the two most important segments are
> (5)   industry and agriculture. However, industry has grown at a
> significantly faster pace than agriculture.
>   The growth in industry has occurred largely in the
> urban areas of China, and has been primarily spurred by a
> focus on technology and heavy manufacturing. This
> (10) emphasis, however, has not come without costs.

Not surprisingly, the author chose to address the industrial side of the economic growth, in this case by focusing on the segments within industry that have been the most important. Of course, as you continue to read, being correct thus far in your predictions should not cause you to stop reading actively. As the passage progresses you should continue to "look ahead" mentally. For example, the last sentence in the text above suggests that the next topic of discussion will be the costs associated with the industrial economic growth.

As a reader, anticipating what will come next in the passage is a habit you should seek to cultivate. By constantly thinking about the possible directions the author can take, you will gain a richer perspective on the story being told and be better prepared for the twists and turns most passages exhibit. Of course, at times, you might be incorrect in your prediction of what will come next. This is not a problem—you will still be able to absorb what is presented and there is no associated time loss. Simply put, there are tremendous benefits gained from reading actively.

Active Reading Drill

The following drill is presented to reinforce the valuable habit of reacting to identifiable verbal cues. Most students are likely to be familiar with the meanings of common transitional words such as "furthermore" and "however," but again, the most effective readers are responsive when they see these sorts of transitions, actively predicting the passage's next lines. After each of the following examples, take a moment to consider what is likely to come next in the passage, and write down your expectations. *Answers on page 38*

1. After developing her initial hypothesis, early studies yielded consistently positive results; in fact,…

   _____

   _____

   _____

2. As a result of his childhood accomplishments, Rhee found many opportunities that would have been inaccessible to lesser known talents. Notwithstanding his early successes,…

   _____

   _____

   _____

3. Martindale was generally scorned by his contemporaries, who characterized him as an artist who lacked the imagination to create anything truly original, as well as the self-awareness to perceive his own shortcomings. Modern critics, however…

   _____

   _____

   _____

   _____

4. Many American constitutional scholars argue that in making legal determinations, the Supreme Court should comply whenever possible with the original intent of the drafters of the Constitution. At the same time,…

   _____

   _____

   _____

   _____

   _____

5. Most experts in the field who were first told of Dr. Jane's hypothesis were initially skeptical, but…

   _____

   _____

   _____

   _____

   _____

Active Reading Drill Answer Key

1. After developing her initial hypothesis, early studies
    yielded consistently positive results; in fact,...

    > In this case, the words "in fact" tell us that the next information provided will likely continue
    > to support the positive results yielded by early studies.

2. As a result of his childhood accomplishments, Rhee
    found many opportunities that would have been
    inaccessible to lesser known talents. Notwithstanding
    his early successes,...

    > "Notwithstanding," which basically means "in spite of," tells us that the passage is about to
    > take a turn; although Rhee did apparently enjoy early success, we are soon likely to be told of
    > some challenge(s) that appeared in spite of Rhee's early achievements and opportunities.

3. Martindale was generally scorned by his
    contemporaries, who characterized him as an artist
    who lacked the imagination to create anything truly
    original, as well as the self-awareness to perceive his
    own shortcomings. Modern critics, however...

    > The word "however" in this example is a clear indication that there is contrast between
    > contemporaries' characterizations and those of modern critics, so it is likely that modern
    > critics are going to have nicer things to say about Martindale.

4. Many American constitutional scholars argue that
    in making legal determinations, the Supreme Court
    should comply whenever possible with the original
    intent of the drafters of the Constitution. At the same
    time,...

    > If taken out of context, "at the same time" might appear to continue a thought, but the phrase
    > is often more akin to "on the other hand." Here, the author begins by telling us that, according
    > to many, Supreme Court decisions should be based on the Constitution's original intent. "At
    > the same time" is likely in this case to be followed by some limitation on the advisability of
    > this notion (e.g., "At the same time, many facets of modern life were not envisioned by the
    > founders.").

5. Most experts in the field who were first told of Dr.
    Jane's hypothesis were initially skeptical, but...

    > "But" is a fairly obvious clue that the passage is about to take a new turn. If we are told of
    > skepticism at first, followed by "but," then it is likely that the author is about to discuss how
    > the hypothesis was confirmed, or possibly how Dr. Jane was able to overcome the initial
    > skepticism of the experts.

Decoding Text

Killer Sentences

One of the most powerful weapons the test makers possess is the ability to manipulate language, and specifically to create sentences that contain a large amount of information while simultaneously being difficult to understand and interpret. Anyone who has completed an LSAT has run across portions of text in Reading Comprehension (and Logical Reasoning) that are tough to understand, or elicit a "what did that just say?" reaction. Those are killer sentences, and they not only slow you down, they can also hinder your ability to understand what was said by each player in the passage. Here is an example:

> The survival strategies of various classes of vertebrates demonstrate that, contrary to the claims of early zoologists, physical similarity does not produce strategic similarity: for example, the strategies that an electric eel uses to defend itself from attack are significantly different from those used by the hagfish, an eel-like fish also known as a slime eel, but both manifest the same basic morphological appearance to predators.

If you encountered that sentence in a passage it would surely cause some issues! So let's talk about how to decode that type of sentence.

Uncovering Meaning: Context, Simplification, and Rephrasing

The key to conquering difficult language is to use a combination of context, simplification, and rephrasing. In other words, you must examine the surroundings for clues, break down the ideas into smaller pieces, and then rephrase it all in a way that makes sense to you. All readers do this naturally to some extent, where as you read you typically reduce the ideas presented to something more readily digestible. But with the complex constructions of the LSAT, there is an inclination to immediately skip over, or even ignore, these sentences because you know your speed matters. After all, if you can't get a handle on the author's meaning how can you simplify or rephrase it? Because of this, many students are too quick to give up on killer sentences, when in fact there are proven strategies that can help you make sense of them!

As mentioned a few pages earlier, some parts of a passage may simply be too confusing to understand at first, and if so, it's not a problem to bypass that portion. But of course the preference is to always know what was said, and in this section we talk about ways to help achieve that goal.

To combat killer sentences, follow these steps as you break them down:

1. Slow down and relax. When you encounter a sentence as convoluted as the example in the prior section, you should automatically know you cannot speed through it with perfect clarity. In fact, the test makers are hoping you will attempt to rush through it or disregard it entirely, so you need to take action to defeat them. The first step is to slow your pace slightly. Don't freeze completely—you still want to maintain an aggressive reading speed and can't get paralyzed by complexity—but details matter on the LSAT, and it is not only acceptable but advisable to spend time at critical points getting your facts straight. And, while easier said than done, you should also try to relax (or at least avoid becoming more stressed by the presence of something obviously difficult). Give yourself a few extra seconds to decode the meaning of the sentence. Be patient! And, crucially, keep in mind that all the information you need to unlock the meaning of the sentence is right there on the page. That fact, more than anything else, should help you maintain your composure.

2. Recognize that killer sentences are really a collection of connected thoughts, meaning you can break down the sentence into smaller, component pieces. To do so, use the punctuation marks in the sentence as natural separators. Commas, dashes, semi-colons, and colons each indicate natural stopping points in the text, and thus you can usually divide each sentence into more manageable sections. For example, let's partition that sample sentence so that each segment that ends with punctuation is on its own line:

    > The survival strategies of various classes of vertebrates demonstrate that,
    >
    > contrary to the claims of early zoologists,
    >
    > physical similarity does not produce strategic similarity:
    >
    > for example,
    >
    > the strategies that an electric eel uses to defend itself from attack are significantly different from those used by the hagfish,
    >
    > an eel-like fish also known as a slime eel,
    >
    > but both manifest the same basic morphological appearance to predators.

Seen from this perspective, you can immediately tell that this sentence contains a large number of ideas! However, each piece is obviously not of equal weight, and some of the ideas are new while some simply expand or clarify earlier points. To analyze this sentence, let's first recall that not all punctuation has the same value. Here's how punctuation marks typically work inside a sentence:

Comma [,]: Commas appear in many sentences, and usually serve to separate ideas in some manner. As such, they are natural stopping points, and help divide a sentence into smaller pieces. Two commas in a sentence often bookend a standalone idea that is related to but separate from the main idea being expressed.

Colon [:]: A colon typically precedes either an explanation of the point prior to the colon, or introduces a list of some sort. Examples:

> The tip on the company's violations came from an unlikely source: the company's CEO.

> Each applicant must demonstrate three talents: communication, creativity, and organization.

This grammar refresher may seem elementary, but spotting differences as subtle as a comma versus a semi-colon can make a world of difference when interpreting complex phrases on the LSAT.

Semi-colon [;]: The ideas on either side of a semi-colon are related but also could stand on their own as complete sentences. In this sense, a semi-colon is stronger than a comma, but less definitive than a period. Example:

> Professional athletes are paid for their time and services; amateur athletes are typically not paid.

Parentheses [( )]: The information in parentheses usually expands upon and adds additional details to the sentence. Example:

> I arrived just before the library closed at 4 P.M. (a surprisingly early closing time in my opinion).

Note: these descriptions are not exhaustive. The point of this discussion is to provide a quick reminder; for more in-depth punctuation analyses refer to an English grammar textbook.

Dash [—]: Dashes are extremely versatile, and are often used in place of other punctuation marks (most notably commas, colons, and parentheses), but the purpose is typically to set apart a particular idea. Example:

> The culmination of her career was a show at the Tate Modern—the premier modern art museum in England.

The phrase "for example" is a very helpful one because it typically expands and clarifies the idea that immediately precedes it, often by providing an individual instance of a broader idea or belief. Thus, the main idea of the sentence (or the passage) is not usually in the "for example" section, but instead just before it.

Returning to the example sentence, you can see that there's a natural dividing point in the center, with the colon. Everything *after* the colon is a clarification and expansion of the now-italicized portion:

> The survival strategies of various classes of vertebrates demonstrate that, contrary to the claims of early zoologists, *physical similarity does not produce strategic similarity*:

> for example, the strategies that an electric eel uses to defend itself from attack are significantly different from those used by the hagfish, an eel-like fish also known as a slime eel, but both manifest the same basic morphological appearance to predators.

So, we can divide this sentence into two big pieces, the first part and then the second, post-colon portion. Let's start by looking at the first part:

> The survival strategies of various classes of vertebrates demonstrate that, contrary to the claims of early zoologists, physical similarity does not produce strategic similarity:

In this section, we have a pair of commas where the thought inside is not integral to the sentence, but, as is often the case, instead expands on our knowledge. Re-ordered with the "contrary to..." clause at the end, the sentence appears as follows:

> The survival strategies of various classes of vertebrates demonstrate that physical similarity does not produce strategic similarity:

> > *The point here is that just because different vertebrates look the same physically does not mean they use the same survival strategies. So, for example, a zebra and a horse might appear physically similar, but not use the same methods to survive.*

> contrary to the claims of early zoologists,

> > *This provides us with information about what zoologists used to think, specifically that early*

zoologists must have thought differently from the author's point (we know this from "contrary to"). So, early zoologists thought that physical similarity meant the survival strategies would be the same.

Since the second part of the sentence clarifies the idea that "physical similarity does not produce strategic similarity," we can now analyze the second half expecting that it will provide an example of that difference, with the additional knowledge that this is a view that early zoologists did not share:

for example, the strategies that an electric eel uses to defend itself from attack are significantly different from those used by the hagfish, an eel-like fish also known as a slime eel, but both manifest the same basic morphological appearance to predators.

The first step here is to realize that again there is a pair of commas that expands on our knowledge of the prior term. In this case, the hagfish is "an eel-like fish also known as a slime eel." In other words, the hagfish is a fish that looks like an eel.

The remainder of the clause simply states that the electric eel uses a different defense mechanism (which is another way of saying "survival strategy") than the hagfish.

But wait, what about that reference to "morphological appearance"? This can be a tough one because there's no direct definition given in the sentence. So we need to use context to understand what it means. We know the author is talking about vertebrates with similar physical appearance having different survival strategies, and the first part of this clause references different survival strategies; thus, this portion must be referring to physical appearance, and that point is reinforced when the section uses "manifest the same basic... appearance." And, indeed, "morphological" relates to form, so this is just an intentionally confusing way of saying that the electric eel and hagfish look the same.

Let's now simplify each part of the sentence in order to complete the analysis:

> The first portion states that although different vertebrates look the same physically, that doesn't mean they use the same survival strategies, although that's not what early zoologists thought.

> The second portion states that eels and hagfish are an example of vertebrates using different survival strategies even though physically they look the same.

That's a lot of work to get to a statement that at its core is fairly basic. But this is how the LSAT tests you: it purposefully dresses up comprehensible ideas and expresses them in ways that are not obvious at a glance. The test makers' hope is that you will give up, but if you can maneuver through the language with a reliable simplification process you will usually find that a clearer understanding is both possible as you read and beneficial as you answer questions. So make it any early goal to practice decoding tough sentences and passage sections: they can always be reduced to simpler forms.

3. Given that you already know the sentence, or series of sentences, presents a challenge, mark that text either by highlighting the passage itself with the digital tools, or jot a quick note on your scratch paper indicating where in the passage you struggled (such as, "P3 second half??" for the second half of paragraph 3; be concise but clear). This helps you keep tabs on where the hardest parts of the passage are, and also helps you quickly locate those areas when questions are asked that reference that information.

How much-or how little-to mark up a passage is discussed in Chapter Five.

Notations of this sort are important to not only indicate where you found difficulty in the passage in case you need to confirm information for an answer choice, but also to provide diagnostic insights into any elements that tend to give you trouble: if you are frequently underlining or highlighting highly-punctuated sentences, or unfamiliar terminology, or dense lists, or specific examples, for instance, you can more reliably adjust your attention and pace when you encounter those situations in the future.

Finally, we provide a targeted exercise—the Prediction Test—in Chapter Ten to further refine your skills at recognizing the passage elements most likely to be asked about, so you will have continued opportunities to explore how the test makers use killer sentences as the source of subsequent questions.

Chapter Three: What to read for— VIEWSTAMP

Chapter Three: What to read for— VIEWSTAMP

POWERSCORE
BY BARBRI

What to Read For

Thus far we've discussed some of the basic ideas behind how to approach the passages, mostly focusing on the mindset you need to adopt when attacking each passage set. Let's now turn to the specific elements you must look for while reading.

One of the points in the last chapter was that your reading speed does not determine your final RC score. This isn't to suggest you do not need to change anything about how you read! Instead, the focus is on *how* you read and what you look for as you read. In other words, it's not about reading faster but about reading better.

To achieve the goal of reading better, you must concentrate on the basic passage elements that generate the majority of questions. These identifiable elements are not difficult to understand, but they are easy to lose in the thicket of information that is a Reading Comprehension passage. So, to help you track those elements you should ask yourself a set of questions while reading, and at the end of the passage you should be able to answer each of the following:

- What is the Main Point of the passage? What is the author driving at? Why was this written?

- Which groups are speaking or are talked about in the passage? In other words, who said what?

- What's the tone or attitude of each group? Angry? Disappointed? Neutral?

- What is the basic position or argument of each group? Nothing complex, more along the lines of, "The environmentalists are for the passage of the bill and the opponent's think the bill will hurt the economy. The author is neutral."

- Last, but not least, what's the structure of the passage? Can you make a mental map of where the ideas appear in the passage and how they fit together?

The questions here are fairly simple, and once you are used to considering them as you read they become quite easy to remember.

Note too that many RC test questions will be answered directly as you satisfy the inquiries listed here.

We will talk about each point in detail on the following pages, but these basic questions help distill the passage information into a simple, usable format that allows you to effectively attack the questions.

Reading The Tablet Screen ▮▮▮

Due to the length of each passage, Reading Comprehension appears differently on the digital tablet than does the text in other sections, and the test makers have therefore taken unique steps to allow for a more comfortable reading experience.

In both Logical Reasoning and Logic Games, you can see the entirety of the stimulus or game scenario and rules on the left side of the screen. But in Reading Comprehension, the passage is so long that you cannot see the entirety of it without scrolling down. This is accomplished by either swiping on the passage text itself, or by pulling down the vertical slider in the center of the screen (see page 14 for a picture of the interface). So when viewed side-by-side with a question in the "Passage with Question" view, there is quite a bit of scrolling involved to get from beginning to end of the full passage text.

Alternately, you have the option to use a "Passage Only" button in the upper left-hand of the interface to remove the question and view the passage across both the left and right columns of the screen. This allows you to see more of the passage at once by replacing the question and answer column with additional passage text, but still does not allow you to see the entire passage on a single screen (you have to click an arrow to see any remaining passage text).

Given the limited nature of how much text is visible at once in a single column and the degree of scrolling required to read in "Passage with Question," the "Passage Only" option can be a great way to read a passage for the first time. And any marks you make on the passage (underlining or highlighting) will remain when you toggle back to "Passage with Question" view (and through the subsequent questions as well).

Prior to taking the LSAT, you should experiment with the digital interface and decide if you prefer the "Passage Only" view or the "Passage with Question" view for your initial reading of each passage.

Once you determine which layout to use to read, you want to focus on controlling all of the elements discussed on the prior page. With that in mind, let's talk about the mental tool we use to help keep everything straight: VIEWSTAMP.

What is VIEWSTAMP? ▄▄▄▄▄▄▄

The basic questions on the first page of this chapter all relate to the primary elements that generate the questions for every LSAT Reading Comprehension passage. With the time pressure and overall complexity involved in RC passages sometimes one can forget to think about these simple questions, so we use the acronym VIEWSTAMP to help you remember each item.

The acronym uses letters from each of these five critical components:

VIEW = the different **VIEW**points in the passage

S = the **S**tructure of the passage

T = the **T**one of the passage

A = the **A**rguments in the passage

MP = the **M**ain **P**oint

Ultimately, VIEWSTAMP is a mental tracking tool that focuses your attention on the ideas and elements most likely to produce questions.

Analyzing the Passage Using VIEWSTAMP ▆▆▆▆▆▆▆▆

In its basic form, VIEWSTAMP is a mnemonic device that helps remind you of what to look for in each passage. But in practice we use this device as a diagnostic instrument that helps us constantly apply a rigorous analysis to each paragraph of the passage. Thus, it is important to discuss exactly when and how to ask these questions, and what to look for as a satisfactory response.

When to Apply VIEWSTAMP

VIEWSTAMP is designed to be a constant companion as you move through the passage. You are always looking for the presence of each element, and at the end of *each paragraph* you should consider the main elements of what you just read as well as what information relates to the VIEWSTAMP goals. Seek to understand not just *what* the author said in the paragraph, but *why* the author made those statements. What's the greater point that's being presented? How does each element function in service of that point?

This paragraph-by-paragraph analysis culminates when you finish the last paragraph, at which point you should have a relatively good sense of what was said, and by whom. As you conclude your reading, pause to make sure you have all of the information straight. If you do not, you risk being swayed by clever answer choices with tempting but inaccurate phrasing. So, if you are at all uncertain about something that feels significant, take a moment to lock down the facts!

How to Apply VIEWSTAMP

One of the keys of applying VIEWSTAMP is to not seek too much detail for each item. An excessive amount of detail will slow you down, and become hard to juggle mentally. Instead, what you want is a very generalized answer to each question. We'll go into the details of each element in the remainder of this chapter, but for now think about each question as a broad query seeking a single sentence answer if possible.

For example, consider the idea of the main point of the passage. While LSAT Reading Comprehension passages are all unique, in every instance you can summarize the main point in a sentence or two at most. So, at the end of the passage when you are looking to answer the question of what is the main point, keep your answer simple and broadly encompassing of the entirety of the text.

You do not need to summarize every few sentences or go into the nuances of each passage; fine shades of meaning are not useful at this level because they are too easy to forget. Thus, a main point summary such as the following would fail our goal:

> The passage argues for the adoption of the new Geisen-Tremaine standards for measuring educational progress among American schoolchildren because these standards take into account cultural and socioeconomic factors that can impact some students more than others. The author pays particular attention to the deficiencies of current measures in addressing underprivileged youth achievement.

Instead, seek something along these lines:

> The main point is that the new standards for measuring the progress of American schoolchildren should be adopted.

The second summary, while short and relatively generalized, would allow you to answer any question about the primary purpose or main point of the passage (which are questions that appear frequently), and would also clue you in to the author's overall intent and belief set. The keys are clarity and simplicity since those will provide maximum recall when you are attacking the questions.

Now, the natural question to ask is: won't a broad summary leave me vulnerable to questions about details or specific sections of the passage? The happy answer is No. When you encounter specific questions you have free rein to return to the passage text, and in fact you are encouraged to do so. Every high scorer returns to the passage to confirm information because there are simply too many details in the passage to remember in full. This process is made easier because one of the five elements being tracked is Structure, so when you encounter a detail question and must return to the passage your already-existing structural knowledge of where to find the information in the passage will help you move more quickly and decisively, particularly when coupled with the marking and notation strategies covered in Chapter Five.

So, at the *end* of each passage you should be able to briefly summarize the five elements within VIEWSTAMP in short, succinct sentences. If you cannot accomplish this goal, you will likely struggle with some or all of the questions. As you practice reading passages, constantly ask yourself these questions, and seek to refine your approach until you are comfortable with each of the five points.

It's not that this first summary is bad; it's actually quite good. The problem is that it's not a distillation of the essence of the passage, and if you apply this level of detailed analysis to each element within the passage, you won't have a simple analysis but instead an extremely complicated analysis that might be difficult to remember.

The analogy we often use for how VIEWSTAMP works is one where you act as an air traffic controller. In that role, you know that you will be tracking planes, but each night the pattern will change and the number and density of planes will be different.

In a similar fashion, you know that certain elements always appear in Reading Comprehension passages, but in each passage those elements are presented in different ways. Your job is to track concurrently those elements as they appear.

Finally, consider your analysis of the five elements to be fluid: it will change from passage to passage. In some passages certain elements will appear earlier than others, and in some cases you might determine an element very early on whereas in another passage you may need to wait until the end of the passage to make a judgment. For example, in one passage the author's attitude might be identifiable right from the beginning whereas in another passage that attitude might not be clear until near the end.

Do not try to impose a rigid order onto your reading; instead react to what the test makers give you: the variation in how information is presented in the passage will require you to be flexible in how you read. Your goal as a reader using VIEWSTAMP is not to read each passage in a fixed and unyielding way, but rather to track the five elements and react to them when they appear. In this way, you can adapt to any passage structure and formation, and thereby attack any set of questions successfully!

Read Directly

As we will see in Chapter Six when we discuss question types, the vast majority of Reading Comprehension questions are Must Be True and Main Point variants. Thus, you are typically on a fact-finding mission when reading an RC passage. This means you are reading for knowledge and understanding, and not as much for things such as Assumptions and what would weaken or strengthen the argument (as in Logical Reasoning). Thus, it's less about "reading between the lines" and more about reading directly. Work to get a grasp of what was said and why, and worry less about what weaknesses the passage has or what assumptions were made.

VIEWSTAMP Examined

We've taken a moment to briefly talk about the utility and goals of applying a VIEWSTAMP analysis, so let us now dive into each part in more detailed fashion.

As we do so, we will not examine each part in the order it appears in the acronym. This is not a concern since during your analysis you should not feel an adherence to VIEWSTAMP's order either; rather, you will identify each part as it arises, or possibly at the conclusion of your reading. For example, viewpoints will be presented throughout the passage, and thus you cannot conclude your viewpoint analysis after reading just the first paragraph. Similarly, a discussion of passage structure requires a broad view encompassing the entirety of the text. But, you should be aware of the viewpoints and structure while reading (more on this shortly), and each time a new view appears, or a paragraph presents a new structural element, you should make mental note of it.

Our discussion of VIEWSTAMP will generally take the following order, as this is the most logical order of analysis:

1. The various groups and viewpoints discussed within the passage.

2. The tone or attitude of each group or individual.

3. The argument made by each group or individual.

4. The main point of the passage.

5. The structure of the passage and the organization of ideas.

This is the order that we will typically discuss the five elements in, not the order they appear in the acronym. This is the most logical order for discussion purposes.

With that in mind, let's examine each of these five elements in detail and see how they can help you read more quickly and answer questions more accurately.

1. Viewpoint Identification and Analysis

This section discusses the "VIEW" in VIEWSTAMP. The "VIEW" stands for Viewpoints.

A viewpoint is the position or perspective of a person or group. On the LSAT, Reading Comprehension passages typically contain anywhere from one to six different viewpoints. These viewpoints can be the author's or those of groups discussed by the author.

As you read, you *must* identify each viewpoint that is presented in the passage. This is a fairly easy process—whenever a new group or individual viewpoint is discussed, simply note its appearance. Because viewpoints can be presented at any time, your analysis of viewpoints will not be concluded until you finish reading the passage.

Consider the following opening paragraph of a passage, and seek to identify the various viewpoints present:

File sharing, the practice of allowing the electronic exchange of files over a network such as the Internet, has in recent years led to the emergence of a new and complex set of legal issues for intellectual property owners. The

(5) rapid and often undetectable movement of digital copies of copyrighted material has made identifying offenders particularly difficult, and has made prosecuting such offenses time-consuming and expensive. The owners of certain types of intellectual property, such as music, have

(10) claimed that enforcement of these violations is necessary in order to send a signal to other possible offenders. File sharers, on the other hand, typically claim that they did not know they were sharing copyrighted material, and that regardless, the widespread use of file sharing networks

(15) renders the protection of copyrights impossible.

Let us take a moment to analyze this paragraph, section by section.

Lines 1-8

Many Reading Comprehension passages begin with a Viewpoint Neutral discussion that provides context for the passage.

Not all of the text on the LSAT is presented with a definable viewpoint. Many Reading Comprehension passages begin with a statement of facts or a description of the situation. In these sections, no viewpoint is presented. Throughout this book, we will refer to these sections as "viewpoint neutral." The first eight and a half lines of this passage are viewpoint neutral, simply providing a description of file sharing and the fact that this system raises legal issues. Yes, "intellectual property owners" are mentioned, but since no viewpoint is ascribed to them (as yet), there is no need to note them as a group.

Again, throughout this book we'll supply line references next to the passages to make the analysis of each passage easier to follow.

On the Digital LSAT, the passages do NOT come with line references; however, they aren't needed since any specific part of the passage that is referenced is directly highlighted on screen.

3

Lines 8-11

The eighth line of the paragraph presents the first identifiable viewpoint of the passage, held by "The owners of certain types of intellectual property." These owners have an identifiable viewpoint, namely that "enforcement of these violations is necessary in order to send a signal to other possible offenders." You can note the presence of this viewpoint element by underlining or highlighting the name of the group (we will discuss passage notation in more detail in a later chapter).

Lines 11-15

Not unusually, a second viewpoint is also presented in the first paragraph. This viewpoint, of "File sharers," is somewhat contrary to the previous viewpoint presented.

Test takers might ask, "What is the value of tracking all of the viewpoints in a given Reading Comprehension passage?" There are several important reasons:

1. Tracking the viewpoints will help you disentangle the mass of information contained in every Reading Comprehension passage.

2. Within the questions, you will be asked to identify the viewpoints presented in the passages and to differentiate between those viewpoints. Answer choices will often present different viewpoints in order to test your ability to distinguish between groups.

In the paragraph under examination, the two viewpoints are presented "back-to-back." This is done intentionally so that the test makers can test your ability to compare and contrast different views. Of course, some test takers fail to distinguish these views, and they are much more prone to fall prey to questions that test the difference between these viewpoints.

In the sample paragraph, the views are presented very clearly, and each group is easy to identify. Unfortunately, viewpoints will not always be presented with such clarity.

Consider the following opening paragraph from a different passage:

Literary critics have praised author Toni Morrison
for her deft handling of female character development
in novels that typically feature powerful and troubling
themes. While some have called the author a feminist,
(5)   Morrison has never referred to herself as such, asserting
that she seeks to craft viewpoints which embrace
equality for all. But one of the strengths of her writing
is the uniquely female point of view her characters bring
to situations of intolerance and oppression. By their very
(10)   nature, Morrison's dynamic portrayals assert that women
deserve equal rights in any forum.

The first sentence introduces the view of "Literary critics" and how they
assess the work of Toni Morrison. The second sentence (line 4) begins
with "some have called," a reference to the views of some commentators,
and then the second half of that sentence (line 5) refers to Morrison and
how she sees herself. So, the first two sentences contain three different
groups and viewpoints. The third and fourth sentences may at first appear
to be viewpoint neutral, but in fact this section is an opinion, and as this
opinion is not ascribed to any particular group, it must be the opinion
and viewpoint of the author. Thus, this paragraph contains four separate
viewpoints:

An opinion
presented
without reference
to any group
is typically the
author's opinion.

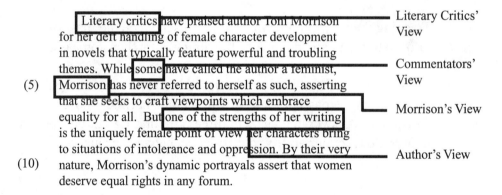

Of course, not all viewpoints are presented in separate sentences. In an
effort to confuse test takers, the test makers sometimes introduce two
viewpoints in a single sentence, as in the following example:

While the proponents of the Futurism art movement
believed that the past was an era to be ignored, some
critics assert that, ironically, for the Futurists to break
from the past would have required a more thorough
(5)   understanding of history on their part.

In the previous sentence, two views are introduced: those of the
proponents of Futurism and of the critics of Futurism. However, although

the sentence contains two opposing views, tracking those elements is no more difficult than when the views are presented in separate sentences. (As mentioned, we will discuss notating the views in a later chapter)

When we begin our discussion of the questions that typically accompany LSAT passages, we will revisit the importance of a viewpoint-based analysis. In the meantime, always remember to identify the various viewpoints that you encounter in a Reading Comprehension passage.

2. Tone/Attitude

Identifying the group or individual behind each viewpoint is usually easy. Identifying the tone or attitude of each group can sometimes be more challenging. Attitude is the state of mind or feeling that each group expresses on the subject matter at hand, and for our purposes, "attitude" and "tone" will be used interchangeably.

The author's attitude is usually revealed through word choice. For example, is the author indifferent? Critical? Convinced? Skeptical? Hopeful? To make a determination of attitude, you must carefully examine the words used by the author. Is the opinion of the author positive or negative? To what degree?

In the vast majority of passages, LSAT authors tend not to be extreme in their opinions (there are exceptions to this rule, which will be discussed later). As mentioned in Chapter Two, most passages are drawn from academic or professional sources, and the authors in these publications attempt to offer reasoned, tempered arguments in support of their position, hoping to sway the average reader. In doing so, they often present counterarguments and acknowledge the position of the other side. This fact does not mean that they cannot have strong opinions; it just means that they will not use extremely passionate or fiery language. Thus, one does not often see an author whose tone would be described as "jubilant," "tempestuous," "exuberant," or "depressed."

Note also that tone is representative of the passage as a whole, and not just of a single section. An author who exhibited strong support for a position throughout a passage but then at the very end of the passage acknowledged that critics existed would not be said to be "concerned" or "negative." In other words, the tone exhibited in the last few lines would not override or outweigh the positive support that the author displayed earlier. Instead, such a section would simply modify the overall tone of the author to something along the lines of "reasoned optimism" or "positive but realistic."

This section discusses the "T" in the VIEWSTAMP acronym. The "T" stands for Tone.

Most LSAT authors do not display an extreme attitude or tone.

Clearly, the author is not the only one who may express a distinct tone. Each viewpoint group can have a tone as well, but determining that tone can sometimes be far more difficult because other positions are filtered through the author's words. That is, the author chooses all of the text in the passage, so the viewpoint of each group is harder to discern at times because non-author views are given to you secondhand. This typically results in a limited range of tones, so, although an author's tone can be quite complex, usually the tone of other viewpoint groups is less so, and can often be reduced to a simple agree/disagree position. Thus, while you must know the viewpoint of each group in the passage, as far as attitude, you are primarily concerned with the attitude of the author.

Let us analyze a few excerpts and examine the idea of tone further.

Consider the following section of text:

> There are signs that the animosity between the two companies is diminishing.

In the section above, the author's attitude towards the occurrence appears to be neutral. The information is presented factually, and no valuation of the diminishing animosity is provided. Consider, however, how this passage would read if one additional word was inserted:

> Fortunately, there are signs that the animosity between the two companies is diminishing.

With the addition of "fortunately," the author's attitude towards the occurrence is now clear—the diminishment of the animosity is a positive occurrence. Other word choices would obviously have a different effect. For example, choosing "unfortunately" instead of "fortunately" would reverse the author's position on the diminishing animosity.
Of course, LSAT passages are comprised of more than a single sentence, and sometimes no indicator words are present. The following segment from the prior section typifies how a passage can begin:

       File sharing, the practice of allowing the electronic
exchange of files over a network such as the Internet,
has in recent years led to the emergence of a new and
complex set of legal issues for intellectual property
(5)   owners. The rapid and often undetectable movement
of digital copies of copyrighted material has made
identifying offenders particularly difficult, and has
made prosecuting such offenses time-consuming and
expensive. The owners of certain types of intellectual
(10)   property, such as music, have claimed that enforcement
is necessary in order to send a signal to other possible
offenders. File sharers, on the other hand, typically
claim to have been unaware that they were sharing
copyrighted material, and that regardless, the widespread
(15)   use of file sharing networks renders the protection of
copyrights impossible.

Lines 1-9 are viewpoint neutral, and thus the tone is neutral as
well. The author simply presents the topic at hand, and he or she
does so in a matter-of-fact manner. One would not say that the
author is "happy," or "serious," or "sad."

Lines 9-12 present the first definable group in the passage,
"Intellectual property owners." We know from prior analysis that
their viewpoint is that enforcement is a necessity, but their tone
is harder to discern. Are they furious? Belligerent? Reasonable?
There is really no way to know because no indication of their
attitude is made other than the obvious fact that they believe
enforcement is important and thus they disagree with other
groups who believe it to be impossible. How they approach that
disagreement, however, is not stated in the passage.

Lines 12-16 present a new viewpoint, that of "File sharers."
However, other than understanding that this group's viewpoint
is somewhat contrary to the owners of intellectual property, we
cannot make a determination of the tone of their argument. There
is no indication that they are focused, or intense, or happy. Like
the previous group, there is simply not enough information to
determine their exact attitude toward the subject matter.

Let's examine another section of text:

    Altering the legal protections available to intellectual
property owners would thus be misguided because it
creates an environment where the consequences of
copyright violation are greater than warranted, and the
mere threat of legal action is enough to create a "chilling
effect" on the creative environment.

Consider the author's position in the example just given. The choice of the word "misguided" reveals the author's attitude to be strongly negative toward changing the legal protections available to the owners. The "negative" part is easy to spot, but how do you know it is "strongly negative"? Think for a moment of some of the other words the author could have chosen instead of "misguided" that would also convey negativity. Here are just a few examples, each of which conveys negativity, but not to the degree implied by "misguided":

> "Altering the legal protections available to intellectual property owners would thus be *concerning* because it..."

> "Altering the legal protections available to intellectual property owners would thus be *troubling* because it..."

> "Altering the legal protections available to intellectual property owners would thus be an *issue* because it..."

In each example, the word chosen to convey negativity is not as strong or as harsh as "misguided." In the annals of LSAT passages, "misguided" is a relatively strong negative term. Of course, the author could have chosen to be even more negative, but that would begin to sound unreasonable:

> "Altering the legal protections available to intellectual property owners would thus be *ridiculous* because..."

> "Altering the legal protections available to intellectual property owners would thus be *preposterous* because..."

> "Altering the legal protections available to intellectual property owners would thus be *disastrous* because..."

These word choices, while possible, tend not to occur on the LSAT because they convey such extreme emotion. Regardless, the point is that in examining attitude, you must carefully consider the word choices used by the author of the passage. The rule is that small changes in word choice can have a large effect on the overall tone of the passage.

Because tracking viewpoints and tone is such a critical ability, the next several pages contain a drill that will help test and strengthen your ability to identify various viewpoints and their accompanying tones.

Viewpoint and Attitude Identification Drill

Read each of the following paragraphs. Then in the spaces that follow each paragraph fill in the proper line references, respective viewpoints, and any associated tone or attitude. There are four viewpoint lines listed for each passage, but *there are not necessarily four viewpoints expressed*; instead, you must determine how many exist for each. *Answers on page 71*

Passage #1:

Federal rules of evidence have long prohibited the presentation in court of many types of "hearsay" (evidence recounted second-hand, rather than reported directly by a witness), based on the notion
(5) that only the most readily verifiable evidence should be allowed consideration by any court in making its determinations. Dr. Kinsley has argued, however, that the rules of evidence as currently written are unacceptably overreaching, defining
(10) as hearsay too many types of evidence whose value would far outweigh any associated detriment if allowed court admissibility. But modern hearsay rules have been written with good reason.

Lines: _____

Viewpoint/Tone: _____

Lines: _____

Viewpoint/Tone: _____

Lines: _____

Viewpoint/Tone: _____

Lines: _____

Viewpoint/Tone: _____

Viewpoint and Attitude Identification Drill

Passage #2:

In the years which preceded Roger Bannister's record breaking performance, it was widely believed that the human body was not equipped to complete a mile-long run in under four minutes;
(5) human lungs, many leading experts asserted, could never deliver sufficient oxygen, and the heart could not undergo such physical stress. Bannister, undeterred, believed that he could reach the goal that he had set in 1952.

Lines: _____

Viewpoint/Tone: _____

Lines: _____

Viewpoint/Tone: _____

Lines: _____

Viewpoint/Tone: _____

Lines: _____

Viewpoint/Tone: _____

Viewpoint and Attitude Identification Drill

Many of Joyce's phrasings are less than readily decipherable, and as a result his works provide seemingly endless opportunity for speculation about construction and meaning. Consensus
(5)   among literary scholars is often elusive, which is why outlier academics sometimes gain notoriety in the short term with questionable but well-publicized claims concerning proper interpretation. For example, one Joyce scholar in Ireland recently
(10)   announced plans to publish "Finn's Hotel," a collection of early notes which he asserts to be "a previously unknown Joyce work," notwithstanding the fact that the stories have all been published before.

Lines: _____

Viewpoint:/Tone _____

Lines: _____

Viewpoint/Tone: _____

Lines: _____

Viewpoint/Tone: _____

Lines: _____

Viewpoint/Tone: _____

Viewpoint and Attitude Identification Drill

Passage #4:

The first cardiac pacemaker was the brainchild of John Hopps, a Canadian electrical engineer who, in 1941, while researching hypothermia and the use of heat from radio frequencies to restore
(5) body temperature, found that mechanical or electrical stimulation can restart a heart that has stopped under conditions of extreme cold. The earliest versions of the pacemaker were heavy pieces of equipment which were far too large for
(10) implantation, and instead had to be rolled on wheels and kept attached to the patient at all times. Modern science has seen a striking decrease in the size of these devices, which are now small enough to be surgically placed under the skin, allowing
(15) them to remain virtually undetectable externally.

Lines: _____

Viewpoint/Tone: _____

Lines: _____

Viewpoint/Tone: _____

Lines: _____

Viewpoint/Tone: _____

Lines: _____

Viewpoint/Tone: _____

Viewpoint and Attitude Identification Drill

Passage #5:

On the other side of the interpretation debate
are those who believe that the Constitution was
meant to be a "living document," whose proper
construction would readily adapt to an evolving
(5) nation. Judges who subscribe to this perspective
are often referred to by strict constructionists as
judicial activists who are trying to take law-making
power away from the legislative branch of
the government. These judges, however, consider
(10) themselves interpreters, not activists. The framers
specifically allowed for constitutional amendment,
and afforded significant power to the judicial
branch; they felt that the Constitution was to
provide a framework but would have to adapt to a
(15) changing nation.

Lines: _____

Viewpoint/Tone: _____

Lines: _____

Viewpoint/Tone: _____

Lines: _____

Viewpoint/Tone: _____

Lines: _____

Viewpoint/Tone: _____

Viewpoint and Attitude Identification Drill

Passage #6:

Critics often accuse Primo Levi of providing a historically incomplete account of the Holocaust in his last book, *The Drowned and the Saved* (1986).
While technically correct, such accusations reveal
(5) a fundamental failure to understand the role of memory—and forgetting—in Levi's outstanding work. Levi regards human memory as a "marvelous but fallacious" instrument, given the inherent subjectivity of personal narration: time can alter
(10) memory, and false memories can emerge. As many psychologists agree, this can be particularly true of traumatic memories. Trauma can often limit precise recall of an injurious experience, and its severity is often predictive of memory status. From that
(15) perspective, the critics are correct: as a survivor of unimaginable horrors, Levi is unlikely to provide a reliably detailed account of his personal experiences. But he never meant to: *The Drowned and the Saved* is, above all, an introspective
(20) account of survival.

Lines: _____

Viewpoint/Tone: _____

Lines: _____

Viewpoint/Tone: _____

Lines: _____

Viewpoint/Tone: _____

Lines: _____

Viewpoint/Tone: _____

Viewpoint and Attitude Identification Drill

Passage #7:

One needs only to look at the vast body of
literary criticism produced during the Cold War
to realize that, as Abbott Gleason aptly observes
in his introduction to George Orwell's *Nineteen*
(5)   *Eighty-Four* (1949), Orwell's novel "has come
to be regarded as one of the great exposes of the
horrors of Stalinism." *Nineteen Eighty-Four* has
indeed transcended its historical occasion, its
themes persisting as ubiquitous elements of popular
(10) culture, political debate, and literary criticism
even after the end of the Cold War. History has
transformed the fictional paradigms contained in
the novel into an allegory of its own factual reality,
an allegory that describes a shared experience
(15) by staying embedded in the collective American
unconscious. If—as Walter Benjamin observes in
his essay, "The Storyteller"—storytelling is the
lost art of the twentieth century, Orwell manages to
find that art precisely at those moments of dramatic
(20) narration when censorship and alienation seem
most oppressive, didactic, and deafening.

Lines: _____

Viewpoint/Tone: _____

Lines: _____

Viewpoint/Tone: _____

Lines: _____

Viewpoint/Tone: _____

Lines: _____

Viewpoint/Tone: _____

Viewpoint and Attitude Identification Drill

Passage #8:

Designed by American architect Frank Lloyd
Wright in the early 1920's, the Hollyhock House
was an odd addition to the suburban landscape of
East Hollywood. Critics deplored its abandonment
(5)   of traditional principles of Western architecture,
noting that the clear inconsistency with its Anglo-
Colonial and Beaux-Arts neighbors. Because its
exterior walls tilted back at 85 degrees, many
felt that the Hollyhock House looked more like a
(10) Mayan temple than a residential building.

Indeed, the Hollyhock House lacked the typical
air of domesticity expected of it. Nevertheless,
the monumental nature of its form should not
have caused such consternation. Although the
(15) geometrically abstract hollyhock motif dominates
the exterior and the interior spaces of the house,
it also creates a rare sense of cohesion between
the two. Thanks to the symmetrical leaves
spaced evenly along its stem, the hollyhock also
(20) establishes an allegorical connection between the
hilly landscape of Southern California and the
building's ornamental design. In sharp contrast
with their predecessors, many modern-day
architects now see the building as organically
(25) inseparable from the Olive Hill on which it sits,
casting a much more favorable light on Frank
Lloyd Wright's ingenious design.

Lines: _____

Viewpoint/Tone: _____

Lines: _____

Viewpoint/Tone: _____

Lines: _____

Viewpoint/Tone: _____

Lines: _____

Viewpoint/Tone: _____

Viewpoint and Attitude Identification Drill

Passage #9:

What is "canon"? Scholars typically label as "canonical" those works of Western literature that have the greatest artistic merit. Critics often complain that canonicity is inherently subjective,
(5) often biased in favor of those who have the power and authority to define what "artistic merit" actually is. Even if the canon does not serve political interests overtly, their argument goes, it provides a perspective that is inherently
(10) exclusionary, if not oppressive.

What such debates fail to acknowledge is that the canon is as much about the past as it is about the present. It creates a fantasy of origin, a shared beginning that has survived the passage
(15) of time thanks to the timeless truth we imagine is contained in it. Much like the painted table in the antique shop, its nicks and chips precious signs of its antiquarian value, the canon provides a compensatory myth whose ambiguities only
(20) contribute to its stature of a classic. They do so by inviting a plethora of interpretations that seek to settle, once and for all, the "real" meaning of the text. The classic is itself a deeply disjointed work that both invites and resists interpretation,
(25) its contradictions exhibiting not a mere lack of adequate philosophical analysis, but rather the symptoms of contingency and incommensurability inherent in its own genealogy.

Lines: _____

Viewpoint/Tone: _____

Lines: _____

Viewpoint/Tone: _____

Lines: _____

Viewpoint/Tone: _____

Lines: _____

Viewpoint/Tone: _____

Viewpoint and Attitude Identification Drill

Passage #10:

For centuries, historians have regarded Vasari's *Life of Michelangelo*, originally published in 1550, as the primary source of information about the marble statue *David*. According to Vasari,
(5) Michelangelo completed the statue in 1504 from a large block of marble previously owned by Piero Soderini, then *gonfaloniere* for life in the city of Florence. Soderini had offered the project to several other Florentine sculptors before offering it
(10) to Michelangelo, Vasari claims, and the numerous attempts at carving the statue had rendered the block of marble virtually unsalvageable.

Although direct proof of Vasari's account was unattainable, he offered enough details to lend
(15) his argument a semblance of rigor. By 1840, however, the consensus among experts was that *David*'s provenance had little to do with Piero Soderini. A newly uncovered document dating back to 1476 showed that it was the Overseers of
(20) the Office of Works of the Duomo (the *Operai*) who commissioned the marble *David* to several sculptors—first to renowned Florentine sculptor Agostino di Duccio, and twelve years later to a younger artist, Antonio Rossellino. The Operai
(25) intended the statue to be part of the century-old "Prophet-project," a monumental series of twelve Old Testament-themed sculptures which would adorn the buttresses of Florence's cathedral church. Unfortunately, Agostino and Rossellino made
(30) little progress for over a decade, prompting the Operai to commission the piece to the 26-year old Michelangelo. Documents from the Duomo dating back to 1501 explicitly refer to the statue's intended purpose and style, leaving no doubt that
(35) Vasari's earlier accounts were factually incorrect.

Lines: _____

Viewpoint/Tone: _____

Lines: _____

Viewpoint/Tone: _____

Lines: _____

Viewpoint/Tone: _____

Lines: _____

Viewpoint/Tone: _____

Viewpoint and Attitude Identification Drill Answer Key

<u>Passage #1:</u>

Federal rules of evidence have long prohibited the presentation in court of many types of "hearsay" (evidence recounted second-hand, rather than reported directly by a witness), based on the notion
(5) that only the most readily verifiable evidence should be allowed consideration by any court in making its determinations. Dr. Kinsley has argued, however, that the rules of evidence as currently written are unacceptably overreaching, defining
(10) as hearsay too many types of evidence whose value would far outweigh any associated detriment if allowed court admissibility. But modern hearsay rules have been written with good reason.

<u>Lines 1-7</u>: This is the view of the federal rules of evidence. The rules allow only the most verifiable evidence to be considered by any court. The implication here is that many types of hearsay do not meet this requirement, and are therefore not allowed under the rules.

<u>Lines 7-12</u>: This is the perspective of Dr. Kinsley. By using the phrase "unacceptably overreaching," Kinsley appears to have a fairly strong negative opinion about the breadth of hearsay prohibitions as currently written.

<u>Lines 12-13</u>: This excerpt is not attributed to anyone, so it is the author at this point who takes issue with Kinsley's argument, asserting that the hearsay rules have a reasonable foundation.

<u>Passage #2:</u>

In the years which preceded Roger Bannister's record breaking performance, it was widely believed that the human body was not equipped to complete a mile-long run in under four minutes;
(5) human lungs, many leading experts asserted, could never deliver sufficient oxygen, and the heart could not undergo such physical stress. Bannister, undeterred, believed that he could reach the goal that he had set in 1952.

<u>Lines 1-7</u>: In the beginning of this paragraph, the author apprises us of a widely held belief about the body's limitations, followed by a more specific attribution of related assertions to many leading experts.

<u>Lines 7-9</u>: Here the author makes the switch to the perspective of Bannister. There is not too much attitude reflected here, although Bannister is characterized as fairly confident.

Viewpoint and Attitude Identification Drill Answer Key

<u>Passage #3:</u>

Many of Joyce's phrasings are less than readily decipherable, and as a result his works provide seemingly endless opportunity for speculation about construction and meaning. Consensus
(5) among literary scholars is often elusive, which is why outlier academics sometimes gain notoriety in the short term with questionable but well-publicized claims concerning proper interpretation. For example, one Joyce scholar in Ireland recently
(10) announced plans to publish "Finn's Hotel," a collection of early notes which he asserts to be "a previously unknown Joyce work," notwithstanding the fact that the stories have all been published before.

<u>Lines 1-5</u>: Author's view. Joyce's works are difficult to interpret and consensus among literary scholars is therefore elusive.

<u>Lines 5-8</u>: Author's view. This lack of consensus allows outlier academics to make questionable interpretations.

<u>Lines 8-12</u>: The viewpoint presented here is that of the Irish Joyce scholar.

<u>Lines 12-14</u>: This final clause is the author's view. The use of the phrase "notwithstanding the fact" shows that the author disagrees with the Joyce scholar's assertion.

<u>Passage #4:</u>

The first cardiac pacemaker was the brainchild of John Hopps, a Canadian electrical engineer who, in 1941, while researching hypothermia and the use of heat from radio frequencies to restore
(5) body temperature, found that mechanical or electrical stimulation can restart a heart that has stopped under conditions of extreme cold. The earliest versions of the pacemaker were heavy pieces of equipment which were far too large for
(10) implantation, and instead had to be rolled on wheels and kept attached to the patient at all times. Modern science has seen a striking decrease in the size of these devices, which are now small enough to be surgically placed under the skin, allowing
(15) them to remain virtually undetectable externally.

<u>Lines 1-15</u>: This excerpt does not provide multiple viewpoints; it is simply the author's presentation of information about the history of the cardiac pacemaker and its inventor. As is sometimes the case with Science passages, this selection reflects a relatively neutral tone.

Viewpoint and Attitude Identification Drill Answer Key

<u>Passage #5</u>:

On the other side of the interpretation debate
are those who believe that the Constitution was
meant to be a "living document," whose proper
construction would readily adapt to an evolving
(5)   nation. Judges who subscribe to this perspective
are often referred to by strict constructionists as
judicial activists who are trying to take law-making
power away from the legislative branch of
the government. These judges, however, consider
(10)   themselves interpreters, not activists. The framers
specifically allowed for constitutional amendment,
and afforded significant power to the judicial
branch; they felt that the Constitution was to
provide a framework but would have to adapt to a
(15)   changing nation.

Lines 1-5: This is the viewpoint of the "living document" proponents, and the tone is fairly matter-of-fact.

Lines 5-9: Here the author presents the perspective of the strict constructionists, who take a negative tone with regard to the "living document" judges.

Lines 9-10: At this point we are presented with the perspective of the so-called "judicial activists," who believe that they are simply offering interpretations rather than newly made laws.

Lines 10-15: Here we are provided with information about the beliefs of the framers, with an attitude that lends more support to the idea of the Constitution as a living document.

Viewpoint and Attitude Identification Drill Answer Key

Passage #6:

    Critics often accuse Primo Levi of providing a historically incomplete account of the Holocaust in his last book, *The Drowned and the Saved* (1986).
(5) While technically correct, such accusations reveal a fundamental failure to understand the role of memory—and forgetting—in Levi's outstanding work. Levi regards human memory as a "marvelous but fallacious" instrument, given the inherent subjectivity of personal narration: time can alter
(10) memory, and false memories can emerge. As many psychologists agree, this can be particularly true of traumatic memories. Trauma can often limit precise recall of an injurious experience, and its severity is often predictive of memory status. From that
(15) perspective, the critics are correct: as a survivor of unimaginable horrors, Levi is unlikely to provide a reliably detailed account of his personal experiences. But he never meant to: *The Drowned and the Saved* is, above all, an introspective
(20) account of survival.

Lines 1-3: The viewpoint presented here is that of the critics, who accuse Levi of providing an incomplete account of the Holocaust.

Lines 3-7: This section is crucial: the author concedes that the critics are "technically correct," but takes a strong stance against their position. The author also embraces Levi's book as an "outstanding work."

Lines 7-10: This excerpt clarifies Levi's viewpoint.

Lines 10-14: A new viewpoint is introduced—that of psychologists.

Lines 14-20: The author elaborates on her earlier claim about why the critics are "technically correct," but fail to grasp the purpose of Levi's account. We also learn more about Levi's purpose, as understood by the author.

Viewpoint and Attitude Identification Drill Answer Key

Passage #7:

One needs only to look at the vast body of
literary criticism produced during the Cold War
to realize that, as Abbott Gleason aptly observes
in his introduction to George Orwell's *Nineteen*
(5) *Eighty-Four* (1949), Orwell's novel "has come
to be regarded as one of the great exposes of the
horrors of Stalinism." *Nineteen Eighty-Four* has
indeed transcended its historical occasion, its
themes persisting as ubiquitous elements of popular
(10) culture, political debate, and literary criticism
even after the end of the Cold War. History has
transformed the fictional paradigms contained in
the novel into an allegory of its own factual reality,
an allegory that describes a shared experience
(15) by staying embedded in the collective American
unconscious. If—as Walter Benjamin observes in
his essay, "The Storyteller"—storytelling is the
lost art of the twentieth century, Orwell manages to
find that art precisely at those moments of dramatic
(20) narration when censorship and alienation seem
most oppressive, didactic, and deafening.

Lines 1-7: This excerpt introduces Gleason's views on George Orwell. The author quotes
Gleason, suggesting an overlap of viewpoints.

Lines 7-16: This section elaborates on the author's interpretation of *Nineteen Eighty-Four*. The
attitude is scholarly, the views—erudite.

Lines 16-21: The author mentions Walter Benjamin, but the reference only serves to lend
further credibility to the author's own views regarding Orwell.

Viewpoint and Attitude Identification Drill Answer Key

<u>Passage #8</u>:

(5)

(10)

Designed by American architect Frank Lloyd Wright in the early 1920's, the Hollyhock House was an odd addition to the suburban landscape of East Hollywood. Critics deplored its abandonment of traditional principles of Western architecture, noting that the clear inconsistency with its Anglo-Colonial and Beaux-Arts neighbors. Because its exterior walls tilted back at 85 degrees, many felt that the Hollyhock House looked more like a Mayan temple than a residential building.

(15)

(20)

(25)

Indeed, the Hollyhock House lacked the typical air of domesticity expected of it. Nevertheless, the monumental nature of its form should not have caused such consternation. Although the geometrically abstract hollyhock motif dominates the exterior and the interior spaces of the house, it also creates a rare sense of cohesion between the two. Thanks to the symmetrical leaves spaced evenly along its stem, the hollyhock also establishes an allegorical connection between the hilly landscape of Southern California and the building's ornamental design. In sharp contrast with their predecessors, many modern-day architects now see the building as organically inseparable from the Olive Hill on which it sits, casting a much more favorable light on Frank Lloyd Wright's ingenious design.

<u>Lines 1-4</u>: The author acknowledges the Hollyhock House is an "odd addition" to East Hollywood.

<u>Lines 4-10</u>: Introduce the critics' viewpoint, which is critical of the Hollyhock House.

<u>Lines 11-22</u>: This is the author's main point. The author concedes that the building is not as "domestic" as expected, but views the critics as too harsh. The author goes on to provide positive aspects of the hollyhock motif to support this view.

<u>Lines 22-27</u>: Juxtapose the critics' views mentioned in the first paragraph to those of modern-day architects, whose views mirror the author's own view.

Viewpoint and Attitude Identification Drill Answer Key

Passage #9:

What is "canon"? Scholars typically label as "canonical" those works of Western literature that have the greatest artistic merit. Critics often complain that canonicity is inherently subjective,
(5) often biased in favor of those who have the power and authority to define what "artistic merit" actually is. Even if the canon does not serve political interests overtly, their argument goes, it provides a perspective that is inherently
(10) exclusionary, if not oppressive.

What such debates fail to acknowledge is that the canon is as much about the past as it is about the present. It creates a fantasy of origin, a shared beginning that has survived the passage
(15) of time thanks to the timeless truth we imagine is contained in it. Much like the painted table in the antique shop, its nicks and chips precious signs of its antiquarian value, the canon provides a compensatory myth whose ambiguities only
(20) contribute to its stature of a classic. They do so by inviting a plethora of interpretations that seek to settle, once and for all, the "real" meaning of the text. The classic is itself a deeply disjointed work that both invites and resists interpretation,
(25) its contradictions exhibiting not a mere lack of adequate philosophical analysis, but rather the symptoms of contingency and incommensurability inherent in its own genealogy.

Lines 1-3: Define "canon" from a scholarly perspective.

Lines 3-10: Outline the critics' argument against canonicity.

Lines 11-28: Introduce and elaborate on the author's perspective regarding canonical works.

Viewpoint and Attitude Identification Drill Answer Key

Passage #10:

For centuries, historians have regarded Vasari's *Life of Michelangelo*, originally published in 1550, as the primary source of information about the marble statue *David*. According to Vasari,
(5) Michelangelo completed the statue in 1504 from a large block of marble previously owned by Piero Soderini, then *gonfaloniere* for life in the city of Florence. Soderini had offered the project to several other Florentine sculptors before offering it
(10) to Michelangelo, Vasari claims, and the numerous attempts at carving the statue had rendered the block of marble virtually unsalvageable.

Although direct proof of Vasari's account was unattainable, he offered enough details to lend
(15) his argument a semblance of rigor. By 1840, however, the consensus among experts was that *David*'s provenance had little to do with Piero Soderini. A newly uncovered document dating back to 1476 showed that it was the Overseers of
(20) the Office of Works of the Duomo (the *Operai*) who commissioned the marble *David* to several sculptors—first to renowned Florentine sculptor Agostino di Duccio, and twelve years later to a younger artist, Antonio Rossellino. The Operai
(25) intended the statue to be part of the century-old "Prophet-project," a monumental series of twelve Old Testament-themed sculptures which would adorn the buttresses of Florence's cathedral church. Unfortunately, Agostino and Rossellino made
(30) little progress for over a decade, prompting the Operai to commission the piece to the 26-year old Michelangelo. Documents from the Duomo dating back to 1501 explicitly refer to the statue's intended purpose and style, leaving no doubt that
(35) Vasari's earlier accounts were factually incorrect.

Lines 1-4: Introduce Vasari's importance to historians.

Lines 4-12: Outline Vasari's version of events regarding the provenance of Michelangelo's *David*.

Lines 13-15: Imply the author's position regarding Vasari's historical account: it *seems* rigorous (but probably isn't).

Lines 15-18: Introduce the experts' position, which is in direct disagreement with Vasari's.

Lines 18-32: Mention the Operai's purpose for commissioning the piece, which functions as evidence for the author's main point.

Lines 32-35: Re-assert the author's main point: Vasari's account is factually incorrect.

3. Passage Argumentation ▐███

Identifying viewpoints and tone is critical in establishing a generalized feel for how a passage unfolds. Understanding the arguments will help you understand the details of the passage. To better help you analyze passage arguments, let's first focus on the broader nature of argumentation itself.

LSAT Reading Comprehension passages consist of premises and conclusions just as in the Logical Reasoning section. In the *PowerScore LSAT Logical Reasoning Bible* we detail how to identify premises and conclusions. Herein, we present a summary of the main points from that section, with additional notes and adjustments to account for the fact that Reading Comprehension passages are longer and more complex than Logical Reasoning stimuli.

Identifying Premises and Conclusions

For LSAT purposes, a premise can be defined as:

> "A fact, proposition, or statement from which a conclusion is made."

Premises support and explain the conclusion. Literally, the premises give the reasons why the conclusion should be accepted. To identify premises, ask yourself, "*What reasons has the author used to persuade me? Why should I believe this argument? What evidence exists?*"

A conclusion can be defined as:

> "A statement or judgment that follows from one or more reasons."

Conclusions, as summary statements, are supposed to be drawn from and rest upon the premises. To identify conclusions, ask yourself, "*What is the author driving at? What does the author want me to believe? What point follows from the others?*"

Because language is the test makers' weapon of choice, you must learn to recognize the words that indicate when a premise or conclusion is present.

This section discusses the "A" in VIEWSTAMP. The "A" stands for Arguments.

LSAC says you are expected to possess, in their words, "a college-level understanding of widely used concepts such as argument, premise, assumption, and conclusion."

A premise gives a reason why something should be believed.

A conclusion is the point the author tries to prove by using another statement.

In expressing arguments, authors often use the following words or phrases to introduce premises and conclusions:

Make sure to memorize these word lists. Recognizing argument elements is critical!

3

Premise Indicators	Conclusion Indicators
because	thus
since	therefore
for	hence
for example	consequently
for the reason that	as a result
in that	so
given that	accordingly
as indicated by	clearly
due to	must be that
owing to	shows that
this can be seen from	conclude that
we know this by	follows that

Because there are so many variations in the English language, these lists cannot be exhaustive, but they do capture many of the premise and conclusion indicators used by LSAT authors. As for frequency of appearance, the top two words in each list are used more than any of the other words listed.

When you are reading, always be aware of the presence of the words catalogued above. These words are like road signs; they tell you what is coming next. Consider the following example:

Humans cannot live on Venus because the surface temperature is too high.

Identifying conclusions often helps in identifying the main point of a passage.

As you read the first portion of the sentence, "Humans cannot live on Venus," you cannot be sure if you are reading a premise or conclusion. But, as soon as you see the word "because"—a premise indicator—you know that a premise will follow, and at that point you know that the first portion of the sentence is a conclusion. In the argument above, the author wants you to believe that humans cannot live on Venus, and the reason is that the surface temperature is too high.

In our daily lives, we make and hear many arguments (when we say "argument," we do not mean a fight!). However, unlike on the LSAT, the majority of these arguments occur in the form of a two-person dialogue where you are actively involved. But with a slight adjustment, LSAT arguments can attain that same form:

Author: "Humans cannot live on Venus."

Respondent: "Really? Why is that?"

Author: "The surface temperature of Venus is too high."

So if you struggle to identify argumentative elements, you can always resort to thinking about the argument as an artificial conversation where you're a participant, and that may assist you in not only locating the conclusion, but also recognizing potential flaws in a speaker's reasoning.

Here are more examples of premise and conclusion indicators in use:

1. "The economy is in tatters. Therefore, we must end this war."

    "Therefore" introduces a conclusion; the first sentence is a premise.

2. "We must reduce our budget due to the significant cost overruns we experienced during production."

    "due to" introduces a premise; "We must reduce our budget" is the conclusion.

3. "Fraud has cost the insurance industry millions of dollars in lost revenue. Thus, Congress will pass a stricter fraud control bill since the insurance industry has one of the most powerful lobbies."

    This argument contains two premises: the first premise is the first sentence and the second premise follows the word "since" in the second sentence; the conclusion is "Congress will pass a stricter fraud control bill."

Notice that premises and conclusions can be presented in any order—the conclusion can be first, last, or elsewhere—and the relationship between the premises and the conclusion remains the same. For example, if the order of the premise(s) and conclusion were switched in any of the prior examples, the logical structure and validity of the arguments would not change.

Also notable is that the premise(s) and the conclusion can appear in the same sentence, or can be separated out into multiple sentences. Whether the ideas are together or separated has no effect on the logical structure of the argument. This is especially important to recognize in Reading Comprehension passages, because sections of an argument can be separated by many lines or spread out over an entire passage.

One Confusing Sentence Form

Because the job of the test makers is to determine how well you can interpret information, they will sometimes arrange premise and conclusion indicators in a way that is designed to be confusing. One of their favorite forms places a conclusion indicator and premise indicator back-to-back, separated by a comma, as in the following examples:

"Therefore, since..."

"Thus, because..."

"Hence, due to..."

A quick glance would seemingly indicate that what will follow is both a premise and a conclusion. In this instance, however, the presence of the comma creates a clause that, due to the premise indicator, contains a premise. The end of that premise clause will be closed with a second comma, and then what follows will be the conclusion, as seen here:

"Therefore, since higher debt has forced consumers to lower their savings, banks now have less money to loan."

"Higher debt has forced consumers to lower their savings" is the premise; "banks now have less money to loan" is the conclusion. So, in this instance "therefore" still introduces a conclusion, but one that is interrupted by a clause that contains a premise.

Additional Premise Indicators

Aside from previously listed premise and conclusion indicators, there are other argument indicator words you should learn to recognize. In the Reading Comprehension section, the author will often make an argument and then for good measure add other premises that lend support to the argument but are non-essential to the conclusion. These are known as additional premises:

Additional Premise Indicators (Continuing the same idea)
furthermore
moreover
besides
in addition
what's more
after all

Following are two examples of additional premise indicators in use:

1. "Every professor at Fillmore University teaches exactly one class per semester. Fillmore's Professor Jackson, therefore, is teaching exactly one class this semester. Moreover, I heard Professor Jackson say she was teaching only a single class."

   The first sentence is a premise. The second sentence contains the conclusion indicator "therefore" and is the conclusion of the argument. The first sentence is the main proof offered by the author for the conclusion. The third sentence begins with the additional premise indicator "moreover." The premise in this sentence is non-essential to the argument, but provides additional proof for the conclusion and could be, if needed, used to help prove the conclusion separately (this would occur if an objection was raised to the first premise).

2. "The city council ought to ease restrictions on outdoor advertising because the city's economy is currently in a slump. Furthermore, the city should not place restrictions on forms of speech such as advertising."

The first sentence contains both the conclusion of the argument and the main premise of the argument (introduced by the premise indicator "because"). The last sentence contains the additional premise indicator "furthermore." As with the previous example, the additional premise in this sentence is non-essential to the argument but provides additional proof for the conclusion.

Counter-argument Indicators

In a passage, an author will sometimes bring up a counter-argument—an argument that contains an idea that is in opposition to the prior argument discussed by the author. In Reading Comprehension passages, counter-argument indicators usually introduce an entirely new viewpoint, and thus tracking these indicators is critical.

Counter-argument indicators can also introduce ideas that compare and contrast with the argument, or work against a previously raised point. In this sense, the counter-argument will generally present an idea that is in some way different from another part of the argument.

Counter-argument indicators, also called adversatives, bring up points of opposition or comparison.

Note that some terms, such as "After all," can appear on multiple indicator lists because the phrase can be used in a variety of ways. As a savvy LSAT taker, it is up to you to identify the exact role that the phrase is playing in the argument.

Counter-argument Indicators (Introducing a new idea)
but
yet
however
on the other hand
admittedly
in contrast
although
even though
still
whereas
in spite of
despite
after all

The following is an example of a counter-argument indicator in use:

1. "The United States prison population is the world's largest and consequently we must take steps to reduce crime in this country. Although other countries have higher rates of incarceration, their statistics have no bearing on the dilemma we currently face."

> The first sentence contains a premise and the conclusion (which is introduced by the conclusion indicator "consequently"). The third sentence offers up a counter-argument as indicated by the word "although."

Recognizing Conclusions Without Indicators

Many of the arguments we have encountered up until this point have had indicator words to help you recognize the conclusion. And, many of the arguments you will see on the LSAT will also have conclusion indicators. But you will encounter arguments that do not contain conclusion indicators. The following is an example:

> "The best way to eliminate traffic congestion will not be easily found. There are so many competing possibilities that it will take millions of dollars to study every option, and implementation of most options carries an exorbitant price tag."

An argument like the one above can be difficult to analyze because no indicator words are present to highlight the presence and location of a viewpoint. How then, would you go about determining if a conclusion is present, and if so, how would you identify that conclusion? Fortunately, there is a fairly simple trick that can be used to handle this situation, and any situation where you are uncertain of the conclusion (including those with multiple conclusions, as will be discussed next).

Aside from the questions you can use to identify premises and conclusions (described earlier in this chapter), the easiest way to determine the conclusion in an argument is to use the Conclusion Identification Method™:

Take the statements under consideration for the conclusion and place them in an arrangement that forces one to be the conclusion and the other(s) to be the premise(s). Use premise and conclusion indicators to achieve this end. Once the pieces are arranged, determine if the arrangement makes logical sense: if the assigned conclusion follows from the premises, and the assigned premises are given in order to support that conclusion. If so, you have made the correct identification. If not, reverse the arrangement and examine the relationship again. Continue until you find an arrangement that is the most logical.

Let's apply this method to the previous argument. For our first arrangement we will make the first sentence the premise and the second sentence the conclusion, and supply indicators (in italics):

Because the best way to eliminate traffic congestion will not be easily found, *we can conclude that* there are so many competing possibilities that it will take millions of dollars to study every option, and implementation of most options carries an exorbitant price tag.

Does that sound right? No. So we'll try again, this time making the first sentence the conclusion and the second sentence the premise:

Because there are so many competing possibilities that it will take millions of dollars to study every option, and implementation of most options carries an exorbitant price tag, *we can conclude that* the best way of eliminating traffic congestion will not be easily found.

Clearly, the second arrangement is superior because it makes more sense. In most cases when you have the conclusion and premise backward, the arrangement will be confusing. The correct arrangement always sounds more reasonable.

Inferences and Assumptions

When working through LSAT questions, you will frequently see the words *inference* and *assumption*. Because these ideas are so prevalent, we should take a moment to define the meaning of each term in the context of LSAT argumentation.

Most people have come to believe that the word *inference* means probably true or likely to be true. Indeed, in common usage *infer* is often used in the same manner as *imply*. On the LSAT these uses are incorrect. In logic, an inference can be defined as something that *must be true*. Thus, if you are asked to identify an inference of or from the passage, you must find an item that must be true based on the information presented.

In argumentation, an assumption is simply the same as an *unstated* premise—what must be true in order for the argument to be true. Put another way, assumptions are ideas that are *required* for the author's argument to be potentially acceptable. They don't guarantee the correctness of the argument, but they do prevent the argument from being immediately dismissible as false. Thus assumptions can often have a great effect on the validity of arguments.

Separating an inference from an assumption can be difficult because the definition of each refers to what "must be true." The difference is simple: an inference is what follows from a set of known premises (in other words, a conclusion) whereas an assumption is what is taken for granted while making an argument. In one sense, an assumption occurs "before" the argument, that is, while the argument is being made. An inference is made "after" the initial information is known, and follows from the given facts/ argument. Note that all authors make assumptions when creating their arguments, and all fact sets and arguments have inferences that can be derived from them.

Complex Argumentation

Up until this point, we have only discussed simple arguments. Simple arguments contain a single conclusion. While many of the arguments that appear on the LSAT are simple arguments, Reading Comprehension passages are typically made up of more complex arguments containing more than one conclusion. In these instances, one of the conclusions is the main conclusion, and the other conclusions are subsidiary conclusions (also known as sub-conclusions or intermediate conclusions).

While complex argumentation may sound daunting at first, you make and encounter complex argumentation every day in your life. In basic terms, a complex argument makes an initial conclusion based on a premise. The author then uses that conclusion as the foundation (or premise) for another conclusion, thus building a chain, or a ladder with several levels. Let's take a look at the two types of arguments in diagram form:

In abstract terms, a simple argument appears as follows:

Conclusion

Premise

As discussed previously, the premise supports the conclusion, hence the arrow from the premise to the conclusion.

By comparison, a complex argument takes an initial conclusion and then uses it as a premise for another conclusion:

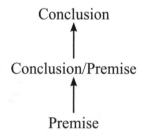

Conclusion

Conclusion/Premise

Premise

Thus, a statement can be both a conclusion for one argument and a premise for another. In this sense, a complex argument can appear somewhat like a ladder, where each level or "rung" represents the next level. Given enough time you could build an argument with hundreds of levels. In LSAT Reading Comprehension passages, however, there are typically four or five levels at most.

Here is an example of a complex argument:

> "Because the Colts have the best quarterback in football, they therefore have the best offense in football. Because they have the best offense in football, they will win the Super Bowl next year."

In this argument, the first sentence contains a premise followed by a conclusion. This initial conclusion is then used in the second sentence as a premise to make a larger conclusion:

Premise: "Because the Colts have the best quarterback in football,"

Sub-Conclusion (conclusion of the previous premise/premise for the following conclusion): "they therefore have the best offense in football."

Main Conclusion: "they will win the Super Bowl next year."

In this argument, the two premises lead directly to the conclusion. Unlike some of the previous argument examples, the author's conclusion seems reasonable based on the two premises. Note that the strength of this argument is based solely on the degree to which the premises prove the conclusion. The truth of the premises themselves is not an issue in determining whether the argument is valid or invalid.

Relationship Indicators

A central purpose of the LSAT is to test how closely you read. One of the ways the LSAT tests whether you have this skill is to probe your knowledge of exactly what the author said. Because of this, you must at times read parts of a passage incredibly closely, and you must pay special attention to words that describe the relationships under discussion. For example, if an author concludes, "Therefore, the refinery can achieve a greater operating efficiency," do not make the mistake of thinking the author implied that greater operating efficiency *will* or *must* be achieved.

When it comes to relationships, the makers of the LSAT have a wide variety of modifiers in their arsenal. The following are two lists of words that should be noted when they appear, regardless of where they appear in the passage.

Quantity Indicators	Probability Indicators
all	must
every	will
most	always
many	not always
some	probably
several	likely
few	would
sole	not necessarily
only	could
not all	rarely
none	never

Quantity Indicators refer to the amount or quantity in the relationship, such as "some people" or "many of the laws." Probability Indicators refer to the likelihood of occurrence, or the obligation present, as in "The Mayor should resign" or "The law will never pass." Many of the terms fit with negatives to form an opposing idea, for example, "some are not" or "most would not."

Words such as the Quantity and Probability Indicators are critical because they are a ripe area for the LSAT makers to exploit. There are numerous examples of incorrect answer choices that have attempted to capitalize on the meaning of a single word in the passage, and thus you must commit yourself to carefully examining every word on the test.

A Word About Indicator Words

Over the past several pages, we presented lists of indicator words. These indicator lists are important for several reasons:

1. They help you identify the main elements of the author's argument.

2. They help you identify supplementary argument points made by the author.

3. They show you when the author introduces viewpoints other than his or her own.

4. They alert you to changes in the direction of the argument.

5. They alert you to the strength of the various points made by the author.

Your ability to track the flow and direction of the argumentation is critical, and thus we strongly recommend that you become extremely familiar with the words presented in each indicator list. These words will serve as road signs as you navigate your way through each passage.

Because of their importance, we will also discuss indicator words again in the chapter on marking passages (Chapter Five).

4. The Main Point

This section discusses the "MP" in the VIEWSTAMP acronym. The "MP" stands for Main Point.

In the previous Passage Argumentation section, our analysis of passage argumentation was at the detail level, discussing the words that authors use to introduce certain types of argumentative elements. Identifying ideas at the elemental level is an important skill, and one that will serve you well throughout the LSAT, as well as in law school. However, a large number of Reading Comprehension questions will ask you broad questions such as the Main Point of the author's argument. Consequently, you must also see the "big picture" as you read, and develop an ability to track the author's major themes and intents.

The main point of a passage is the central idea that the author is attempting to prove or relay.

The main point of a passage is the central idea, or ultimate conclusion, that the author is attempting to prove. Although in the majority of passages the main point is stated in the first paragraph, it is not always the case that the main point appears at the very outset. The main point of many passages has appeared in the final sentence of the first paragraph or in the first sentence of the second paragraph, or, at times, in the last paragraph. So, although the main point is often found early in the first paragraph, the test makers have the ability to place the main point anywhere in the passage.

As you read, you must identify the author's conclusions and track how they link together. What is the ultimate aim of the author's statements? What is he or she attempting to prove? Are some conclusions used to support others? If so, which is the primary conclusion? The key to identifying a main point is to remember that, although the main point may be stated succinctly in a sentence or two, all paragraphs of the passage must support the main point. Thus, the main point will not just reflect the argument contained in a single paragraph, but will instead represent the author's objectives for the entirety of the passage.

When we discuss Main Point questions in Chapter Six, we will cover this part of passage identification more thoroughly, and then as we break down actual passage sets we will also examine main points in detail.

5. Passage Structure

Many students, when they first begin working with Reading Comprehension passages, attempt to remember every single detail of the passage. Given the limits of human short-term memory and the test's intensive time pressure, this is an impossible task. Fortunately, it is also an unnecessary one. Built into your test taking strategy should be the expectation that you will frequently return to the passage during the questions to confirm and disconfirm answer choices.

This section discusses the "S" in the VIEWSTAMP acronym. The "S" stands for Structure.

In order to successfully return to the passage, however, you must attempt to identify the underlying logical structure of the passage as you read. This will help you quickly find information once you begin to answer the questions. For example, some passages open by stating the background of a thesis that will be challenged later in the passage. In the following paragraphs the author will then present an alternative viewpoint to the thesis and perhaps specific counterexamples which provide support for the alternative view. Awareness of this general structure will allow you to reduce the time you spend searching for information when you refer back to the text.

Fortunately, identifying the logical structure of a passage does not require any training in logic or logical terminology. You simply need to be able to describe in general terms the order in which things are presented in the passage. This is most often connected to specific paragraphs, as in, "The first paragraph introduces the jury unanimity requirement, and then presents the viewpoints of the critics of unanimity. At the start of the second paragraph, the author takes a strong position that jury unanimity is essential. The second and third paragraphs support that position— paragraph two states that the costs of hung juries are minimal, and paragraph three states that requiring unanimous verdicts leads to fairer verdicts and thus fairer trials." With a brief synopsis such as this one, you could confidently return to the passage as needed. Question about the critic's position? Most likely the answer will be found in the first paragraph. Question about verdict fairness? Most likely the answer will be found in the last paragraph.

Don't worry that you will not be able to recall every detail. The answers to every problem are already on the page, and thus your task is simply to be able to identify the correct answer, not to remember every single thing about the passage.

Note that your structural analysis is *not* written down in full during the exam; instead, you simply hold the idea in your mind as you read and then move to the questions. Thus, in a nutshell, your structural analysis must be compact enough to be mentally retained, and it must also provide enough basic detail to serve as a guide when you return to the passage. Also keep in mind that if you need to refresh your memory, you can glance at any marks or notes you made about the passage itself for clues (we will discuss this in more detail in Chapter Five).

Of course, the Viewpoint Analysis approach we discussed briefly before will also help you identify and understand the structure of the passage. Recognizing the views of the various players in the passage will greatly assist in your ability to comprehend the passage as a whole. Identifying the main point and author's tone will also make this task easier.

Here is an example using the opening paragraph from an LSAT passage:

The Canadian Auto Workers' (CAW) Legal Services Plan, designed to give active and retired autoworkers and their families access to totally prepaid or partially reimbursed legal services, has
(5)   been in operation since late 1985. Plan members have the option of using either the plan's staff lawyers, whose services are fully covered by the cost of membership in the plan, or an outside lawyer. Outside lawyers, in turn, can either sign up with the plan as a
(10) "cooperating lawyer" and accept the CAW's fee schedule as payment in full, or they can charge a higher fee and collect the balance from the client. Autoworkers appear to have embraced the notion of prepaid legal services: 45 percent of eligible union
(15) members were enrolled in the plan by 1988. Moreover, the idea of prepaid legal services has been spreading in Canada. A department store is even offering a plan to holders of its credit card.

A written analysis of the paragraph would appear as follows:

The paragraph opens by introducing the concept of a prepaid legal service plan, and specifically the one used by Canadian Auto Workers (CAW). There are several important elements that define the plan:

1. Members receive prepaid or partially reimbursed legal services.

2. Plan staff lawyers are fully covered by the plan.

3. Members can use outside lawyers, who may or may not charge an additional fee.

The plan has operated since 1985, and as of 1988 included 45 percent of eligible CAW members, so it seems there has been a good response to the plan in the short term. The idea is also spreading—other organizations are starting to offer similar plans.

The prior analysis is too much to keep in your head while reading, so you must distill the essence of the paragraph into a more concise description that is easier to remember (and of course, you may choose to underline or highlight parts of the passage that will help reinforce certain points you deem notable). Such an analysis would probably consist of:

> The prepaid legal service plan for Canadian Auto Workers covers legal costs for members and has been successful.

Does this description capture every detail of the first paragraph? No, but it does not need to! You simply need to get the gist of what is occurring in this paragraph so you can quickly return if needed to answer a question.

Let us examine the second paragraph of the same passage:

(20)　　While many plan members seem to be happy to get reduced-cost legal help, many lawyers are concerned about the plan's effect on their profession, especially its impact on prices for legal services. Some point out that even though most lawyers have not joined the plan as cooperating lawyers, legal fees
(25)　in the cities in which the CAW plan operates have been depressed, in some cases to an unprofitable level. The directors of the plan, however, claim that both clients and lawyers benefit from their arrangement. For while the clients get ready access to
(30)　reduced-price services, lawyers get professional contact with people who would not otherwise be using legal services, which helps generate even more business for their firms. Experience shows, the directors say, that if people are referred to a firm and
(35)　receive excellent service, the firm will get three to four other referrals who are not plan subscribers and who would therefore pay the firm's standard rate.

Bypassing a complete written analysis for the moment, our distilled, structural analysis of this paragraph would be along the lines of:

> Lawyers are concerned about the plan's effect on prices; directors of the plan claim that everyone benefits.

Again, this description omits certain details, but it does indicate that there are two viewpoints presented in this paragraph, and that those two viewpoints are opposing. Should a question ask about the views of lawyers, you would know to return to the first half of this paragraph. On the other hand, should a question ask about the plan's directors, the second half of this paragraph would be the proper starting point.

Consider, for example, the following question which accompanied this passage:

5. The passage most strongly suggests that, according to proponents of prepaid legal plans, cooperating lawyers benefit from taking clients at lower fees in which one of the following ways?

   (A) Lawyers can expect to gain expertise in a wide variety of legal services by availing themselves of the access to diverse clientele that plan participation affords.
   (B) Experienced cooperating lawyers are likely to enjoy the higher profits of long-term, complex cases, for which new lawyers are not suited.
   (C) Lower rates of profit will be offset by a higher volume of clients and new business through word-of-mouth recommendations.
   (D) Lower fees tend to attract clients away from established, nonparticipating law firms.
   (E) With all legal fees moving downward to match the plans' schedules, the profession will respond to market forces.

With regard to this question, it is valuable to be familiar with the passage organization, since the proponents' (directors') arguments can all be found in the second paragraph. Further, since the author presents conflicting viewpoints in that paragraph, we should focus on the second half, in which the author presents proponents' arguments in favor of the plan (The correct answer to the question above is answer choice (C), which summarizes the argument presented in lines 33-37 of the passage).

Let's complete our analysis by reviewing the final paragraph of the passage:

> But it is unlikely that increased use of such plans
> will result in long-term client satisfaction or in a
> (40) substantial increase in profits for law firms. Since
> lawyers with established reputations and client bases
> can benefit little, if at all, from participation, the
> plans function largely as marketing devices for
> lawyers who have yet to establish themselves. While
> (45) many of these lawyers are no doubt very able and
> conscientious, they will tend to have less expertise
> and to provide less satisfaction to clients. At the same
> time, the downward pressure on fees will mean that
> the full-fee referrals that proponents say will come
> (50) through plan participation may not make up for a
> firm's investment in providing services at low plan
> rates. And since lowered fees provide little incentive
> for lawyers to devote more than minimal effort to
> cases, a "volume discount" approach toward the
> (55) practice of law will mean less time devoted to
> complex cases and a general lowering of quality for
> clients.

Again, we can bypass a complete written breakdown, and instead look at the distilled, structural analysis of this paragraph:

> The author concludes that the plan is unlikely to benefit clients or lawyers, and then offers reasons why.

As before, this synopsis intentionally leaves out some details, but that is immaterial. The point is to understand the general idea of what happened in the passage. You should also note that the first several lines of this paragraph contain the author's main point.

Putting all three analyses together, the entire structure appears as:

> The prepaid legal service plan for Canadian Auto Workers covers legal costs for members and has been successful.

> Lawyers are concerned about the plans effect on prices; directors of the plan claim that everyone benefits.

> The author concludes that the plan is unlikely to benefit clients or lawyers, and then offers reasons why.

Note that this summation not only describes the structural elements—viewpoints, for example—but also provides basic details of each. Compare this to a more logic-based analysis that eliminates the details of each viewpoint:

Paragraph 1:   Introduce one example of a prepaid legal service plan

Paragraph 2:   Present arguments for and against this type of plan

Paragraph 3:   Assess these plans as unlikely to be beneficial, listing several specific reasons for this assertion.

This analysis is factually correct, but for our purposes it would not provide a very helpful guide when answering the questions. For example, the above characterization of the second paragraph is perfectly accurate, but as a mental tool for use in returning to the passage it would be inadequate.

Never forget the rule of structural analysis stated earlier:

Your structural analysis must be compact enough to be mentally retained, and it must also provide enough basic detail to serve as a guide when you return to the passage.

Basic Summary and Purpose Drill

After each of the following short passages, provide a basic summary of the material presented, followed by a basic analysis of the author's purpose. *Answers on page 107*

Example:

> Chinchillas, which are native to the Andes Mountains in South America, are rare in the wild due to overhunting. The trade in chinchilla fur extends as far back as the 1500s, but by the early 1900s demand for chinchilla pelts was so great that chinchillas became almost extinct. A series of trade prohibitions that outlawed the trade of chinchilla fur slowed the decline. Today, Chinchillas are still endangered but no longer on the brink of extinction.

Basic Summary: Chinchillas, native to the South American Andes, are rare because of the demand for their pelts, which began in the 1500s and put them near extinction in the 1900s. Trade prohibitions have slowed the decline.

Purpose: Introduce the Chinchilla, its overhunting, and the trade prohibitions which saved the animal from the verge of extinction.

Passage #1:

> Many early scientists operated under the mistaken assumption that the continents were fixed in place, static and incapable of independent movement. As a result most ignored the fact that the east coast of South America and the west coast of Africa appeared to line up, mocking assertions that the two continents had at one time been part of a larger mass. Later, scientists began to consider the possibility of continental drift, and the likelihood that the two continents had indeed been linked at some point in the past.

Basic Summary: _____

_____

_____

_____

_____

Purpose: _____

_____

_____

_____

Basic Summary and Purpose Drill

Passage #2:

    Political commentators have long advocated direct
monetary aid as an effective way to help resolve the political
and economic struggles of many African nations. In her
recent book, however, Dambisa Moyo makes the startling
argument that western nations should discontinue direct
governmental aid on the grounds that such aid actually
worsens conditions for the general population. Although
she grants that some direct investment in the economies
of Africa—in the form of business loans and credit—is
desirable, her belief is that debt levels have become
intolerably high and that foreign aid has facilitated the
creation of corrupt regimes. Critics have labeled her views
cruel and callous, attacking her for providing a rationale for
western neglect of Africa.

Basic Summary: _____

_____

_____

_____

_____

Purpose: _____

_____

_____

_____

Basic Summary and Purpose Drill

<u>Passage #3</u>:

    The success of a small local business can often depend on issues different from those which determine the success of a large or national business. Although many factors can contribute to the failure of a local business, experts point to three significant areas that commonly cause problems. First, poor management of business operations can doom even the best small business to failure. Management covers a gamut of items, from accounting to customer service to employee management, and a weakness or lack of oversight in any of these areas can quickly lead to serious problems. Second, a local business must often rely on a good location. A poor location fails to attract customers, which translates directly into low sales. Finally, small businesses must rely heavily on advertising for success, so a weak (or nonexistent) marketing strategy can have an exaggerated impact on the health of the business.

Basic Summary: _____

_____

_____

_____

_____

Purpose: _____

_____

_____

_____

Basic Summary and Purpose Drill

Passage #4:

The integral role played by the law in promoting public health is irrefutable. Eliminating lead in paints, banning smoking in public buildings, and requiring the posting of nutritional content on food labels are just a few types of public protection that have resulted from public health legislation. Within the nutritional law community, experts agree that these legal efforts have produced demonstrable benefits nationally. One burgeoning area of nutritional law is obesity law; proposed legislation in this area focuses largely on food warnings and additional labeling to apprise the public of risks associated with the overconsumption of certain foods. Participants in this debate must weigh the needs of all stakeholders, considering the rights of food producers while also considering the health of the general population.

Basic Summary: _____

_____

_____

_____

_____

Purpose: _____

_____

_____

_____

Basic Summary and Purpose Drill

Passage #5:

The fall of the Berlin Wall in 1989 is interpreted differently by different groups, depending in many cases on their ideology and their location. Observers in the United States often credit Ronald Reagan with the fall, due to his aggressive anti-communist agenda and large military budget. Europeans tend to perceive the event differently, believing that a policy of accommodation and productive engagement towards East Germany ultimately lead to the political upheaval that resulted in the fall of the Wall. Russians often view the event in a negative light, with a concomitant loss of geopolitical influence and control. Many Russians argue that post-fall events left Russia on the periphery of European politics, while Europe enjoyed an atmosphere that was more inclusive and cooperative.

Basic Summary: _____

_____

_____

_____

_____

Purpose: _____

_____

_____

_____

Basic Summary and Purpose Drill

Passage #6:

Aeronautics really might be called the "other NASA," distinct in its charge, methodologies, and scale. Aeronautics research is not mission-oriented in the same way that going to the Moon or Mars is. It is interested in learning about physical phenomena, such as turbulence, and how to do something, such as quieting the noise of helicopter blades. Aeronautics' mission is not about going somewhere specific or building one particular thing; it is about supporting the country's commercial and military needs with respect to aviation. The contrast with the space program is telling: where NASA has gone to considerable lengths to justify the space program and explain how space innovations feed into the country's more terrestrial needs, aeronautics research has had a direct and undeniable impact on commercial and military technology development.

Basic Summary: _____

_____

_____

_____

_____

Purpose: _____

_____

_____

_____

Basic Summary and Purpose Drill

<u>Passage #7</u>:

Many of the world's mythologies explain landforms as the legacies of struggles among giants, time out of mind. Legend accounts for the Giant's Causeway, a geological formation off the coast of Northern Ireland, as the remains of an ancient bridge that giants made between Ireland and Scotland. In Native American mythologies, landforms of the American West cohere as the body parts of vast divinities, whose death precedes the emergence and growth of peoples and cultures. Contemporary Americans of many backgrounds, too, use names for body parts to label geographic forms, naming heads of hollows, gorges of rivers, or mouths of mines. Unwittingly, then, our words suggest that we likewise inhabit landscapes formed from the sundered bodies of giants.

Basic Summary: _____

_____

_____

_____

_____

Purpose: _____

_____

_____

_____

Basic Summary and Purpose Drill

<u>Passage #8:</u>

There was great rejoicing all over the land when the Lords of the Council went down to Hatfield, to hail the Princess Elizabeth as the new Queen of England. Weary of the barbarities of Mary's reign, the people looked with hope and gladness to the new Sovereign. The nation seemed to wake from a horrible dream; and Heaven, so long hidden by the smoke of the fires that roasted men and women to death, appeared to brighten once more. Queen Elizabeth was five-and-twenty years of age when she rode through the streets of London, from the Tower to Westminster Abbey, to be crowned. Her countenance was strongly marked, but on the whole, commanding and dignified. She was not the beautiful creature her courtiers made out; but she was well enough, and no doubt looked all the better for coming after the dark and gloomy Mary. She was well educated, but a roundabout writer, and rather a hard swearer and coarse talker. She was clever, but cunning and deceitful, and inherited much of her father's violent temper.

Basic Summary: _____

_____

_____

_____

_____

Purpose: _____

_____

_____

_____

Basic Summary and Purpose Drill Answer Key

Note: It is unlikely that your answers will exactly match the answers below; these are merely suggested analyses of the passage excerpts. However, you should focus on whether your analysis of each excerpt provides similar basic details and can be easily understood and retained.

Passage #1:

Many early scientists operated under the mistaken assumption that the continents were fixed in place, static and incapable of independent movement. As a result most ignored the fact that the east coast of South America and the west coast of Africa appeared to line up, mocking assertions that the two continents had at one time been part of a larger mass. Later, scientists began to consider the possibility of continental drift, and the likelihood that the two continents had indeed been linked at some point in the past.

Basic Summary: Early scientists believed that continents couldn't move on their own, and thus failed to see the relationship between the coasts of South America and Africa. Later scientists considered the possibility that the continents had been linked in the past.

Purpose: Introduce the misconceived perspective among "many early scientists" regarding static continents, these scientists' failure to note the evidence, and later scientists' considerations of a possible continental link.

Passage #2:

Political commentators have long advocated direct monetary aid as an effective way to help resolve the political and economic struggles of many African nations. In her recent book, however, Dambisa Moyo makes the startling argument that western nations should discontinue direct governmental aid on the grounds that such aid actually worsens conditions for the general population. Although she grants that some direct investment in the economies of Africa—in the form of business loans and credit—is desirable, her belief is that debt levels have become intolerably high and that foreign aid has facilitated the creation of corrupt regimes. Critics have labeled her views cruel and callous, attacking her for providing a rationale for western neglect of Africa.

Basic Summary: While many have advocated direct financial aid as a way to help Africa, Moyo disagrees, asserting that debt levels have grown too great, and foreign aid had led to corruption among the powerful. Moyo's critics attack her views, saying that these views justify western neglect.

Purpose: Introduce traditional beliefs regarding economic aid to Africa, followed by contrary perspective of Moyo, who sees this traditional approach as detrimental. Finally, introduce viewpoint of Moyo's critics, who consider her perspective to have damaging consequences.

Basic Summary and Purpose Drill Answer Key

Passage #3:

The success of a small local business can often depend on issues different from those which determine the success of a large or national business. Although many factors can contribute to the failure of a local business, experts point to three significant areas that commonly cause problems. First, poor management of business operations can doom even the best small business to failure. Management covers a gamut of items, from accounting to customer service to employee management, and a weakness or lack of oversight in any of these areas can quickly lead to serious problems. Second, a local business must often rely on a good location. A poor location fails to attract customers, which translates directly into low sales. Finally, small businesses must rely heavily on advertising for success, so a weak (or nonexistent) marketing strategy can have an exaggerated impact on the health of the business.

Basic Summary: Small, local businesses' success can depend on different factors than those of large, national businesses. Factors that commonly lead to problems are as follows: poor management of business operations, poor location, and weak or non-existent marketing strategy.

Purpose: Assert that small local businesses and large businesses can often rely on different factors for success. Introduce and briefly discuss three factors that can cause problems for small local businesses.

Basic Summary and Purpose Drill Answer Key

Passage #4:

The integral role played by the law in promoting public health is irrefutable. Eliminating lead in paints, banning smoking in public buildings, and requiring the posting of nutritional content on food labels are just a few types of public protection that have resulted from public health legislation. Within the nutritional law community, experts agree that these legal efforts have produced demonstrable benefits nationally. One burgeoning area of nutritional law is obesity law; proposed legislation in this area focuses largely on food warnings and additional labeling to apprise the public of risks associated with the overconsumption of certain foods. Participants in this debate must weigh the needs of all stakeholders, considering the rights of food producers while also considering the health of the general population.

Basic Summary: The law plays an important part in protecting public health, with regard to such examples as lead paint and second hand smoke. Recently some have proposed expanding legislation regarding food labeling and warnings. The decision will require consideration of the producers' perspective as well as that of the general public.

Purpose: Discuss importance of public health law; provide specific examples. Introduce new area of consideration—that of obesity law, the question of expanded labeling legislation, and the sides of the issue to be considered.

Basic Summary and Purpose Drill Answer Key

Passage #5:

The fall of the Berlin Wall in 1989 is interpreted differently by different groups, depending in many cases on their ideology and their location. Observers in the United States often credit Ronald Reagan with the fall, due to his aggressive anti-communist agenda and large military budget. Europeans tend to perceive the event differently, believing that a policy of accommodation and productive engagement towards East Germany ultimately lead to the political upheaval that resulted in the fall of the Wall. Russians often view the event in a negative light, with a concomitant loss of geopolitical influence and control. Many Russians argue that post-fall events left Russia on the periphery of European politics, while Europe enjoyed an atmosphere that was more inclusive and cooperative.

Basic Summary: Different groups interpret the fall of the Berlin Wall in different ways, often depending on their ideology and location. Americans tend to credit Reagan, who had a large military budget to back a strongly anti-communist sentiment. In Europe they tend to credit "productive engagement" and eventual political upheaval, while Russians often perceive the event negatively, believing that it put Russia out on the political fringe.

Purpose: Introduce general topic of differing viewpoints on the fall of the Berlin Wall, and reasons for differences in perspective. Briefly expand on the general viewpoints on the matter in the US, Europe, and Russia.

Basic Summary and Purpose Drill Answer Key

<u>Passage #6</u>:

Aeronautics really might be called the "other NASA," distinct in its charge, methodologies, and scale. Aeronautics research is not mission-oriented in the same way that going to the Moon or Mars is. It is interested in learning about physical phenomena, such as turbulence, and how to do something, such as quieting the noise of helicopter blades. Aeronautics' mission is not about going somewhere specific or building one particular thing; it is about supporting the country's commercial and military needs with respect to aviation. The contrast with the space program is telling: where NASA has gone to considerable lengths to justify the space program and explain how space innovations feed into the country's more terrestrial needs, aeronautics research has had a direct and undeniable impact on commercial and military technology development.

Basic Summary: Aeronautics could be referred to as the "other NASA," because its goals and methods are different from those of NASA's space program. Aeronautics focuses not on a specific destination, but rather on supporting the country's aviation needs, by understanding physical phenomena and working toward beneficial accomplishments such as noise reduction. The contrast, says the author, is telling, because while NASA has worked hard to justify the space program, the benefits of the organization's research in aeronautics, commercially and militarily, is undeniable.

Purpose: Discuss the aeronautics branch of NASA, contrast with NASA's space program regarding focus, methods, and goals of serving the country's commercial and military needs, leaving the space program on the defensive while the accomplishments of aeronautics research on development is beyond question.

NASA's First A, by Robert G. Ferguson. This article incorporates public domain material from websites or documents of NASA

Basic Summary and Purpose Drill Answer Key

Passage #7:

Many of the world's mythologies explain landforms as the legacies of struggles among giants, time out of mind. Legend accounts for the Giant's Causeway, a geological formation off the coast of Northern Ireland, as the remains of an ancient bridge that giants made between Ireland and Scotland. In Native American mythologies, landforms of the American West cohere as the body parts of vast divinities, whose death precedes the emergence and growth of peoples and cultures. Contemporary Americans of many backgrounds, too, use names for body parts to label geographic forms, naming heads of hollows, gorges of rivers, or mouths of mines. Unwittingly, then, our words suggest that we likewise inhabit landscapes formed from the sundered bodies of giants.

Basic Summary: Landforms are sometimes mythologized as remnants of fights between giants, as with Ireland's Giant's Causeway, said to have been originally made by giants, and with the American West landforms, characterized as the body parts of gods from the past. Today we still assign the names of body parts to geographic forms, so aware or not, we carry on the same tradition.

Purpose: Introduce the fact that people often explain various geographic formations as the remains of past giants and gods. Provide two examples of regions where this has occurred, point out that the tradition is carried on even today, perhaps unwittingly.

Basic Summary and Purpose Drill Answer Key

Passage #8:

There was great rejoicing all over the land when the Lords of the Council went down to Hatfield, to hail the Princess Elizabeth as the new Queen of England. Weary of the barbarities of Mary's reign, the people looked with hope and gladness to the new Sovereign. The nation seemed to wake from a horrible dream; and Heaven, so long hidden by the smoke of the fires that roasted men and women to death, appeared to brighten once more. Queen Elizabeth was five-and-twenty years of age when she rode through the streets of London, from the Tower to Westminster Abbey, to be crowned. Her countenance was strongly marked, but on the whole, commanding and dignified. She was not the beautiful creature her courtiers made out; but she was well enough, and no doubt looked all the better for coming after the dark and gloomy Mary. She was well educated, but a roundabout writer, and rather a hard swearer and coarse talker. She was clever, but cunning and deceitful, and inherited much of her father's violent temper.

Basic Summary: When Elizabeth became the new Queen of England, there was a national celebration. After the horrors and the darkness of Mary's reign, Elizabeth, only twenty-five, had command and dignity, and her courtiers played up her beauty, which was that much brighter relative to the "gloomy Mary." Elizabeth had a good education but swore and used coarse language, and was sharp but deceitful, with a bad temper that she got from her father.

Purpose: Provide a basic description of Elizabeth at the time of her ascent to the throne, as well as the nationwide celebratory mood. Describe the new queen's appearance and personality, contrast with the former queen, Mary, and her dark, barbarian reign.

Excerpted from A Child's History of England by Charles Dickens

A Sample Passage Analyzed

Take several minutes to read the following LSAT passage (time is not critical for this exercise). Look for the five crucial elements of VIEWSTAMP that we discussed within this chapter:

1. The various groups and viewpoints discussed within the passage. (VIEW)
2. The tone or attitude of each group or individual. (T)
3. The argument made by each group or individual. (A)
4. The main point of the passage. (MP)
5. The structure of the passage and the organization of ideas. (S)

Please note that we will not examine the questions just yet.

Economists have long defined prosperity in terms of monetary value, gauging a given nation's prosperity solely on the basis of the total monetary value of the goods and services produced annually.
(5) However, critics point out that defining prosperity solely as a function of monetary value is questionable since it fails to recognize other kinds of values, such as quality of life or environmental health, that contribute directly to prosperity in a broader sense.
(10) For example, as the earth's ozone layer weakens and loses its ability to protect people from ultraviolet radiation, sales of hats, sunglasses, and sunscreens are likely to skyrocket, all adding to the nation's total expenditures. In this way, troubling reductions in
(15) environmental health and quality of life may in fact initiate economic activity that, by the economists' measure, bolsters prosperity.

It can also happen that communities seeking to increase their prosperity as measured strictly in
(20) monetary terms may damage their quality of life and their environment. The situation of one rural community illustrates this point: residents of the community value the local timber industry as a primary source of income, and they vocally protested
(25) proposed limitations on timber harvests as a threat to their prosperity. Implicitly adopting the economists' point of view, the residents argued that the harvest limitations would lower their wages or even cause the loss of jobs.
(30) But critics of the economists' view argue that this view of the situation overlooks a crucial consideration. Without the harvest limitations, they say, the land on which the community depends would be seriously damaged. Moreover, they point out that the residents

(35) themselves cite the abundance of natural beauty as one of the features that make their community a highly desirable place to live. But it is also extremely poor, and the critics point out that the residents could double their incomes by moving only 150 kilometers
(40) away. From their decision not to do so, the critics conclude that their location has substantial monetary value to them. The community will thus lose much more—even understood in monetary terms—if the proposed harvest limits are not implemented.
(45) Economists respond by arguing that to be a useful concept, prosperity must be defined in easily quantifiable terms, and that prosperity thus should not include difficult-to-measure values such as happiness or environmental health. But this position dodges the
(50) issue—emphasizing ease of calculation causes one to disregard substantive issues that directly influence real prosperity. The economists' stance is rather like that of a literary critic who takes total sales to be the best measure of a book's value—true, the number of
(55) copies sold is a convenient and quantifiable measure, but it is a poor substitute for an accurate appraisal of literary merit.

This passage begins with the introduction of the viewpoint of the economists, who have long defined a nation's prosperity solely in terms of exact monetary value. In line 5, the opposing viewpoint of the critics is introduced, namely that defining prosperity in just economic terms is a poor measure because it fails to include important non-economic measures of prosperity, such as quality of life. The remainder of the first paragraph provides an example that supports the position of the critics.

In the first paragraph, the author does not make a strong statement of position, but there is a suggestion that the author supports the critics: in line 14, the author uses the term "troubling" in reference to reductions in environmental health and quality. This modifier suggests that the author agrees with the critics that non-economic measures of prosperity have value.

From a tone standpoint, thus far we simply have the economists and critics disagreeing over the measure of prosperity, with the author possibly on the side of the critics. No main point has been presented yet (that is, no conclusion has been drawn by the author). Structurally, we have two opposing views and an example supporting the critics' view.

The second paragraph suggests more strongly that the author agrees with the critics. The paragraph opens by indicating that communities who measure prosperity in strictly monetary terms can jeopardize their quality of life and their environment. The author's use of the words "It can also happen" and "may damage" suggest that the author believes these communities are harming themselves (and thus that the critics are correct in measuring prosperity in other terms besides just economic ones). The remainder of the paragraph is devoted to an example where a community uses an economic justification to oppose limits on timber harvests.

From a viewpoint, tone, and main idea standpoint, this paragraph adds very little. Structurally, the paragraph is comprised of a sentence that supports the critics, and an example that shows a community using an economic justification for a decision.

The third paragraph opens with the critics' response to the example in the second paragraph, namely that residents of the community have failed to consider that scenic beauty is a critical factor in their choice of residence. The community thus stands to lose a considerable amount if timber harvest limits are not imposed.

Similar to the second paragraph, this paragraph adds very little new information in the way of viewpoint, tone, or main point. The third paragraph is simply a continuation of the critics' view.

The final paragraph returns to the view of the economists, indicating that they believe that prosperity must be defined in easily quantifiable terms, and that therefore prosperity should not be defined to include quality of life values. At this point, the author finally enters and presents a defined viewpoint, that the economists' position is weak. The phrasing used in line 49—"But this position..."—attributes the view to no particular group, and thus the view must be that of the author. The passage then ends with further criticism of the economists. This final criticism reveals the main point of the passage, which is that the economists have defined prosperity too narrowly. Structurally, the last paragraph opens with the economists' position on how to define prosperity, and ends with the author's rebuttal of that position.

Let us take a moment to review each of the five critical VIEWSTAMP elements in the passage:

1. The various groups and viewpoints discussed within the passage.

   There are three main viewpoints presented in the passage: the economists', the critics', and the author's. The critics and the author are in agreement, and both oppose the economists.

2. The tone or attitude of each group or individual.

   The economists and the critics are at odds, but the tone of the disagreement does not appear to be acrimonious. For example, critics "point out" and "argue." Those are fairly mild words that simply indicate general disagreement, not animosity or particularly strong opposition.

   The author appears to disagree with the economists to a greater degree. In lines 49-57, the author uses terms like "dodges the issue" and "poor substitute" to indicate that he or she has a fairly negative view of the economists' position.

3. The argument made by each group or individual.

   The economists argue that prosperity should be defined in solely economic terms. Any measure of prosperity must be easily quantifiable, and thus any difficult-to-measure value should be rejected.

The critics and the author disagree with the economists, and argue that a solely economic stance fails to account for other values that contribute to prosperity (such as quality of life), which are difficult to quantify but nonetheless important.

4. The main point of the passage.

Noting the main point of the passage will always be valuable, in part because recognition of the main point is vital to a complete understanding of the passage, and in part because a very significant percentage of Reading Comprehension passages are accompanied by a Main Point question—including this one. In this case, the main point is presented at the end of the passage, where the author indicates that the economists' definition of prosperity is too narrowly drawn.

1. Which one of the following most accurately states the main point of the passage?

(A) According to critics, communities that seek to increase their prosperity recognize the need to gauge the value and ensure the long-term health of their local environment.

(B) Economists' definition of prosperity strictly in terms of monetary value is too narrow to truly capture our ordinary conception of this notion.

(C) If economists were to alter and expand their definition of prosperity, it is likely that the economic and environmental health of most communities would appear worse under the new definition than under the old definition.

(D) In contrast with the views of economists, some critics believe that prosperity can be neither scientifically measured nor accurately defined, and as a concept is therefore of little use for economists.

(E) While they are generally an accurate and practical measure of current economic prosperity, figures for the total expenditures of a nation do not aid in providing an indication of that nation's future economic prospects.

As prephrased above, the main point of the passage is that a monetary definition is too narrow to cover our notion of prosperity, so the correct answer choice is (B).

5. The structure of the passage and the organization of ideas.

    The structure of the passage is as follows: The first paragraph presents the economists' view of prosperity, the critics' opposing view, and a supporting example of the critics' viewpoint. The second paragraph is a sentence that supports the critics, and an example that shows a community using an economic justification for a decision. The third paragraph is a further criticism of the economists, framed against the example from the second paragraph. The last paragraph opens with a further discussion of the economists' position on how to define prosperity, and ends with the author's main point—a rebuttal of the economists' position.

Overall, this is a solid passage—several viewpoints exist, clear authorial position and attitude are presented, and reasonably clear structure and argumentation exist. Granted, the topic may not be the most exciting, but the examples given are not uninteresting and you can engage yourself by focusing on the disagreement between the parties.

One final note: If you can consistently apply the five VIEWSTAMP ideas we have discussed throughout this chapter, you will be in an excellent position to attack the questions. And, our discussions of passage formations and passage notations in the next two chapters will only serve to make you an even stronger test taker. By the time we begin examining the questions in a few chapters, you will have a powerful arsenal of tools to dissect each problem, and, in many cases, you will discover that you know what the correct answer will say before you even begin reading the five answer choices.

Chapter Four: Passage Elements and Formations

Chapter Four: Passage Elements and Formations

Chapter Preview

This chapter will cover sources of passage difficulty and examine the elements and formations in passages which tend to generate questions. That is, we will look at what makes passages hard and what passage elements the test makers most commonly ask about. In this sense, this chapter continues the discussion begun in Chapter Three. Chapter Three introduced the "big picture" elements that you must always track, whereas here we will discuss the more detailed elements that you should note. The next two chapters will then talk about how to physically notate these elements when they appear, and the individual question types that follow.

Sources of Difficulty: The Test Makers' Arsenal

There are a number of ways the makers of the test can increase the level of difficulty of any given passage, and indeed of the section as a whole, but before we examine the specific elements they employ, reviewing the general methods that can be used to increase difficulty is helpful.

The following five items are the primary ways the test makers use to alter your perception of passage and overall section difficulty:

Challenging Topic or Terminology

In some passages, the choice of topic makes the passage seem more difficult to test takers. For example, many students fear the appearance of a Science-related passage on the LSAT. As we will discuss later, you should not be afraid or unduly worried by Science passages (or any passage, for that matter). That said, an unfamiliar or complex topic can make a passage harder, but only incrementally so because the test makers must explain the main concepts of the passage, regardless of the topic. Thus, there may be a few moments of anxiety while you are forced to adjust to an unknown topic, but they should be fleeting since the test makers will always give you the information needed to answer the questions. So this is more of a psychological challenge than one of genuine difficulty.

The use of complicated terminology usually concerns students as well. Reading a passage that contains words or ideas that you do not recognize is intimidating and often confusing. As mentioned in Chapter Two however, you should not be alarmed by unknown concepts, mainly because the test makers must *always* define any term or concept not in common public usage.

When you encounter unknown words, they will fall into one of two categories: new terms related to the concept under discussion or unknown vocabulary words. In the case of terms directly related to the topic at hand (such as *Scar Art* or *LHB*), the test makers will explain the term or concept for you in the text, sometimes briefly using synonyms, other times in greater detail. Unknown vocabulary words can be more challenging, but you can use context clues from the surrounding text to help determine the meaning of words you do not know. We will briefly discuss this point again later in this chapter.

Challenging Writing Style

The test makers carefully choose whether a passage will have a clear, easy-to-follow form, or a more dense, convoluted construction. Obviously, writing style has a tremendous effect on passage difficulty because even the easiest of concepts can become hard to understand if the presentation is intentionally complex.

In the first few lines of a passage, it is difficult to tell whether the writing style will be challenging. If you do encounter a passage that has a very difficult-to-read style, use some of the tips in the next section to focus on the elements most likely to be tested.

There is no easy way to combat a passage written in an intentionally convoluted style, but slowing down slightly, reading carefully, and focusing primarily on the overall structure will help.

Multiple Viewpoints

We first discussed the importance of tracking passage viewpoints in Chapter Three, and readdress them here because a common and easy way for the test makers to increase difficulty is to add *more* viewpoints. Tracking viewpoints in a passage with only one or two viewpoints is easy; tracking viewpoints in a passage with six viewpoints is considerably more challenging. The more viewpoints present, the easier it is for readers to confuse them, or forget who said what. This is especially true because when more viewpoints are present, the test makers typically insert extensive compare-and-contrast sections, which makes separating and mastering each view more difficult.

Later in this chapter we will address "compare and contrast" sections, and in Chapter Five we will discuss further methods for tracking viewpoints in a concrete and easy-to-identify fashion.

Difficult Questions/Answers

The difficulty of a passage set is also affected by the nature of the questions. For example, if there are a large number of questions, or if the questions are unusual in nature, or, most frequently, if the answer choices are difficult to separate from one another as right or wrong, then the passage set itself will be difficult or time-consuming. Thus, even an easily-understood passage can turn challenging once you start answering its questions. In Chapter Six we will discuss question types in detail, and provide you with an effective approach for attacking every question you could face.

Order of Passage Presentation

Another important factor is one that will inform your choices throughout the entire Reading Comprehension section. There is a common misconception among test takers that RC passages are presented in order of difficulty from first to fourth. But LSAC is rarely interested in making things easy on the reader (indeed, even if this were their intent, certain topics/passages are easy for some readers and difficult for others). Thus, sometimes the hardest passage on the test is last, but it may also appear first, second, or third. To combat this situation, you can use the navigation bar at the bottom of the screen to quickly jump to the first question in each passage to scan for content if needed—so, for example, if you can tell after reading the first few lines of a passage that it looks particularly challenging, consider moving on to another passage. This can be a bit disconcerting at first, because by the time you decide that a passage is difficult, you may feel that you have already invested significant time and effort into that passage. This is an understandable worry, but typically unfounded: if moving on allows you to face easier passages first then the initial investment was well worth it, and students tend to overestimate the amount of time it takes to read the first portion of a passage and decide. In reality, within 10 to 15 seconds of *reading* a passage (not skimming), it is often possible to assess two key factors:

1. Whether or not the topic is one of inherent interest to you.

2. Whether the passage is written in a style that you find relatively easy to understand from the outset.

Although ideally you will be reading all of the passages in the section at some point, it can be far more efficient to start with those that you find most enjoyable and accessible!

4

This test makers' weapon (the order of the passages) is one of the easiest to overcome: If you know that the passages might not be presented in an ideal order, simply choose your favorite(s) first!

Some students prefer the Comparative Reading passages, which tend to be shorter, so those are the first they consider when beginning the Reading Comprehension section.

Passage Elements That Generate Questions

As you read, there are certain specific, consistent passage elements that should jump out at you, primarily because history has reflected the test makers' tendency to use these elements as the basis for questions. That means recognizing these moments when you first encounter them can allow you to predict with confidence what matters most in the passage and what questions are likely to follow it! In fact, so crucial is this anticipatory skill that Chapter Ten includes a dedicated exercise known as the Prediction Test to help you refine your approach.

For purposes of clarity in this overview, we will divide these elements into two types: viewpoint-specific elements and text-based elements.

Viewpoint-specific Elements

Analysis of viewpoints is one of the major techniques we use in attacking the passages, and in Chapter Three we discussed this approach in depth. Separating viewpoints allows you to divide the passage into logical, trackable components, and helps you to more easily understand the passage and to disentangle the many disparate ideas presented. Viewpoints also play a central role in the main themes of the passage, so naturally they serve as the source of many of the questions asked by the test makers. For example, questions about the main point, authorities cited by the author, or the perspective of any of the players in the passage are all related to viewpoints, and thus tracking viewpoints not only makes understanding the passage itself easier, it automatically assists you in answering a *significant* portion of the questions. Thus, while reading you must always focus on identifying each viewpoint in the passage.

Competing perspectives offer differing opinions on the same subject.

When considering viewpoints, be aware that one of the test makers' favorite tricks is to use competing perspectives, a tactic that involves presenting two or more viewpoints on the same subject, with each view containing slightly different elements (while also offering moments of overlap and similarity).

Here is an example:

Topic: Nuclear power

Viewpoint 1: Nuclear power plants are efficient generators of energy, but they present serious long-term environmental concerns because of the problems associated with storing radioactive waste in the form of spent fuel.

Viewpoint 2: Nuclear power is the most efficient way to produce energy, and the waste problems associated with them, while significant, are lesser than those associated with more traditional energy production methods, such as those involving coal.

In the paragraphs above, the differences and similarities in viewpoints are easy to identify, even with some less obvious subtleties included ("efficient generators of energy" vs "most efficient way to produce energy," and "serious long-term environmental concerns" vs "waste problems...while significant, are lesser," to name two). But imagine for a moment that the two views are woven together in a passage, and some extraneous information is also interspersed. When you finally attack the questions a few minutes later, it would be very easy to have forgotten the exact similarities and differences, especially in the presence of additional viewpoints.

Since competing perspectives can be quite tricky to follow—it is easy to confuse or misremember different views in the context of entire passages—it should come as no surprise that questions about these elements closely test whether you understand the *exact* differences between the various viewpoints on offer. So precision is paramount!

Because viewpoint analysis was a main feature in Chapter Three we will move on for the moment, but in all of the passages we explore in later chapters this element will be a cornerstone of our analysis.

Text-based Questions

In one sense, all questions are based on the text. In using the name "text-based," we're referring to elements that appear directly in the text as an identifiable part—definitions, lists, compare/contrast sections, and specific dates, for example—and not the broader and somewhat more abstract elements such as main point, author's purpose, or passage structure. Under this definition, text-based questions will often be smaller pieces, sometimes just a single word, other times a short section of the text. In this sense, these are the "nuts and bolts" components that you should be aware of when reading.

These are the elements we will discuss (not in order of importance):

Note these elements as you encounter them in the passages; you are likely to see them again in the questions.

1. Initial Information/Closing Information

2. Dates and Numbers

3. Definitions

4. Examples

5. Difficult words or phrases

6. Enumerations/Lists

7. Text Questions

Please note that the itemized list above is *not* a checklist to use when attacking passages. You simply can't read while also looking for a seven-part, numbered list. Instead, you must ingrain an understanding of these elements into your Reading Comprehension world view, and then simply take notice of them when they appear. This requires practice, but it is easily achievable with a little work. Approaching passages in this fashion allows you to read broadly for the VIEWSTAMP elements while simultaneously noting the ideas above when they appear. To reiterate an analogy introduced in Chapter Three, you are like an air traffic controller looking at a radar screen: you only worry about these elements when they appear, and you only react to them when you have to do so.

Let's talk about each item in more detail.

1. Initial Information/Closing Information

The information presented in the first five lines of a passage—especially fine details—is often forgotten by students. This occurs because at the very beginning of a passage you are focused on figuring out the topic and the author's general position, and thus seemingly minor details are hard to retain.

Similarly, the information presented in the last five lines is often forgotten because the average student is eager to jump to the questions and thus skims over the material at the very end of the passage.

The test makers are well aware of these tendencies, so they occasionally question you on your knowledge of information seen at the very beginning or end of the passage. To combat this, make sure to check these areas if you are having difficulty answering a question, especially when you seem to have no idea where in the passage the answer comes from (again, this would most likely occur with detail or fact-based questions).

2. Dates and Numbers

Dates often provide useful markers within a passage, allowing you "before" and "after" points to return to when searching for answers. While in some passages the use of dates is incidental, in other passages a clear chronology is created, and then some of the questions will test your ability to understand the timeline.

The general rule is that the more dates you see in a passage, particularly if they are given in regular intervals or serve as identifiers of progress or change, the more important it is that you make note of them.

Numbers are usually less important than dates, but when numbers are used in a comparative sense, or as part of an explanation, the test makers will sometimes check your comprehension of their meaning.

When an LSAT author references more than one date or era, creating a simple timeline can be an effective way to maintain relative perspective, whether the comparisons span days or centuries.

3. Definitions

Identifying definitions serves two purposes: in those cases where you do not understand the term or concept it helps you to clarify the idea, and even when you do understand the concept the test makers will frequently test you on your understanding of the definition, so noting its location is extremely useful.

The typical definition is presented in the immediate vicinity of the word or concept it represents, like so:

> This landmark case established that in order to prevail against a publisher for defamation and libel, a public figure must be able to prove "actual malice," which means that the publisher either knowingly printed false statements about the public figure in question, or showed reckless disregard with respect to the truth or falsity of such statements when publishing them.

In the text above, the clause after the comma provides the definition for the legal term *actual malice*. Of course, some definitions are much shorter, such as this sentence which includes the one-word definition of *mitigate*:

> While the plaintiff does have legal rights in such cases, there also exists a duty when possible to mitigate, or reduce, damages sustained as a result of negligence on the part of the defendant.

Regardless of the length of a definition, you should make sure that you are comfortable with the term being defined. If you encounter an idea or term that you think should be defined but do not see a definition in the immediate vicinity, then the definition will probably be presented relatively soon (explicitly or through context clues), and the test makers are simply trying to trick you with a "trap of separation," which we will discuss later in this chapter.

Whenever you see a brand new term or concept defined, be sure to take note; if the test makers have provided a clear definition or description, they generally expect you to be able to locate the reference (and thus often ask questions related to it).

4. Examples

LSAT authors often use examples to explain or underscore or even attempt to prove the points they are making. Logically, these examples serve as concrete (often real-world) premises that support the broader conclusion of the author. Functionally, they help you to understand the typically more abstract point that the author is making, and so they can be quite helpful especially when you are having difficulty understanding an argument.

Examples can be short and specific to a single point, or they can be substantial and involved and appear throughout the passage. Always remember, though, that the example is not the main conclusion or point of the author; generally, examples are provided to *support or explain* the main conclusion.

The words "for example" are the most common way that examples are introduced, but the following phrases all have been used:

> For example
> For instance
> A case in point is
> As shown by
> As demonstrated by

Whenever you see these terms, immediately note what point is being illustrated. Consider this:

> In science, serendipity often plays a crucial role in discoveries. For instance, Teflon was discovered by a scientist attempting to find a new gas for use in refrigeration.

Above, the author introduces a concept (that good luck often plays a crucial role in new discoveries), and immediately exemplifies that belief with the introductory phrase "for instance" and the specific case of Teflon.

Examples are not the main conclusion or point of the author; the point being supported or explained by the example is the author's central belief.

5. Difficult words or phrases

As mentioned earlier, challenging words or phrases are items that you should note while reading, but you should not become overly distressed if you do not immediately know what the terms mean. Terms outside the common public domain of knowledge (such as *circumpolar vortex*) are always explained, and unknown vocabulary words (such as *vituperate*) can often be defined by the context of usage. Acronyms, too, are always explained.

The key thing to remember is that even if you do not understand a word or idea, you will still understand virtually all other words and ideas in the passage, and so the potential downside of not knowing one element is very small. If you cannot make sense of something reasonably quickly, simply move on and see if clarity is made possible via some subsequent portion of text.

6. Lists and Enumerations

A number of passages feature sections where the author presents a view by providing a list of points that support or explain the position, or that are possible outcomes of a course of action. When these lists occur, you are almost always tested on your understanding of some or all of the items on the list. In fact, of the seven items discussed in this section, Lists and Enumerations are generally the most reliable question producer: when a passage contains a list of two or more items, chances are nearly 100% that at least one question will be asked in reference to it.

The listed items do not appear as bullet points. Rather, they tend to appear using constructions similar to one of the following:

"First...Second...Third..."
"First...Second...In addition..."
"First...Second...Third...Last..."
"(1)...(2)..."
"Initially...And...Further..."
"One possibility is...another possibility is...A final possibility..."

The lists usually contain one of two types of items: a list of reasons (premises) that explain why an action was taken or why a circumstance came into being, or a list of examples that relate to the point at hand. But note that any type of enumerated grouping is possible, and a likely source for the questions that follow.

A list of premises may appear as follows:

> The move towards political systems less dependent on monarchical structures came about for several reasons. First, the monetary and military abuses of the royalty placed several governments in severe financial hardship and created a strong undercurrent of discontent and resentment among the populace. Second, the uncertainty over personal human and property rights caused select elements within the upper class to become convinced that a more concrete and accountable political system was necessary, one insulated from the vagaries of royalty. And finally, problems with succession created a political environment fraught with uncertainty and turmoil.

A list of examples might appear as follows:

> Developing nations have used a number of ingenious methods to increase energy production—and therefore gross economic capacity—while at the same time maintaining a commitment to sustaining the environment. Microfinanced solar projects in India, Brazil, and Vietnam have all yielded power systems able to sustain towns and villages in remote areas, all without a material impact on local resources. A wind farm in Morocco is a successful collaboration between three commercial firms and the government, and now outputs 50 megawatts. In Tibet, where there are no significant or obtainable fossil fuel resources, the Nagqu geothermal energy field provides 300 kilowatts of power in a more cost-effective fashion than could any fossil fuel generators.

In the example above, the listed items are not numbered or introduced as list items, but a list of examples connected to specific countries is presented nonetheless. When reading, you must be prepared to encounter lists of items that are not clearly marked as such in the text. Any time an author presents a series of examples (or a series of *anything*, for that matter), you should recognize it and expect to refer back to it when you begin answering the questions.

7. Text Questions

When an author poses a question in the passage, in most instances the author goes on to immediately answer that question. Thus, tracking the presence of text questions is critical because it provides you with an outline for where the passage will go next. And, because these questions are often central to the theme of the passage, there is usually a post-passage question that centers on the answer to the question the author posed.

Most often, text questions are raised in the traditional, explicit manner, with a question mark, as follows:

> So, what was the ultimate impact of the court's ruling on property rights for the Aleutian Islanders?

Text questions can be explicitly or implicitly presented in the passage.

However, questions can be posed without the traditional question mark, as in this example:

> And thus, researchers concluded that some other explanation was needed to account for the difference in temperatures.

In this example, the sentence implies that there is a question regarding the temperature difference, and this implicit question is likely to then be answered in the text.

Two Broad Reasoning Structures ▬

Causal reasoning and conditional reasoning appear frequently in the Logical Reasoning sections of the LSAT, but less so in the Reading Comprehension section. Still, recognizing each reasoning type when it appears is extremely helpful because it provides a framework for understanding the arguments being made.

Let's briefly review causal and conditional reasoning:

Causal Reasoning

Cause and effect reasoning asserts or denies that one thing causes another, or that one thing is caused by another. The cause is the event that makes the other occur; the effect is the event that follows from the cause. By definition, the cause must occur before the effect, and the cause is the "activator" or "ignitor" in the relationship. The effect always happens at some point in time after the cause.

Causality in Reading Comprehension usually is discussed in the context of why certain events occurred. The terms that typically introduce causality—such as *caused by*, *reason for*, *led to*, or *product of*—are still used, but then the author often goes on to discuss the reasons behind the occurrence in depth.

Causality, when it appears in Reading Comprehension, is not normally viewed as inherently flawed reasoning, and LSAT authors usually make an effort to explain the thinking behind their causal assertions.

Conditional Reasoning

Conditional reasoning is the broad name given to logical relationships composed of sufficient and necessary conditions. Any conditional relationship consists of at least one sufficient condition and at least one necessary condition. A sufficient condition is an event or circumstance whose occurrence indicates that a necessary condition must also occur. A necessary condition is an event or circumstance whose occurrence is required in order for a sufficient condition to occur. In other words, if a sufficient condition occurs, you automatically know that the necessary condition also occurs. If a necessary condition occurs, then it is possible but not certain that the sufficient condition will occur. However, if a necessary condition *fails* to occur, you then know that the sufficient condition cannot occur either.

The PowerScore LSAT Logical Reasoning Bible contains chapters on causality and conditionality that are considerably more extensive than the short section in this book. This is because those reasoning forms appear far more frequently in the Logical Reasoning section than in the Reading Comprehension section.

4

Conditional relationships in Reading Comprehension passages tend to be unobtrusive, usually occurring as a sideline point to a larger argument. For example, a passage might discuss monetary policy, and in the course of doing so make a conditional assertion such as, "The only way to decrease monetary volatility is to tightly control the supply of money." In this sense, conditionality is usually not the focus or main point of a passage, but instead it is a type of reasoning that occurs while discussing or supporting other points.

Of the two types of reasoning, causal reasoning appears more frequently than conditional reasoning in the Reading Comprehension section. This difference is due to the fact that many passages attempt to address why certain events occurred, and in doing so they naturally fall into causal explanations.

When either of the two reasoning types are present, they are usually discussed in more expansive terms, and the causal or conditional argument is broad and seldom based on single words or sentences. For example, consider the following paragraph:

> While prescriptions for medications are at an all-time high, hyperactivity in children appears to be attributable in many cases to diet. Excessive ingestion of processed sugars, for example, has been linked to various disorders. In a recent study of children diagnosed with hyperactivity, many subjects displayed a more positive response to sugar restriction than to traditionally prescribed medication.

In the first sentence, a cause-and-effect relationship is asserted, and then the remainder of the paragraph builds the case for the assertion. Of course, causal or conditional reasoning arguments need not be limited to a single paragraph; entire passages can be built around a single causal or conditional idea.

Pitfalls to Avoid

While there are many concrete elements to track when reading a passage, there are also a number of text formations and configurations you should recognize. These constructions are often used by the test makers to create confusion, so in this sense they function as possible "traps" for the unwary test taker. The following section reviews the most frequently appearing traps, and examines each in detail.

Traps of Similarities and Distinctions

This trap occurs when, in a continuous section of text, an author discusses in detail items that have both similarities and differences. By comparing and contrasting the items in close proximity, the test makers create a greater likelihood for confusion (by comparison, if the discussion of the concepts were separated into discrete sections, the information would be easier to keep clear). Here is an example of a compare-and-contrast section of text:

> Geologically, rocks generally fall into one of three categories: igneous, sedimentary, or metamorphic. Igneous rocks are the result of cooled lava or magma, sedimentary rocks are the result of pressures and accumulations that often result in layers, and metamorphic rocks are igneous or sedimentary rocks that undergo a change caused by conditions underground.
>
> The role of heat in the formation of rocks is varied, and somewhat dependent on location. Igneous rocks are often formed within the earth, and the release of high levels of heat through cooling leads to the formation of the rock. Sedimentary rocks are formed at the earth's surface (often underwater) by the addition of low levels of heat, and metamorphic rocks are formed in virtually any location by the addition of low or high levels of heat.
>
> Within each classification, texture, "or "microstructure," is an important determinant of type. Texture occurs throughout a rock, and is an important means of identifying the origin of a rock. While sedimentary rock microstructures tend to reveal the condition of the sediment or layer the rock originated from, metamorphic rock microstructures tend to reveal the nature and timing of the change that lead to the creation of the rock. Igneous rock textures depend on several factors, including the cooling rate and mineral composition of the magma or lava. They are often characterized by grains or crystals.

If a list of comparisons and contrasts starts to get complicated, a simple note on your scratch paper ("textures compared") allows you to keep that section in perspective and move on to the rest of the passage.

You should not become bogged down in trying to get every detail straight in a section like the one above. Instead, make some simple notes on your scratch paper, or underline or highlight key points (we will discuss this in the next chapter) so that if you are asked about the details you can quickly return to the passage and sort out the specifics.

Compare-and-contrast sections appear very frequently in Reading Comprehension passages, and you should expect to see one or more on your exam.

Trap of Separation

One favorite trick of the test makers is to take a long discussion of a particular topic and break it up by inserting within it a section of text about a related but distinct topic, effectively creating a separation effect: the main idea bisected by similar but different (and possibly distracting) content in the middle. Then in the questions, the test makers require you to follow and understand the bigger-picture discussion, testing your ability to track the interrupted main concept despite its beginning and end being divided by many lines (or entire paragraphs) in the passage. Consider the following example:

Market control is the ability to affect and influence trends in pricing, quantities available, and other aspects of a given market. Market control factors can lead to four distinct major market structures. In a case of perfect competition, there are many sellers producing similar goods, none of the participants have market control, and there are limited barriers to entry into the market. While such a scenario is considered optimal, it is nearly impossible to achieve or maintain. In a monopoly, a single seller of a particular product or service exists, and that seller has complete control over supply and pricing. Monopolies typically arise in industries that have significant barriers to entry, such as high capital costs or centralized resource control. In both an oligopoly and a duopoly, only a small number of sellers exist, and each maintains a degree of market control.

Within monopolistic and oligopolistic market structures, the potential for market abuse is significant. Monopolists face no competition and can thus restrict supply in order to maintain artificially high prices. Each member of an oligopoly is typically aware of the decisions and actions of other members, increasing the prospects for collusion and other such restrictive trade practices. Because both monopolies and oligopolies can work against the general public interest, industrialized societies often put in place legal restrictions to control the behavior of such firms, in some cases preventing the formation of monopolies or oligopolies altogether.

A fourth market structure tends to require less governmental oversight. Monopolistic competition, also known as a competitive market, exists when there are many producers and many consumers, with products and services that might be similar but are sufficiently distinctive to allow for continued competition in the marketplace. Such a system is preferable to the monopoly and the oligopoly, each of which is conducive to unfair degrees of market manipulation.

In the previous passage, the author introduces the idea of four major market structures, and goes on to immediately expand upon three of the four (perfect competition, monopoly, duopoly) in the first paragraph. Following this partial coverage, the entire second paragraph is used to discuss potential market abuses and restrictions to protect the public interest. Then in the last paragraph, the author returns to the topic of the first paragraph's list, presenting monopolistic competition as the fourth and final portion of the discussion of major market structures.

In some especially insidious instances, the question stems will specifically refer you to just one of the places where the concept is discussed (for example, "In the final sentence of the first paragraph, the author..."), but this will not be the place in the passage that contains the information needed to answer the question. This trap, known as the Trap of Question Misdirection, can be very difficult to handle because most questions that specifically refer you to a place in the passage are indeed referring you to the area where the information needed to answer the question resides. (In Chapter Six we will discuss specific reference questions in more detail and outline strategies to attack them)

One reason this trick works is that there is a natural tendency on the part of readers to assume that pieces of information that are related should be in close proximity. The logical and linear writing style used in newspapers and textbooks tends to reinforce this belief, thus many students regrettably approach the LSAT with these misguided expectations. However, as we have already discussed, the test makers want to present passages that test your ability to comprehend difficult, nonlinear material, and so they use certain methods to create greater complexity in the passages.

Of course, just as information that is separated can be related, information that is in close proximity does not have to be connected, as discussed next.

Trap of Proximity

Just because two ideas are presented in close physical proximity to one another within a passage does not mean that they are related. In the Market Structures passage on the previous page, we noted that the second paragraph provided a discussion that was not particularly relevant to the classification list in paragraph 1. And yet this digression is cleverly sandwiched between the first three classifications in the opening paragraph, and the fourth classification in the last paragraph.

As mentioned in the prior section, the expectation of most readers is that information that is physically close together will be related. This does not have to be the case, and the makers of the LSAT will set up situations to test your ability to make that distinction.

The Trap of Question Misdirection occurs when the test makers use a specific line reference in the question stem to direct you to a place in the passage where the correct answer will not be found.

Trap of Inserted Alternate Viewpoint

Another ploy the test makers favor is to present several different viewpoints in a single passage, even a single paragraph, forcing readers to track both the topical information and the various perspectives. For example:

> Some critics have complained that Faulkner's storytelling in *The Sound and the Fury* was "disorganized and incoherent" to such a degree that understanding the novel seems "deliberately incomprehensible." What such critics fail to see is that Faulkner's use of different narrators was meant to provide a broader perspective, through alternative views of the story. Faulkner himself admitted, however, that he had failed in his attempt to tell the story in a way he found satisfactory, and some critics agree.

In the above excerpt, the author quickly jumps from the perspective of "some critics" to that of the passage author, to Faulkner's own view (a perspective with which some critics agree!). This technique is meant to test your ability to track different perspectives and to understand who said or believed what. As discussed in Chapter Three's VIEWSTAMP analysis, multiple viewpoints in a passage require a heightened level of clarity and precision, as opportunities to misattribute beliefs are sure to feature heavily in the questions.

Traps of Chronology

Traps of chronology relate to the placement and order of items within the passage, and the tendency of many readers to believe that when one item is presented before another, then the first item occurred first or caused the second. These two traps are called the Trap of Order and the Trap of Cause, respectively:

Trap of Order

Some students make the mistake of believing that because an event or situation is discussed before another event, the first event likely predated the second. Unless explicitly stated or inherently obvious, this does not have to be the case.

Trap of Cause

Some students also mistakenly assume that when one scenario is discussed before another, then the first item must have caused the second item. This assumption is unwarranted. The easiest way to discern the author's intention is to carefully examine the language used because causal relationships almost always feature one or more of the words that indicate causality (such as *caused by*, *produced by*, *determined*, *led to*, *resulted in*, etc).

The simple truth is that the order of presentation of the items in the passage does not necessarily indicate any temporal or causal relationship between them.

Passage Topic Traps

Previously we discussed how passages on any topic could be easy or difficult. Passage difficulty is more a function of writing style, the number of viewpoints, and the exact concepts under discussion than of the general topic of the passage. That said, the test makers will occasionally use the topic to catch test takers off-guard. This technique of theirs works because when the typical student begins reading a passage, the topic often frames their expectations. For example, Science passages are thought to be challenging whereas passages about humanities are less feared. The test makers are well aware of these ingrained expectations, and they at times play a sort of "bait and switch" game with students, especially by making a passage initially look hard or easy and then radically changing the level of difficulty after the first few lines or first paragraph.

An example occurred on the June 2006 LSAT. The last passage opened with a discussion of the cultivation of maize, and most students immediately relaxed. After all, this was a passage about corn, and we are all familiar with good ol' corn, so how hard could it be? After the first paragraph, however, the passage became brutally difficult. On the other hand, on the September 2006 LSAT the second passage began with a discussion of modern bankruptcy law that looked rather ominous. However, as the passage unfolded, the argument was easy to follow and the passage as a whole was fairly simple to understand. There are, of course, myriad other examples from LSAT history.

The point to take from this discussion is that you should not assume that a passage will be easy or hard solely from its topic, and certainly not from reading just the first line or paragraph. The test makers love to play with the expectations of test takers, and one of their favorite tricks is to turn those expectations on their head.

As you develop the ability to see through the topic and focus on the writing style, you will notice that many passages are not as complex as their topics might suggest.

Final Chapter Note

In review, the approach we advocate is a multi-level one. While reading, you should constantly track the five major VIEWSTAMP elements discussed in Chapter Three: the various groups and viewpoints within the passage, the tone or attitude of each group or individual, the argument(s) made by each group or individual, the main point of the passage, and the structure of the passage and organization of its ideas.

At the same time, you must also keep an eye on the more singular features that appear throughout the text; items such as examples and definitions, itemized lists, and forms of reasoning, to name a few.

While this approach may sound complicated, with practice it becomes second nature, and soon you will find that you are able to answer many questions very quickly and with more confidence. In Chapter Seven we will present a review of all of the ideas from the first few chapters in order to give you a concise guide to approaching any passage.

In addition, to help you juggle all of this information, in the next chapter we will discuss how to effectively track all of the key ideas. Prior to that, however, on the following pages is a drill that will test your ability to recognize the various elements discussed in this chapter.

Passage Elements and Formations Recognition Drill

Analyze the following passage excerpts, noting the components discussed in this chapter. In the space provided, list any of the notable passage formations, elements, or reasoning structures, and then provide a brief summary of the material in each excerpt. *Answers on page 151*

Passage #1:

The quagga, an extinct subspecies of the zebra, was initially classified as an entirely separate species (*Equus quagga*) in 1778, based in part on its distinctive coat, which included stripes on only the front half of the animal's body. Recent DNA studies conducted at the Smithsonian Institution, however, indicate that the animal was actually a subspecies of the plains zebra (*Equus burcelli*). Based on the discovery of the close relationship between quaggas and extant zebra species, those conducting the "Quagga Project" in South Africa began selectively breeding existing plains zebras and have successfully produced animals whose outward appearance is very similar to that of preserved quagga specimens.

Analysis: _____

_____

_____

_____

_____

_____

_____

_____

_____

_____

_____

_____

_____

_____

_____

_____

Passage Elements and Formations Recognition Drill

Passage #2:

What is the "right" that the Second Amendment to
the US Constitution was intended to protect? This
amendment, which states that "A well regulated
militia, being necessary to the security of a free
state, the right of the people to keep and bear arms,
shall not be infringed," has largely been subject
to two very different interpretations. Some argue
that the amendment guarantees every citizen the
right to own a gun. Others believe that the founders
intended to assure the right to those who were
members of the necessary "well-regulated militia,"
but that this right does not necessarily extend to
every individual citizen.

Analysis: _____

_____

_____

_____

_____

_____

_____

_____

_____

_____

_____

_____

_____

_____

_____

_____

Passage Elements and Formations Recognition Drill

Passage #3:

The Great Depression was an era of nationwide
financial devastation which led to a significant
increase in the number of married women working
outside the home; the percentage of wives in the
workplace increased from 12% in the early 1930's,
to 15% by the start of World War II. After the war,
the expansion of business and public sectors led
to an increase in the number of jobs available, and
by 1960 almost one third of married women were
working outside the home.

4

Analysis: _____

_____

_____

_____

_____

_____

_____

_____

_____

_____

_____

_____

_____

_____

_____

Passage Elements and Formations Recognition Drill

Passage #4:

Radioactivity causes many nuclei to be unstable, leading to a chain of *decay* (emission of atomic particles), which occurs until a stable nucleus is achieved. Radioactive decay generally takes one of three forms: The first type is known as Alpha decay, which describes the emission of an alpha particle from the nucleus. The second type is called Beta decay, which takes place when the ratio of neutrons to protons is too great, which can lead to the emission of an electron or a positron. Gamma decay is the third class of radioactive decay, which takes place when excessive energy is present in the nucleus and involves the emission of a gamma particle.

Analysis: _____

_____

_____

_____

_____

_____

_____

_____

_____

_____

_____

_____

_____

_____

Passage Elements and Formations Recognition Drill

One alternative to antibiotics is the use of localized bioactive phytochemicals. Certain plant species have an almost limitless ability to synthesize aromatic substances (phytochemicals), which in many cases serve as plant defense mechanisms against predation by insects, herbivores, and, most significantly, micro-organisms. Scientists investigating this antimicrobial activity have found that these phytochemicals can also inhibit the growth of pathogenic bacteria in humans, and, since these agents appear to have structures and operational effects that are distinct from currently utilized antibiotics, the effects of pre-existing antibiotic resistance on phytochemicals should be minimal.

4

Analysis: _____

_____

_____

_____

_____

_____

_____

_____

_____

_____

_____

_____

_____

_____

Passage Elements and Formations Recognition Drill

Passage #6:

Scholarly analysis of the comparative prevalence of epithets—words and phrases used to describe a person or thing, e.g., "rosy-fingered" dawn—in the seminal works of Virgil and Homer has raised fundamental questions about the interpretation of epic poetry. Virgil used epithets rarely, except in his translations into Latin of Homer's *Iliad* and the *Odyssey*, in which epithets abound. Some scholars argue that the performance constraints of preliterate ancient Greece explain Homer's frequent use of epithets, which served as lyrical and mnemonic aids for the orator. Virgil's infrequent use of epithets in the *Aeneid*, these scholars claim, results from the context of a later, literate Roman society. This distinction has led to a debate regarding the propriety of interpreting epithets in the works of Homer and Virgil using the same aesthetic criteria.

Analysis: _____

_____

_____

_____

_____

_____

_____

_____

_____

_____

_____

_____

_____

_____

_____

Passage Elements and Formations Recognition Drill

Passage #7:

Recently, several Hopi katsina kwaatsi have been placed for sale in European auction houses. These Hopi ceremonial masks are sacred objects to the Hopi, who use them to connect with spiritual intermediaries to their gods. The Hopi Tribe argue that these masks are sacred and should be returned to them. The auction houses argue that these objects have previously been sold at auction without objection, and that the Hopi Tribe should appreciate the fact that non-Hopi collectors seek the masks in an effort to learn more about the Hopi culture. Some who support the Hopi cause suggest that, in the event the courts refuse to return the masks to the Tribe, the Tribe should purchase them back at auction, though the Tribal Council has indicated that to do so would only serve to support the false idea that the masks are commercial, rather than sacred objects.

Analysis: _____

_____

_____

_____

_____

_____

_____

_____

_____

_____

_____

_____

_____

_____

Passage Elements and Formations Recognition Drill

Passage #8:

Paleontologists have assumed that they could rely on microscopic observation of round and oblong structures, identified as melanosomes, found in the preserved feathers of ancient birds, to accurately identify the birds' coloring. This is because melanosomes contain melanin, a complex polymer derived from the amino acid tyrosine, that determines skin and feather color. However, recent research involving a fossilized feather from an avian dinosaur known as *Gansus yumenensis* has cast doubt on that assumption. Rather than appearing on the surface of the feather, melanosomes are shielded by the protein keratin. Only after the keratin has been degraded can the melanosome be examined. Yet, the microbes involved in the decomposition process required to expose the melanosomes have round and oblong microscopic structures visually indistinguishable from the melanosomes themselves, even under sophisticated microscopic observation.

Analysis: _____

_____

_____

_____

_____

_____

_____

_____

_____

_____

_____

_____

_____

_____

Passage Elements and Formations Recognition Drill

Passage #9:

Do mandatory seatbelt laws actually increase the total number of traffic fatalities? Some researchers have reached this surprising conclusion based on the theory of "compensating behavior." Under this theory, drivers restrained by a seatbelt feel more secure, and therefore engage in riskier driving behaviors. This change in driving style leads to a higher number of accidents and a concomitant increase in the number of traffic fatalities. Others argue that the data currently available from the widespread adoption of seatbelt laws definitively prove that these laws reduce the total number of traffic fatalities. By 1999, mandatory seatbelt laws had been adopted in all 50 states and the District of Columbia, a marked increase from the first adoption of such laws by just two states in 1985. The next year, 19 more states adopted seatbelt laws. By 1987, more than half of the states had adopted similar laws.

Analysis: _____

_____

_____

_____

_____

_____

_____

_____

_____

_____

_____

_____

_____

Passage Elements and Formations Recognition Drill

Passage #10:

Recently, the reliability of breath tests used as scientific evidence in drunk driving cases has been called into question. The testing machines typically use infrared spectroscopy to identify molecules according to their absorption of infrared light. Defendants have attacked alleged weaknesses in the testing procedures as well as the machines' sophisticated programming. A breath sample must be obtained from deep within the lungs, known as the "end expiratory air," in order to guarantee the machine is able to accurately determine the fraction of alcohol passing from the suspect's bloodstream across a membrane into the alveoli, or hollow cavities, of the lung. The machines then use Henry's Law to extrapolate the suspect's blood alcohol level. Henry's Law states that "the mass of a dissolved gas in a given volume of solvent at equilibrium is proportional to the partial pressure of the gas."

Analysis: _____

_____

_____

_____

_____

_____

_____

_____

_____

_____

_____

_____

_____

Passage Elements and Formations Recognition Drill Answer Key

Passage #1:

The quagga, an extinct subspecies of the zebra, was initially classified as an entirely separate species (*Equus quagga*) in 1778, based in part on its distinctive, which included stripes on only the front half of the animal's body. Recent DNA studies conducted at the Smithsonian Institution, however, indicate that the animal was actually a subspecies of the plains zebra (*Equus burcelli*). Based on the discovery of the close relationship between quaggas and extant zebra species, those conducting the "Quagga Project" in South Africa began selectively breeding existing plains zebras and have successfully produced animals whose outward appearance is very similar to that of preserved quagga specimens.

In this passage we are presented with a scientific topic and many unfamiliar and difficult words (most of which are Latin!). As long as we don't get intimidated by the scientific terminology, the concepts presented here are not overly complex:

> The quagga is a subspecies of the zebra. At first thought a totally different species, it was called *Equus quagga*. Recent DNA studies show it to be a relative of plains zebras—*Equus burcelli*—still in existence today. Thus, members of the "Quagga Project" have selectively bred plains zebras and developed an animal which looks outwardly like the extinct quagga.

Passage #2:

What is the "right" that the Second Amendment to the US Constitution was intended to protect? This amendment, which states that "A well regulated militia, being necessary to the security of a free state, the right of the people to keep and bear arms, shall not be infringed," has largely been subject to two very different interpretations. Some argue that the amendment guarantees every citizen the right to own a gun. Others believe that the founders intended to assure the right to those who were members of the necessary "well-regulated militia," but that this right does not necessarily extend to every individual citizen.

The author opens this passage with a text question. When we see such a question in an LSAT passage, we should always take note; it often presents an inquiry central to the discussion (as is the case here). This passage also provides an example of multiple viewpoints—one of the test makers' methods of adding complexity.

Passage Elements and Formations Recognition Drill Answer Key

The passage can be distilled as follows:

> What is protected by the Second Amendment?
> Some say it protects the right of every individual to own a gun.
> Others say it protects the rights of the "well-regulated militia" but not of every individual citizen.

Passage #3:

The Great Depression was an era of nationwide financial devastation which led to a significant increase in the number of married women working outside the home; the percentage of wives in the workplace increased from 12% in the early 1930's, to 15% by the start of World War II. After the war, the expansion of business and public sectors led to an increase in the number of jobs available, and by 1960 almost one third of married women were working outside the home.

Here the author provides us with the percentage of working married women at three different points in time. Since there are several different dates and numbers to consider, a simple timeline is helpful in tracking information and developing a clear perspective:

Early 1930s	Beginning of WWII	1960
12%	15%	almost 33%

Passage Elements and Formations Recognition Drill Answer Key

Passage #4:

Radioactivity causes many nuclei to be unstable, leading to a chain of *decay* (emission of atomic particles), which occurs until a stable nucleus is achieved. Radioactive decay generally takes one of three forms: The first type is known as Alpha decay, which describes the emission of an alpha particle from the nucleus. The second type is called Beta decay, which takes place when the ratio of neutrons to protons is too great, which can lead to the emission of an electron or a positron. Gamma decay is the third class of radioactive decay, which takes place when excessive energy is present in the nucleus and involves the emission of a gamma particle.

4

The author of this passage discusses a challenging topic—radioactive decay—and provides a definition, which we should note: in this context, decay means particle emission. The author then presents a list of the three different types of such decay. Whenever an LSAT author provides a list, we should take note, because we are likely to see related questions. The three types are as follows:

A. Alpha decay: emission of an alpha particle

B. Beta decay: emission of electron or positron

C. Gamma decay: emission of a gamma particle

Passage #5:

One alternative to antibiotics is the use of localized bioactive phytochemicals. Certain plant species have an almost limitless ability to synthesize aromatic substances (phytochemicals), which in many cases serve as plant defense mechanisms against predation by insects, herbivores, and, most significantly, micro-organisms. Scientists investigating this antimicrobial activity have found that these phytochemicals can also inhibit the growth of pathogenic bacteria in humans, and, since these agents appear to have structures and operational effects that are distinct from currently utilized antibiotics, the effects of pre-existing antibiotic resistance on phytochemicals should be minimal.

Passage Elements and Formations Recognition Drill Answer Key

If there is a common element reflected here it is the author's challenging writing style; this selection is not written in a particularly accessible way, and begins with some unfamiliar and difficult terminology. The passage can be distilled as follows:

> Bioactive phytochemicals (defined as aromatic substances) can be used in place of antibiotics. Certain plants can create such substances, which can defend against plant predators, including micro-organisms. Scientists have found that these substances can also help defend against pathogens in humans. Further, phytochemicals are different enough from antibiotics that antibiotic resistance should have no effect on such substances.

Passage #6:

Scholarly analysis of the comparative prevalence of epithets—words and phrases used to describe a person or thing, e.g., "rosy-fingered" dawn—in the seminal works of Virgil and Homer has raised fundamental questions about the interpretation of epic poetry. Virgil used epithets rarely, except in his translations into Latin of Homer's *Iliad* and the *Odyssey*, in which epithets abound. Some scholars argue that the performance constraints of preliterate ancient Greece explain Homer's frequent use of epithets, which served as lyrical and mnemonic aids for the orator. Virgil's infrequent use of epithets in the *Aeneid*, these scholars claim, results from the context of a later, literate Roman society. This distinction has led to a debate regarding the propriety of interpreting epithets in the works of Homer and Virgil using the same aesthetic criteria.

The difficulty in this passage comes, in part, from the subject matter. While many students are generally more comfortable with the topics of poetry and literature, in this case the passage content deals with a less familiar technical matter, the use of epithets in ancient epic poetry. We refer to this "bait and switch" aspect of the excerpt as a Passage Topic Trap. In addition, this excerpt employs the Trap of Order, because although the excerpt discusses Virgil first, Homer actually preceded Virgil. Despite the apparent complexity of the passage, the concepts are straightforward:

> An epithet is a word or phrase used to describe a person or a thing. Some argue that Homer created his poems at a time before Greece had a written language, and that he used epithets frequently to help people recite his poetry from memory. Virgil used epithets infrequently in his original work, the *Aeneid*, because at the time he created the *Aeneid*, Rome had a written language. So, Virgil did not have the same need for epithets as Homer. Since different causes led to the use of epithets by Homer and Virgil, scholars disagree over how to interpret epithets in their respective works.

Passage Elements and Formations Recognition Drill Answer Key

Passage #7:

Recently, several Hopi katsina kwaatsi have been placed for sale in European auction houses. These Hopi ceremonial masks are sacred objects to the Hopi, who use them to connect with spiritual intermediaries to their gods. The Hopi Tribe argue that these masks are sacred and should be returned to them. The auction houses argue that these objects have previously been sold at auction without objection, and that the Hopi Tribe should appreciate the fact that non-Hopi collectors seek the masks in an effort to learn more about the Hopi culture. Some who support the Hopi cause suggest that, in the event the courts refuse to return the masks to the Tribe, the Tribe should purchase them back at auction, though the Tribal Council has indicated that to do so would only serve to support the false idea that the masks are commercial, rather than sacred objects.

While the concepts involved in this excerpt are not complex, the presence of multiple viewpoints can cause an organizational challenge, and represents the Trap of Inserted Alternate Viewpoints. We can break down this passage as follows:

1. Hopi katsina kwaatsi are ceremonial masks considered by the Hopi to be sacred objects.

2. The Hopi Tribe objects to their sale as commercial objects.

3. Auction houses argue the masks have been sold in the past, and that their sale reflects an interest in Hopi culture.

4. Some Hopi supporters think the Hopi Tribe should itself buy back the masks if the courts decline to return them.

5. But, the Hopi Tribal Council believes that such a solution would still support the notion that the masks are commercial rather than sacred.

Passage Elements and Formations Recognition Drill Answer Key

Passage #8:

Paleontologists have assumed that they could rely on microscopic observation of round and oblong structures, identified as melanosomes, found in the preserved feathers of ancient birds, to accurately identify the birds' coloring. This is because melanosomes contain melanin, a complex polymer derived from the amino acid tyrosine, that determines skin and feather color. However, recent research involving a fossilized feather from an avian dinosaur known as *Gansus yumenensis* has cast doubt on that assumption. Rather than appearing on the surface of the feather, melanosomes are shielded by the protein keratin. Only after the keratin has been degraded can the melanosome be examined. Yet, the microbes involved in the decomposition process required to expose the melanosomes have round and oblong microscopic structures visually indistinguishable from the melanosomes themselves, even under sophisticated microscopic observation.

Here, reasonably simple concepts are camouflaged by the scientific topic and its related technical terms. There is no distinct trap in this example, other than the tendency of many students to shut down when faced with unfamiliar, technical language. In more simplified language, the passage presents this issue:

Paleontologists cannot rely on the microscopic structure of melanosomes to identify the coloring of ancient birds, because the melanosomes can only be seen if microbes with an indistinguishable structure are also present. So, the observer cannot tell if what they are observing are the melanosomes (which produce the coloring), or microbes (which caused the decomposition).

Passage #9:

Do mandatory seatbelt laws actually increase the total number of traffic fatalities? Some researchers have reached this surprising conclusion based on the theory of "compensating behavior." Under this theory, drivers restrained by a seatbelt feel more secure, and therefore engage in riskier driving behaviors. This change in driving style leads to a higher number of accidents and a concomitant increase in the number of traffic fatalities. Others argue that the data currently available from the widespread adoption of seatbelt laws definitively prove that these laws reduce the total number of traffic fatalities. By 1999, mandatory seatbelt laws had been adopted in all 50 states and the District of Columbia, a marked increase from the first adoption of such laws by just two states in 1985. The next year, 19 more states adopted seatbelt laws. By 1987, more than half of the states had adopted similar laws.

This passage excerpt features three common passage elements. The first is a text question, which typically identifies an issue central to the author's argument, as it does here. Next, the excerpt presents multiple viewpoints, which the author uses to discuss the text question. Finally, dates and numbers are offered as evidence. Here, although the dates are *intentionally presented out of order* to make the passage more complex, a timeline shows the correct organization of the data:

1985	1986	1987	1999
2 states	21 states	At least 26 states ("more than half")	All 50 states and the District of Columbia

Passage Elements and Formations Recognition Drill Answer Key

Passage #10:

Recently, the reliability of breath tests used as scientific evidence in drunk driving cases has been called into question. The testing machines typically use infrared spectroscopy to identify molecules according to their absorption of infrared light. Defendants have attacked alleged weaknesses in the testing procedures as well as the machines' sophisticated programming. A breath sample must be obtained from deep within the lungs, known as the "end expiratory air," in order to guarantee the machine is able to accurately determine the fraction of alcohol passing from the suspect's bloodstream across a membrane into the alveoli, or hollow cavities, of the lung. The machines then use Henry's Law to extrapolate the suspect's blood alcohol level. Henry's Law states that "the mass of a dissolved gas in a given volume of solvent at equilibrium is proportional to the partial pressure of the gas."

This excerpt employs a Passage Topic Trap, by combining complex scientific material with a Law-Related passage. The key to attacking a passage such as this is to remember that the questions will focus on the *argumentation* involved, and cannot require a sophisticated understanding of the scientific material. In this case, the proper approach while reading is to mark the location of the scientific details for later reference (if necessary), but to focus on a broad understanding of the central issue:

Criminal defendants have alleged that procedural and technical flaws in breath test machines render them unreliable for use as evidence in drunk driving prosecutions.

Chapter Five:
Tracking
Information

Chapter Five: Tracking Information

Tracking Passage Information ■■■

Because of the amount of information contained in each RC passage, most students seek to make some marks and notes about the text as they read. These notations, when created in an organized and purposeful fashion, allow you to better follow the passage information by providing a "visual summary" of the text. Your notes not only help to mentally organize the structure and flow of the passage, but can also save valuable time when returning to the text because the location of desired information is more obvious. As such, an effective approach to tracking the information in a passage can help you to answer the questions more effectively and efficiently.

In this chapter we discuss the options you have to mark and notate passages, and consider several ways to quickly represent the most important elements of each passage. We present these options for your consideration, so that you are able to develop the passage notation strategy that you find most effective.

To that last point: **the proper approach to tracking information varies from person to person, and there is no universally correct or incorrect way to notate a passage**. The methods we discuss provide an idea of the *types* of diagramming that can be done; they are not meant to suggest that every element *must* be marked. In fact, as you continue to practice and improve we strongly suggest trying to notate less, where you only annotate the passage when absolutely necessary for comprehension and/or future reference. So first become familiar with these tools, and then use your practice time to establish the type and amount of notating that works best for you!

Our diagramming analysis focuses on the two most helpful types: markings and notes. Passage markings are the indicators—underlining or highlighting—made on the text itself, whereas notes are the written words or symbolizations that you show on your scratch paper. The combined product of your marks and notations is what we sometimes term the "passage diagram."

Good information tracking helps to direct you efficiently when you return to the passage. In this sense, it is like road signs that quickly give you a wealth of information. But, also like road signs, when there are too many marks and notes it can become confusing, so avoid the tendency to over-notate!

"Markings" refer to marks made directly on the text of the passage. "Notes" refer to written words or symbolizations made on your scratch paper. "Passage diagrams" include all of the marks and notes for the passage.

5

What You Can Use to Diagram

Per LSAC rules, you have the following options for annotating passages:

On Screen:

Underliner: The digital interface allows you to select words and phrases, and then underline them in black.

Highlighters: The interface has *three* color choices for highlighting sections of the passage or answer choices: yellow, pink, and orange. These colors can be used together interchangeably, a point we will discuss shortly.

On Scratch Paper:

Pen: A pen is built into the stylus that is provided to you at the test center.

Pencil: You are allowed to bring pencils to the center, and they can be used to make notes on your scratch paper.

You are not required to use any of these tools (and many good test takers do not use them) but you must be aware of your options before arriving at the test center. Let's talk next about different strategies for using (or not using) each of these tools.

How To Read and Notate ▮▮▮▮▮▮

The Reading Comprehension section is perhaps the most challenging of the three section types when done in a digital environment. As mentioned in Chapter Three, the entire text of the passage is not visible on a single screen. Thus, you must scroll through the passage to complete it. You can alternately select a "Passage Only" view that allows you to see more of the passage, but even then you cannot see the entire passage on a single screen, and you must click to the next screen to see the remainder of the text.

Even more problematic is that your options for notating directly on the passage are extremely limited. You cannot write or draw on the screen in a freehand manner, restricting you to only the tools discussed on the prior page. Thus, students are faced with a limited set of options for controlling information within a passage.

The best approach will naturally change from person to person, so, again, **you must practice with digital passages in order to find the technique that best suits you**. With that in mind, let's discuss the various options and approaches you can experiment with:

1. Light (or No) Marking and Light (or No) Note Taking

    This approach directs the reader to simply focus on the passage, and to only make minimal marks on the passage screen, and few to no notes on the scratch paper. To apply this strategy, simply begin reading the passage and focus on the VIEWSTAMP elements.

    One concern with this approach is that if you forget parts of the passage, it can be difficult to retrieve that information quickly. However, this weakness is somewhat offset because this approach requires the least amount of time to implement, so you have more time to return to the passage and to answer the questions.

    This is a strategy that is often used by students who are strong readers, or are high scorers with reliable recall. It focuses primarily on the reading aspect, and allows you to trust that you will have the time to return to the passage as needed to find required information.

2. Light Marking but Heavier Note Taking

This strategy primarily relies on using your scratch paper to make notes about the passage, which might include abbreviated references to key elements like viewpoints and shifts in tone, or even short paragraph or passage summaries.

It de-emphasizes use of the digital tools (underlining and highlighting) for help understanding the passage, and is an excellent option for students used to taking extensive notes.

One downside to this approach is that it takes extra time to write out summaries and notes on the scratch paper, so be prepared to move more slowly at first than you may currently be used to.

3. Heavier Marking but Light Note Taking

This strategy is the opposite of the last approach, where now the use of underlining and highlighting is emphasized, and the scratch paper is largely ignored.

While using the screen tools is relatively quick, the limited nature of what you can illustrate with them minimizes the effect. Thus, this approach tends to be most advisable for those with relatively good recall of the overall structure of the passage and just need to note key moments in the text.

4. Heavier Marking and Heavier Note Taking

This is the riskiest of the possible strategies because it is the most time-intensive and involved. Both marking the passage and making side notes will require a significant amount of time and energy, and thus we generally recommend this strategy only for students really struggling with the Reading section. However, for those students, this approach helps consolidate and reduce all of the information to a more manageable, highlighted form, and that can be a big help when answering questions.

Now that we've outlined some of the possible approaches, let's talk about how you can best execute marking and note taking.

Marking the Passage Text ▰▰▰▰

When marking the passage, as outlined previously you have a limited set of options: underlining and highlighting. That's it! Let's discuss the use of each:

Remember, limited markings are generally preferable to heavy markings. The same holds true of the notations discussed later in this chapter.

Underlining

This is the simplest and most common technique of all: select the underline tool, pick out words or phrases that give decisive information or indicate a turning point in the passage, and then underline those portions. Underlining can help crystallize the information, allowing you to more easily handle the material, and draw your eye to the most essential moments in each paragraph. Here is a brief example:

> While the proponents of the Futurism art movement
> believed that <u>the past was an era to be ignored</u>, some
> critics assert that, ironically, for the Futurists to break
> from the past would have required a more thorough
> (5) understanding of history on their part.

The key point to remember is that while *some* underlining is very helpful, a large amount of underlining actually makes things more confusing. So be judicious when choosing what to underline! For example, consider the following:

> While the <u>proponents of the Futurism art movement</u>
> believed that <u>the past was an era to be ignored</u>, some
> <u>critics assert that, ironically, for the Futurists to break</u>
> <u>from the past would have required a more thorough</u>
> (5) <u>understanding of history on their part</u>.

In this case, the underlining has no value because almost all of the text has been marked as important or notable. The key is to mark those few sections that you feel have high value. We will discuss this in more detail when we look at additional examples of passage diagramming shortly.

Highlighting

The other useful on screen tool allows you to highlight sections of the text, and the digital interface gives you three color options for highlighting: yellow, pink, and orange.

Highlighting provides a visual change from underlining, and can make certain elements of the passage stand out more clearly:

> While the proponents of the Futurism art movement
> believed that the past was an era to be ignored, some
> critics assert that, ironically, for the Futurists to break
> from the past would have required a more thorough
> (5)   understanding of history on their part.

On the LSAT, you can use just a single highlighter color to make all of your marks, or you can attempt to use two or three colors as a sort of visual tracking system. For example, you could highlight the author's relevant points in yellow, and then the opposition view could be orange. However, note that an approach like this has some drawbacks, primarily in the amount of time needed to switch colors as you go through the passage. We'd advise using an approach like this only if you are struggling to understand the passage text, and then practicing extensively with multiple colors to ensure you're comfortable switching between them on test day.

Note also that highlighting can be used in place of underlining, or it can be used in conjunction with underlining. This is again a personal preference, and you will need to spend time experimenting with passages in order to determine which methods are most effective for you.

5

Passage Notes

Passage notes are the handwritten comments and short phrases made on your scratch paper. These also included any abbreviations that you use to represent certain common elements within the passage (such as "V" for viewpoint or "MP" for Main Point).

Some students ask if they should always write out full sentences or summations on their scratch paper for each paragraph or important element. In general, the answer is No. In many cases no notes are required, but you can determine through practice the extent to which they serve your needs.

The exception to this rule is when you are having extreme difficulty retaining the structure or main ideas of a passage (this is a problem that non-native English speakers sometimes face, for example). In these cases, the best strategy is often to write out a short description of each paragraph or of the passage as a whole.

If you make scratch paper notes, number the paragraphs of the passage on your page and make the relevant notes beside or under those paragraph numbers. These are some scratch paper notations that you could then use:

"V" for Viewpoint

Typically this is accompanied with a subscript to identify the viewpoint's owner, such as V_A for the viewpoint of the author, or V_C for the viewpoint of a critic. Here is an example, using our sample section:

> While the proponents of the Futurism art movement believed that the past was an era to be ignored, some critics assert that, ironically, for the Futurists to break from the past would have required a more thorough
> (5) understanding of history on their part.

On your scratch paper, you could write out:

¶ 1. V_P = ignore past

V_C = They had to know history

Remember, one of the ways the test makers can make Reading Comprehension passages more challenging is with quick shifts from one perspective to another. So it is vital that you at least recognize the various opinions presented: when you are responding to a question about viewpoints a well-notated passage can lead you directly to the relevant perspectives.

"MP" for Main Point

An "MP" notation can be used whenever you identify the Main Point of the passage. Often, the MP notation appears in conjunction with underlining or highlighting, but that is a personal and contextual choice.

"CC" for Compare and Contrast sections

As discussed in the last chapter, the makers of the LSAT frequently include dense sections of text where ideas or positions are compared and contrasted. Because identifying connected positions using underlining or highlighting is challenging in these sections, often the best approach is to simply place a "CC" notation on your scratch paper in reference to a section of compare and contrast material. This notation then provides a quick reference point to return to if a question comes up about one or more of the groups involved. At that point you can sort out which viewpoint is which. Example:

¶ 2.   CC Proponents and Critics

"Def" for Definitions

Also discussed in the last chapter was the fact that definitions are often tested in the questions, either directly or indirectly. Consequently, notating definitions when they appear is beneficial. The best approach is to simply place a "Def" notation on your scratch paper in reference to the specific paragraph. This notation then provides a quick reference point to return to if a question comes up about that definition. Example:

¶ 1, top.   Def = Dimorphism

"Ex" for Examples

As previously discussed, examples are generally used to support the arguments in the passage, and they help readers gain a greater understanding of the concept under discussion by illustrating broad ideas with concrete instances. Thus, examples are often tested in the questions.

Enumerations

Another point of interest in Chapter Four was the notion of lists: LSAT authors often enumerate the reasons behind a specific action or occurrence, provide multiple options for achieving some desired result, or list possible consequences of a particular plan or approach. When this occurs, you should underline or highlight the word that indicates each item, as in the following example:

(10)   Historians have indicated that support for the legislation was broad-based. <u>First</u>, active members of the armed forces benefited directly from the educational incentives provided by the law. <u>Second</u>, colleges and universities were ardent supporters of the legislation due to the
(15)   financial advantages afforded by thousands of new students. And <u>finally</u>, employers ultimately benefited from the presence of a better educated workforce (albeit not immediately).

You can also list those numbered items in your notes, but at times that can be difficult or too time-consuming.

With practice, many test takers find that marking and notating becomes second nature. When this occurs, the amount of time used for diagramming the passage is minimal. The key, though, is to be extremely familiar with the kinds of marks and notations you prefer to make, and then to be judicious in your application of them.

What to Diagram—Reviewed by Diagram Element

The first rule of passage diagramming is: do not over-diagram! The key to successfully tracking passage information is to mark and note the elements that routinely appear in the questions and to do so consistently. With this in mind, let us take a moment to review the passage diagrams, along with notes on what each diagram element should designate.

Marking Tools:

Underlining

- Use to mark words, phrases or sentences that are important, such as tone indicators.

- Use with indicator words for numbered lists.

Highlighting

- Use to track viewpoints or particularly important or difficult sections of the text.

- There are three color choices, so you can mix and match according to your preference.

Possible Scratch Paper Notation Abbreviations:

V   Viewpoints, with a subscript identifying the group or person.

MP   Use to identify the Main Point of the passage.

CC   Use to denote Compare and Contrast sections.

Def   References definitions of words, phrases, or ideas.

Ex   Used to reference Examples used in the passage.

1, 2, etc. Underline or highlight each item indicator.

Passage Diagramming and Summarization Examples

On the following pages we offer three examples of passages that have accompanying notations. These passages are marked and notated using different approaches—from heavier diagramming to light diagramming—in an effort to demonstrate that **there is no one "correct" method**. Instead, you must use the method that suits you best, as determined by practicing with both copious and minimal notation techniques.

In addition, a brief summary of each passage is included for review purposes.

Some students find heavy diagramming of passages distracting, while others feel that the right types of marks and notations can make it much easier to track the main points and structure. Experiment to find the approach that works best for you!

5

Passage Diagramming and Summarization: Heavy Underlining Example

Below is a sample passage in which underlining is used liberally, and as the primary notation device. The summary is drawn almost exclusively from the underlined portions of the passage:

The <u>Law and Economics movement seeks to apply economic theories to the law</u>. Within the movement there are <u>two approaches</u>: the positive and the normative. Positive economic analysis of law <u>attempts to predict</u> the economic <u>outcomes of different legal rules</u>. For example, a product liability case would require examination of the various economic outcomes produced under negligence claims, as compared with those produced under statutory claims. Normative economic analysis <u>incorporates</u> the <u>positive</u> economic analysis <u>and adds</u> to it by making policy <u>recommendations based on the various outcomes</u>. The defining guideline under a normative analysis is to advocate for the most efficient outcome in economic terms.

Critics of the Law and Economics movement compellingly argue that academic <u>economic models are unsuitable</u> for the analysis of <u>real-world legal scenarios</u>. Because the most complicated economic models, they argue, are still unable to reflect the <u>complexities of actual human behavior</u> and motivations, an economic analysis can never produce fully accurate results. In addition, because a number of desirable <u>social values</u>—such as free speech—<u>cannot be easily</u> <u>quantified</u>, the economic <u>values assigned</u> are somewhat arbitrary and most likely egregiously <u>inaccurate</u>.

Defenders of the Law and Economics movement argue that the <u>general value</u> of an economic analysis is <u>enough to justify</u> adopting the approach, and that <u>precise outcomes are hard to predict</u> regardless of the model used. Further, advocates argue that the <u>field is developing</u>, and recent developments attempt to account for some of the criticisms. These arguments provide some defenses against the critics, but in the main fall short of validating the movement.

Summary:

The Law and Economics Movement applies economic theory to the law; two approaches:

1. Positive analysis: tries to predict outcomes of different rules (ex: negligence vs. statutory claims).
2. Normative analysis: incorporates positive analysis and adds recommendations seeking efficiency.

There are three viewpoints:

Critics: Such models don't apply to complex real world behavior, social values are hard to quantify.

Defenders: Analysis has general value; outcomes are often unpredictable, the field is still developing.

Author: Defenders have some defense, but not enough to validate the movement (joins the critics).

Passage Diagramming and Summarization: Underlining and Scratch Paper Notes Example

In this example, underlining and scratch paper notes are combined; note that much of the general summarization has been completed once the passage is outlined in this fashion:

Passage:

Scratch Paper Notes:

The World Anti-Doping Agency defines "<u>Gene Doping</u>" as "the non-therapeutic use of cells, genes, genetic elements, or of the modulation of gene expression, having the capacity to improve athletic performance." <u>Some argue</u> that the best way to gain any degree of control over the problem of gene doping, which can be both costly and difficult to detect, <u>is to legalize it</u>. After all, they assert, if a professional golfer can have eye surgery to improve his game, then perhaps other types of athletes should be allowed certain limited genetic modifications. Moreover, the argument goes, legalization and regulation would bring the imposition of safety standards.

But isn't gene doping different? <u>Doesn't it violate the basic spirit</u> of fair competition? The overwhelming consensus is that it does. <u>The Olympic committee</u> believes that gene doping is wrong, and this perspective is shared by several professional and college sports leagues, all of which have added gene doping to their lists of official prohibitions. <u>It is quite doubtful, however, that all of these groups will be able to match strong objection with practical enforcement.</u>

¶1. Def = Doping

V_s = Legalization

Golf eye ex

Safer

¶2. It's a violation

V_{OC} = It's wrong

Other groups agree

V_A = They can't enforce it

Summary:

The first paragraph opens with a definition of gene doping, followed by the viewpoint of "some" who suggest legalization and regulation, comparing gene doping to eye surgery. Safety standards are offered as another possible justification.

The second paragraph begins with the point that gene doping violates the spirit of fair competition, presenting the viewpoint of the Olympic committee and many other athletic organizations who oppose the practice. The closing sentence reflects the viewpoint of the author, who is skeptical about prospects for practical enforcement.

Passage Diagramming and Summarization: Minimal Diagramming Example

A more minimalistic approach to diagramming is exemplified below; just a few properly placed notations can help to highlight the overall structure and general content of the passage:

Although there has been progress in attempting to attain equality for women in the workplace, there is still much to be done before equality is achieved. In particular, certain workplace initiatives would likely attract more women, including those with families. Accordingly, experts have identified several areas where employers should improve job options and benefits. The two most notable recommendations in regards to working mothers are increased flex-time options and expansion of the virtual workplace.

Flex-time, which allows for a variable work schedule, addresses the needs of working mothers by helping to foster a balance between work and family obligations. Schedules can accommodate four-day work weeks, irregular hours (including nights and weekends), and rotating schedules subject to routine changes. The flex-time option, which should be mandatory where possible, benefits employers as well: happy, satisfied workers have been proven to be more productive, and offering this option makes the employer more attractive in the labor market.

Another worthy initiative is the expansion of the virtual workplace. The advent of the internet, more easily available high-speed digital data transfer, and new telecommunications technology has made working from home a viable option for many. Working mothers benefit from time saved (less travel time between work and home, less time needed to get ready for work) and from the convenience of working in an environment where family emergencies can be countered or even avoided. The virtual workplace, in combination with flex-time, offers the flexibility required by many working mothers, and employers should be legally compelled to offer these options.

Summary:

There is still much to be done before women have achieved equality in the workplace. The author believes employers should improve job options and benefits, with two specific recommendations:

1. Flex-time: variable and rotating work schedules foster balance between work and family.

2. Virtual workplace: technology allows working from home, more efficient and convenient.

The author's viewpoint is that these two recommendations provide much greater flexibility and thus should be legally required.

5

Final Chapter Note

The marks and notes discussed in this chapter are not the only possible ones; they are simply common ones we have found useful. If you have a different system or technique that you find helpful, by all means use it. Developing a system that works for you is one of the primary goals of this book!

Keep in mind that when it comes to diagramming, practice can play an important role in perfecting the approach that works best for you: By taking practice sections or reading practice passages, you can quickly increase your familiarity with the type of language the test makers use and the sorts of questions you are likely to encounter. Beyond that, you can use your test reviews to hone your summarization and notation skills, and to help determine the diagramming approach that is most effective for you. Don't be afraid to try out different levels of notation and diagramming, and as you review your Reading Comprehension results, review your diagrams and notations as well! As you look over all of the questions (the ones that you missed and the ones you answered correctly), also consider your passage notations. Could you have done a better job? Did you over-notate in some cases, or perhaps fail to note crucial information in others? If so, go back with the right answers in hand and fix or improve your notations, and then apply the lessons you've learned to the next passage you attack.

Remember, diagramming systems are simply a helpful tool to keep track of the information in each passage. Although they will help you organize and quickly locate information, you are still responsible for identifying the main conclusion, tone and viewpoints of the speakers, and overall structure of the passage.

And finally, once you've established what seems to be the most appropriate diagramming style for you (in terms of elements marked and overall volume of notes), work to be consistent in your notations. By always representing the same elements in the same way, you can move through the test as quickly as possible with maximum accuracy.

Chapter Six:
The Questions
and Answers

Chapter Six: The Questions and Answers

POWERSCORE
BY BARBRI

The Questions

In this chapter, we will focus solely on the questions that tend to accompany single passage sets. In the Comparative Reading chapter, we will discuss in detail two additional question types that more frequently appear with dual passage sets.

In single passage sets, a group of five to eight questions follows each passage, and each of the questions is directed at the passage. The question stems cover a wide range of tasks, and will variously ask you to:

- describe the main point or primary purpose of the passage

- describe the structure and organization of the passage

- identify the viewpoint of the author or the viewpoint of subjects discussed within the passage

- identify details of the passage or statements proven by the passage

- describe the meaning, function, or purpose of words or phrases in the passage

- strengthen, weaken, or parallel elements of the passage

- augment or expand the passage

On average, you typically have less than 1 minute to complete each question.

6

Analyzing the Question Stem

At first glance, Reading Comprehension sections appear to have a multitude of different types of question stems. The test makers create this impression by varying the words used in each question stem. As we will see shortly, even though they use different words, many of these question stems are identical in terms of what you are asked to do.

In order to easily handle the different questions, we categorize the question stems that appear on the LSAT. Fortunately, every question stem can be defined as a certain type, and the more familiar you are with the question types, the faster you can respond when faced with individual questions. Thus, one of your tasks is to learn each question type and become familiar with the characteristics that define each type. We will help you accomplish this goal by including a variety of question type identification drills and by examining each type of question in detail.

The Location Element™

Make sure
to read each
question stem
very carefully.
Some stems
direct you to
focus on certain
areas of the
passage and
if you miss
these clues, the
problem becomes
much more
difficult.

All Reading Comprehension question stems provide some insight into where in the passage you should begin your search for the correct answer. This element is called "location," and you should always establish location as you read each question stem.

Location can be divided into three categories—Specific Reference, Concept Reference, and Global Reference:

Specific Reference (SR). These question stems refer you to a specific line, sentence, or paragraph. For example:

> "The author of the passage uses the phrase 'rational expectations' (last sentence of the first paragraph) primarily in order to"

> "Which one of the following best defines the word 'pragmatic' as it is used in the second paragraph of the passage?"

> "Which one of the following would best exemplify the kind of theory referred to in the final paragraph of the passage?"

On the digital LSAT, when Specific Reference questions include a word, phrase, or sentence, that point of reference will be highlighted in both the question stem and in the passage itself. For instance, the following question stem would highlight the word "academics" in both the question and in the passage's final paragraph, making for easy identification as you consider the original usage in the text:

> Which one of the following, in its context in the passage, most clearly reveals the attitude of the author toward the 'academics' described in the final paragraph of the passage?

Although the correct answer to a Specific Reference question is not always found in the exact lines referenced, those reference points are always an excellent starting point for your analysis.

To attack
Specific
Reference
questions, return
to the passage
and start
reading three to
five lines above
the reference,
or from the
most logical
nearby starting
point such as
the start of a
paragraph.

To attack Specific Reference questions that refer to an exact word, phrase, or sentence, always return to the passage and start reading three to five lines above the reference, or from the most logical nearby starting point such as the start of a paragraph. To attack Specific Reference questions that refer to a paragraph, return to the passage and consider the paragraph in question. We will discuss this approach in more detail when we begin dissecting individual passages.

Concept Reference (CR). Some questions refer you to ideas or themes within the passage that are not identified by a specific line or paragraph reference, but that are identifiable because the ideas are clearly enunciated or expressed within one or two areas of the passage. When reading questions that contain concept references, you should typically know where to search in the passage for the relevant information even though no line reference is given. Examples include:

"The passage suggests which one of the following about the behavior of elk in conflict situations?"

"The author's discussion of telephone answering machines serves primarily to..."

"The passage indicates that prior to the use of carbon dating, at least some historians believed which one of the following?"

In each of the above instances, although no specific location reference is given, an engaged student would know where in the passage to begin searching for the correct answer, and he or she would then return to the passage and take a moment to review the relevant information.

Global Reference (GR). Global Reference questions ask about the passage as a whole, or they fail to identify a defined area or isolated concept within the question stem. For example:

"Which one of the following most accurately expresses the main point of the passage?"

"The primary purpose of the passage is to..."

"Information in the passage most strongly supports which one of the following statements?"

Although they might at first seem intimidating, many Global questions can be answered from your initial reading of the passage. For example, you know that you are always seeking to identify the main point of the passage as you read, so the presence of a Main Point question should not alarm you or cause you any undue work. On the other hand, Global questions that ask you to prove statements drawn from the passage can be time-consuming because they typically require you to return to the passage and cross-check each answer choice.

A thorough understanding of the organization of the passage allows for quick access to the information necessary to attack Concept Reference questions.

6

Understanding the "big picture" is vital, since at least half of the questions on any given passage are likely to be Global Reference questions.

Note that not every question stem that refers to a concept is a Concept Reference question. For example, if an entire passage is about the poet Rita Dove, and the question stem asks about the views of Rita Dove, that question would be classified as Global. We will discuss this classification in more detail when we examine individual questions.

Throughout this book, all questions are first classified as one of these three types. There are also additional indicators designating question type, etc.

As we classify Reading Comprehension questions, location will always appear as the first element of the classification. Thus, every question classification in this book will begin with the shorthand reference of SR, CR, or GR.

The concept of location should not be an unexpected one. Reading Comprehension passages are roughly 50-60 lines in length (in standard font), and with a passage of that size, you should expect that the test makers will want to ask about different parts of the passage.

Throughout this section we will indicate how frequently each type of question appears. Assessing just the Location element, this is the frequency of appearance per section (the typical section is 26-28 questions in length):

Frequency of SR Questions: 25 - 30% overall

Frequency of CR Questions: 25 - 30% overall

Frequency of GR Questions: 40 - 50% overall

Location Designation Drill

Each of the following items contains a sample Reading Comprehension question stem. In the space provided, categorize each stem into one of the three Location designations: Specific Reference (SR), Concept Reference (CR), and Global Reference (GR). While we realize that you have not yet worked directly with each question type, by considering the designations you will now have an advantage as you attack future questions. Later in this chapter we will present more comprehensive Identify the Question Stem drills to further strengthen your abilities. *Answers on page 184*

1. Which one of the following most accurately describes the organization of the material presented in the passage?

   Location Designation:

   _____

2. The third paragraph of the passage provides the most support for which one of the following inferences?

   Location Designation:

   _____

3. The discussion of Muniz' first theory is intended to perform which of the following functions in the passage?

   Location Designation:

   _____

4. The author mentions the number of species (last two sentences of the third paragraph) primarily in order to support which of the following claims?

   Location Designation:

   _____

5. Which of the following is mentioned in the passage as an important characteristic of each of the three theories discussed in the passage?

   Location Designation:

   _____

6. Which one of the following titles most completely and accurately describes the contents of the passage?

   Location Designation:

   _____

Location Designation Drill Answer Key

The typical student misses a few questions in this drill. Do not worry about how many you miss; the point of this drill is to acquaint you with the idea of Location as it is presented in different question stems. As you see more examples of each type of question, your ability to correctly identify the Location element will improve.

1. Which one of the following most accurately describes the organization of the material presented in the passage?

    Location Type: Global Reference

    Because this stem asks about the "organization of the material presented in the passage," it references the passage as a whole and is thus best described as a Global Reference question.

2. The third paragraph of the passage provides the most support for which one of the following inferences?

    Location Type: Specific Reference

    This stem specifically references the "third paragraph of the passage," and so this is a Specific Reference question.

3. The discussion of Muniz' first theory is intended to perform which of the following functions in the passage?

    Location Type: Concept Reference

    This question stem does not refer to a specific line or paragraph, so it cannot be a Specific Reference question. The reference to a particular theory is enough to suggest that this is more specific than a Global Reference question, so this example can be classified a Concept Reference question.

Location Designation Drill Answer Key

4. The author mentions the number of species (last two sentences of the third paragraph) primarily in order to support which of the following claims?

Location Type: Specific Reference

This stem specifically references the last two sentences of the third paragraph, and therefore this is a Specific Reference question.

---

5. Which of the following is mentioned in the passage as an important characteristic of each of the three theories discussed in the passage?

Location Type: Concept Reference

This question stem does not refer to a specific line or paragraph, so it cannot be a Specific Reference question. However, the question also does not refer to the passage in general, and the idea mentioned in the stem is specific enough to suggest that this is a Concept Reference question.

---

6. Which one of the following titles most completely and accurately describes the contents of the passage?

Location Type: Global Reference

This stem discusses the "contents of the passage," and is thus best described as a Global Reference question.

Main Reading Comprehension Question Types

Many of the question types discussed in the LSAT Logical Reasoning Bible are also covered here.

After establishing Location, the next element you must identify when reading question stems is the type of question that you face. The questions in the Reading Comprehension section are similar to the questions asked in the Logical Reasoning section, and virtually all question stems that appear in the Reading Comprehension section of the LSAT can be classified into one of six different types:

1. Must Be True/Most Supported

2. Main Point

3. Strengthen

4. Weaken

5. Parallel Reasoning

6. Cannot Be True

Note that some of the other question types that appear in the Logical Reasoning section, such as Justify the Conclusion or Resolve the Paradox, *could* appear in the Reading Comprehension section, but they appear so infrequently that a discussion of those types is not useful. Further, keep in mind that we will discuss two additional question types when we look at Comparative Reading in Chapter Eight; the initial discussion here is specific to single passages.

You must correctly analyze and classify every question stem because the question stem ultimately determines the nature of the correct answer choice. A mistake in analyzing the question stem almost invariably leads to a missed question. Properly identifying the question stem type will allow you to proceed quickly and with confidence, and in some cases it will help you determine the correct answer before you read any of the five answer choices.

Occasionally, students ask if we refer to the question types by number or by name. We always refer to the questions by name, as that is an easier and more efficient approach. Numerical question type classification systems force you to add two unnecessary levels of abstraction to your thinking process. For example, consider a question that asks you to "weaken" the argument. In a numerical question classification system, you must first recognize that the question asks you to weaken the argument, then you must classify that question into a numerical category (say, Type 4), and then you must translate Type 4 to mean "Weaken." Literally, numerical classification systems force you to perform an abstract, circular translation of the meaning of the question, and this translation process is both time-consuming and valueless.

On the following pages we will briefly discuss each of the primary Reading Comprehension question types.

1. <u>Must Be True/Most Supported</u>

    This category is simply known as "Must Be True." Must Be True questions ask you to identify the answer choice that is best proven by the information in the passage. Question stem examples:

    > "If the statements above are true, which one of the following must also be true?"

    > "Which one of the following can be properly inferred from the passage?"

    Note that while the second question stem above falls under the category of Must Be True, it asks for the answer choice that can be *properly inferred* from the passage; in Reading Comprehension, again, a valid or proper inference is something that *must be true* based on the information provided in the passage.

    Must Be True questions are the dominant type in the Reading Comprehension section; over 75% of the questions you face in each section can be categorized as Must Be True. Although at first glance this might seem like an unusually high percentage, keep in mind that Reading Comprehension is about measuring how well you understand a lengthy passage of text. The best way to test your comprehension of this information is to ask a series of questions aimed at determining whether you properly interpreted the facts that you read, and can make accurate assessments both of and from them. It also means that when selecting an answer, you must find one directly supported by the information in the passage. We call this the Fact Test™: the correct answer to a Must Be True question can always be proven by referring to the facts stated in the passage.

    Many of the Must Be True questions in the Reading Comprehension section ask you to perform a more specific action, such as to identify the author's viewpoint or the function of a word or phrase. In the next section we will examine these attributes in more detail and discuss each type of Must Be True question.

Must Be True is the premier question category in the Reading Comprehension section, and that reflects the directness of your task: knowing what you read and what it tells you.

2. Main Point

Main Point questions are a variant of Must Be True questions. As you might expect, a Main Point question asks you to find the primary focus of the passage. Question stem example:

"The main point of the argument is that..."

Roughly 75% of LSAT Reading Comprehension passages are accompanied by a Main Point question.

Main Point questions most often appear as the very first question in each passage set. This placement is beneficial because as you conclude your reading of the passage, you should already know the main point of what you have read.

As a total in the section, Main Point questions appear approximately 11% of the time, but they appear in approximately 75% of all passages. When considered in combination with Must Be True questions, therefore, the operation of finding facts and proving conclusions represents over 85% of the questions in a Reading Comprehension section.

3. Strengthen

These questions ask you to select the answer choice that provides support for the author's argument or strengthens it in some way. Question stem examples:

"Which one of the following, if true, most strengthens the argument?"

"Which one of the following, if true, most strongly supports the statement above?"

4. Weaken

Weaken questions ask you to attack or undermine the author's argument. Question stem example:

"Which one of the following, if true, most seriously weakens the argument?"

Considered together, Strengthen and Weaken questions only appear about 5% of the time.

5. Parallel Reasoning

Parallel Reasoning questions ask you to identify the answer choice that contains reasoning most similar in structure to the reasoning presented in the stimulus. Question stem example:

> "Which one of the following arguments is most similar in its pattern of reasoning to the argument above?"

Over the past several years Parallel Reasoning questions have appeared more frequently. Even so, these questions are still relatively rare, with usually no more than two or three per section.

6. Cannot Be True

Cannot Be True questions ask you to identify the answer choice that cannot be true or is most weakened based on the information in the stimulus. Question stem example:

> "If the statements above are true, which one of the following CANNOT be true?"

These questions often appear with the modifier "Least," which will be discussed in more detail in a later section of this chapter.

Other question elements will also be discussed, most notably question variants (such as Author's Perspective questions) and overlays (such as Principle questions). Those will be covered later in this chapter.

Rephrasing Question Stems

As you may have noticed in examining the question stem examples presented for each type, not all stems are phrased in the form of a question. Clearly the test makes are quite fond of variety, but this goes beyond a simple preference for diverse constructions: students often have greater difficulty completing a sentence than answering a direct question!

So we encourage you to get in the habit of rephrasing—translating partial-statement stems into their equivalent question forms—so that you are always responding to a precise *inquiry* rather than a more abstract unfinished sentence. Many readers perform this step naturally, but if you find yourself struggling to properly anticipate the nature of right and wrong answers following question stems lacking a question, formalizing this approach will likely help.

To assist you with this translation exercise we've included rephrased question stems in the answer key for the drill on the following page (where appropriate).

Question Classification (Up to this point)

From a classification standpoint, we have now established that every question in the Reading Comprehension section has two elements: Location and Question Type. When questions are classified in this book, those two elements are always listed in order, as follows: Location, Question Type.

Here are several sample question classifications featuring both elements:

SR, Must   (Location: Specific Reference, Type: Must Be True)

CR, Strengthen   (Location: Concept Reference, Type: Strengthen)

GR, MP   (Location: Global Reference, Type: Main Point)

SR, Parallel   (Location: Specific Reference, Type: Parallel Reasoning)

The next several pages contain a drill designed to strengthen your ability to correctly classify questions.

Identify the Question Stem Drill

Each of the following items contains a sample Reading Comprehension question stem. In the space provided, categorize each stem as one of the three Location designations: Specific Reference (SR), Concept Reference (CR), and Global Reference (GR), and then categorize each stem into one of the six main Reading Comprehension Question Types: Must Be True, Main Point, Strengthen, Weaken, Parallel Reasoning, or Cannot Be True. While we realize that you have not yet worked directly with each question type, by considering the designations now you will have an advantage as you attack future questions. *Answers on page 194*

1. Which of the following, if true, would lend most support to the view attributed to Norton's critics?

   Classification:

   _____

2. The author would most likely disagree with which one of the following statements?

   Classification:

   _____

3. Which one of the following most accurately describes the author's purpose in referring to Johnson as being "unfairly criticized by his contemporaries" in the first sentence of the passage?

   Classification:

   _____

4. Which one of the following most accurately expresses the main point of the passage?

   Classification:

   _____

5. Which one of the following, if true, would most call into question the author's assertion in the last sentence of the passage?

   Classification:

   _____

6. The author's description of the relationship between the conductor and the orchestra in the second-to-last sentence of the passage is most closely analogous to which of the following?

   Classification:

   _____

7. Which one of the following most accurately describes the organization of the passage?

   Classification:

   _____

8. Which one of the following, if true, would most weaken the author's argument against international aid as a first line of defense?

   Classification:

   _____

6

Identify the Question Stem Drill

9. The author of the passage would be most likely to agree with which one of the following statements?

Classification:

_____

10. Which one of the following would, if true, most strengthen the claim made by the author in the last sentence of the passage?

Classification:

_____

11. Which one of the following, if true, offers, the most support for Harper's hypothesis?

Classification:

_____

12. According to the passage, which one of the following is an obstacle to the creation of an effective treatment plan for patients in third world nations?

Classification:

_____

13. Which one of the following is most similar to the relationship described in the passage between the new methods of the building industry and pre-twentieth-century construction?

Classification:

_____

14. The third paragraph of the passage most strongly supports which one of the following inferences?

Classification:

_____

15. Which one of the following most accurately describes the function of the second paragraph of the passage?

Classification:

_____

16. Which one of the following most accurately expresses the central point of the passage?

Classification:

_____

17. The author lists each of the following as a characteristic of modern commerce EXCEPT:

Classification:

_____

6

Identify the Question Stem Drill

18. Which one of the following, if true, would most undermine the hypothesis presented in the last paragraph of the passage?

Classification:

_____

19. The passage provides information to answer all of the following questions EXCEPT:

Classification:

_____

20. The author's central thesis is that

Classification:

_____

Identify the Question Stem Drill Answer Key

The typical student misses about half of the questions in this drill. Do not worry about how many you miss; the point of this drill is to acquaint you with the different question stems. As you see more examples of each type of question, your ability to correctly identify each stem will improve.

1. Which of the following, if true, would lend most support to the view attributed to Norton's critics?

    CR, Strengthen

    Location: Here we are asked to find the answer choice that would support a particular view referenced from the passage, so this is a Concept Reference question.

    Type: The presence of the phrase "Which of the following, if true," generally introduces either a Strengthen or a Weaken question. In this case, since the correct answer will support the referenced view, this is clearly a Strengthen question.

---

2. The author would most likely disagree with which one of the following statements?

    GR, Cannot

    Location: This example provides no direction, conceptual or otherwise, to a location in the passage. It is therefore a Global Reference question.

    Type: This question requires you to find the answer choice with which the author would disagree. Because the correct answer choice will be inconsistent with the author's attitude, this question stem can be classified as a Cannot Be True question (that is, "according to the author, which of the following cannot be true?").

---

3. Which one of the following most accurately describes the author's purpose in referring to Johnson as being "unfairly criticized by his contemporaries" in the first sentence of the passage?

    SR, Must

    Location: This example provides the exact location of the referenced quote, so this is a Specific Reference question.

    Type: The correct answer must pass the Fact Test; in this case it must provide an accurate description of the referenced quote's purpose in the passage. Therefore this question stem falls under the Must Be True category.

6

Identify the Question Stem Drill Answer Key

4. Which one of the following most accurately expresses the main point of the passage?

   GR, MP

   Location: This common question stem refers to the passage as a whole and is therefore a Global Reference question.

   Type: Since this question stem asks for the main point of the passage, this is a clear example of a Main Point question. The correct answer choice will be the one which most accurately and completely reflects the central focus of the passage.

5. Which one of the following, if true, would most call into question the author's assertion in the last sentence of the passage?

   SR, Weaken

   Location: Although no line reference is provided in this example, the reader is directed specifically to the last sentence of the passage, so this is a Specific Reference question.

   Type: A question stem that begins with "Which of the following, if true" is nearly certain to be a Strengthen or Weaken question. In this case, the information in the correct answer will call the referenced assertion into question, so this should be classified as a Weaken question.

6. The author's description of the relationship between the conductor and the orchestra in the second-to-last sentence of the passage is most closely analogous to which of the following?

   SR, Parallel

   Location: Since an exact location is provided, this is a Specific Reference question.

   Type: Here the reader is asked to find the answer choice which is most closely analogous to the referenced discussion, which makes this a Parallel question. The correct answer choice will reflect a relationship or other element similar to that discussed in the passage.

Identify the Question Stem Drill Answer Key

7.   Which one of the following most accurately describes
     the organization of the passage?

   GR, Must

   Location: Since this question stem deals with the entire passage, this is a <u>Global Reference</u>
   question.

   Type: This question requires that the reader understand the overall structure of the given
   passage, and the correct answer choice must reflect that structure. This is a <u>Must Be True</u>
   question.

8.   Which one of the following, if true, would most
     weaken the author's argument against international
     aid as a first line of defense?

   CR, Weaken

   Location: Although this question does not provide a line reference, it refers to a very specific
   argument advanced by the author. It is thus a <u>Concept Reference</u> question.

   Type: This is one of the more readily recognizable question types, since the word "weaken"
   is in the question stem; this is a standard <u>Weaken</u> question which in this case requires that the
   correct answer choice reduce the credibility of the author's referenced criticism.

9.   The author of the passage would be most likely to
     agree with which one of the following statements?

   GR, Must

   Location: This question deals with the passage as a whole, so this is a <u>Global Reference</u>
   question.

   Type: This common question requires that the reader understand the author's perspective.
   The correct answer choice must reflect the author's attitude, and pass the Fact Test, so this is
   a <u>Must Be True</u> question.

10. Which one of the following would, if true, most strengthen the claim made by the author in the last sentence of the passage?

SR, Strengthen

Location: The reference at the end of this question stem to the passage's last sentence identifies this example as a <u>Specific Reference</u> question.

Type: The fact that we are asked to strengthen a claim means that this is a <u>Strengthen</u> question, and the correct answer choice must assist the author's argument in some way.

---

11. Which one of the following, if true, offers, the most support for Harper's hypothesis?

GR, Strengthen

Location: Without reading the passage, it might be difficult to assess the scope of this question's reference (although you should immediately recognize that this is not a Specific Reference question). If the passage is largely focused on the referenced hypothesis, this is a <u>Global Reference</u> question.

Type: The correct answer choice will support the hypothesis, so this is a <u>Strengthen</u> question.

---

12. According to the passage, which one of the following is an obstacle to the creation of an effective treatment plan for patients in third world nations?

CR, Must

Location: This question stem requires the reader to identify a particular obstacle but does not provide its specific location in the passage, so this is a <u>Concept Reference</u> question.

Type: In this case, the correct answer choice will come directly from information provided in the passage, so this is a <u>Must Be True</u> question.

Identify the Question Stem Drill Answer Key

13. Which one of the following is most similar to the relationship described in the passage between the new methods of the building industry and pre-twentieth-century construction?

CR, Parallel

Location: This question refers to a specific relationship but offers no line references, thus it is a <u>Concept Reference</u> question.

Type: The question stem asks you to find an answer that is "most similar to the relationship" in the passage, and thus this is a <u>Parallel</u> question.

---

14. The third paragraph of the passage most strongly supports which one of the following inferences?

SR, Must

Location: Specification of "the third paragraph" makes this a <u>Specific Reference</u> question.

Type: Although this question stem uses the word "supports," the correct answer choice will be the one which, based on the passage, <u>Must Be True</u>.

---

15. Which one of the following most accurately describes the function of the second paragraph of the passage?

SR, Must

Question Location: Since this question stem refers specifically to the second paragraph of the passage, it is a <u>Specific Reference</u> question.

Question Type: This question requires you to determine the function, or purpose, of the second paragraph, so this is a <u>Must Be True, Purpose</u> question.

16. Which one of the following most accurately expresses the central point of the passage?

   GR, Main Point

   Question Location: This question refers to the passage as a whole, making it a <u>Global Reference</u> question.

   Question Type: Since the question requires you to find the central point of the passage, this is a <u>Main Point</u> question.

---

17. The author lists each of the following as a characteristic of modern commerce EXCEPT:

   CR, Cannot

   Question Location: This question refers to the characteristics of modern commerce, so it is a <u>Concept Reference</u> question.

   Question Type: Since the question has the word "except," this is a <u>Cannot Be True</u> question. Each of the incorrect answer choices in this case would provide a characteristic of modern commerce, while the correct answer choice would not.

   Rephrased: Which of the following does the author not list as a characteristic of modern commerce?

---

18. Which one of the following, if true, would most undermine the hypothesis presented in the last paragraph of the passage?

   SR, Weaken

   Question Location: This question refers specifically to the last paragraph of the passage, so this is a <u>Specific Reference</u> question.

   Question Type: Since this example asks you to select the choice that would undermine a given hypothesis, this is a <u>Weaken</u> question.

6

Identify the Question Stem Drill Answer Key

19. The passage provides information to answer all of the
    following questions EXCEPT:

   GR, Cannot

   Question Location: This question points to no specific location or concept within the
   passage, so this is a <u>Global Reference</u> question.

   Question Type: The presence of the word "except" makes this a <u>Cannot Be True</u> question;
   the four incorrect choices will provide questions that *can* be answered by the information in
   the passage, while the correct answer choice will be the only one that is *not* answered by the
   passage.

   Rephrased: Which of the following questions does the passage not provide information to
   answer?

---

20. The author's central thesis is that

   GR, Main Point

   Question Location: This question provides no particular line or concept reference, so it is
   clearly a <u>Global Reference</u> question.

   Question Type: This question asks for the author's "central thesis." The test makers can find
   various ways to phrase the same concept; regardless of the specific phrasing, this question
   requires the answer that reflects the <u>Main Point</u> of the passage.

   Rephrased: What is the author's central thesis? (Alternatively: What is the author's main
   point?)

Reading Comprehension Question Types Examined in Detail ■■■■

Must Be True/Most Supported Questions ■■■■■■■■

Percentage of passages containing Must Be True Questions: 100%

Must Be True questions are, by far, the most important Reading Comprehension question type, representing approximately 75% of all of the questions in each section. Thus, to achieve a high score, you must dominate Must Be True. In this section we will examine Must Be True questions, and then examine a variety of specific Must Be True subtypes. In each instance we will provide helpful tips and strategies to attack the type and subtype.

Must Be True questions require you to select an answer choice that is proven by the information presented in the passage. The correct answer choice can be a paraphrase of part of the passage or it can be a logical consequence of one or more parts of the passage. However, when selecting an answer, you must have proof from the passage that supports it. As mentioned, this is called the Fact Test:

> The correct answer to a Must Be True question can always be proven by referring to the facts stated in the passage.

The test makers will try to entice you with incorrect answer choices that could possibly occur or are likely to occur, but are not *certain* to occur. You must avoid those answers and instead select the choice that is most clearly supported by what you read. Similarly, do not bring in information from outside the passage (aside from commonsense assumptions); all of the information necessary to answer the question is included in the text.

Must Be True questions are considered the foundation of the LSAT because the skills required to answer Must Be True are also required for every other LSAT question: read text, and understand the facts that logically follow. To Weaken or Strengthen an argument, for example, you first need to correctly ascertain its details and what reasonable conclusions can be drawn; this allows you to recognize any invalid conclusions on the part of the author, and then to attack or resolve those potential mistakes, respectively. And the same goes for every other type of question.

The statistics presented at the start of each section reference the percentage of all passages that contain the listed question type. In this instance, for example, every single LSAT passage is accompanied by at least one Must Be True question.

6

The vast majority of the questions in the Reading Comprehension section are Must Be True questions.

In the Reading Comprehension section from the June '05 LSAT, 100% of the questions fell under the category of Must Be True and its sub-types.

Because every question type relies on the fact-finding skill used to answer Must Be True questions, your performance with Must Be True dictates your overall Reading Comprehension score. For this reason, you must master this question category now! The pages that follow will provide the tools necessary to do so.

Attacking Must Be True Questions

Your approach to Must Be True questions will, in part, be determined by the Location element specified in each question stem. That is, your approach to an SR, Must question will necessarily be different from your approach to a GR, Must question. Here we examine how the difference in Location affects how you attack Must Be True questions.

Specific Reference

As mentioned in the Location section:

> To attack Specific Reference Must Be True questions—those which refer to an exact word, phrase, sentence, or paragraph—always return to the passage and start reading three to five lines above the reference, or from the most logical nearby starting point such as the start of a paragraph.

As we will see when discussing specific passages and questions, the "three to five line" recommendation is open-ended because what you are seeking is the most logical starting point for your reading, and that starting point is typically the prior complete sentence or two.

For Specific Reference questions that refer to a paragraph, remember the following rule:

> To attack Specific Reference questions that refer to a paragraph, return to the passage and consider the paragraph in question.

Concept Reference

With Concept Reference Must Be True questions, you must return to the areas in the passage mentioned in the question stem and quickly review the information. These questions are more vague than Specific Reference questions and so you must rely on your passage diagramming or memory to return to the correct area.

Global Must Be True questions are usually Main Point, Purpose, or Organization questions (this subtype will be discussed in a few pages), and you will typically not need to refer back to the passage prior to attacking the answer choices because you should already know the answer from your reading. Remember, if you seek to identify the five critical elements of each passage as identified in Chapter Three, you will automatically know the answer to every Global Must Be True question. Thus, you would only need to refer back to the passage to eliminate or confirm individual answer choices.

Must Be True Question Subtypes ▬▬

Percentage of passages containing Must Be True Question Subtypes: 100%

Although many of the questions in the Reading Comprehension section are straightforward Must Be True questions (this category comprises roughly 30% of all questions), about 60% of all questions are subtypes of the Must Be True category. Fundamentally, these subtypes are approached in exactly the same manner as regular Must Be True questions. That is, the Fact Test applies and you must still be able to justify your answer with evidence from the passage. However, some of these subtypes ask for very specific information, and thus an awareness of each subtype is essential.

Main Point Questions (MP)

Percentage of passages containing a Main Point Question: 75%

Main Point questions may be the question type most familiar to test takers. Many standardized tests that you have already encountered, such as the SAT and ACT, contain questions that ask you to ascertain main points, where you summarize the central focus of a passage. Such questions are common on the LSAT, accompanying most Reading Comprehension passages, and appearing in the Logical Reasoning sections of the test as well. Regardless of the context, the ability to recognize an author's main conclusion is a crucial part of understanding any stimulus or passage, and the right approach is vital if you want to attack Main Point questions effectively and efficiently.

After reading any given question, you should seek to quickly form a rough conception of the answer before you have moved on to consider the choices provided. When you have created an effective prephrase, in many cases you will find that you are able to scan the answers and quickly zero in on the right one—a process that is *far* more efficient than considering the answer choices one by one.

A complete understanding of any passage requires that you identify the main point, even in the rare case that a passage does not include a Main Point question.

In the context of Reading Comprehension, the proper approach to forming an effective prephrase is sometimes a bit different from what is required when responding to such questions on the Logical Reasoning sections of the test; in Logical Reasoning, the author's main point is often stated quite succinctly (which makes sense considering each stimulus is no more than a few sentences long). As a result, LR Main Point questions are often particularly conducive to prephrasing—if you've isolated the main point or conclusion of the stimulus, and it is clearly relayed among the answer choices, you will generally know it when you see it, enabling you to sidestep many of the test makers' clever wrong answer choices.

In Reading Comprehension, on the other hand, Main Point questions often work a bit differently. The passages are generally much longer than a Logical Reasoning stimulus, and in many cases the main point will not appear in a single sentence or even in any one location within the passage. So, determining the main point may take a bit more effort, but it is still vital that you attempt to do so. Since the main point is often not stated succinctly within the passage, prephrasing the answer with perfect precision is often nearly impossible, so remember that you often need to be flexible as you scan through the answer choices.

The takeaway is this: In Logical Reasoning, finding the main point will often involve quickly isolating the author's conclusion and then simply recognizing it among the answer choices. In Reading Comprehension, the main point is less likely to be expressed in a single sentence; forming an effective prephrase will often require a broad understanding of the passage as a whole, and a search for the answer choice that *most closely* relays your prephrased answer. So, when you encounter Main Point questions in Reading Comprehension, always prephrase an answer, but prepare to be a bit more open-minded as you consider the choices provided.

The Main Point question stem format is remarkably consistent, requiring you in each case to identify the conclusion or point of the argument, as in the following examples:

> "Which one of the following most accurately expresses the main point of the passage?"

> "Which one of the following statements best expresses the main idea of the passage?"

Two types of *incorrect* answers frequently appear with Main Point questions:

1. Answers that are true but do not encapsulate the author's point.

2. Answers that repeat portions of the passage but not the Main Point.

Each answer type is attractive because they are true based on what you have read. However, neither summarizes the author's main point and therefore both are incorrect. Fortunately, these traps are also easily recognized and avoided, as we will discuss shortly.

Purpose/Function Questions (P)

Percentage of passages containing a Purpose Question: 87%

At the Specific Reference and Concept Reference level, Purpose questions ask why the author referred to a particular word, phrase, or idea. To determine the reasons behind the author's use of words or ideas, refer to the context around the reference, using context clues and your knowledge of the viewpoints and structure of the passage. Here are several example question stems:

> "The author of the passage uses the phrase "clearly insufficient" (last sentence of the passage) primarily in order to..."

> "The author's discussion of feline maternal instinct in the second paragraph functions primarily to..."

> "The author's discussion of increased erosion over the last decade serves primarily to..."

> "Which one of the following best states the function of the third paragraph of the passage?"

Global Purpose questions are almost always phrased using the words "primary purpose" and ask for the author's main purpose in writing the passage. These questions ask you to describe why the author wrote the passage, and the correct answer is often an abstract version of the main point (and if not, at the very least the answer to a Global Purpose question will agree with the Main Point). For instance:

> "The primary purpose of the passage is to..."

> "In the passage, the author seeks primarily to..."

Perspective Questions

Percentage of passages containing a Perspective Question: 95%

This category contains questions about two of the five VIEWSTAMP elements identified in Chapter Three: viewpoints and tone. These two elements are very closely related, and we combine these two elements in our question classification, using the term "perspective" to capture the idea behind both elements.

Historically, Purpose/Function questions have comprised approximately 1/5 of all Reading Comprehension questions.

6

Perspective questions can be divided into two categories: questions that ask about the author's views and tone, and questions that ask about the views and tone of one of the other groups discussed in the passage. These two types are discussed below.

Author's Perspective Questions (AP)

Understanding the author's viewpoint is an integral part of mastering any passage. About 25% of Reading Comprehension questions concern the Author's Perspective.

Percentage of passages containing an Author's Perspective Question: 84%

Author's Perspective questions ask you to select the answer choice that best reflects the author's views on a subject or the author's attitude toward a subject. Because identifying the position of the author is a critical part of your strategy when reading, normally these questions should be relatively painless.

> "The author of the passage would most likely agree with which one of the following statements?"

> "It can be inferred that the author of the passage believes which one of the following about the history of modern art?"

> "It can be reasonably inferred from the passage that the author's attitude is most favorable toward which one of the following?"

Subject Perspective Questions (SP)

Percentage of passages containing a Subject Perspective Question: 29%

Subject Perspective questions make up about 10% of Reading Comprehension questions overall.

In this question type, we use the term "subject" to refer to a person or group who is discussed in the passage. Subject Perspective questions ask you to select the answer choice that best reflects the views or attitude of one of the other groups in the passage. Because identifying all views is a critical part of your strategy when reading, you should be well-prepared for these questions.

> "Given the information in the passage, which one of the following is Kantor most likely to believe?"

> "It can be inferred that Peter Goodrich would be most likely to agree with which one of the following statements concerning common law?"

These questions are considered Must Be True questions because the correct answer follows directly from the statements in the passage.

Organization Questions (O)

Percentage of passages containing an Organization Question: 25%

These questions usually appear in reference to either a specific paragraph or to the passage as a whole, and refer less frequently to specific lines.

At the line or sentence level, you are normally asked to identify the way in which pairs of lines relate to each other:

> "The logical relationship of the first sentence of the passage to the final two sentences of paragraph three is most accurately described as..."

At a specific paragraph level, you will either be asked to identify the structure of the paragraph, or to identify how one paragraph relates to another paragraph. Question examples include:

> "Which one of the following most accurately describes the relationship between the second paragraph and the final paragraph?"

> "Which one of the following most accurately describes the organization of the material presented in the second and third paragraphs of the passage?"

At the Global level, these questions ask you to describe the overall structure of the passage. For example:

> "Which one of the following best describes the organization of the passage?"

> "Which one of the following most accurately describes the organization of the material presented in the passage?"

> "Which one of the following sequences most accurately and completely corresponds to the presentation of the material in the passage?"

In both the Specific and Global versions, these questions are similar to the Method of Reasoning questions in the Logical Reasoning section, but they are generally broader. Given that you must track structure as you read, these questions should be fairly straightforward exercises in matching answer choices to what you already know occurred in the passage.

Although questions which specifically reference Passage Organization make up only about 4% of questions in this section, a strong grasp of the structure of a passage will allow you to attack Concept Reference and Specific Reference questions far more efficiently.

6

Expansion Questions (E)

Percentage of passages containing an Expansion Question: 10%

Expansion questions require you to extrapolate ideas from the passage to determine one of three elements: where the passage was drawn from or how it could be titled, what sentence or idea could come before the passage, and what sentence or idea could follow the passage. The following examples show the range of phrasing in these questions:

"Which one of the following would be most suitable as a title for this passage if it were to appear as an editorial piece?"

"Which one of the following titles most completely summarizes the contents of the passage?"

"If this passage had been excerpted from a longer text, which one of the following predictions regarding the future of aeronautics would be most likely to appear in that text?"

"Which one of the following sentences would most logically begin a paragraph immediately following the end of the passage?"

"Which one of the following is the most logical continuation of the last paragraph of the passage?"

"Which one of the following sentences could most logically be appended to the end of the last paragraph of the passage?"

Questions about the title or source of the passage typically reflect the Main Point of the passage. Questions asking you to identify pre- or post-passage sentences, however, are usually immediately dependent upon the two or three sentences at the beginning or end of the passage, and then more generally dependent upon the passage as a whole. These questions can be difficult because they ask you to infer the flow and direction of the passage from a somewhat limited set of clues.

In fact, broadly speaking, any questions that require you to infer an answer from the text rather than pull an answer directly from it—whether an Author's or Subject's Perspective (AP or SP), or an Expansion question (E) discussed above—are commonly felt to be the most challenging questions in a Reading Comprehension section.

Correct Answers in Must Be True Questions

Let us take a moment to discuss two types of answers that will always be correct in a Must Be True question and any Must Be True subtype (except for Main Point questions, as discussed previously).

1. Paraphrased Answers

   Paraphrased Answers are answers that restate a portion of the passage in different terms. Because the language is not exactly the same as in the passage, Paraphrased Answers can be easy to miss. Paraphrased Answers are designed to test your ability to discern the author's exact meaning. Sometimes the answer can appear to be almost too obvious since it is drawn directly from the passage.

2. Combination Answers

   Answers that are the sum of two or more passage statements

   Any answer choice that would result from combining two or more statements in the passage will be correct.

Should you encounter either of the above as an answer choice in a non-Main Point, Must Be True question, select the answer with confidence.

Incorrect Answers in Must Be True Questions

There are several types of answers that appear in Must Be True questions that are incorrect. These answers appear frequently enough that we have provided a review of the major types below. Each answer category below is designed to attract you to an incorrect answer choice. As we begin to look at actual passages and questions in the next chapter, we will examine instances of these types of answers.

1. Could Be True or Likely to Be True Answers

   Because the criteria in the question stem require you to find an answer choice that Must Be True, answers that merely could be true or are even likely to be true are incorrect. These answers are attractive because there is nothing demonstrably wrong with them (for example, they do not contain statements that are counter to the passage). Regardless, like all incorrect answers, these answers fail the Fact Test. Remember, you must select an answer choice that must occur based on what you have read.

   This category of "incorrect answers" is very broad, and some of the types mentioned on the next page will fall under this general idea but place an emphasis on a specific aspect of the answer.

2. Exaggerated Answers

   Exaggerated Answers take information from the passage and then stretch that information to make a broader statement that is not supported by the passage. In that sense, this form of answer is a variation of a Could Be True answer since the exaggeration is possible, but not proven based on the information. Here is an example:

   > If the passage states, "*Some* software vendors recently implemented more rigorous licensing procedures."
   >
   > An incorrect answer would exaggerate one or more of the elements: "*Most* software vendors recently implemented more rigorous licensing procedures." In this example, *some* is exaggerated to *most*. While it could be true that most software vendors made the change, the passage does not prove that it must be true. This type of answer is often paraphrased, creating a deadly combination where the language is similar enough to be attractive but different enough to be incorrect.

Here is another example:

> If the passage states, "Recent advances in the field of molecular biology make it *likely* that many school textbooks will be rewritten."

> The exaggerated and paraphrased version would be: "Many school textbooks about molecular biology will be re-written." In this example, *likely* has been dropped, and this omission exaggerates the certainty of the change. The paraphrase is also problematic because the passage referenced school textbooks whereas the paraphrased answer refers to school textbooks *about molecular biology*.

3. "New" Information Answers

Because correct Must Be True answers must be based on information in the passage or the direct result of combining statements in the passage, be wary of answers that present so-called new information—that is, information not mentioned explicitly in the passage or information that would not fall under the umbrella of a statement made in the passage. For example, if a passage discusses the economic policies of Japan, be careful with an answer that mentions U.S. economic policy. Look closely at the passage—does the information about Japanese economic policy apply to the U.S., or are the test makers trying to get you to fall for an answer that sounds logical but is not directly supported?

4. The Shell Game

The LSAT makers have a variety of psychological tricks they use to entice test takers to select an answer choice. One of their favorites is one we call the Shell Game: an idea or concept is raised in the passage, and then a very similar idea appears in an answer choice, but the idea is changed just enough to be incorrect but still attractive. This trick is called the Shell Game because it abstractly resembles those street corner gambling games where a person hides a small object underneath one of three shells, and then scrambles them on a flat surface while a bettor tries to guess which shell the object is under (similar to Three-card Monte). The object of a Shell Game is to trick the bettor into guessing incorrectly by mixing up the shells so quickly and deceptively that the bettor mistakenly selects the wrong shell. The intent of the LSAT makers is the same.

Shell Game answers occur in all LSAT question types, not just Must Be True.

5. The Opposite Answer

As the name suggests, the Opposite Answer provides an answer that is completely opposite of the stated facts of the passage. Opposite Answers are very attractive to students who are reading too quickly or carelessly.

6. The Reverse Answer

Here is a simplified example of how a Reverse Answer works, using italics to indicate the reversed parts:

Reverse Answers can occur in any type of question.

> The passage might state, "*Many* people have *some* type of security system in their home."

> An incorrect answer then reverses the elements: "*Some* people have *many* types of security systems in their home."

The Reverse Answer is attractive because it contains familiar elements from the passage, but the reversed statement is incorrect because it rearranges those elements to create a new, unsupported statement.

7. The Wrong View

Wrong View answers frequently appear in Perspective questions. For example, the question will ask you to identify a statement that agrees with the author's view, but then places one or more answers that would agree with the view of another group in the passage. You can avoid these answers by carefully tracking viewpoints as discussed earlier.

8. Hidden References

In some Specific Reference questions, you will be sent to a certain location in the passage but the information needed to answer the question will reside elsewhere in the passage, in a section that also touches on the issue in the Specific Reference. This can be difficult to handle if the information is a large number of lines away.

Non-Must Be True Question Types ■

In this section we examine all other Reading Comprehension question types. As mentioned earlier, these questions appear with far less frequency than Must Be True questions.

Non-Must Be True Questions appear approximately 12% of the time.

Strengthen Questions ■■■■■■■

Percentage of passages containing a Strengthen Question: 8%

Strengthen questions ask you to identify the answer choice that best supports a section of the passage or a particular view from the passage. The correct answer choice does not necessarily prove the argument beyond a shadow of a doubt, nor is the correct answer choice necessarily an assumption of the argument. The correct answer choice simply helps the argument in some way.

Following are several Strengthen question stem examples:

50% of the LSAT is devoted exclusively to Logical Reasoning, so questions which test your critical reasoning ability, such as Strengthen or Weaken questions, are less common in the Reading Comprehension section.

> "Which one of the following would, if true, most strengthen the author's position regarding the practical applicability of the theory presented in the passage?"

> "Which one of the following would, if true, most strengthen the claim made by the author in the last sentence of the passage?"

> "Which one of the following, if true, would lend the most support to the claims of critics discussed in the second paragraph?"

How to Strengthen an Argument

Use the following points to effectively strengthen arguments:

1. Identify what you are trying to strengthen!

   Before you can examine the answer choices, you must know what it is that you must strengthen. When evaluating an answer, ask yourself, "Would this answer choice assist the position in question in some way?" If so, you have the correct answer.

2. Personalize the argument.

   Personalizing allows you to see the argument from a very involved perspective and can clarify your perspective as you assess the strength of each answer.

3. Look for weaknesses in the argument.

   This may seem like a strange recommendation since your task is to strengthen the argument, but a weak spot in an argument is tailor-made for an answer that eliminates that weakness. If you see a weakness or flaw in the argument, look for an answer that eliminates the weakness.

   In other words, close any gap or hole in the argument.

   Many Strengthen questions require students to find the missing link between a premise and the conclusion. These missing links are assumptions made by the author or by the party in question, and bringing an assumption to light strengthens the argument because it validates part of the author's thinking.

4. Remember that the correct answer can strengthen the argument just a little or a lot. This variation is what makes these questions difficult.

Three Incorrect Answer Traps

The following types of wrong answer traps frequently appear in Strengthen questions:

1. Opposite Answers. These answers do the exact opposite of what is needed—they weaken the position in question. Because of their direct relation to the argument they are tempting, despite the fact that they result in consequences opposite of those intended.

2. Shell Game Answers. Remember, a Shell Game occurs when an idea or concept is raised in the passage and then a very similar idea appears in the answer choice, but the idea is changed just enough to be incorrect but still attractive. In Strengthen questions, the Shell Game is usually used to support a conclusion or position that is similar to, but slightly different from, the one presented in the passage.

3. Out of Scope Answers. These answers simply miss the point of the argument and support issues that are either unrelated to the argument or tangential to the argument.

Some of the wrong answer types from the Must Be True section do not apply to Strengthen and Weaken questions. For example, the New Information answer is usually wrong in a Must Be True question, but not in a Strengthen or Weaken question because new information is acceptable in the answer choices.

6

These three incorrect answer traps are not the only forms that an attractive wrong answer may take, but they appear frequently enough that you should be familiar with each form.

Because the same types of wrong answer traps appear in Strengthen as in Weaken questions, the three items above apply to both this section and the following section on Weaken questions.

Weaken Questions

Percentage of passages containing a Weaken Question: 14%

You do not need to find an answer that destroys the author's position. Instead, simply find an answer that hurts the argument.

Weaken questions require you to select the answer choice that undermines a position as decisively as possible. In this sense, Weaken questions are the polar opposite of Strengthen questions.

Note that the makers of the LSAT can use a variety of words to indicate that your task is to weaken the argument:

> weaken
> attack
> undermine
> refute
> argue against
> call into question
> cast doubt
> challenge
> damage
> counter

Here are two Weaken question stem examples:

> "Which one of the following, if true, would most weaken Hart's argument regarding the recently excavated fossils?"

> "Which one of the following, if true, would most seriously challenge the position of the critics mentioned in the third sentence of the final paragraph?"

When approaching Weaken questions, always remember to:

1. Isolate and assess the position you are attacking. Only by understanding the structure of the position can you gain the perspective necessary to attack that position.

2. Know the details of what was said in the passage.

3. Accept the answer choices as given, even if they include "new" information. Unlike Must Be True questions, Weaken answer choices can bring into consideration information outside of or tangential to the stimulus. Just because a fact or idea is not mentioned in the passage is not grounds for dismissing an answer choice. Your task is to determine which answer choice best attacks the position.

By focusing on the points above, you will maximize your chances of success on Weaken questions.

Weaken question stems tell you to accept the answer choices as true, so you cannot throw out an answer because it doesn't seem possible.

6

Parallel Reasoning Questions ▮▮▮

Percentage of passages containing a Parallel Reasoning Question: 32%

Parallel Reasoning questions ask you to identify the answer choice that contains reasoning most similar in structure to the reasoning in a section of the passage. Because each answer choice is a wholly new argument, these questions force you to evaluate five arguments in one question, and as such they can be quite time consuming (a fact known to and exploited by the test makers).

In the *LSAT Logical Reasoning Bible*, we detail a sophisticated and highly effective method for solving Logical Reasoning Parallel Reasoning questions. This method, while effective for Reading Comprehension questions, tends to be too advanced. The typical Reading Comprehension Parallel Reasoning question asks you to parallel the structure of a section or paragraph, and thus you usually need only understand the basic outline of what occurred in the section. Then, select the answer choice that contains the same structure. If you find yourself choosing between two or more answer choices, then simply compare some of the other elements in the passage—intent of the author or group, force and use of premises, the relationship of the premises to a conclusion, and the soundness of the argument.

Question stem examples:

"Which one of the following is most analogous to the artistic achievements that the author attributes to Mangino?"

"As described in the passage, the approach suggested by the Modernists is most similar to which one of the following?"

"Based on the passage, the relationship between attorney and client is most analogous to the relationship between:"

Cannot Be True Questions ■■■■

Percentage of passages containing a Cannot Be True Question: 16%

As you can see, Cannot Be True questions occur infrequently in Reading Comprehension sections. Nonetheless, a familiarity with the principles behind these questions is helpful.

In Cannot Be True questions your task is to identify the answer choice that cannot be true or is most weakened by the information in the passage. Thus, instead of using the information in the passage to prove that one of the answer choices must be true, you must instead prove that one of the answer choices cannot occur, or that it disagrees with the information in the passage.

From an abstract standpoint, Cannot Be True questions can be viewed in two ways:

1. Polar Opposite Must Be True Questions

   Cannot Be True questions are the polar opposite of Must Be True questions: instead of proving an answer choice, you disprove an answer choice.

2. Reverse Weaken Questions

   Cannot Be True questions are like reverse Weaken questions: use the information in the stimulus to attack one of the answers.

Both question descriptions are similar, and neither sounds very difficult. In practice, however, Cannot Be True questions are tricky because the concept of an answer choice being possibly true and therefore wrong is counterintuitive. This type of question appears very infrequently, but the test makers are savvy and they know Cannot questions can catch test takers off-guard and consume more time than the average question. When you encounter a Cannot Be True question, you must mentally prepare yourself to eliminate answers that could be true or that are possible, and select the one answer choice that cannot be true or that is impossible.

Question types that appear infrequently, such as Cannot Be True (which occur in about 3% of all questions), tend to consume more time because students are not used to seeing those types of questions.

6

Cannot Be True questions can be worded in a variety of ways, but the gist of the question type is to show that an answer cannot follow, as in the following examples:

"Which one of the following, if true, is LEAST consistent with Alaimo's theory about aggressive behavior in wasps?"

"Given the information in the passage, the author is LEAST likely to believe which one of the following?"

Question Modifiers and Overlays

Certain words that appear in question stems can have a powerful impact on the nature of the answer choice you are seeking. The most important of these words are discussed below.

"Most" and "Best" in Question Stems

Many question stems contain the qualifiers "most" or "best." For example, a question stem might ask, "Which one of the following most accurately expresses the main point of the passage?" or "Which one of the following best expresses the main idea of the passage?" Astute test takers realize that the presence of "most" or "best" opens up a Pandora's box of sorts: by including "most" or "best," there is a possibility that other answer choices will also meet the criteria of the question stem (Main Point, Strengthen, Parallel, etc.), albeit to a lesser extent. In other words, if a question stem says "most weakens," the possibility is that every answer choice weakens the argument and you would be in the unenviable position of having to choose the best from a bunch of decent answer choices. *Fortunately, this is not how it works*. Even though "most" or "best" will appear in a number of stems, you can rest assured that only one answer choice will meet the criteria. So, if you see a "most weakens" question stem, only one of the answers will weaken the argument to any legitimate degree. So, then, why does "most" or "best" appear in so many question stems? Because in order to maintain test integrity the test makers need to make sure their credited answer choice is as airtight and defensible as possible. Imagine what would occur if a question stem, let us say a Weaken question, did not include a "most" or "best" qualifier: any answer choice that weakened the argument, even if only very slightly, could then be argued to meet the criteria of the question stem. A situation like this would make constructing the test exceedingly difficult because any given problem might have multiple correct answer choices. To eliminate this predicament, the test makers insert "most" or "best" into the question stem, and then they can always claim there is one and only one correct answer choice.

"Except" and "Least" in Question Stems

The word "except" has a dramatic impact when it appears in a question stem. Because "except" means "other than," when "except" is placed in a question it negates the logical quality of the answer choice you seek. Literally, it turns the intent of the question stem upside down. For example, if a question asks you what must be true, the one correct answer must be true and the other four answers are not necessarily true. If "except" is added to the question stem, as in "Each of the following must be true EXCEPT," the stem is turned around and instead of the correct answer having the characteristic of must be true, the four incorrect answers must be true and the one correct answer is not necessarily true.

"Except" is used more frequently in LSAT Reading Comprehension question stems than "least."

Many students, upon encountering "except" in a question stem, make the mistake of assuming that the "except" charges you with seeking the polar opposite. For example, if a question stem asks you to weaken a statement, some students believe that a "Weaken EXCEPT" question stem actually asks you to strengthen the statement. This is incorrect. Although weaken and strengthen are polar opposites, because except means "other than," when a "Weaken EXCEPT" question stem appears, you are asked to find any answer choice other than Weaken. While this could include a strengthening answer choice, it could also include an answer choice that has no effect on the statement. Thus, in a "Weaken EXCEPT" question, the four incorrect answers Weaken the statement and the one correct answer does not weaken the statement (could strengthen or have no effect). Here is another example:

The true effect of "except" is to logically negate the question stem.

6

"Which one of the following, if true, strengthens the argument above?"

One correct answer: Strengthen
Four incorrect answers: Do not Strengthen

"Each of the following, if true, strengthens the argument above EXCEPT:"

One correct answer: Does not Strengthen
Four incorrect answers: Strengthen

As you can see from the example, the presence of except has a profound impact upon the meaning of the question stem. Because "except" has this powerful effect, it always appears in all capital letters whenever it is used in an LSAT question stem. This is also an excellent example of why it is often wise to Rephrase question stem statements, as noted previously!

The word "least" has a similar effect to "except" when it appears in a question stem. Although "least" and "except" do not generally have the same meaning, when "least" appears in a question stem you should treat it *exactly the same* as "except." Note: this advice holds true only when this word appears in the question stem! If you see the word "least" elsewhere on the LSAT, consider it to have its usual meaning of "in the lowest or smallest degree."

Because "least," like "except," has such a strong impact on the meaning of a question stem, the test makers kindly place "least" in all capital letters when it appears in a question stem.

In the answer keys to this book, we will designate questions that contain "except" or "least" by placing an "X" at the end of the question stem classification. For example, a "Must Be True EXCEPT" question stem would be classified as "MustX." A "Parallel EXCEPT" question stem would be classified as "ParallelX" and so on. The only exception to this rule will be a question that states, "Each of the following could be true EXCEPT." Those questions will be designated "Cannot Be True."

Except and *Least* Identify the Question Stem Mini-Drill

Each of the following items contains a sample question stem. In the space provided, note the common Reading Comprehension question type and notate any Except (X) identifier you see. *Answers on page 224*

1. The passage supports each of the following inferences EXCEPT:

   Question Type:

   _____

2. The passage indicates that each of the following can be an effect of global warming EXCEPT:

   Question Type:

   _____

3. It can be inferred from the passage that Van Gogh would have been LEAST likely to choose which of the following as a subject of his work?

   Question Type:

   _____

4. The passage explicitly mentions each of the following as a characteristic of early American art EXCEPT:

   Question Type:

   _____

5. Based on the passage, the author would be LEAST likely to refuse which one of the following topics for a public television show?

   Question Type:

   _____

6

Except and *Least* Identify the Question Stem Mini-Drill Answer Key

1. The passage supports each of the following inferences
   EXCEPT:

   Question Type: MustX

   The four incorrect answer choices will be inferences that are supported by the passage; the correct answer choice will be the only one to provide an inference that is *not* supported by the passage.

2. The passage indicates that each of the following can be an effect of global warming EXCEPT:

   Question Type: Cannot Be True

   Note that the "can be true EXCEPT" construction is classified as Cannot Be True. This is because the four incorrect answers Could Be True, and the remaining answer choice is the opposite—Cannot Be True. In this case, the four incorrect answer choices will list possible effects of global warming; the correct answer choice will not.

3. It can be inferred from the passage that Van Gogh would have been LEAST likely to choose which of the following as a subject of his work?

   Question Type: MustX

   The four incorrect answer choices will provide subjects that Van Gogh would likely have chosen; the correct answer choice will present a subject which, according to the passage, Van Gogh would *not* likely have chosen.

4. The passage explicitly mentions each of the following as a characteristic of early American art EXCEPT:

   Question Type: MustX

   The four incorrect answer choices will feature a characteristic of early American art that is explicitly mentioned in the passage; the correct answer will be the only one *not* explicitly mentioned in the passage.

5. Based on the passage, the author would be LEAST likely to refuse which one of the following topics for a public television show?

   Question Type: Cannot Be TrueX

   The four incorrect answer choices will feature topics that the author would refuse for public television, and rejecting an answer is a characteristic of Cannot Be True questions. The correct answer choice will provide a topic that the author would *not* likely refuse.

Principle Questions

Percentage of passages containing a Principle Question: 13%

Principle questions (PR) are not a separate question type but are instead an "overlay" that appears in a variety of question types. For example, there are Must Be True Principle questions (Must—PR), Strengthen Principle questions (Strengthen—PR), and Parallel Principle questions (Parallel—PR), among others. In a question stem, the key indicator that the Principle concept is present is the word "principle." Here are two examples of Principle question stems:

> "Which one of the following principles can be most clearly said to underlie the author's arguments in the third paragraph?"

> "Given the information provided in the second paragraph, the author can most reasonably be said to use which one of the following principles to support the scientists' claims?

A principle is a broad rule that specifies what actions or judgments are correct in certain situations. For example, "Some companies are profitable" is not a principle because no rule is involved and no judgment can be drawn from the statement. "All companies should strive to be profitable" is a principle, and one that can be applied to any company.

The degree of generality of principles can vary considerably, and some are much narrower than others. For example, "Children at Smith Elementary School must wear uniforms" is a principle restricted to children attending Smith. The principle does not apply to a child attending a different school. On the other hand, the principle "Any person of voting age has an obligation to vote" applies to a large number of people regardless of background, education, wealth, etc.

Because a principle is by definition a broad rule (usually conditional in nature), the presence of the Principle indicator serves to broaden the scope of the question. The question becomes more abstract, and you must analyze the problem to identify the underlying relationships. Functionally, you must take a broad, global proposition and apply it in a specific manner, either to the answer choices (as in a Must or Parallel question) or to the passage (as in a Strengthen or Weaken question).

The word "proposition" or "precept" can be used in place of "principle."

6

Question Type Variety

One of the aims of the test makers is to keep you off-balance. An unsettled, flustered test taker is prone to make mistakes. By mixing up the types of questions you face as well as the location you must search in order to find the proper information, the makers of the test can keep you from getting into a rhythm. Imagine how much easier the Reading Comprehension section would be if you faced eight consecutive Local Must Be True questions with each passage. For this reason, you will always see a range of questions within each section, and you will rarely see the same exact question type twice in a row.

Since this situation is guaranteed to occur on your LSAT, before the test begins prepare yourself mentally for the quick shifting of mental gears that is required to move from question to question.

6

Location, Type, and Sub-type Drill

The following is another collection of sample Reading Comprehension questions. In the space provided, categorize each stem into one of the three Location designations: Specific Reference (SR), Concept Reference (CR), and Global Reference (GR), and then categorize each stem into one of the six main Reading Comprehension Question Types: Must Be True, Main Point, Strengthen, Weaken, Parallel Reasoning, or Cannot Be True. In addition, include any relevant sub-type designations as discussed in this chapter: Purpose (P), Organization (O), Author's Perspective (AP), Subject Perspective (SP), Passage Expansion (E), Except (X), or Principle (PR). *Answers on page 230*

1. It can be reasonably inferred from the passage that the author's attitude is most favorable toward which one of the following?

    Question Type:

    _____

2. Which one of the following views can most reasonably be attributed to the experts cited in the second sentence of the first paragraph?

    Question Type:

    _____

3. As described in the passage, the approach used by FEMA in collecting the data is most analogous to which of the following?

    Question Type:

    _____

4. Based on information in the passage, it can be inferred that which one of the following sentences could most logically be added to the passage as a concluding sentence?

    Question Type:

    _____

5. Which one of the following, if true, would most weaken the author's argument against contracts similar to those described in the passage?

    Question Type:

    _____

6. Which of the following, if true, lends the most credence to the author's argument in the last paragraph of the passage?

    Question Type:

    _____

7. Which one of the following best states the main idea of the passage?

    Question Type:

    _____

6

Location, Type, and Sub-type Drill

8. Which one of the following most accurately describes the organization of the passage?

   Question Type:

   _____

9. The passage provides information that answers each of the following questions EXCEPT:

   Question Type:

   _____

10. The author's primary purpose in the passage is...

    Question Type:

    _____

11. The logical relationship of the first sentence of the third paragraph to the final sentence of the third paragraph is most accurately described as

    Question Type:

    _____

12. Which one of the following, if true, would most cast doubt on the author's interpretation of the study involving the family discussed in the second paragraph?

    Question Type:

    _____

13. The passage contains information sufficient to justify inferring which one of the following?

    Question Type:

    _____

14. The author's attitude toward Zeno's development of a new hypothesis about atomic processes can most aptly be described as...

    Question Type:

    _____

15. Which one of the following institutions would NOT be covered by the multi-tier classification system proposed by Jacobs?

    Question Type:

    _____

16. Which one of the following most closely expresses the author's intended meaning in using the term "unabashedly" (final sentence of the passage)?

    Question Type:

    _____

17. The author's attitude toward the studies mentioned in the first paragraph is most likely...

    Question Type:

    _____

Location, Type, and Sub-type Drill

18. Based on the passage, the author would probably hold that which one of the following principles is fundamental to long-term reduction of recidivism rates?

Question Type:

_____

19. Which one of the following most accurately describes the organization of the material presented in the first and second paragraphs of the passage?

Question Type:

_____

20. In discussing the tangential details of events, the passage contrasts their original significance to witnesses with their possible significance in the courtroom (last two sentences of the fourth paragraph). That contrast is most closely analogous to which one of the following?

Question Type:

_____

Location, Type, and Sub-type Drill Answer Key

The typical student misses at least half of the questions in this drill. Do not worry about how many you miss; the point of this drill is to acquaint you with the different question stems. As you see more examples of each type of question, your ability to correctly identify each stem will improve.

1. It can be reasonably inferred from the passage that the author's attitude is most favorable toward which one of the following?

    GR, Must, AP

    Location: This question stem provides no reference points, so this is a Global Reference Question.

    Type: The correct answer to this question must reflect the author's attitude as described in the passage, and it must pass the Fact Test. This is a Must Be True question.

    Sub-Type: Since the question deals with the author's attitude, this is an Author's Perspective question.

2. Which one of the following views can most reasonably be attributed to the experts cited in the second sentence of the first paragraph?

    SR, Must, SP

    Location: This question stem provides a clear sentence reference, so this is a Specific Reference question.

    Type: The correct answer must be consistent with the passage's description of the referenced experts, so this is a Must Be True question.

    Sub-Type: Here we are asked about the views of experts cited in the passage, so we must understand their perspective to find the answer to this Subject Perspective question.

3. As described in the passage, the approach used by FEMA in collecting the data is most analogous to which of the following?

    CR, Parallel

    Location: This question stem refers to a particular approach discussed somewhere in the passage, so this is a Concept Reference question.

    Type: Here we are asked to parallel the referenced approach, so this is a Parallel Reasoning question (as with most questions that contain the word "analogous").

6

Location, Type, and Sub-type Drill Answer Key

4. Based on information in the passage, it can be inferred that which one of the following sentences could most logically be added to the passage as a concluding sentence?

    SR, Must, E

    Location: This question stem specifies the location by asking for a logical concluding sentence.

    Type: The correct answer to this question must provide a logical conclusion, which can be determined based on information from the passage, so this is a Must Be True question.

    Sub-Type: This question requires that a logical conclusion be added to the end of the passage, which makes this a Passage Expansion question.

5. Which one of the following, if true, would most weaken the author's argument against contracts similar to those described in the passage?

    CR, Weaken

    Location: This question deals with a particular argument made by the author, so this is a Concept Reference question (if the entire passage were focused on this one argument, this would then be a Global Reference question).

    Type: Since this question asks for the answer choice which will weaken the author's argument, this is of course a Weaken question.

6. Which of the following, if true, lends the most credence to the author's argument in the last paragraph of the passage?

    SR, Strengthen

    Location: The line reference makes this a Specific Reference question.

    Type: In this case we are asked to "lend credence" to an argument (otherwise known as "strengthening"). This is a Strengthen question.

Location, Type, and Sub-type Drill Answer Key

7. Which one of the following best states the main idea
    of the passage?

    GR, MP

    Location: This question stem regards the passage as a whole, so this is a Global Reference
    Question.

    Type: Since this question asks for the central focus of the passage, this is a Main Point
    question.

8. Which one of the following most accurately describes
    the organization of the passage?

    GR, Must, O

    Location: As this question provides no specific reference points, it is a Global Reference
    question.

    Type: The answer to this question stem comes directly from information in the stimulus, so
    this is a Must Be True question.

    Sub-Type: This is a clear example of an Organization question, which requires that you have
    an understanding of the overall structure of the passage.

9. The passage provides information that answers each
    of the following questions EXCEPT:

    GR, MustX

    Location: This question references the passage in its entirety, so this is a Global Reference
    question.

    Type: The information needed to answer this question comes directly from the passage, so
    this is a Must Be True question.

    Sub-Type: This is an Except question, so the four incorrect answers in this case will be those
    choices that can be answered with information provided in the passage. The correct answer
    choice will be the one that cannot be answered by the passage.

Location, Type, and Sub-type Drill Answer Key

10. The author's primary purpose in the passage is...

   GR, Must, P

   Location: This common question stem refers to the passage as a whole, and is therefore a Global Reference question.

   Type: The answer to this question will be based on information from the passage (and should be prephrased). This is a Must Be True question.

   Sub-Type: Since this question asks for the author's main purpose, this is a Purpose question.

---

11. The logical relationship of the first sentence of the third paragraph to the final sentence of the third paragraph is most accurately described as

   SR, Must, O

   Location: This question refers us specifically to various locations in the passage, so this is a Specific Reference question.

   Type: The answer comes from information from the passage, making this a Must Be True question.

   Sub-Type: Because this question requires that you understand the structure of the passage, as well as the relationship between various sections of the passage, this is an Organization question.

---

12. Which one of the following, if true, would most cast doubt on the author's interpretation of the study involving the family discussed in the second paragraph?

   SR, Weaken

   Location: The reference to the second paragraph makes this a Specific Reference question.

   Type: When we see a question begin with "Which of the following, if true," we can generally expect either a Strengthen or a Weaken question. In this case, because the correct answer will "cast doubt," this is a Weaken question.

Location, Type, and Sub-type Drill Answer Key

13. The passage contains information sufficient to justify inferring which one of the following?

   GR, Must

   Location: This stem gets no more specific than "The passage," so this is a Global Reference question.

   Type: Although the wording in this case is somewhat convoluted, if an answer choice must be a "sufficiently justified inference," then it Must Be True.

---

14. The author's attitude toward Zeno's development of a new hypothesis about atomic processes can most aptly be described as...

   CR, Must, AP

   Location: This question stem refers to a particular hypothesis, which makes this a Concept Reference question.

   Type: A proper description of the author's attitude will come directly from information in the passage (and therefore should certainly be prephrased), so this is a Must Be True question.

   Sub-Type: This question requires an understanding of the author's attitude, so it is an Author's Perspective question.

---

15. Which one of the following institutions would NOT be covered by the multi-tier classification system proposed by Jacobs?

   CR, Cannot

   Location: This question stem deals with a proposed classification system. If this system were the focus of the passage as a whole, this would be a Global Reference question. In the actual passage, however, that is not the case, making this a Concept Reference question.

   Type: Since the correct answer choice cannot be covered by the proposed classification, this is a Cannot question.

Location, Type, and Sub-type Drill Answer Key

16. Which one of the following most closely expresses the author's intended meaning in using the term "unabashedly" (final sentence of the passage)?

SR, Must, P

Location: This question refers us to the passage's last sentence, which makes this a Specific Reference question.

Type: The answer to this question should be prephrased, as it will come directly from information offered in the passage. It is a Must Be True question.

Sub-Type: Since this question stem requires that we consider the intended meaning of the given term, it is a Function/Purpose question.

17. The author's attitude toward the studies mentioned in the first paragraph is most likely...

SR, Must, AP

Location: This question stem specifies that the study is mentioned in the first paragraph, so this is a Specific Reference question.

Type: This question regards information about the author which comes directly from the stimulus, and the answer must pass the Fact Test. This is a Must Be True question.

Sub-Type: This example requires an understanding of the author's attitude, so it is an Author's Perspective question.

18. Based on the passage, the author would probably hold that which one of the following principles is fundamental to long-term reduction of recidivism rates?

GR, Must, AP, PR

Location: If this question deals with a passage which focuses on recidivism rates, then this is a Global Reference question. If recidivism had only made up a part of the discussion, this would have been a Concept Reference question.

Type: The answer to this question will come from the information offered in the passage, so this is a Must Be True question.

Sub-Type: Since this question regards the author's attitude, it is an Author's Perspective question, and because the answer will involve fundamental principles, it is also a Principle question.

Location, Type, and Sub-type Drill Answer Key

19. Which one of the following most accurately describes the organization of the material presented in the first and second paragraphs of the passage?

SR, Must, O

Location: This question refers to a specific portion of the passage, so it is a Specific Reference question.

Type: The answer to this Must Be True question will come from information provided in the passage, and should be prephrased.

Sub-Type: This question stem requires an understanding of the structure of the passage, as it is a Passage Organization question.

20. In discussing the tangential details of events, the passage contrasts their original significance to witnesses with their possible significance in the courtroom (last two sentences of the fourth paragraph). That contrast is most closely analogous to which one of the following?

SR, Parallel

Location: Since this question refers to the end of the fourth paragraph, it is a Specific Reference question.

Type: This question requires that we find an "analogous contrast," which basically means that we have to find a parallel scenario. This is a Parallel Reasoning question.

6

Prephrasing Answers

Most students tend to simply read the question stem and then move on to the answer choices without further thought. This is disadvantageous because these students run a greater risk of being tempted by the expertly constructed incorrect answer choices. One of the most effective techniques for quickly finding correct answer choices and avoiding incorrect answer choices is prephrasing. Prephrasing an answer involves quickly speculating on what you expect the correct answer will be based on the information in the passage.

Although every answer you prephrase may not be correct, there is great value in considering for a moment what elements could appear in the correct answer choice. Students who regularly prephrase find that they are more readily able to eliminate incorrect answer choices, and of course, many times their prephrased answer is correct. In part, prephrasing puts you in an attacking mindset: if you look ahead and consider a possible answer, you are forced to involve yourself in the problem. This process helps keep you alert and in touch with the elements of the problem.

Keep in mind that prephrasing is directly related to attacking the passage; typically, students who closely analyze the five critical elements of the passage can more easily prephrase an answer.

Keep in mind, however, that while the answers to *many* questions can be prephrased, not *all* answers can be prephrased. A question that asks, "Which one of the following most accurately states the main point of the passage?" should immediately bring an answer to mind. On the other hand, if a question asks, "To which one of the following questions does the passage most clearly provide an answer?" you cannot prephrase an answer, because you are not given sufficient information to pre-form an opinion. Yes, you will have some general knowledge based on your reading, but because the test makers can choose any angle from the passage, you will probably not come up with a strong prephrase to this question. This should not be a concern—prephrase when you can, and if you cannot, move ahead.

Finally, if you find that you are still struggling to prephrase effectively as your test date approaches, we have provided the Prephrasing Test in Chapter Ten: a targeted exercise designed to help you master this critical skill!

Prephrasing is the LSAT version of the old adage, "An ounce of prevention is worth a pound of cure."

All high-scoring test takers are active and aggressive. Passive test takers tend to be less involved in the exam and therefore more prone to error.

Because of the LSAT's time constraints, some students are afraid to pause between reading the questions and assessing the answers. Always prephrase when possible! Prephrasing is far more efficient, and makes you less susceptible to the test makers' cleverly worded incorrect answer choices.

6

6

The Answer Choices

All LSAT questions have five lettered answer choices and each question has only one correct, or "credited," response. As with other sections, the correct answer in a Reading Comprehension question must meet the Uniqueness Rule of Answer Choices™, which states that "Every correct answer has a unique logical quality that meets the criteria in the question stem. Every incorrect answer has the opposite logical quality." The correctness of the answer choices themselves conforms to this rule: there is one correct answer choice; the other four answer choices are the opposite of correct, or incorrect. Consider the following specific examples:

1. Logical Quality of the Correct Answer: Must Be True

   Logical Quality of the Four Incorrect Answers:

   > The opposite of Must Be True = Not Necessarily True (could be not necessarily the case or never the case)

2. Logical Quality of the Correct Answer: Strengthen

   Logical Quality of the Four Incorrect Answers:

   > The opposite of Strengthen = Not Strengthen (could be neutral or weaken)

3. Logical Quality of the Correct Answer: Weaken

   Logical Quality of the Four Incorrect Answers:

   > The opposite of Weaken = Not Weaken (could be neutral or strengthen)

Even though there is only one correct answer choice and this answer choice is unique, you still are faced with a difficult task when attempting to determine the correct answer. The test makers have the advantage of time and language on their side. Because identifying the correct answer at first glance can be quite hard, you must always read all five of the answer choices. Students who fail to read all five answer choices open themselves up to missing questions without ever having read the correct answer. There are many classic examples of LSAC placing highly attractive wrong answer choices just before the correct answer. If you are going to make the time investment of analyzing the stimulus and the question stem, you should also make the wise investment of considering each answer choice.

As you read through each answer choice, sort them into Contenders and Losers. If an answer choice appears somewhat attractive, interesting, or even confusing, keep it as a contender and quickly move on to the next answer choice. You do not want to spend time debating the merits of an answer choice only to find that the next answer choice is superior. However, if an answer choice immediately strikes you as incorrect, classify it as a loser and move on. Once you have evaluated all five answer choices, return to the answer choices that strike you as most likely to be correct and decide which one is correct.

The Contender/Loser separation process is exceedingly important, primarily because it saves time. Consider two students—1 and 2—who each approach the same question, one of whom uses the Contender/Loser approach and the other who does not. Answer choice (D) is correct:

Student 1 (using Contender/Loser)

Answer choice A: considers this answer for 10 seconds, keeps it as a Contender.

Answer choice B: considers this answer for 5 seconds, eliminates it as a Loser.

Answer choice C: considers this answer for 10 seconds, eliminates it as a Loser.

Answer choice D: considers this answer for 15 seconds, keeps it as a Contender, and mentally notes that this answer is preferable to (A).

Answer choice E: considers this answer for 10 seconds, would normally keep as a contender, but determines answer choice (D) is superior.

After a quick review, Student 1 selects answer choice (D) and moves to the next question. Total time spent on the answer choices: 50 seconds (irrespective of the time spent on the passage).

Student 2 (considering each answer choice in its entirety)

Answer choice A: considers this answer for 10 seconds, is not sure if the answer is correct or incorrect. Returns to stimulus and spends another 15 seconds proving the answer is wrong.

Answer choice B: considers this answer for 5 seconds, eliminates it.

Answer choice C: considers this answer for 10 seconds, eliminates it.

Answer choice D: considers this answer for 15 seconds, notes this is the best answer.

Answer choice E: considers this answer for 10 seconds, but determines answer choice (D) is superior.

After a quick review, Student 2 selects answer choice (D) and moves to the next question. Total time spent on the answer choices: 65 seconds.

Comparison: both students answer the problem correctly, but Student 2 takes 15 more seconds to answer the question than Student 1.

Some students, on reading this comparison, note that both students answered the problem correctly and that the time difference was small, only 15 seconds more for Student 2 to complete the problem. Doesn't sound like that big a difference, does it? But, the extra 15 seconds was for just one problem. Imagine if that same thing occurred on every single Reading Comprehension problem in the section: that extra 15 seconds per question would translate to a loss of 6 minutes and 45 seconds when multiplied across 27 questions in a section! And that lost time would mean that student 2 would get to four or five fewer questions than Student 1, just in this one section. This example underscores an essential LSAT truth: little things make a big difference, and every single second counts. If you can save even five seconds by employing a certain method, then do so!

Occasionally, students will read and eliminate all five of the answer choices. If this occurs, return to the passage and re-evaluate what you have read. Remember—the information needed to answer the question always resides in the passage, either implicitly or explicitly. If none of the answers are attractive, then you must have missed something key in the passage.

Analyzing the Answer Choices

We've talked about prephrasing prior to attacking the answers, but let's take a moment to consider how to best analyze the answers once you have arrived at them.

First, it's worth remembering why you should prephrase for each question. Many students approach the answers with the idea that they will use the answer choices against each other, that is, the answers will suggest to them what the correct choice will be. But, to be blunt, that is a terrible strategy because it allows the test makers to manipulate and influence you with the incorrect answer choices (which are 80% of what you see in each question). So, instead of being passive and inviting manipulation or deceit, instead try to take control early and attack the answers based on your own informed expectations. Force the answer choices to match your prediction when possible, rather than letting the answers make suggestions to you.

The point above is worth mentioning because it's a reminder that the test makers are attempting to control you with each incorrect answer choice. They want to draw your attention to incorrect answers when possible, and have you bypass the correct answer when you do read it. There are certain tricks they use to accomplish these goals, including:

6

- The use of identical and synonymous phrases.

   In many answer choices the test makers will use exact words from the passage, but often only in wrong answers. In the correct answer they will use a synonymous phrase in order to force you to parse meaning and equate ideas stated in different terms. The exact duplication in wrong answers is appealing and fools unsuspecting test takers.

- The mixing of Global and Specific ideas in the answers.

   Watch the question stem to see whether the question is a Global Reference (and thus about the whole passage) or a more Specifically Referenced idea (and thus about a sentence or a paragraph). Global Reference questions will almost always have incorrect answers that then refer to attitudes or ideas from only one or two paragraphs (in other words, answers that capture only part of the overall attitude being expressed). This Global/Specific distinction can often trap unwary test takers who don't realize the scope of what they are being asked about.

- The mixing of groups and viewpoints.

Watch for wrong answers that mix up the group in question. A favorite tactic is to have an answer that perfectly captures the ideas or viewpoint of a group in the passage, but not the group the question specifies. Make sure you are clear on who is being asked about and then anticipate trap answers designed to entice you with the views of a different group.

The above items tend to be about mixing ideas up in the answer choices and then making the test taker determine which combination matches the exact question being asked. That should not surprise you—the majority of Reading Comprehension questions are Must Be True-based, and thus each correct answer has to pass the Fact Test. In other words, if the test makers are going to claim a certain position or attitude is correct, you have to be able to point to the section or sections of the passage that support or prove that thinking. Don't waver on using the Fact Test as a decisive separating tool. Too many students allow answers to get by as "close enough," or try to prove their answer right despite warning signs that it's wrong, or even fight for it long after it should have been dismissed. That's the wrong approach—the answer needs to prove itself to you, not the other way around!

6

Tricks of the Trade ▄▄▄▄▄▄

The Digital LSAT: Problem Flagging and Answer Marking

There are two tools available to you in the digital interface that work well together when you are working with questions and answer choices:

Flagging

To the right of each question stem is a small flag icon that, when selected, marks the question for you. The flag darkens, and, more importantly, a small blue flag appears above the question number at the bottom of the screen in the navigation bar. This allows you to instantly see all the problems you have flagged, and using the navigation bar, to return to them instantly. Simply click on the flagged question at the bottom and you will immediately return to that problem.

Answer Markout

Another tool available to you on the Digital LSAT allows you to "mark out" individual answer choices that you deem incorrect. By selecting the circle with a slash through it that sits to the right of each answer, the entire answer will be greyed out (readable still, but clearly dimmed on-screen). The answer choice bubble itself then appears with a slash through it, indicating that you have chosen to eliminate the answer (this can be overridden by tapping the answer bubble).

For many students, the markout tool is a helpful substitute for their normal approach to eliminating answers visually: simply crossing through the lettered answer choice in their test booklet. Perhaps most useful, if you leave the question and return to it later, the markouts remain, which helps you quickly identify the answers you disliked on your first read-through. This tool, when combined with the flagging of questions, allows you to instantly return to uncertain questions and re-engage with the problem.

Because these tools allow you to navigate both questions and answer choices more easily, we strongly recommend that you use them both!

Flagging Questions vs Dwelling on Problems

The individuals who construct standardized tests are called *psychometricians*. We know this job title sounds ominous, but it's actually quite revealing: breaking the word into its two parts tells you a great deal about the nature of the LSAT!

While we could make a number of jokes about the *psycho* part (and often do in class!), this portion of the word merely refers to psychology; the *metrician* piece relates to metrics or measurement. Thus, the purpose of these individuals is to create a test that measures you in a precise, psychological way.

As part of this process, the makers of the LSAT carefully analyze reams of data from every test administration in order to assess the tendencies and behavior of test takers. As Sherlock Holmes observed, "You can, for example, never foretell what any one man will do, but you can say with precision what an average number will be up to." By studying the actions of all past test takers, the makers of the exam can reliably predict where you will be most likely to make errors. And throughout this book we will reference those pitfalls as they relate to specific passage and question types.

For the moment, we would like to highlight one mental trap you must avoid at all times in any LSAT section: the tendency to dwell on past problems and allow them to subvert your concentration going forward. Many students fall prey to "answering" a question, and then continuing to replay it in their minds as they start the next question, and the next. Obviously, this is distracting and creates an environment where missing subsequent problems becomes far more likely. So be sure to separate the notions of reusing your prior work within a passage and learning as you go—approaches that are crucial for success!—from the psychological pitfall we're describing here: when you finish a question, you must move to the next question with 100% focus, clarity, and confidence.

Remember, if you are uncertain of your answer on a problem, simply flag that question electronically and then, time permitting, return to it later for further review (use the navigation bar at the bottom of the screen to quickly jump to your flagged questions). This allows you to track any difficulties that may arise, but also immediately set them aside as you move on to the remaining questions and the continued insights and assistance they often provide.

Practicing with Time

In the last chapter of this book we will discuss time management in detail. However, most students begin practicing with the ideas in this book before reaching that chapter, and we would like to take a moment to give you advice on how to properly practice for the timed element of the LSAT.

Students often ask if they should time themselves while practicing. While every student should take a timed practice LSAT at the very start of their preparation in order to gauge where they stand, not all preparation should be composed of timed exercises. When you learn a new concept or are practicing with a certain technique, you should begin by doing the first several problems untimed in order to get a feel for how the idea operates. Once you feel comfortable with the concept, begin tracking the time it takes you to complete each question. At first, do not worry about completing the passages within a specified time frame, but rather examine how long it takes you to do each passage when you are relaxed. How long does it take you to read the passage? How long to do each question? After doing several passages in this fashion, then begin attempting to read each passage and question set in the time frame allowed on the test (8 minutes and 45 seconds). Thus, you can "ramp up" to the appropriate time per passage.

Note that, while the *average* time allowed per passage set is 8 minutes and 45 seconds, we recommend you use a "number of questions + 2" timing approach for each passage (thus, you'd have 8 minutes to complete a passage with 6 questions, 9 minutes to complete a passage with 7 questions, etc). More on this "Plus 2 Timing Formula" in Chapter Ten.

We are also often asked if every LSAT PrepTest must be done as a full, timed exercise. The answer is No. Although we recommend doing as many PrepTests as possible, you can break up individual tests and do section challenges (completing just one or two sections in the required time) or simply work through a section as a challenge exercise where you focus on answering a variety of question types without worrying about the time component.

Because these ideas are so critical, we will address them again near the end of this book in Chapter Ten.

Average completion times for the other two sections:

Logic Games: 8 minutes and 45 seconds per game.

Logical Reasoning: 1 minute and 25 seconds per question.

6

A number of LSAT PrepTests can be purchased through our website, powerscore.com.

Final Chapter Note ▆▆▆▆▆▆▆▆▆▆

This concludes our general discussion of the single passages that appear in the Reading Comprehension section. In the next chapter we will briefly review all of the ideas from Chapters One through Six, and then we will use those techniques to work through several complete single passages and question sets. If, in the future, you find yourself unclear about some of these ideas, please return to these initial chapters and re-read them.

If you feel as if you are still hazy on some of the ideas discussed so far, do not worry. When discussing the theory that underlies all questions and approaches, the points can sometimes be a bit abstract and dry. In the remaining chapters we will focus more on the application of these ideas to real questions, and working with actual questions often helps a heretofore confusing idea become clear.

6

Chapter Seven: Putting It All Together

Chapter Seven: Putting It All Together

Chapter Preview

Up to this point we have focused on the methods needed to analyze the passages, and in doing so we have isolated individual sections of text that relate directly to each discussion. Now it is time to combine all of the strategies you have learned and analyze some complete passage sets. Accordingly, this chapter contains three sections:

1. A review of the approach we use for single passages.

2. A Mini-Passage Drill focusing on the individual VIEWSTAMP components.

3. Two actual LSAT passages, each with a detailed breakdown of the passage text and questions.

Reading Approach Review

The following section briefly reviews the reading approaches discussed in the Chapters Three and Four of this book.

Chapter Three Review

After you have ascertained the topic, as you move deeper into the passage you must carefully track the following five key VIEWSTAMP elements:

1. The various groups and viewpoints discussed within the passage (**VIEW**)
   Ask yourself: Which groups are speaking or are talked about in the passage?

2. The structure of the passage and the organization of ideas (**S**)
   Ask yourself: What's the structure of the passage? Can I make a mental map of where the ideas appear in the passage?

3. The tone or attitude of each group or individual (**T**)
   Ask yourself: What's the tone or attitude of each group?

4. The argument made by each group or individual (**A**)
   Ask yourself: What is the very basic position or argument of each group?

5. The main point of the passage (**MP**)
   Ask yourself: What is the Main Point of the passage? What is the author driving at? Why was this written?

Chapter Four Review

Sources of Difficulty

There are five general ways the makers of the test can increase the difficulty of any given passage set:

1. Challenging Topic or Terminology

2. Challenging Writing Style

3. Multiple Viewpoints

4. Difficult Questions/Answers

5. Order of Passage Presentation

Passage Elements That Generate Questions

As you read, there are certain specific, consistent passage elements that should jump out at you, primarily because history has reflected the test makers' tendency to use these elements as the basis of questions. For purposes of clarity, we will divide these elements into two types:

Viewpoint-specific Elements

1. Track all viewpoints

2. Be wary of competing perspectives

Text-based Elements

Text-based elements will often be smaller pieces, sometimes just a single word, but sometimes short sections of the text. In this sense, these are the "nuts and bolts" elements that you should be aware of when reading.

These are the seven elements (not in order of importance):

1. Initial Information/Closing Information

2. Dates and Numbers

3. Definitions

4. Examples

5. Difficult words or Phrases

6. Enumerations/Lists

7. Text Questions

Two Broad Reasoning Structures

Causal reasoning and conditional reasoning appear frequently in the Logical Reasoning sections of the LSAT, but less so in the Reading Comprehension section.

Causal Reasoning

Cause and effect reasoning asserts or denies that one thing causes another, or that one thing is caused by another. The cause is the event that makes the other occur; the effect is the event that follows from the cause. By definition, the cause must occur before the effect, and the cause is the "activator" or "ignitor" in the relationship. The effect always happens at some point in time after the cause.

Causality in Reading Comprehension usually is discussed in the context of why certain events occurred. The terms that typically introduce causality—such as *caused by*, *reason for*, *led to*, or *product of*—are still used, but then the author often goes on to discuss the reasons behind the occurrence in depth.

Conditional Reasoning

Conditional reasoning is the broad name given to logical relationships composed of sufficient and necessary conditions. Any conditional relationship consists of at least one sufficient condition and at least one necessary condition.

Conditional relationships in Reading Comprehension passages tend to be unobtrusive, usually occurring as a sideline point to a larger argument.

Of the two types of reasoning, causal reasoning appears more frequently than conditional reasoning in the Reading Comprehension section.

Pitfalls to Avoid

There are a number of text formations and configurations you should recognize. These constructions are often used by the test makers to create confusion, so in this sense they function as possible "traps" for the unwary test taker.

Traps of Similarities and Distinctions

This trap occurs when, in a continuous section of text, an author discusses in detail items that have both similarities and differences. By comparing and contrasting the items in close proximity, the test makers create a greater likelihood for confusion.

Trap of Separation

One favorite trick of the test makers is to take a long discussion of a particular topic and break it up by inserting within it a section of text about a related but distinct topic, effectively creating a separation effect: the main idea bisected by similar but different (and possibly distracting) content in the middle. Then questions will test your ability to track the interrupted main concept despite its beginning and end being divided by many lines (or entire paragraphs) in the passage.

The Trap of Question Misdirection

This trap occurs when the test makers use a specific line reference in the question stem to direct you to a place in the passage where the correct answer will not be found.

Trap of Proximity

Just because two ideas are placed in physical proximity in a passage does not mean that they are related. Similarly, items widely separated in the passage are not necessarily unrelated.

Trap of Inserted Alternate Viewpoint

Another ploy the test makers favor is to present several different viewpoints in a single passage, even a single paragraph, forcing readers to track both the topical information and the various perspectives.

Traps of Chronology

Traps of chronology relate to the placement and order of items within the passage, and the tendency of many readers to believe that when one item is presented before another, then the first item occurred first or caused the second. These two traps are called the Trap of Order and the Trap of Cause, respectively:

Trap of Order

Some students make the mistake of believing that because an event or situation is discussed before another event, the first event likely predated the second. Unless explicitly stated or inherently obvious, this does not have to be the case.

Trap of Cause

Some students also mistakenly assume that when one scenario is discussed before another, then the first item must have caused the second item. This assumption is unwarranted. The easiest way to discern the author's intention is to carefully examine the language used because causal relationships almost always feature one or more of the words that indicate causality (such as *caused by*, *produced by*, *determined*, *led to*, *resulted in*, etc).

The simple truth is that the order of presentation of the items in the passage does not indicate any temporal or causal relationship between them.

Passage Topic Traps

Passage difficulty is more a function of writing style, the number of viewpoints, and the exact concepts under discussion than of the general topic of the passage. That said, the test makers will occasionally use the topic to catch test takers off-guard. This technique of theirs works because when the typical student begins reading a passage, the topic often frames their expectations. The test makers are well aware of these ingrained expectations, and they at times play a sort of "bait and switch" game with students, especially by making a passage initially look hard or easy and then radically changing the level of difficulty after the first few lines or first paragraph.

Mini-Passage Drill: The Elements of VIEWSTAMP

The following short passages are provided for practice with the reading and notating strategies discussed in previous chapters, with each passage followed by a short question set focused on one of five major elements of the VIEWSTAMP analysis (don't worry about your pacing just yet; full-length passage and question sets will follow shortly). *Answers on page 259*

Mini-Passage #1:
Viewpoints

The Vienna Circle, an association of philosophers gathered around the University of Vienna in 1922, pioneered a "positivist" philosophy of science. Their aim was to present
(5) a unified vision of the world, where knowledge can only derive from experience through the application of logical analysis. Not surprisingly, most members of the Vienna Circle eschewed metaphysics, embracing a decidedly empiricist
(10) attitude toward the pursuit of scientific truth. Their attitude was shared by other prominent scientists such as Albert Einstein, whose works were frequently cited in monographs published by members of the Circle. Ironically, by the time the
(15) Vienna Circle "discovered" an intellectual bond with Einstein, he had departed from his positivist views to pursue less optimistic answers to the question of political, philosophical and scientific unity.

1. It can be inferred from the passage that Albert Einstein would be most likely to agree with which one of the following statements concerning the "positivist" philosophy of science, pioneered by the Vienna Circle in 1922?

   (A) Though theoretically valuable, it erroneously embraced an empiricist attitude toward the pursuit of scientific truth.
   (B) Its rejection of metaphysics resulted in a quest for scientific unity that was too optimistic.
   (C) Its emphasis on empirical knowledge was laudable, even if the goal of presenting a unified vision of the world was ultimately unrealistic.
   (D) Its quest for political, philosophical and scientific unity was detrimental to its pursuit of scientific truth.
   (E) Though initially promising, its quest for scientific unity was a failure.

2. This passage suggests which one of the following about metaphysics?

   (A) It was a reaction against the positivist philosophy of science.
   (B) It failed to present a unified vision of the world.
   (C) It did not necessarily seek to derive knowledge through experience alone.
   (D) It was initially embraced by prominent scientists such as Einstein.
   (E) It was regarded by members of the Vienna Circle as intellectually suspect.

Mini-Passage Drill: The Elements of VIEWSTAMP

Mini-Passage #2:
Structure

In establishing economic policy, policy makers usually rely on preexisting models of development and tend to adopt the dominant development theory of their era. With dominant theories quickly
(5) losing credibility as a result of flaws exposed through their application, alternative theories often take hold. Such intellectual shifts are welcome in academia, but can adversely affect the economic development of developing nations.

(10) Unlike most first-world countries whose economic policies are subject to scrutiny by democratically-elected government officials and tend to change gradually, developing nations can be easily compelled to accept structural
(15) adjustment policies by international regimes such as the World Trade Organization (WTO) and the International Monetary Fund (IMF). In the early 1980's, for instance, the IMF forced many developing countries to accept
(20) neoclassical policies in return for funding. This quickly devalued the states' currency, cut government spending, raised prices, and phased out agricultural subsidies. By compelling developing countries to abolish trade protections
(25) and participate in free trade regimes, the IMF left those markets vulnerable to exploitation and predation.

1. Which one of the following best describes the organization of the passage?

   (A) A predicament is outlined, factors leading up to the predicament are scrutinized, and an example of the predicament is offered.
   (B) A phenomenon is described, an implication of the phenomenon is suggested, and an illustration of that implication is offered.
   (C) A problem is presented, an example of the problem is provided, and a course of action addressing the problem is suggested.
   (D) A generalization is made, evidence supporting the generalization is presented, and a particular instance illustrating the generalization is evaluated.
   (E) A particular worldview is explained, its shortcomings are discussed, and an evaluation of these shortcomings is presented.

2. Which one of the following best describes the relationship of the second paragraph to the passage as a whole?

   (A) It predicts a future development.
   (B) It qualifies an assertion made earlier by the author.
   (C) It introduces a hypothesis that the author later expands upon.
   (D) It clarifies a claim made in the preceding paragraph.
   (E) It presents a counterexample to a general thesis.

7

Mini-Passage Drill: The Elements of VIEWSTAMP

Mini-Passage #3:
Tone, Purpose

In 1996, the State of Arizona introduced a statute that divests the juvenile court of jurisdiction over juvenile offenders fifteen years of age or older who are accused of first- or
(5) second-degree murder, forcible sexual assault, armed robbery or other violent felony offenses. Opponents have rightfully argued that by assigning automatic criminal responsibility to juveniles based solely on their age and the type
(10) of offense with which they are charged, many of the extenuating circumstances that would have previously been considered by a juvenile court judge are now largely irrelevant. In fact, if the prosecution finds sufficient grounds for
(15) charging a juvenile offender with, say, armed robbery, juvenile court review will be entirely bypassed and the offender will automatically be tried in criminal court as an adult. The choice of court, therefore, rests entirely in the discretion
(20) of the prosecution. Regrettably, courts have been reluctant to question the constitutionality of such discretion, and little hope remains that they would subject it to judicial review any time soon.

1. The author mentions armed robbery (lines 15-16) primarily in order to

    (A) provide an example of a type of offense with which offenders are rarely charged in juvenile court
    (B) show how the prosecution can automatically decide a jurisdictional issue involving some juvenile offenders
    (C) illustrate a type of offense that the new statute will make more difficult to prosecute
    (D) explain why extenuating circumstances must be considered when assigning criminal responsibility to juvenile offenders
    (E) emphasize the severity of the offenses that are typically considered only in cases tried in criminal court

2. Which one of the following words employed by the author is most indicative of the author's attitude toward the ability of prosecutors to bypass juvenile court review following the passage of the new statute?

    (A) rightfully
    (B) hope
    (C) regrettably
    (D) reluctant
    (E) divests

3. The passage suggests which one of the following about a sixteen-year old offender charged with armed robbery in the state of Arizona prior to 1996?

    (A) The offender could be prosecuted either in juvenile or in criminal court.
    (B) The prosecution did not have sufficient grounds to charge the offender with a more serious crime.
    (C) The court would consider all extenuating circumstances relevant to his case.
    (D) The prosecution could decide to bypass juvenile court review and try the offender in criminal court.
    (E) The choice of courts did not rest entirely in the discretion of the prosecution.

4. The author's main purpose in the passage is to

    (A) defend a proposed statutory change against criticism
    (B) explain the unforeseen consequences of a legal reform
    (C) support a critical evaluation of a statute
    (D) criticize the constitutionality of judicial discretion
    (E) articulate opposing arguments and propose a reconciliation

7

Mini-Passage Drill: The Elements of VIEWSTAMP

Mini-Passage #4:
Main Point and Argumentation

Many of the most popular diets today, including the so-called "Paleo diet," are premised on the dubious assumption that increased consumption of meat and meat by-products pose minimal health
(5) risks to the human body. Proponents of such diets correctly observe that cholesterol intake does not directly correlate with the concentration of harmful low-density lipoprotein (LDL) cholesterol particles in the blood plasma. Studies show,
(10) however, that cholesterol intake exacerbates the negative effect of saturated fatty acids on LDL concentrations, thus increasing LDL levels indirectly. Furthermore, there is evidence suggesting that the oxidation of low-density
(15) lipoproteins in human beings is itself atherogenic, and there appears to be a consistent positive association between the consumption of saturated animal fats and the oxidation of LDL particles. Although antioxidants and dietary fiber can help
(20) prevent oxidative modification of LDL, most diets fail to recommend sufficient amounts of either supplement.

1. Which one of the following most accurately states the main point of the passage?

   (A) Increased consumption of meat and meat by-products may be harmful to one's health.
   (B) Cholesterol intake can exacerbate the negative effects of saturated fatty acids on LDL concentrations.
   (C) Most diets are not as healthful as their proponents are led to believe.
   (D) Although cholesterol intake is not directly responsible for increasing the concentration of LDL particles in the blood plasma, it can cause such an increase indirectly.
   (E) The healthiest diets are those that eliminate meat and meat by-products.

2. Which one of the following most accurately describes the role played in the argument by the claim that cholesterol intake does not directly correlate with the concentration of harmful low-density lipoprotein (lines 6-8)?

   (A) It is a claim on which the argument depends but for which no support is given.
   (B) It is used to refute the causal explanation described by the conclusion of the argument.
   (C) It summarizes a position that the argument as a whole is directed toward discrediting.
   (D) It acknowledges a possible objection to the recommendation put forth in the argument.
   (E) It is a proposition for which the argument seeks to advance a causal explanation.

3. Which one of the following, if true, would most strengthen the proponents' argument that increased consumption of meat and meat by-products pose minimal health risks to the human body?

   (A) Excessive consumption of salt, often found in meat by-products, is associated with increased risk of cardiovascular disease.
   (B) Some animal fat contains large amounts of omega-3 fatty acids, which mitigate the ill effects of increased LDL concentrations.
   (C) Of all plant-based diets, those that exclude meat and meat by-products are the most protective against atherosclerosis.
   (D) Drugs that lower cholesterol levels can also prevent cardiovascular disease, but carry the risk of adverse side effects.
   (E) Antioxidants and dietary fiber are not the only substances that can prevent oxidative modification of LDL.

7

Mini-Passage Drill: The Elements of VIEWSTAMP

Mini-Passage #5:
Main Point

Socialist realism, the officially approved style of realistic art developed in the Soviet Union during the 1930's, had a relatively simple political objective. As the primary instrument of state
(5) propaganda, it sought to promote the goals of socialism and communism through positive images of rapidly changing villages, grandiose public projects, and well-groomed wholesome youth. Form and content were strictly regulated
(10) by a vast army of cultural bureaucrats, whose only job was to ensure conformity to state doctrine. Accordingly, impressionism and abstraction were quickly abolished, replaced by ostensibly truthful representation of reality in its "revolutionary"
(15) development.

Ultimately, censorship was fated to collaborate in its own undoing. The state correctly perceived the interpretive potential of art to be inherently dangerous, but the effort to contain artistic
(20) ambiguity only amplified the disconnect between reality and fiction. As the Soviet Union's centrally planned economy led to increasingly inefficient resource distribution, the utopian vision of a "revolutionary" world became easy to mock. The
(25) art of socialist realism did provide a refuge from the bleak reality of most ordinary Russians, if only because irony and laughter (unlike bread and butter) were always abundant, and required no food stamps to procure.

1. Which one of the following most accurately states the main point of the passage?

(A) Socialist realism had, as its chief objective, the furtherance of socialist and communist ideology.

(B) Because of censorship, socialist realism never fulfilled its artistic potential.

(C) The art of socialist realism was a welcome distraction from the bleak reality of ordinary Russians.

(D) Conformity to state doctrine led to an ostensibly truthful representation of reality in its revolutionary development.

(E) The proliferation of uniformly positive images of a fictional world impeded, rather than promoted, the political objectives of socialist realism.

Mini-Passage Drill: The Elements of VIEWSTAMP Answer Key

Mini-Passage #1: _Viewpoints_

The passage explicitly presents two viewpoints (the Vienna Circle's and Einstein's), and alludes to a third (metaphysicists').

Question #1: CR, Must Be True, SP. The correct answer choice is (C)

Answer choice (A) is incorrect, because Einstein shared the philosophers' empiricist attitude toward the pursuit of scientific truth. Nowhere in the passage do we have evidence that Einstein considered such attitude to be "erroneous."

Answer choice (B) is incorrect. While Einstein might perceive the quest for scientific unity as overly optimistic, the positivists' rejection of metaphysics has nothing to do with that. This answer choice assumes a causal relationship for which there is no evidence in the passage.

Answer choice (C) is the correct answer choice. Einstein shared the Vienna Circle's "decidedly empiricist attitude toward the pursuit of scientific truth" (lines 9-10), suggesting that he would find their emphasis on empirical knowledge to be "laudable." But, as we learn at the end of the passage, Einstein later "departed from his positivist views to pursue _less_ optimistic answers to the question of political, philosophical and scientific unity" (lines 16-19). It is likely, therefore, that he would regard the goal of presenting an unified vision of the world as _too_ optimistic (i.e. as "ultimately unrealistic").

Answer choice (D) is incorrect, because Einstein does not perceive the quest for unity to be particularly harmful: it is merely too optimistic.

Answer choice (E) is incorrect, because "failure" is too strong of a word, for which no evidence is presented in the passage.

Mini-Passage Drill: The Elements of VIEWSTAMP Answer Key

Question #2: CR, Must Be True. The correct answer choice is (C)

Answer choice (A) is incorrect, because there is no evidence that metaphysics was a reaction against positivism. If anything, the relationship seems to be inverted: it is the positivists that rejected metaphysics, not the other way around.

Answer choice (B) is incorrect: the failure to present a unified vision of the world concerns Einstein's views on positivism.

Answer choice (C) is the correct answer choice. Metaphysics is mentioned on line 9 as a philosophical movement eschewed (i.e. rejected) by the members of the Vienna Circle, who instead embraced a more *empiricist* attitude toward the pursuit of scientific truth, where knowledge can only derive from experience (line 6). Thus, it is reasonable to conclude that metaphysicists held a contrary belief, i.e. that it did not necessarily seek to derive knowledge through experience alone.

Answer choice (D) is incorrect, because it is positivism—not metaphysics—that was initially embraced by Einstein (lines 9-12).

Answer choice (E) is attractive, but also incorrect. While the Vienna Circle rejected metaphysics (presumably because of the latter's disregard for experiential knowledge), we have little evidence that the Vienna Circle would regard metaphysics as "intellectually suspect." This is too strong of a label, and insufficient evidence is presented to substantiate such a definitive claim.

7

Mini-Passage Drill: The Elements of VIEWSTAMP Answer Key

Mini-Passage #2: _Structure_

The passage has the following structure:

> Paragraph 1: Describe a policy behavior and suggest that it adversely affects developing nations.

> Paragraph 2: Explain why developing nations are particularly affected, and present an example to illustrate this effect.

Question #1: GR, Organization. The correct answer choice is (B)

Before you attack the answer choices to an Organization question, it is important to have a general understanding of passage structure. As described above, the first paragraph outlines a phenomenon that adversely affects developing nations. The second paragraph explains why such nations are particularly affected, and illustrates this proposition with an example. Answer choice (B) comes the closest to matching our prephrase, and is therefore correct.

Answer choice (A) is incorrect, because the author does not examine the factors leading up to the predicament described in the beginning of the passage. We do not know, for instance, _why_ policy makers tend to adopt the dominant development theory of their era. The passage is only concerned with examining the effects, not the causes, of the phenomenon outlined in the first paragraph.

Answer choice (B) is the correct answer choice. The phenomenon of policy makers adopting the dominant theory of their era is described, its implication affecting developing nations is suggested, and an illustration of that implication is offered (lines 18-27).

Answer choice (C) is incorrect, because no course of action addressing the problem is suggested.

Answer choice (D) is incorrect. Although the author uses evidence to explain how developing nations are adversely affected by the intellectual shifts described in the first paragraph, the observation regarding these adverse effects does not constitute a generalization. Rather, it is a specific _implication_ of the generalization that policy makers tend to adopt the dominant development theory of their era. No example of this generalization is ever presented.

Answer choice (E) is incorrect. Even if the negative consequences of the worldview outlined in lines 1-7 can be described as "shortcomings," the author does not _evaluate_ these shortcomings. She merely explains them by virtue of an example.

Mini-Passage Drill: The Elements of VIEWSTAMP Answer Key

Question #2: SR, Organization. The correct answer choice is (D)

Answer choice (A) is incorrect, because the second paragraph makes no predictions about any future developments.

Answer choice (B) is incorrect, because the second paragraph does not *qualify* the assertion made in the first paragraph. Qualifying an assertion usually requires examining its potential limitations or applicability. In the second paragraph, the author attempts to explain, not qualify, the assertion that developing nations are adversely affected by the policy of adopting the dominant development theory of their era.

Answer choice (C) is incorrect, because it describes the function of the first, not the second paragraph.

Answer choice (D) is the correct answer choice. This question concerns the function of the second paragraph within the passage as a whole. As previously mentioned, the second paragraph explains why developing nations in particular are adversely affected by the intellectual shifts outlined in the first paragraph. As such, the second paragraph can be said to clarify a claim made earlier. This prephrase agrees with answer choice (D), which is correct.

Answer choice (E) is incorrect, because the second paragraph presents an example, not a counterexample, to the thesis outlined in the first paragraph.

7

Mini-Passage Drill: The Elements of VIEWSTAMP Answer Key

Mini-Passage #3: _Tone, Purpose_

The author's attitude is one of resignation and disappointment with the passage of the 1996 statute. The purpose of the passage is to support the critics who oppose the statute by explaining its ramifications to the criminal justice system.

Question #1: SR, Must, Purpose. The correct answer choice is (B)

Answer choice (A) is incorrect, because it is perfectly possible that, up until 1996, offenders tried in juvenile court were frequently charged with armed robbery (among other violent felony offenses). Just because the new statute makes it impossible to do so does not mean that it rarely happened in the past.

Answer choice (B) is the correct answer choice. The author mentions armed robbery in order to illustrate how easily the prosecution can divest the juvenile court of jurisdiction over juvenile offenders. All the prosecutor needs to do is charge the juvenile offender with a violent felony, such as armed robbery. Answer choice (B) is consistent with this prephrase and is therefore correct.

Answer choice (C) is incorrect, because there is no evidence that prosecuting a juvenile offender as an adult is somehow more _difficult_ than prosecuting him in juvenile court.

Answer choice (D) is incorrect. The author regrets that "many of the extenuating circumstances that would have previously been considered by a juvenile court judge are now largely irrelevant" (lines 10-13), but never explicitly states that such circumstances _must_ be considered when assigning criminal responsibility to juvenile offenders. Furthermore, it is unclear how charging someone with armed robbery explains the need to consider extenuating circumstances.

Answer choice (E) is incorrect, because the author never intends to draw a line between juvenile and criminal court with respect to the severity of the crimes being prosecuted there. In fact, up until the passage of the new statute, it is reasonable to infer that juvenile offenders charged with violent felonies were tried in juvenile court.

7

Mini-Passage Drill: The Elements of VIEWSTAMP Answer Key

Question #2: GR, Must, Tone. The correct answer choice is (C)

Answer choices (A) and (B) are incorrect, because the author clearly opposes the ramifications of the recently passed statute.

Answer choice (C) is the correct answer choice. In line 20, the author expresses regret over the court's reluctance to question the constitutionality of a statute that allows prosecutors to bypass juvenile court review. The word "regrettably" captures the author's attitude and tone, proving answer choice (C) correct.

Answer choice (D) is incorrect, because the author is not reluctant to take a stance (the courts are).

Answer choice (E) indicates the effect of the new statute on the juvenile court, not the author's *attitude* toward this effect.

Question #3: CR, Must. The correct answer choice is (E)

Answer choice (A) is incorrect, because prior to 1996 the juvenile court would have had jurisdiction over the juvenile offender (the statute stripped the court of such jurisdiction). We have no reason to believe that the offender could *also* have been prosecuted in criminal court.

Answer choice (B) describes a hypothetical that cannot be proven with the information available.

Answer choice (C) contains an exaggeration. While the juvenile court would have likely considered many of the extenuating circumstances that would have been irrelevant in criminal court (lines 10-13), we cannot prove that it would have considered *all* extenuating circumstances relevant to the offender's case.

Answer choice (D) describes how the offender would be tried following the passage of the new statute, i.e. *after* 1996.

Answer choice (E) is the correct answer choice. The author regrets that, following the 1996 statute, "The choice of court, [...] rests entirely in the discretion of the prosecution" (lines 18-20), adding that "courts have been reluctant to question the constitutionality of such discretion" (lines 20-22). We can infer that *prior* to 1996 this was not the case, which agrees with answer choice (E).

Mini-Passage Drill: The Elements of VIEWSTAMP Answer Key

Question 4: GR, Purpose/Function. The correct answer choice is (C)

Answer choice (A) is incorrect, because the author does not defend the statute against criticism: on the contrary, she supports the criticism (line 7).

Answer choice (B) is attractive, but incorrect. The author certainly alludes to the consequences of the newly introduced statute (lines 7-18); however, we have no way of knowing if these consequences are necessarily *unforeseen*. This answer choice fails the Fact Test, and is therefore incorrect.

Answer choice (C) is the correct answer choice. The author begins by introducing a statute, which is immediately criticized ("opponents have rightfully argued that…"). The remainder of the passage explains why the opponents' argument is a reasonable one. Answer choice (C) agrees with this prephrase, and is therefore correct.

Answer choice (D) is incorrect, because the constitutionality of *judicial* discretion is not in question. The author only questions the constitutionality of *prosecutorial* discretion (lines 18-22).

Answer choice (E) is incorrect, because the argument in favor of the new statute is never outlined, and no reconciliation between the two positions is provided.

7

Mini-Passage Drill: The Elements of VIEWSTAMP Answer Key

Mini-Passage #4: *Main Point and Argumentation*

The main point of the passage is that increased consumption of meat and meat by-products may pose more health risks than the proponents of such diets assume (Their assumption is "dubious," line 3). The argument is structured as follows:

Proponents of the Paleo diet:

Premise: Cholesterol intake does not directly correlate with the concentration of harmful low-density lipoprotein.

Conclusion: Increased consumption of meat and meat by-products pose minimal health risks to the human body.

Counterargument (author's):

Premise: Cholesterol intake can increase LDL levels indirectly.

Premise: Consumption of saturated animal fats may cause the oxidation of LDL particles, which is itself atherogenic.

Conclusion: Increased consumption of meat and meat by-products may pose more health risks than the proponents of such diets assume.

Question #1: GR, Main Point. The correct answer choice is (A)

Answer choice (A) is the correct answer choice. This passage opens with a critique of some popular diets, whose proponents incorrectly believe that increased consumption of meat and meat by-products pose minimal health risks to the human body. The key word here is "dubious," suggesting the author's disagreement with those views. Answer choice (A) agrees with this prephrase, suggesting that increased consumption of meat and meat by-products *may* be harmful to one's health. The remainder of the passage supports this view, which therefore represents the main point of the passage.

Answer choice (B) is incorrect. Although cholesterol intake can indeed exacerbate the negative effects of saturated fatty acids on LDL concentrations (lines 9-13), this is a *premise* for the author's conclusion that meat products may be harmful to one's health.

Answer choice (C) is incorrect, because it contains an exaggeration. While *many* of the most popular diets are not as healthful as their proponents are led to believe, we cannot reliably conclude that about *most* diets.

Mini-Passage Drill: The Elements of VIEWSTAMP Answer Key

Answer choice (D) is incorrect, because it is a subsidiary conclusion for the main argument. Although the indirect effects of cholesterol intake are supported by the studies described in lines 9-13, these effects, in turn, serve to support a more general criticism of diets that promote increased consumption of meat and meat by-products.

Answer choice (E) is incorrect. While the author seems to believe that consuming meat and meat-by-products can be harmful to one's health, no argument is made for their complete *elimination*, and no statement is made regarding which diets are the *healthiest*.

Question #2: SR, Purpose/Function. The correct answer choice is (D)

The stem asks us to identify the role played in the argument by the claim that cholesterol intake does not directly correlate with the concentration of harmful low-density lipoprotein (lines 6-9). To answer this question correctly, it is imperative to have a solid understanding of argument structure. As described in our discussion of argumentation (above), the cited claim is simply a premise used by the proponents of the Paleo diet in support of their conclusion. Unfortunately, this prephrase does not produce a close match to any of the answer choices, as there are many ways to describe the function of any given argument part. Nevertheless, as long as you understand the broader function of the cited claim, you will be able to eliminate four of the five answer choices relatively quickly.

Answer choice (A) is incorrect, because the claim in question supports a position that the argument as a whole is directed towards discrediting.

Answer choice (B) is incorrect, because the cited claim does not *refute* the causal link between cholesterol intake and increased LDL levels. The author clearly believes that a causal link still exists.

Answer choice (C) is incorrect, because the author acknowledges that the claim in question is factually correct. As such, it only provides *support* for the position that the argument as a whole is directed toward discrediting; it is not a *summary* of that position.

Answer choice (D): This is the correct answer choice. As mentioned above, the cited claim represents an observation advanced by the proponents of the Paleo diet in support of their conclusion. The author concedes that the observation is correct, but argues that their conclusion is not (cholesterol intake can still increase LDL concentrations indirectly). As such, the cited claim represents a possible objection to the recommendation put forth in the argument.

Answer choice (E): The author makes no attempt of explaining why there is no direct correlation between cholesterol intake and increased LDL levels. Instead, she argues that the two are causally related *despite* the absence of such a direct correlation.

7

Mini-Passage Drill: The Elements of VIEWSTAMP Answer Key

Question #3: CR, Strengthen. The correct answer choice is (B)

The question stem asks us to strengthen the proponents' position that increased consumption of meat and meat by-products pose minimal health risks to the human body. The correct answer choice is likely to show that the consumption of meat and meat by-products somehow mitigates the ill effects of increased LDL levels, or else prevents the oxidative modification of LDL.

Answer choice (A) is incorrect, because it is an Opposite Answer. If excessive consumption of salt, often found in meat by-products, is associated with increased risk of cardiovascular disease, this would strengthen the author's position that increased consumption of meat and meat by-products is harmful to one's health.

Answer choice (B) is the correct answer choice. If omega-3 fatty acids, often found in animal fat, can protect against the effects of increased LDL levels, then meat-based diets may not be as hazardous as the author fears them to be.

Answer choice (C) is incorrect, because it is an Opposite Answer. If diets that exclude meat are the most protective against atherosclerosis, the author's claim that meat consumption poses certain health risks cannot be ignored.

Answer choice (D) is incorrect, because it provides further evidence that elevated cholesterol levels are associated with the risk of cardiovascular disease. One could argue that such drugs can lower the risk of consuming meat and meat by-products, but that does not mean that the consumption of meat *itself* poses minimal health risks (which is what the proponents seem to believe). Furthermore, since the drugs in question carry the risk of adverse side effects, the costs may ultimately outweigh the benefits.

Answer choice (E) is incorrect. Just because there are substances besides antioxidants and dietary fiber that can prevent oxidative modification of LDL does not mean that these substances are readily available to those who follow the Paleo diet.

Mini-Passage Drill: The Elements of VIEWSTAMP Answer Key

Mini-Passage #5: *Main Point*

Question #1: GR, Main Point. The correct answer choice is (E)

Answer choice (A) is incorrect, because it does not represent a summary of the passage. The author does not try to *convince* us that socialist realism sought to further socialist and communist ideology; the fact that it did is merely stated as a fact in the first paragraph.

Answer choice (B) is incorrect, because the artistic potential of socialist realism is not under discussion.

Answer choice (C) is incorrect, because it is not the main point of the passage. While socialist realism did provide a refuge from the bleak reality of ordinary Russians (lines 24-26), the rest of the passage does not seek to support this claim.

Answer choice (D) is incorrect, because the effects of censorship on artistic representation are not the main point of the passage. Furthermore, as the discussion in the second paragraph shows, censorship led to a *fictitious* representation of reality, which compromised its primary objectives.

Answer choice (E) is the correct answer choice. The passage opens with a description of the central objectives of socialist realism, and elaborates on the importance of censorship in aligning them to those of the state. The second paragraph changes direction: censorship led to its own undoing. The rest of the paragraph supports this statement by explaining how that occurred, making the first sentence of the second paragraph the main point of the passage. Answer choice (E) most closely parallels the idea that by censoring artistic expression, the state amplified the disconnect between reality and fiction, which ultimately compromised the objectives of socialist realism.

7

7

Two Passages Analyzed ▮▮▮▮

On the following pages two actual LSAT passages are presented, along with a complete analysis of each passage and all of the corresponding questions.

To most effectively benefit from this section, time yourself on the first passage. Attempt to finish the passage in 8 minutes and 45 seconds, but if you cannot, continue working until you complete all of the questions and note your time. Then, read the entire explanation section. After reviewing the first passage, proceed to the second passage and try again.

If you experience trouble with time, do not worry. Your pace will naturally pick up the more you practice applying the strategies you've been learning. At the end of the book we will discuss timing and time management to further increase your speed, if necessary.

Remember that maintaining a positive attitude is critical! Approach the passages with energy and enthusiasm and you will see your performance improve.

Final note:

> In doing these passages, **use scratch paper instead of writing directly on the passage!** This will prepare you for the Digital LSAT format where you cannot write directly on the screen.

7

Practice Passage I—June 2006 Passage #1

Attempt to finish each passage in 8 minutes and 45 seconds, but if you cannot, continue working until you complete all of the questions and note your time. Then, read the corresponding explanation section. *Answers on page 276*

The use of computer-generated visual displays in courtrooms is growing as awareness of their ability to recreate crime scenes spreads. Displays currently in use range from still pictures in series that mimic
(5) simple movement to sophisticated simulations based on complex applications of rules of physics and mathematics. By making it possible to slow or stop action, to vary visual perspectives according to witnesses' vantage points, or to highlight or enlarge
(10) images, computer displays provide litigators with tremendous explanatory advantages. Soon, litigators may even have available graphic systems capable of simulating three dimensions, thus creating the illusion that viewers are at the scene of a crime or accident,
(15) directly experiencing its occurrence. The advantages of computer-generated displays derive from the greater psychological impact they have on juries as compared to purely verbal presentations; studies show that people generally retain about 85 percent of visual
(20) information but only 10 percent of aural information. This is especially valuable in complex or technical trials, where juror interest and comprehension are generally low. In addition, computers also allow litigators to integrate graphic aids seamlessly into
(25) their presentations.

Despite these benefits, however, some critics are urging caution in the use of these displays, pointing to a concomitant potential for abuse or unintentional misuse, such as the unfair manipulation of a juror's
(30) impression of an event. These critics argue further that the persuasive and richly communicative nature of the displays can mesmerize jurors and cause them to relax their normal critical faculties. This potential for distortion is compounded when one side in a trial
(35) does not use the technology—often because of the considerable expense involved—leaving the jury susceptible to prejudice in favor of the side employing computer displays. And aside from the risk of intentional manipulation of images or deceitful use
(40) of capacities such as stop-action and highlighting, there is also the possibility that computer displays can be inherently misleading. As an amalgamation of data collection, judgment, and speculation, the displays may in some instances constitute evidence unsuitable
(45) for use in a trial.

To avoid misuse of this technology in the courtroom, practical steps must be taken. First, counsel must be alert to the ever-present danger of its misuse: diligent analyses of the data that form the
(50) basis for computer displays should be routinely

performed and disclosed. Judges, who have the discretion to disallow displays that might unfairly prejudice one side, must also be vigilant in assessing the displays they do allow. Similarly, judges should
(55) forewarn jurors of the potentially biased nature of computer-generated evidence. Finally, steps should be taken to ensure that if one side utilizes computer technology, the opposing side will also have access to it. Granting financial aid in these circumstances
(60) would help create a more equitable legal arena in this respect.

1. Which one of the following most accurately states the main point of the passage?

    (A) Those involved in court trials that take advantage of computer-generated displays as evidence need to take steps to prevent the misuse of this evidence.

    (B) The use of computer-generated displays has grown dramatically in recent years because computer aids allow litigators to convey complex information more clearly.

    (C) The persuasive nature of computer-generated displays requires that the rules governing the use of these displays be based on the most sophisticated principles of jurisprudence.

    (D) Litigators' prudent use of computer-generated displays will result in heightened jury comprehension of complex legal issues and thus fairer trials.

    (E) Any disadvantages of computer-generated visual displays can be eliminated by enacting a number of practical procedures to avoid their intentional misuse.

2. Which one of the following most accurately describes the organization of the passage?

(A) The popularity of a new technology is lamented; criticisms of the technology are voiced; corrective actions to stem its use are recommended.

(B) A new technology is endorsed; specific examples of its advantages are offered; ways to take further advantage of the technology are presented.

(C) A new technology is presented as problematic; specific problems associated with its use are discussed; alternative uses of the technology are proposed.

(D) A new technology is introduced as useful; potential problems associated with its use are identified; recommendations for preventing these problems are offered.

(E) A new technology is described in detail; arguments for and against its use are voiced; recommendations for promoting the widespread use of the technology are advanced.

3. As described in the passage, re-creating an accident with a computer-generated display is most similar to which one of the following?

(A) using several of a crime suspect's statements together to suggest that the suspect had a motive

(B) using an author's original manuscript to correct printing errors in the current edition of her novel

(C) using information gathered from satellite images to predict the development of a thunderstorm

(D) using a video camera to gather opinions of passersby for use in a candidate's political campaign advertisements

(E) using detailed geological evidence to design a museum exhibit depicting a recent volcanic eruption

4. Based on the passage, with which one of the following statements regarding the use of computer displays in courtroom proceedings would the author be most likely to agree?

(A) The courts should suspend the use of stop-action and highlighting techniques until an adequate financial aid program has been established.

(B) Computer-generated evidence should be scrutinized to ensure that it does not rely on excessive speculation in depicting the details of an event.

(C) Actual static photographs of a crime scene are generally more effective as displays than are computer displays.

(D) Verbal accounts by eyewitnesses to crimes should play a more vital role in the presentation of evidence than should computer displays.

(E) Computer displays based on insufficient or inaccurate input of data would not seem realistic and would generally not persuade jurors effectively.

5. The author states which one of the following about computer displays used in trial proceedings?

(A) Despite appearances, computer displays offer few practical advantages over conventional forms of evidence.

(B) Most critics of computer-generated evidence argue for banning such evidence in legal proceedings.

(C) Judges should forewarn jurors of the potentially biased nature of computer-generated displays.

(D) Computer displays are used primarily in technical trials, in which jury interest is naturally low.

(E) Litigators who utilize computer-generated displays must ensure that the opposing side has equal access to such technology.

6. The author mentions each of the following as an advantage of using computer displays in courtroom proceedings EXCEPT:

(A) They enable litigators to slow or stop action.

(B) They can aid jurors in understanding complex or technical information.

(C) They make it possible to vary visual perspectives.

(D) They allow litigators to integrate visual materials smoothly into their presentations.

(E) They prevent litigators from engaging in certain kinds of unjustified speculation.

7

One of the intriguing questions considered by anthropologists concerns the purpose our early ancestors had in first creating images of the world around them. Among these images are 25,000-year-

(5) old cave paintings made by the Aurignacians, a people who supplanted the Neanderthals in Europe and who produced the earliest known examples of representational art. Some anthropologists see these paintings as evidence that the Aurignacians had a

(10) more secure life than the Neanderthals. No one under constant threat of starvation, the reasoning goes, could afford time for luxuries such as art; moreover, the art is, in its latter stages at least, so astonishingly well-executed by almost any standard of excellence

(15) that it is highly unlikely it was produced by people who had not spent a great deal of time perfecting their skills. In other words, the high level of quality suggests that Aurignacian art was created by a distinct group of artists, who would likely have spent

(20) most of their time practicing and passing on their skills while being supported by other members of their community.

Curiously, however, the paintings were usually placed in areas accessible only with extreme effort

(25) and completely unilluminated by natural light. This makes it unlikely that these representational cave paintings arose simply out of a love of beauty or pride in artistry—had aesthetic enjoyment been the sole purpose of the paintings, they would presumably

(30) have been located where they could have been easily seen and appreciated.

Given that the Aurignacians were hunter-gatherers and had to cope with the practical problems of extracting a living from a difficult environment, many

(35) anthropologists hypothesize that the paintings were also intended to provide a means of ensuring a steady supply of food. Since it was common among pretechnological societies to believe that one can gain power over an animal by making an image of it,

(40) these anthropologists maintain that the Aurignacian paintings were meant to grant magical power over the Aurignacians' prey—typically large, dangerous animals such as mammoths and bison. The images were probably intended to make these animals

(45) vulnerable to the weapons of the hunters, an explanation supported by the fact that many of the pictures show animals with their hearts outlined in red, or with bright, arrow-shaped lines tracing paths to vital organs. Other paintings clearly show some

(50) animals as pregnant, perhaps in an effort to assure plentiful hunting grounds. There is also evidence that ceremonies of some sort were performed before these images. Well-worn footprints of dancers can still be discerned in the clay floors of some caves, and

(55) pictures of what appear to be shamans, or religious leaders, garbed in fantastic costumes, are found among the painted animals.

1. Which one of the following most accurately describes the author's position regarding the claims attributed to anthropologists in the third paragraph?

(A)   implicit acceptance
(B)   hesitant agreement
(C)   noncommittal curiosity
(D)   detached skepticism
(E)   broad disagreement

2. The passage provides information that answers which one of the following questions?

(A)   For how long a period did the Neanderthals occupy Europe?
(B)   How long did it take for the Aurignacians to supplant the Neanderthals?
(C)   Did the Aurignacians make their homes in caves?
(D)   What are some of the animals represented in Aurignacian cave paintings?
(E)   What other prehistoric groups aside from the Aurignacians produced representational art?

7

3. The author would be most likely to agree with which one of the following statements?

    (A) The cave paintings indicate that the Aurignacians lived a relatively secure life compared to most other hunter-gatherer cultures.
    (B) Skill in art was essential to becoming an Aurignacian shaman.
    (C) Prehistoric hunter-gatherers did not create any art solely for aesthetic purposes.
    (D) All art created by the Aurignacians was intended to grant magical power over other beings.
    (E) The Aurignacians sought to gain magical power over their prey by means of ceremonial acts in addition to painted images.

4. The author mentions the relative inaccessibility of the Aurignacian cave paintings primarily to

    (A) stress the importance of the cave paintings to the lives of the artists who painted them by indicating the difficulties they had to overcome to do so
    (B) lay the groundwork for a fuller explanation of the paintings' function
    (C) suggest that only a select portion of the Aurignacian community was permitted to view the paintings
    (D) help explain why the paintings are still well preserved
    (E) support the argument that Aurignacian artists were a distinct and highly skilled group

5. The passage suggests that the author would be most likely to agree with which one of the following claims about the Aurignacians?

    (A) They were technologically no more advanced than the Neanderthals they supplanted.
    (B) They were the first humans known to have worn costumes for ceremonial purposes.
    (C) They had established some highly specialized social roles.
    (D) They occupied a less hostile environment than the Neanderthals did.
    (E) They carved images of their intended prey on their weapons to increase the weapons' efficacy.

7

On the following pages you will find both practice passages, each followed by an outline of the passage and complete explanations of the questions.

The use of computer-generated visual displays in courtrooms is growing as awareness of their ability to recreate crime scenes spreads. Displays currently in use range from still pictures in series that mimic
(5) simple movement to sophisticated simulations based on complex applications of rules of physics and mathematics. By making it possible to slow or stop action, to vary visual perspectives according to witnesses' vantage points, or to highlight or enlarge
(10) images, computer displays provide litigators with tremendous explanatory advantages. Soon, litigators may even have available graphic systems capable of simulating three dimensions, thus creating the illusion that viewers are at the scene of a crime or accident,
(15) directly experiencing its occurrence. The advantages of computer-generated displays derive from the greater psychological impact they have on juries as compared to purely verbal presentations; studies show that people generally retain about 85 percent of visual
(20) information but only 10 percent of aural information. This is especially valuable in complex or technical trials, where juror interest and comprehension are generally low. In addition, computers also allow litigators to integrate graphic aids seamlessly into
(25) their presentations.

Despite these benefits, however, some critics are urging caution in the use of these displays, pointing to a concomitant potential for abuse or unintentional misuse, such as the unfair manipulation of a juror's
(30) impression of an event. These critics argue further that the persuasive and richly communicative nature of the displays can mesmerize jurors and cause them to relax their normal critical faculties. This potential for distortion is compounded when one side in a trial
(35) does not use the technology—often because of the considerable expense involved—leaving the jury susceptible to prejudice in favor of the side employing computer displays. And aside from the risk of intentional manipulation of images or deceitful use
(40) of capacities such as stop-action and highlighting, there is also the possibility that computer displays can be inherently misleading. As an amalgamation of data collection, judgment, and speculation, the displays may in some instances constitute evidence unsuitable
(45) for use in a trial.

To avoid misuse of this technology in the courtroom, practical steps must be taken. First, counsel must be alert to the ever-present danger of its misuse: diligent analyses of the data that form the
(50) basis for computer displays should be routinely performed and disclosed. Judges, who have the discretion to disallow displays that might unfairly prejudice one side, must also be vigilant in assessing the displays they do allow. Similarly, judges should
(55) forewarn jurors of the potentially biased nature of computer-generated evidence. Finally, steps should be taken to ensure that if one side utilizes computer technology, the opposing side will also have access to it. Granting financial aid in these circumstances
(60) would help create a more equitable legal arena in this respect.

7

Practice Passage I—June 2006 Passage #1 Answer Key

Paragraph One:

This passage begins with a presentation of facts from the author. Computer-generated visual displays are effective at recreating crime scenes, so they are becoming more widely used, in forms ranging from still pictures to complex simulations. These visual aids (soon available in 3-D) provide significant advantages, since people only retain 10% of what they hear, versus 85% of what they see, and trials are often complicated and uninteresting to jurors. Visual displays can be seamlessly integrated into a litigator's presentation.

Paragraph Two:

Having outlined the benefits of these displays, the author turns to the subject of potential for abuse, shifting to the viewpoint of "some critics," who warn that mesmerizing displays might throw off the jury's reasoning abilities, especially in a long, boring trial. The critics are also concerned that these displays are potentially unfair when only presented on one side of the argument, since juries might tend to be prejudiced in favor of the side with the visual displays. Displays that require too much speculation would be unsuitable for trial.

Paragraph Three:

In this paragraph the passage shifts to the author's viewpoint, that the following list of steps must be taken to avoid misuse:

1. Lawyers must avoid misuse of computer visual displays by analyzing and disclosing data used, and judges must prohibit prejudicial displays and analyze admissible ones.

2. Judges should forewarn jurors of the potential for bias.

3. Computer displays should be accessible to both sides; financial aid may ensure this.

VIEWSTAMP Analysis:

The **Viewpoints** presented in this passage are those of "some critics urging caution," (line 26) and the perspective of the author, who agrees with those critics about the need for prudence.

7

Practice Passage I—June 2006 Passage #1 Answer Key

The author's **Tone** is even-handed, discussing both pros and cons, but certainly cautionary with regard to court use of computer displays.

The main **Argument** in this passage is that these displays, though advantageous, should be used prudently in the court system to ensure equitability.

The **Main Point** of this passage is that these computer displays provide some advantage, but we must guard against their misuse.

The **Structure** of this passage is as follows:

> Paragraph One: Introduce the concept of computer-generated visual displays, and discuss several advantages associated with their seamless presentation and visual nature.

> Paragraph Two: Discuss the disadvantages, including potential for abuse, potential to prejudice the jury, and potentially speculative basis for some such displays.

> Paragraph Three: Provide three steps that must be taken to avoid misuse of the displays: analyze the data, prohibit prejudicial use, forewarn juries, and allow access to both sides.

Question #1: GR, Main Point. The Correct answer is (A)

We already know the Main Point, so this question should be relatively straightforward.

Answer choice (A): This is the correct answer choice. Those who make use of the advantages must guard against potential for abuse.

Answer choice (B): This statement does not reflect the main point of the passage, and we cannot even confirm its accuracy based on the passage; the author says that use of the displays is growing, but nothing about dramatic growth.

Answer choice (C): The author believes that the legal community should guard against abuse, but says nothing about basing rules on "the most sophisticated principles of jurisprudence."

Answer choice (D): While prudent use of the displays might increase jury comprehension, the author is concerned about the prospect for unfairness, so it would be inaccurate to claim that use of the displays would inherently result in fairer trials.

7

Practice Passage I—June 2006 Passage #1 Answer Key

Answer choice (E): The author provides a list of steps that must be taken to guard against misuse of the visual displays, but avoidance of intentional misuse would not guarantee this outcome—the author specifies the prospect of unintentional misuse as well.

Question #2: GR, O. The correct answer choice is (D)

Again, we should seek to prephrase an answer. The organization of this passage is basically as follows: the author introduces the concept of computer visual displays, discusses advantages, possible problems, and steps to take to guard against misuse.

Answer choice (A): The popularity of the displays is not lamented; the author simply wishes to guard against their misuse. And the author does not necessarily want to stop their use, but rather to take steps to ensure proper use.

Answer choice (B): This answer choice overstates the author's perspective; the author does not endorse the displays, as much as present pros, cons, and protective measures. This answer choice does not even mention the disadvantages of the displays, which is an integral part of the passage.

Answer choice (C): The author does not discuss alternative uses of the computer visual displays, but rather suggests ways to ensure fairness in the way they are used.

Answer choice (D): This is the correct answer choice, as it restates our prephrase: new technology is introduced with pros, cons, and steps to avoid unfairness in its application.

Answer choice (E): In this passage, the author does describe a new technology, followed by a discussion of its benefits and potential problems, but this is not quite the same as arguing against its use in general. The author just believes that we need to take care in the use of visual displays. Further, the author is not necessarily interested in promoting its widespread use, but rather that the courts be prudent as the use of the displays grows in popularity.

Question #3: GR, Parallel. The correct answer choice is (E)

Here we are looking for something analogous to the use of computer generated displays, which translate information into a more visual re-creation.

Answer choice (A): Using a suspect's statements to suggest a motive does not even contain a visual component, so this is not analogous to the use of courtroom visual displays.

Answer choice (B): Using an original to correct printing errors is not parallel, because in such a case there would be no reason for concerns about accuracy or speculation. Also, there is no visual re-creation in this scenario, so this answer choice is incorrect.

Answer choice (C): This answer choice provides a scenario that involves prediction, as opposed to re-creation or representation, so this choice is not parallel.

Answer choice (D): While this answer choice does involve a visual component, this scenario does not involve a re-creation of any sort, so it is not analogous.

Answer choice (E): This is the correct answer choice. Here we have a situation where evidence is being gathered for the presentation of a visual re-creation, which is much like that created by computer-generated courtroom visual displays.

Question #4: GR, Must, AP. The correct answer choice is (B)

To answer this question, we must have a solid grasp on the author's tone, which is precautionary.

Answer choice (A): The author discusses the possible applicability of a financial aid program in the context of the newer technologies that are less accessible to those with less resources. Stop-action and highlighting would seem more broadly accessible, and the author does not discuss this matter specifically, so this answer choice is incorrect.

Answer choice (B): This is the correct answer choice. One of the reasons for caution specified by the author is the speculative content of computer-generated displays presented as evidence.

Answer choice (C): The author never makes this comparison, and in any case it seems unlikely that the author would agree with this assertion.

Answer choice (D): The author does not assert that computer displays should play a less vital role. Rather, the author is primarily concerned with the responsible use of this technology which can be used very effectively in court.

Answer choice (E): The author never discusses the persuasiveness of inaccurate data, but since the author is concerned that this evidence may be unfairly prejudicial, presumably this is based on the concern that inaccurate data could effectively persuade the jury, so this answer choice is incorrect.

Question #5: GR, Must: The correct answer choice is (C)

For a Must Be True question, we can apply the Fact Test to confirm the correct answer choice.

Answer choice (A): There is specific discussion of the possible advantages of the computer-generated visual displays, so the author would not agree with this assertion.

Answer choice (B): Critics of the technology don't necessarily want to see it banned; some just want to ensure that the courts are responsible in allowing and monitoring its use.

Answer choice (C): This is the correct answer choice. This is one of the steps the author provides in the list of steps which must be taken to avoid misuse in the courts.

Answer choice (D): The word that makes this answer choice incorrect is "primarily." We know that the computer-generated displays are used in technical trials, but the author provides no insight into how often the displays may be used in non-technical trials.

Answer choice (E): This answer choice provides a clever pitfall: the author believes in the principle of equal access to the modern displays, but does not place the burden on the litigators. The author asserts that the job of counsel (litigators) is to analyze the data and disclose findings, and it would appear to be the job of the court system to provide for financial aid and ensure equal access to the technology.

Question #6: GR, MustX. The correct answer choice is (E)

In this Must Be True Except question, among the five answer choices, the four incorrect answer choices will be accurate based on the information in the passage, and the correct answer choice is the one that is not necessarily true.

Answer choice (A): The author mentions this advantage in line 7, so this answer choice is incorrect.

Answer choice (B): This advantage is discussed in line 21, so this accurate assertion is another incorrect answer.

Answer choice (C): This advantage is specifically mentioned in line 8 of the passage, so this answer choice is incorrect.

Answer choice (D): This is discussed at the end of the first paragraph, in lines 23-25. Since this answer choice is confirmed by the Fact Test, it must be incorrect in response to this Except question.

Answer choice (E): This is the correct answer choice. The author does not make this assertion—in fact the author is specifically concerned with the prospect of too much speculation going into the creation of the computer-generated displays. Since the assertion in this answer choice is definitely not true, this is the correct answer choice to this Must Be True Except question.

One of the intriguing questions considered by anthropologists concerns the purpose our early ancestors had in first creating images of the world around them. Among these images are 25,000-year-
(5) old cave paintings made by the Aurignacians, a people who supplanted the Neanderthals in Europe and who produced the earliest known examples of representational art. Some anthropologists see these paintings as evidence that the Aurignacians had a
(10) more secure life than the Neanderthals. No one under constant threat of starvation, the reasoning goes, could afford time for luxuries such as art; moreover, the art is, in its latter stages at least, so astonishingly well-executed by almost any standard of excellence
(15) that it is highly unlikely it was produced by people who had not spent a great deal of time perfecting their skills. In other words, the high level of quality suggests that Aurignacian art was created by a distinct group of artists, who would likely have spent
(20) most of their time practicing and passing on their skills while being supported by other members of their community.

Curiously, however, the paintings were usually placed in areas accessible only with extreme effort
(25) and completely unilluminated by natural light. This makes it unlikely that these representational cave paintings arose simply out of a love of beauty or pride in artistry—had aesthetic enjoyment been the sole purpose of the paintings, they would presumably
(30) have been located where they could have been easily seen and appreciated.

Given that the Aurignacians were hunter-gatherers and had to cope with the practical problems of extracting a living from a difficult environment, many
(35) anthropologists hypothesize that the paintings were also intended to provide a means of ensuring a steady supply of food. Since it was common among pretechnological societies to believe that one can gain power over an animal by making an image of it,
(40) these anthropologists maintain that the Aurignacian paintings were meant to grant magical power over the Aurignacians' prey—typically large, dangerous animals such as mammoths and bison. The images were probably intended to make these animals
(45) vulnerable to the weapons of the hunters, an explanation supported by the fact that many of the pictures show animals with their hearts outlined in red, or with bright, arrow-shaped lines tracing paths to vital organs. Other paintings clearly show some
(50) animals as pregnant, perhaps in an effort to assure plentiful hunting grounds. There is also evidence that ceremonies of some sort were performed before these images. Well-worn footprints of dancers can still be discerned in the clay floors of some caves, and
(55) pictures of what appear to be shamans, or religious

leaders, garbed in fantastic costumes, are found among the painted animals.

7

Practice Passage II—December 2005 Passage #1 Answer Key

Paragraph One:

The author begins this Science passage with a factual, viewpoint-neutral tone, introducing the anthropological question of why our early ancestors created artistic images of their world. The Aurignacians, who emerged in Europe after the Neanderthals, created the first known representational art in cave paintings 25,000 years ago. At line 8, the author shifts to the viewpoint of "some anthropologists," who claim that the art speaks to the Aurignacians' secure environment, since they were able to focus on something beyond survival.

Paragraph Two:

In this paragraph the author presents evidence which weighs against artistic appreciation as the driving force of the cave paintings. Since the paintings were placed inaccessibly in unlit caves, it seems unlikely that aesthetic concern was the sole purpose for the creation of the cave paintings.

Paragraph Three:

In the final paragraph the author presents the viewpoint of "many anthropologists." The Aurignacians did have a difficult living environment, so they may have created the paintings to ensure a steady food supply; like other pretechnological societies, the Aurignacians may have believed that creation of an animal's image gives one power over that animal. This assertion is supported by images of animals being killed, images of pregnant animals, and evidence of ceremonial dances, which included costumed religious figures and took place near the cave paintings.

VIEWSTAMP Analysis:

These are the three **Viewpoints** presented in the passage: Those of "some anthropologists," discussed in the first paragraph, who believe that the cave paintings spoke to the Aurignacians' secure lifestyle; that of the author, who uses the second paragraph to question this belief; and the perspective of "many anthropologists," discussed in the third paragraph, who think the paintings were meant to gain power over the animals depicted.

7

The author's **Tone** is somewhat academic, considering and then dismissing one hypothesis in favor of a different explanation for the cave paintings.

The **Arguments** in the passage are those of the first group of anthropologists mentioned, who assert that the cave paintings meant security, that of the author, who presents evidence to refute the notion that the paintings were purely aesthetic, and that of the second group of anthropologists, who believe they were meant to bring power.

The **Main Point** of the passage is to discuss what may have caused the Aurignacians to create the first known representational art; it was probably not aesthetics (they were low-lit and not readily accessible), but rather the Aurignacians' efforts to gain power over the animals depicted in the paintings.

The **Structure** of the passage is as follows:

Paragraph One: Introduce question of why early peoples created images, and the first known representational art, the Aurignacians' cave paintings. Discuss hypothesis that such art reflects a secure lifestyle.

Paragraph Two: Point out that the cave paintings were poorly lit and inaccessible, so aesthetics were probably not their primary purpose.

Paragraph Three: Discuss the possibility that the paintings were intended to gain power over the animals depicted.

Practice Passage II—December 2005 Passage #1 Answer Key

Question #1: SR, Must, AP. The correct answer choice is (A)

To answer this question, it is helpful to have recognized the author's tone with regard to the various hypotheses. The author appears to agree with the reasoning of the anthropologists discussed in the third paragraph.

Answer choice (A): This is the correct answer choice. The author presents the hypothesis of "many anthropologists" at the beginning of the third paragraph, provides their evidence, takes a supportive tone, and never questions the validity of their argument. This is implicit acceptance.

Answer choice (B): The author does not appear hesitant to agree with the anthropologists, but rather supportive of their beliefs, so this answer choice is incorrect.

Answer choice (C): "Non-committal" does not describe the tone here; the author appears to agree with the reasoning of the anthropologists discussed in the third paragraph, so this answer choice is incorrect.

Answer choice (D): The author is skeptical about the theory in the first paragraph, but with regard to the anthropologists discussed in the third paragraph the author is neither detached nor skeptical.

Answer choice (E): Broad disagreement is certainly not reflected by the author in the third paragraph of this passage; the author appears to agree with the hypothesis and the supporting evidence, so this answer choice is incorrect.

Question #2: GR, Must. The correct answer choice is (D)

Answer choice (A): Although the author tells us that the Aurignacians supplanted the Neanderthals, the length of the Neanderthals' occupation of Europe is never discussed in the passage.

Answer choice (B): Again, the author mentions this supplanting, but does not specify how long it took, so this answer choice is incorrect.

Answer choice (C): The images discussed in the passage were created in caves, but the author never discusses whether or not the Aurignacians lived in caves.

Answer choice (D): This is the correct answer choice. In lines 42-43, the author tells us that some of the animals represented were large, dangerous animals such as mammoths and bison.

Answer choice (E): The only representational art discussed in the passage is that of the Aurignacians, the earliest known creators of such images. Since the author provides no information about other artistic prehistoric groups, this answer choice is incorrect.

Practice Passage II—December 2005 Passage #1 Answer Key

Question #3: GR, AP. The correct answer choice is (E)

Answer choice (A): The first group of anthropologists, discussed in the opening paragraph, make this hypothesis, but the author appears to disagree, providing evidence to the contrary in the second paragraph.

Answer choice (B): The author maintains that the creators of the cave paintings were highly skilled, but these artists were not necessarily the same people as the shamans discussed in the last paragraph of the passage, so this answer choice is incorrect.

Answer choice (C): The word that makes this answer choice incorrect is "any." The author doesn't go so far as to say that *no* art was created for solely aesthetic reasons, only that the cave paintings' placement suggests that *they* weren't created just for artistic enjoyment.

Answer choice (D): Again, one word takes this question out of contention: "all." The discussion in the passage is limited to the cave paintings, and the author makes no such broad assertions regarding "all art" that the people created.

Answer choice (E): This is the correct answer choice. This answer choice is supported by the third paragraph of the passage, and discussed as a likely reason for the creation of the cave paintings.

Question #4: CR, Must. The correct answer choice is (B)

This is another question conducive to prephrasing, so we should try to get a good idea of the answer before considering the choices provided. In this case, the author discusses the relative inaccessibility of the cave paintings to show that they were probably not produced solely for artistic appreciation, leading to another explanation of what drove the Aurignacians to create the images.

Answer choice (A): The author does not delve into the personal lives of the artists, beyond mentioning the likelihood that these people apparently made up a distinct group in the Aurignacian society.

Answer choice (B): This is the correct answer choice, and is perfectly aligned with our prephrase. The author mentions the inaccessibility in order to set the stage for the alternative explanation that the images were created as part of the Aurignacians' ceremonial efforts to master their prey.

Answer choice (C): There is no suggestion that any segment of the Aurignacian society was prohibited from seeing the paintings—only that the images were placed in unlit, relatively inaccessible places.

Answer choice (D): While the placement of the paintings does provide a reasonable explanation for their preservation, this is not what led the author to discuss their placement, so this answer choice is incorrect.

Answer choice (E): The author does believe that the artists were a distinct group, but this is based on the quality of the work, and has nothing to do with the author's discussion of inaccessibility.

7

Question #5: GR, Must, AP. The correct answer choice is (C)

Answer choice (A): While both groups may have been nontechnological societies, the author makes no comparison of the technological advancement of the two groups. We know that the Aurignacians supplanted the Neanderthals, but that does not provide information about their respective technological advances, so this answer choice is incorrect.

Answer choice (B): The author does not assert that the Aurignacians were the first humans known to wear costumes for ceremonies, but rather that they were the first to create representational art. No information is provided concerning whether the Aurignacians' costumed ceremonies were preceded by such ceremonies in other cultures.

Answer choice (C): This is the correct answer choice. The author does support the belief that the artists played a distinct role, based on the level of excellence of the art, so this answer choice is supported by the information in the passage.

Answer choice (D): This is the assertion of the anthropologists discussed in the first paragraph of the passage. The author goes on to discuss the inaccessibility of the cave paintings to show that they were not necessarily reflective of a more secure lifestyle, but of a desire to gain power over their prey.

Answer choice (E): Weapon carving is not discussed in the passage, so this answer does not pass the Fact Test, and is incorrect.

7

Chapter Eight: Comparative Reading Passages

Chapter Eight: Comparative Reading Passages

Dual Passages

In the first seven chapters of this book we have focused on single passages. We now turn our attention to the dual passages—also known as Comparative Reading—that also appear on the LSAT.

Starting with the June 2007 LSAT, the makers of the test introduced the dual passage format to the exam, and every LSAT now features exactly one dual passage set per RC section. The dual passages can appear anywhere within the section (first, second, third, or last), and, as with single passages, the number of questions varies from five to eight.

Comparative Reading passages were first introduced on the June 2007 LSAT.

Dual passages are very similar to the single passages in tone and topic, but rather than present just one excerpt from a single author, two passages are given on a duplicate or related subject by two separate authors (generally with somewhat different points of view). Comparative Reading sets are also distinguished from the single passages because the two passages are labeled, "**Passage A**" and "**Passage B**," respectively. In total the two passages are also roughly the same length as a standard single passage (approximately 450-500 words) and line number references are provided every five lines. The line numbering does not restart for the second passage, but continues on from Passage A.

The first thing to keep in mind when approaching Comparative Reading is that the strategies you have learned thus far for the single passages still apply extremely well! That is, you must still read the dual passages for ideas like viewpoints, tone, argumentation, main point, and general passage structure and function. Similarly, the approach that you have taken towards the single passages—reading the passage first, making relevant notations within the passage, actively seeking viewpoints and main point ideas—is identical in Comparative Reading. So this is less a "new task" and more a natural extension of the skills you've been developing.

All of the strategies we discussed in the single passage sections apply to Comparative Reading.

8

In fact, many students come to enjoy the dual passages more than the single passage format, as the two passages provide a more complete and balanced perspective on the topic being discussed. This typically leads to a better understanding of the ideas presented and, consequently, a better performance on the questions that follow. Further, because each passage is shorter, the arguments and viewpoints developed in each tend to be less complex than in single passages, and thus the reading itself is often easier.

As you examine the passages, remember that they will relate to each other in some way, and will almost always have at least one or two points of both conflict and agreement: authors are never in complete accord, however even in instances where the authors seem fiercely opposed, some common ground is all but guaranteed. Thus, finding moments of overlap and uniqueness is the key to performing well in Comparative Reading.

There are, however, a variety of relationships that can exist between passage A and passage B. As the test makers note, "In some cases, the authors of the passages will be in general agreement with each other, while in others their views will be directly opposed. Passage pairs may also exhibit more complex types of relationships: for example, one passage might articulate a set of principles, while the other passage applies those or similar principles to a particular situation." So, regrettably, no single form or template is sufficiently representative of the dual passage dynamic.

Regardless, the primary goal for Comparative Reading is to identify the main point and purpose of each passage and then to relate those ideas to each other, focusing on the passages' similarities and differences.

So let's take a moment now to analyze how single and dual passages compare.

Similarities between Comparative Reading Passage Sets and Single Passages

- General reading strategy remains the same for all passage types

- Difficulty of the subject matter is the same for single and dual passages, and the subject matter will be drawn from the same disciplines: humanities, social sciences, biological and physical sciences, and issues related to law

- Dual passage length and the number of accompanying questions are comparable to those of a single passage, so the total amount of reading is similar

- Question difficulty is roughly equivalent for single and dual passages

- Question types are generally similar to those seen in the single passages, however the emphasis is more on global questions (main point, author's attitude, function) and passage relationship questions (as we'll soon see) in Comparative Reading

- The same reading challenges, sources of difficulty, and trap answers appear in all passage types

- Questions should be answered exclusively on the basis of the information provided in the selection(s); no specific, subject-based knowledge is necessary

- Single and dual passages can all be diagrammed in the same ways

Differences between Comparative Reading Passage Sets and Single Passages

- There are two related passages in Comparative Reading as opposed to a single passage

- Two authors contribute to the reading selection in comparative reading, while single passage selections are drawn from only one author

- The majority of the Comparative Reading questions deal with the relationship between the two passages, while single passage questions tend to have a higher percentage of local questions

- The theme or main point of the Comparative Reading passages will often change from passage A to passage B, as opposed to the more consistent, singular purpose of an author in a single passage

- The ability to compare and contrast is paramount to success in Comparative Reading; success in singular passage reading comprehension is largely dependent upon a reader's ability to identify passage structure and organization

- The complexity of argumentation in each of the dual passages tends to be less than the complexity developed in a single passage. This is logical because there are fewer words in each of the individual dual passages

Passage Diagramming

You can use the same system of markings and notations for the dual passages as you use for single passages. Simply recognize that with two passages there will be two authors' viewpoints, two main points, etc.

The diagramming system we discussed in Chapter Five applies to Comparative Reading as well.

One additional practice strategy that some students have found helpful (especially those struggling with the Reading Comprehension), is to make two columns in the small space available in the lower margin of their scratch paper: the first column for Similarities, and the second column for Differences. This diagram allows you to write out the various points on which the passages agree and disagree, and better delineate the sometimes subtle differences on which the questions tend to focus.

Where Comparative Reading Appears

Historically, Comparative Reading passages tend not to appear first in the section, and have been most likely to appear third:

Comparative Reading Passage Placement June 2007 - November 2019*		
# of Passage 1	3	7.69%
# of Passage 2	8	20.51%
# of Passage 3	19	48.72%
# of Passage 4	9	23.08%

In addition, the typical Comparative Reading passage contains 6 or 7 questions (as opposed to 5 or 8 questions):

Comparative Reading Passage Question Count June 2007 - November 2019*		
# of 5 questions	6	15.38%
# of 6 questions	15	38.46%
# of 7 questions	14	35.90%
# of 8 questions	4	10.26%

*These statistics do not include nondisclosed LSAT administrations.

8

One Special Dual Passage Strategy

As mentioned, Comparative Reading questions are generally the same as single passage set questions, with the difference that the emphasis is on how well you can understand the similarities and differences between the two passages. And since many of the questions that follow dual passages test your compare and contrast abilities, we cannot overstress the importance of keeping track of precisely where the authors are alike and where they differ. In our passage explanations we will highlight this comparison by setting aside the normal VIEWSTAMP analysis in favor of a similarities and differences analysis to help you better understand the crucial nature of this idea.

If you're concerned about becoming confused by the similarities in the two passages and misattributing viewpoints or details, there is a solution strategy that can help.

After reading passage A, pause briefly to organize your thoughts about what you have just read and then go and complete each question that is focused *solely* on passage A. There may not be any with a passage A-only focus, but chances are good that at least one or two will be exclusive to the first author's text. Then go back and read passage B with the intention of both understanding B on its own and establishing the relationship between the two authors. After completing passage B, attempt each question that focuses solely on passage B (again, there will likely be at least one). Thereafter, complete the remaining questions which deal with the relationships between the two passages. This strategy allows you to isolate the passages first, making it more likely that you will answer single-passage questions correctly.

While there are occasions where every question addresses both passages, the approach above is still potentially useful: by pausing after passage A and considering the questions you inevitably compartmentalize what you have just read, reducing the potential for confusion as you then move on to passage B.

You must be aware of how the passages are similar and how they differ.

This strategy is especially effective because Passage A is always shorter than a regular RC passage, meaning that the information is fresher and more readily understood. Answering the questions about Passage A immediately after reading Passage A maximizes your chances of answering them correctly.

8

Two Comparative Reading Question Types

The number of Point at Issue and Point of Agreement questions varies considerably from LSAT to LSAT. Some Comparative passage sets have none, while other dual passage sets have two or three.

Because Comparative Reading passages are written by two authors discussing a related subject but from different perspectives, they often serve as the source for a pair of unique question types: Point at Issue and Point of Agreement. These questions center on the compare and contrast nature of dual passages, where Point at Issue ask you to find a belief about which the authors differ, and Point of Agreement have you choose an idea about which the two authors concur. Let's take a closer look at both.

Point at Issue Questions

Point at Issue questions are a variant of the Must Be True questions at the heart of Reading Comprehension (and examined at length in Chapter Six). Like all Must question types, you can only use the information in the passages to evaluate the answer choices, meaning you must *know* with a reasonable degree of certainty what each speaker believes strictly from what is written. Success relies on choosing answers about which the views of the sources are both known and in direct opposition of one another. The question stem of a Point at Issue question typically refers to a disagreement or point of contention between the two authors/passages.

Question stem examples:

"The authors would be most likely to disagree over whether"

"On the basis of their statements, the authors of passage A and passage B are committed to disagreeing over whether"

"Given the statements about cross-examination in the last sentence of passage B, the author of passage B would be most likely to take issue with which one of the following claims by the author of passage A?"

8

Incorrect Answers in Point at Issue Questions

Finding the correct answer in most Point at Issue questions involves examining the conclusion of each speaker. And while this itself is a familiar process, because Point at Issue questions require the more demanding task of selecting a statement relevant to *both* sources, there are a number of common traps available to the test makers:

1. Ethical versus Factual Situations

   When a pair of passages address an issue that is ethical (or motivational, behavioral, etc.) in nature, answer choices that are strictly factual cannot be correct. For example, imagine that two passages disagree about whether doctors should inform their patients of a terminal illness. An answer such as the following would clearly be incorrect:

   > Every medical school includes ethics training in its curriculum.

   This answer, factual in nature, cannot address the underlying judgment issues that form an ethical or moral debate.

   The reverse is also true: when passage disputes are more factual in nature, answer choices that are non-factual—*why* something should happen, or whether it is right or wrong—cannot be correct.

   For example, consider the following brief debate:

   > Damon: World War I began in 1910.

   > Tania: No, World War I began in 1914.

   The gist of the disagreement is clear: did the war begin in 1910 or 1914? (1914 is correct). In a factual debate like this, an answer choice that addresses an ethical or interpretational issue (such as "should nations go to war?" or "what led to World War I?") would be incorrect.

   However, disagreements over facts occur infrequently because they are generally easy for students to spot, so be prepared for disputes to largely center on the interpretation of facts, rather than the strict circumstances or events described.

2. Dual Agreement or Dual Disagreement

   Often, incorrect answer choices will supply statements that *both* authors agree with, or that both authors disagree with. These answer choices are typically quite attractive because they raise issues that are indeed addressed in the passages, but remember: just because both speakers discuss the issue does not mean that it is an issue about which the two would disagree.

3. The View of One Speaker is Unknown

   Another crafty trick used by the test makers is to offer an answer where the view of only one of the authors is known. In these instances one passage did not address the issue in the answer choice, or at least failed to do so clearly enough that the author's opinion on it can be known. Since the correct answer must contain a point of disagreement, these "one unknown" answers are always incorrect since there is no way to determine the feelings of both speakers.

The Agree/Disagree Test™

Because of the specific nature of the correct answer choice, you can double-check answers in Point at Issue using the Agree/Disagree Test™:

> The correct answer must produce responses where one speaker would say, "I agree, this statement is correct" and the other speaker would say, "I disagree, this statement is incorrect." If those two responses are not produced, then the answer is incorrect.

The Agree/Disagree Test crystallizes the essence of Point at Issue questions by forcing you to concretely identify both speakers' position on an answer choice. It should also feel reasonably familiar: because the correct answer to a Point at Issue question can always be proven by referring to the viewpoints in the passages, the Agree/Disagree Test is really just an extension of the analysis we can apply to all Must Be True-type questions.

8

After succeeding with the Agree/Disagree Test, some students become enamored of the process and want to apply it to every answer choice. But this is an overuse of the technique! Using the Agree/Disagree Test for every answer choice will reveal the correct answer, but the process will take too much time. Like other "litmus tests" for answer choices, the Agree/Disagree Test is designed to either confirm you have selected the correct answer choice or to help you decide between two or three remaining options. So use the Test judiciously.

Point of Agreement Questions ▰▰▰

Point of Agreement questions require you to identify the issue or statement with which the two authors would both agree. Point of Agreement questions are thus the opposite of Point at Issue questions, where instead of being asked to identify a *disagreement*, you are asked to identify the point of *agreement* between two authors. At the same time, Point of Agreement questions are also closely related to Point at Issue questions, in that both require a comparison of the views of two speakers.

Note that, as with Point at Issue, this is an active task: You are looking for the answer choice about which both speakers have the same view (they might agree that the statements are correct, or they might both agree that the statements are incorrect).

Question stem examples:

> "The authors of the passages would be most likely to agree with which one of the following statements?"
>
> "Borges and the author of passage B would be most likely to agree with which one of the following statements?"
>
> "It can be inferred that each author would agree that if judges conduct independent research, that research"

Point of Agreement questions appear roughly as often as Point at Issue questions in Comparative Reading passage sets.

8

Note the similarities in Point of Agreement and Point at Issue question stems: the only differentiating factor is that with Point of Agreement you're seeking to find common ground instead of a dispute. This degree of kinship allows us to attack Point of Agreement in much the same way we approached Point at Issue, as we will see on the following page.

The Agree/Agree Test™

Because these questions are so similar to Point at Issue questions, we can use a similar (but slightly altered) test to help determine the correct answer. This test is known as The Agree/Agree Test™:

> The correct answer choice must be one about which both speakers would say, "Yes, I agree with that statement." If each speaker does not produce that response, the answer is incorrect.

Again, this test should not be used on all five answers, but only on those remaining after removing the obvious failures, or on any you wish to confirm as correct.

Finally, note that, as with Point at Issue answer choices, if the view of one speaker is unknown, then that answer is automatically incorrect.

A Final Tip: Explicit versus Implicit Beliefs

Point at Issue and Point of Agreement questions are particularly clever in how they test your understanding of viewpoints, in that they tend to focus far more on authors' implied beliefs, rather than dealing strictly with views stated directly. This should come as little surprise, as the test makers prefer to avoid the superficially obvious whenever possible, and explicitly-given viewpoints are easy to both identify and understand. But it also means that you must read between the lines, somewhat literally, when analyzing a speaker's position!

To give you a better sense of what we mean by "explicit" and "implicit" views, consider the following statement and what you can determine based on it:

> "The only way to score well on the LSAT is through intensive study."

The immediate takeaway is that intensive studying is required to score well on the LSAT (and a contrapositive of sorts: if you don't study intensively you will not score well). But look deeper! In using the word "only" the speaker is implying that any other, non-study approach to the test will be insufficient for scoring well: you cannot score well on the LSAT by merely cheating, for instance, or by getting lucky, or by having a tremendous amount of natural ability. Those beliefs aren't expressly mentioned, but the nature of the statement allows them each to be known all the same. And that is precisely how most of these questions operate.

A Comparative Reading Passage Analyzed

On the following pages an actual LSAT Comparative Reading passage is presented, along with a complete analysis of the passage and all of the corresponding questions.

To most effectively benefit from this section, time yourself on the passage set. Attempt to finish the passage and questions in 8 minutes and 45 seconds, but if you cannot, continue working until you complete all of the questions and note your time. While reading, remember to look for the VIEWSTAMP elements within each passage, but concentrate equally on the similarities and differences between the two passages as those will be the focus of the questions. Then, read the entire explanation section and consider what elements you missed, and what you need to do to improve. Within the passage analysis we will directly discuss the passage similarities and differences.

If you experience trouble with time, do not worry. At the end of the book we will discuss timing and time management.

8

Passage Analysis—December 2007 Passage #3

The passages discuss relationships between business interests and university research.

Passage A

As university researchers working in a "gift economy" dedicated to collegial sharing of ideas, we have long been insulated from market pressures. The recent tendency to treat research findings as
(5) commodities, tradable for cash, threatens this tradition and the role of research as a public good.

The nurseries for new ideas are traditionally universities, which provide an environment uniquely suited to the painstaking testing and revision of
(10) theories. Unfortunately, the market process and values governing commodity exchange are ill suited to the cultivation and management of new ideas. With their shareholders impatient for quick returns, businesses are averse to wide-ranging experimentation. And, what
(15) is even more important, few commercial enterprises contain the range of expertise needed to handle the replacement of shattered theoretical frameworks.

Further, since entrepreneurs usually have little affinity for adventure of the intellectual sort, they can
(20) buy research and bury its products, hiding knowledge useful to society or to their competitors. The growth of industrial biotechnology, for example, has been accompanied by a reduction in the free sharing of research methods and results-a high price to pay for
(25) the undoubted benefits of new drugs and therapies.

Important new experimental results once led university scientists to rush down the hall and share their excitement with colleagues. When instead the rush is to patent lawyers and venture capitalists, I
(30) worry about the long-term future of scientific discovery.

Passage B

The fruits of pure science were once considered primarily a public good, available for society as a whole. The argument for this view was that most of
(35) these benefits were produced through government support of universities, and thus no individual was entitled to restrict access to them.

Today, however, the critical role of science in the modern "information economy" means that what was
(40) previously seen as a public good is being transformed into a market commodity. For example, by exploiting the information that basic research has accumulated about the detailed structures of cells and genes, the biotechnology industry can derive profitable
(45) pharmaceuticals or medical screening technologies. In this context, assertion of legal claims to "intellectual property"-not just in commercial products but in the underlying scientific knowledge-becomes crucial.

Previously, the distinction between a scientific
(50) "discovery" (which could not be patented) and a technical "invention" (which could) defined the limits of industry's ability to patent something. Today, however, the speed with which scientific discoveries can be turned into products and the large profits
(55) resulting from this transformation have led to a blurring of both the legal distinction between discovery and invention and the moral distinction between what should and should not be patented.

Industry argues that if it has supported-either in
(60) its own laboratories or in a university-the makers of a scientific discovery, then it is entitled to seek a return on its investment, either by charging others for using the discovery or by keeping it for its own exclusive use.

15. Which one of the following is discussed in passage B but not in passage A?

(A) the blurring of the legal distinction between discovery and invention
(B) the general effects of the market on the exchange of scientific knowledge
(C) the role of scientific research in supplying public goods
(D) new pharmaceuticals that result from industrial research
(E) industry's practice of restricting access to research findings

16. Both passages place in opposition the members of which one of the following pairs?

(A) commercially successful research and commercially unsuccessful research
(B) research methods and research results
(C) a marketable commodity and a public good
(D) a discovery and an invention
(E) scientific research and other types of inquiry

17. Both passages refer to which one of the following?

    (A)   theoretical frameworks
    (B)   venture capitalists
    (C)   physics and chemistry
    (D)   industrial biotechnology
    (E)   shareholders

18. It can be inferred from the passages that the authors believe that the increased constraint on access to scientific information and ideas arises from

    (A)   the enormous increase in the volume of scientific knowledge that is being generated
    (B)   the desire of individual researchers to receive credit for their discoveries
    (C)   the striving of commercial enterprises to gain a competitive advantage in the market
    (D)   moral reservations about the social impact of some scientific research
    (E)   a drastic reduction in government funding for university research

19. Which one of the following statements is most strongly supported by both passages?

    (A)   Many scientific researchers who previously worked in universities have begun to work in the biotechnology industry.
    (B)   Private biotechnology companies have invalidly patented the basic research findings of university researchers.
    (C)   Because of the nature of current scientific research, patent authorities no longer consider the distinction between discoveries and inventions to be clear-cut.
    (D)   In the past, scientists working in industry had free access to the results of basic research conducted in universities.
    (E)   Government-funded research in universities has traditionally been motivated by the goals of private industry.

8

Passage Analysis—December 2007 Passage #3

As with most Comparative Reading passages, we have two authors taking different tones in their discussions of the same general topic: the transformation that has taken place in the way research is developed and brought to market. The first author fears the ramifications of these changes, while the second is more accepting of the increasing role of industry in science's commoditization.

Your job as a reader is to first get a clear picture of passage A. Let's take a moment to analyze the four paragraphs of **Passage A**:

Paragraph One:

The author—who is apparently a university researcher, as indicated by the "we"—states that researchers have long been insulated from market pressures. The author now believes that this tradition has been threatened by the recent tendency to treat research findings like commodities that can be traded for cash. There is some clear tone in this initial paragraph: the author is a traditionalist who yearns for the old days, when universities worked toward the sharing of ideas, in service of the common good.

Paragraph Two:

In this paragraph, the author continues the argument for universities as the ideal developers of new ideas: cultivation of new ideas, the author argues, is uniquely suited to universities. The latter half of this paragraph introduces two of the reasons the author believes businesses are ill-suited to the cultivation and management of new ideas, namely that the market is impatient with experimentation, desiring quick returns on investment and few businesses are expert enough to suggest new theories when old ones are disproved.

Paragraph Three:

Here the author presents another problem—the entrepreneur's incentive to bury information that is potentially useful to the competition. We are also provided with the example of the biotech industry, which has developed new drugs and therapies, but at the cost of reduced sharing of research methods and results. Structurally, this paragraph explains the third of the three reasons businesses are unsuitable to managing new ideas.

Paragraph Four:

In the final paragraph the author reasserts the nostalgic attitude from the first paragraph, along with a concern for the future if new discoveries will lead researchers not to their colleagues, but rather to their lawyers and corporate sponsors.

8

Passage Analysis—December 2007 Passage #3

Overall, this author believes that universities provide a good system of idea development while allowing for freedom to experiment, share ideas, and develop new theories. The author argues that the old system is far preferable to the new system, which faces market pressures for quick returns and is emerging with the trend toward commoditization of research findings, and under which there are incentives to hoard information (as exemplified by the biotech industry). The author is concerned about the future if this trend continues. As a whole, the passage is reasonably interesting and the arguments made are not difficult to understand.

With a strong analysis of passage A in hand, move to the second passage and perform a similar analysis on **Passage B**:

Paragraph One:

This passage starts much like the first, with the author discussing the old days, when scientific discoveries were considered a public good. This perception was based on the fact that such discoveries were facilitated by government support of universities, and thus entitled to no one individual. However, the author separates himself from this view by using the phrase, "The argument for this view..."

Paragraph Two:

With the transitional term "however," the author denotes a change in the direction of the discussion: In contrast to the old days, the author asserts, the "information economy" of today is transforming public goods into market commodities. The author provides the example of the biotech industry, which can take information about cell structures and turn it into profit through drugs or medical screening technologies. In such situations, the question of legal rights to such underlying intellectual property becomes critical.

Paragraph Three:

In this paragraph, the author refers again to the old days, when the right to patent depended on the distinction between discoveries, which could not be patented, and inventions, which could. Today, the author asserts, the speed of the market in transforming discoveries to profitable products has led to a blurring of the previously existing legal and moral distinctions.

Paragraph Four:

In this final paragraph the author presents the viewpoint of "Industry," which argues that if it has sponsored a discovery, on its own or through a university, then it should get a return on this investment, by charging others or maintaining exclusive use of the discovery.

Passage Analysis—December 2007 Passage #3

Overall, this author believes that the new information economy is bringing inevitable change to our system of idea development. The old system was based on the government sponsorship of new scientific discovery; today, such discoveries can be so quickly converted to cash that the old legal and moral lines are becoming blurred. The author presents the argument of Industry: if a business sponsors a discovery, it is entitled to a return, through licensing or exclusive use.

This passage is a bit more difficult than passage A, but you can still break down the passage fairly easily. The third paragraph is probably the one paragraph that causes students to slow down and possibly re-read.

With a clear understanding of the two passages, the next step is to make a basic analysis of the passage relationships:

Passage Similarities:

Both authors believe that the world is changing, and both discuss the changes that are taking place as scientific research is treated increasingly like a commodity. Interestingly, both authors use the example of the biotechnology field in their discussions of developing research results for the market. You should expect this shared biotech example to appear at least once in the questions or answer choices.

Passage Differences:

While the topics of the passages are similar, the authors' tones are quite different. They agree that the world is changing, but where the first author yearns for the past, the second author is clearly more resigned to, and more comfortable with, these changes. The first author discusses the example of biotech in the context of detriment that can come from the incentives of the new system. The second author brings up the example in order to reflect the increasing importance of determinations of intellectual property rights. The first author closes passage A on a somber note, asserting concern for the future. The second author, in contrast, is more accepting of the changes, and closes passage B with a presentation of Industry's argument.

The two passages are each easy to read, and the tone of each author is clear. After taking a moment to consider the similarities and differences between the two passages, you should feel quite confident about moving on to the questions.

Question #15: GR, Must. The correct answer choice is (A)

The first question in the passage provides few specifics but requires you to find the answer choice that is referenced in only the second passage presented.

Answer choice (A): This is the correct answer choice. The author of passage A does not refer to the blurring of legal lines, but the author of passage B discusses this issue in lines 50-59.

Answer choice (B): Both authors bring up the general issue of the effect of the market on the exchange of scientific knowledge, so this answer choice is incorrect.

Answer choice (C): Both passages begin with discussions of the old days, when scientific discoveries were generally considered public goods (line 6 in passage A, and line 33 in passage B), so this response is incorrect.

Answer choice (D): New pharmaceuticals are brought up in different contexts by both authors (in passage A in line 25, and in passage B in line 45), so this cannot be the correct response to this Passage Exclusivity question.

Answer choice (E): The restriction of access to research findings is discussed in lines 20-21 in passage A, and on the last two lines in passage B.

Question #16: CR, Must. The correct answer choice is (C)

The remaining four questions all require you to consider the information in both passages. This particular question asks you to analyze pairs discussed in each passage and choose the group that is presented by both authors as being in opposition to one another over some topic.

Answer choice (A): Neither passage involves discussion of commercially successful versus unsuccessful research, so this answer choice is incorrect.

Answer choice (B): Both passages discuss research in terms of its status as a public good versus a commodity tradable for cash. Neither passage involves discussion of research methods versus research results.

Answer choice (C): This is the correct answer choice. Both authors discuss the old days in contrast with modern times, and the fact that research results are becoming less of a public good as they become more of a commodity. The author of passage A tells us that "the recent tendency to treat research findings as commodities…threatens this tradition…of research as a public good." Passage B provides, "what was previously seen as a public good is being transformed into a market commodity."

Note the Point at Issue nature of this question, as well, where the pair in the correct answer must hold opposing views on some issue or idea.

Answer choice (D): Only the author of passage B discusses the outdated distinction between an invention and a discovery. Passage A does not include this comparison, so this answer choice is incorrect.

Answer choice (E): The author of passage A discusses the difference between university-run and non-university-run research, but neither author discusses any distinction between scientific research and other types of inquiry.

Question #17: GR, Must. The correct answer choice is (D)

This open-ended question tests your ability to seek a reference common to each passage.

Answer choice (A): Passage A refers to theoretical frameworks on line 17, but passage B makes no reference to them, so this answer choice is incorrect.

Answer choice (B): Venture capitalists are referenced in passage A, in line 29, with regard to the author's concern for the future, but they are not discussed in passage B.

Answer choice (C): Neither author discusses physics and chemistry, so this answer choice is incorrect.

Answer choice (D): This is the correct answer choice. The biotech field is discussed in passage A to exemplify the reduced sharing of information (lines 21-25), and in passage B to reflect the importance of intellectual property given the speed of the market (lines 44-48).

Answer choice (E): Shareholders are discussed in passage A as part of the problem (line 13), but they are not discussed by the author of passage B, so this choice is incorrect.

Question #18: CR, Must. The correct answer choice is (C)

Attack this Concept Reference question by prephrasing the answer: both authors believe that this increased constraint comes from the pressures of the market.

Answer choice (A): Both authors credit (or blame) market processes, but neither discusses the increase of research volume, so this answer choice is incorrect.

Answer choice (B): Because neither passage discusses the desire of individual researchers for credit, this cannot be the correct response.

Passage Analysis—December 2007 Passage #3

Answer choice (C): This is the correct answer choice; it is the market's desire for advantage that has led to constraints on access to research findings. Passage A provides, beginning in line 18, "… entrepreneurs…can buy research and bury its products, hiding knowledge useful to society or to their competitors." The author of passage B presents Industry's argument, which is that if Industry has sponsored research, "…then it is entitled to seek a return…either by charging others…or by keeping it for its own exclusive use."

Answer choice (D): There is no discussion regarding moral reservations about research's social impact, so this answer choice is incorrect.

Answer choice (E): Neither author discusses a reduction in government funding for university research.

Question #19: GR, Must. The correct answer choice is (D)

This is likely the hardest question of the passage set. The question stem is a simple Must Be True, but finding the correct answer was challenging for many test takers.

Answer choice (A): Although both authors use the biotech industry to exemplify how research results are brought to today's market, neither makes any claim that researchers are leaving universities to work in biotech.

Answer choice (B): Neither author asserts any claims regarding invalid patents, so this answer choice is incorrect.

Answer choice (C): The blurring of the distinctions of legal lines is discussed only in passage B, and not attributable to the nature of current scientific research—these lines are getting blurred by the speed of the market and the large profits that are now accessible.

Answer choice (D): This is the correct answer choice. Both authors discuss the fact that in the old days, the results of scientific research were generally considered public goods, which implies free access.

Answer choice (E): There are no claims made in either one of the passages regarding the motivations of government-funded research, so this answer choice is incorrect.

8

Two Comparative Reading Practice Passages

The next four pages contain two actual LSAT Comparative Reading passage sets. After the two passages, a complete analysis of each passage and all of the corresponding questions is presented.

To most effectively benefit from this section, time yourself on the first passage set. Attempt to finish the passage and questions in 8 minutes and 45 seconds, but if you cannot, continue working until you complete all of the questions and then note your time. Then, read the entire explanation section for the first passage and look for opportunities to refine your approach. Afterwards, move to the second passage and repeat the process.

8

Practice Passage I—October 2008 Passage #2

The following passages concern a plant called purple loosestrife. Passage A is excerpted from a report issued by a prairie research council; passage B from a journal of sociology.

Passage A

Purple loosestrife *(Lythrum salicaria),* an aggressive and invasive perennial of Eurasian origin, arrived with settlers in eastern North America in the early 1800s and has spread across the continent's
(5) midlatitude wetlands. The impact of purple loosestrife on native vegetation has been disastrous, with more than 50 percent of the biomass of some wetland communities displaced. Monospecific blocks of this weed have maintained themselves for at least 20 years.
(10) Impacts on wildlife have not been well studied, but serious reductions in waterfowl and aquatic furbearer productivity have been observed. In addition, several endangered species of vertebrates are threatened with further degradation of their
(15) breeding habitats. Although purple loosestrife can invade relatively undisturbed habitats, the spread and dominance of this weed have been greatly accelerated in disturbed habitats. While digging out the plants can temporarily halt their spread, there has been little
(20) research on long-term purple loosestrife control. Glyphosate has been used successfully, but no measure of the impact of this herbicide on native plant communities has been made.

With the spread of purple loosestrife growing
(25) exponentially, some form of integrated control is needed. At present, coping with purple loosestrife hinges on early detection of the weed's arrival in areas, which allows local eradication to be carried out with minimum damage to the native plant community.

Passage B

(30) The war on purple loosestrife is apparently conducted on behalf of nature, an attempt to liberate the biotic community from the tyrannical influence of a life-destroying invasive weed. Indeed, purple loosestrife control is portrayed by its practitioners as
(35) an environmental initiative intended to save nature rather than control it. Accordingly, the purple loosestrife literature, scientific and otherwise, dutifully discusses the impacts of the weed on endangered species—and on threatened biodiversity
(40) more generally. Purple loosestrife is a pollution, according to the scientific community, and all of nature suffers under its pervasive influence.

Regardless of the perceived and actual ecological effects of the purple invader, it is apparent that
(45) popular pollution ideologies have been extended into the wetlands of North America. Consequently, the scientific effort to liberate nature from purple loosestrife has failed to decouple itself from its philosophical origin as an instrument to control nature
(50) to the satisfaction of human desires. Birds, particularly game birds and waterfowl, provide the bulk of the justification for loosestrife management. However, no bird species other than the canvasback has been identified in the literature as endangered by
(55) purple loosestrife. The impact of purple loosestrife on

furbearing mammals is discussed at great length, though none of the species highlighted (muskrat, mink) can be considered threatened in North America. What is threatened by purple loosestrife is the
(60) economics of exploiting such preferred species and the millions of dollars that will be lost to the economies of the United States and Canada from reduced hunting, trapping, and recreation revenues due to a decline in the production of the wetland
(65) resource.

7. Both passages explicitly mention which one of the following?

   (A) furbearing animals
   (B) glyphosate
   (C) the threat purple loosestrife poses to economies
   (D) popular pollution ideologies
   (E) literature on purple loosestrife control

8. Each of the passages contains information sufficient to answer which one of the following questions?

   (A) Approximately how long ago did purple loosestrife arrive in North America?
   (B) Is there much literature discussing the potential benefit that hunters might derive from purple loosestrife management?
   (C) What is an issue regarding purple loosestrife management on which both hunters and farmers agree?
   (D) Is the canvasback threatened with extinction due to the spread of purple loosestrife?
   (E) What is a type of terrain that is affected in at least some parts of North America by the presence of purple loosestrife?

9. It can be inferred that the authors would be most likely to disagree about which one of the following?

   (A) Purple loosestrife spreads more quickly in disturbed habitats than in undisturbed habitats.
   (B) The threat posed by purple loosestrife to local aquatic furbearer populations is serious.
   (C) Most people who advocate that eradication measures be taken to control purple loosestrife are not genuine in their concern for the environment.
   (D) The size of the biomass that has been displaced by purple loosestrife is larger than is generally thought.
   (E) Measures should be taken to prevent other non-native plant species from invading North America.

8

10. Which one of the following most accurately describes the attitude expressed by the author of passage B toward the overall argument represented by passage A?

(A) enthusiastic agreement
(B) cautious agreement
(C) pure neutrality
(D) general ambivalence
(E) pointed skepticism

11. It can be inferred that both authors would be most likely to agree with which one of the following statements regarding purple loosestrife?

(A) As it increases in North America, some wildlife populations tend to decrease.
(B) Its establishment in North America has had a disastrous effect on native North American wetland vegetation in certain regions.
(C) It is very difficult to control effectively with herbicides.
(D) Its introduction into North America was a great ecological blunder.
(E) When it is eliminated from a given area, it tends to return to that area fairly quickly.

12. Which one of the following is true about the relationship between the two passages?

(A) Passage A presents evidence that directly counters claims made in passage B.
(B) Passage B assumes what passage A explicitly argues for.
(C) Passage B displays an awareness of the arguments touched on in passage A, but not vice versa.
(D) Passage B advocates a policy that passage A rejects.
(E) Passage A downplays the seriousness of claims made in passage B.

13. Which one of the following, if true, would cast doubt on the argument in passage B but bolster the argument in passage A?

(A) Localized population reduction is often a precursor to widespread endangerment of a species.
(B) Purple loosestrife was barely noticed in North America before the advent of suburban sprawl in the 1950s.
(C) The amount by which overall hunting, trapping, and recreation revenues would be reduced as a result of the extinction of one or more species threatened by purple loosestrife represents a significant portion of those revenues.
(D) Some environmentalists who advocate taking measures to eradicate purple loosestrife view such measures as a means of controlling nature.
(E) Purple loosestrife has never become a problem in its native habitat, even though no effort has been made to eradicate it there.

8

Practice Passage II—September 2007 Passage #2

Passage A

Readers, like writers, need to search for answers.
Part of the joy of reading is in being surprised, but
academic historians leave little to the imagination. The
perniciousness of the historiographic approach became
(5) fully evident to me when I started teaching. Historians
require undergraduates to read scholarly monographs
that sap the vitality of history; they visit on students
what was visited on them in graduate school. They
assign books with formulaic arguments that transform
(10) history into an abstract debate that would have been
unfathomable to those who lived in the past. Aimed
so squarely at the head, such books cannot stimulate
students who yearn to connect to history emotionally
as well as intellectually.

(15) In an effort to address this problem, some historians
have begun to rediscover stories. It has even become
something of a fad within the profession. This year, the
American Historical Association chose as the theme
for its annual conference some putative connection to
(20) storytelling: "Practices of Historical Narrative."
Predictably, historians responded by adding the word
"narrative" to their titles and presenting papers at
sessions on "Oral History and the Narrative of Class
Identity," and "Meaning and Time: The Problem of
(25) Historical Narrative." But it was still historiography,
intended only for other academics. At meetings of
historians, we still encounter very few historians telling
stories or moving audiences to smiles, chills, or tears.

Passage B

Writing is at the heart of the lawyer's craft, and so,
(30) like it or not, we who teach the law inevitably teach
aspiring lawyers how lawyers write. We do this in a few
stand-alone courses and, to a greater extent, through the
constraints that we impose on their writing throughout
the curriculum. Legal writing, because of the purposes
(35) it serves, is necessarily ruled by linear logic, creating a
path without diversions, surprises, or reversals.
Conformity is a virtue, creativity suspect, humor
forbidden, and voice mute.

Lawyers write as they see other lawyers write, and,
(40) influenced by education, profession, economic
constraints, and perceived self-interest, they too often
write badly. Perhaps the currently fashionable call for
attention to narrative in legal education could have an
effect on this. It is not yet exactly clear what role
(45) narrative should play in the law, but it is nonetheless
true that every case has at its heart a story—of real
events and people, of concerns, misfortunes, conflicts,
feelings. But because legal analysis strips the human
narrative content from the abstract, canonical legal
(50) form of the case, law students learn to act as if there is
no such story.

It may well turn out that some of the terminology
and public rhetoric of this potentially subversive
movement toward attention to narrative will find its

(55) way into the law curriculum, but without producing
corresponding changes in how legal writing is actually
taught or in how our future colleagues will write. Still,
even mere awareness of the value of narrative could
perhaps serve as an important corrective.

7. Which one of the following does each of the passages
display?

(A) a concern with the question of what teaching
methods are most effective in developing
writing skills

(B) a concern with how a particular discipline tends
to represent points of view it does not typically
deal with

(C) a conviction that writing in specialized
professional disciplines cannot be creatively
crafted

(D) a belief that the writing in a particular profession
could benefit from more attention to storytelling

(E) a desire to see writing in a particular field purged
of elements from other disciplines

8. The passages most strongly support which one of
the following inferences regarding the authors'
relationships to the professions they discuss?

(A) Neither author is an active member of the
profession that he or she discusses.

(B) Each author is an active member of the
profession he or she discusses.

(C) The author of passage A is a member of the
profession discussed in that passage, but the
author of passage B is not a member of either of
the professions discussed in the passages.

(D) Both authors are active members of the
profession discussed in passage B.

(E) The author of passage B, but not the author of
passage A, is an active member of both of the
professions discussed in the passages.

9. Which one of the following does each passage indicate is typical of writing in the respective professions discussed in the passages?

    (A)   abstraction
    (B)   hyperbole
    (C)   subversion
    (D)   narrative
    (E)   imagination

10. In which one of the following ways are the passages NOT parallel?

    (A)   Passage A presents and rejects arguments for an opposing position, whereas passage B does not.
    (B)   Passage A makes evaluative claims, whereas passage B does not.
    (C)   Passage A describes specific examples of a phenomenon it criticizes, whereas passage B does not.
    (D)   Passage B offers criticism, whereas passage A does not.
    (E)   Passage B outlines a theory, whereas passage A does not.

11. The phrase "scholarly monographs that sap the vitality of history" in passage A (lines 6-7) plays a role in that passage's overall argument that is most analogous to the role played in passage B by which one of the following phrases?

    (A)   "Writing is at the heart of the lawyer's craft" (line 29)
    (B)   "Conformity is a virtue, creativity suspect, humor forbidden, and voice mute" (lines 37-38)
    (C)   "Lawyers write as they see other lawyers write" (line 39)
    (D)   "every case has at its heart a story" (line 46)
    (E)   "Still, even mere awareness of the value of narrative could perhaps serve as an important corrective" (lines 57-59)

12. Suppose that a lawyer is writing a legal document describing the facts that are at issue in a case. The author of passage B would be most likely to expect which one of the following to be true of the document?

    (A)   It will be poorly written because the lawyer who is writing it was not given explicit advice by law professors on how lawyers should write.
    (B)   It will be crafted to function like a piece of fiction in its description of the characters and motivations of the people involved in the case.
    (C)   It will be a concise, well-crafted piece of writing that summarizes most, if not all, of the facts that are important in the case.
    (D)   It will not genuinely convey the human dimension of the case, regardless of how accurate the document may be in its details.
    (E)   It will neglect to make appropriate connections between the details of the case and relevant legal doctrines.

8

Passage A

Paragraph One:

This paragraph opens with a description of the passage's central focus: purple loosestrife, a Eurasian plant brought to eastern North America in the early 1800s. After a brief introduction, the author's attitude toward the spread of the perennial plant becomes clear, calling it "disastrous," discussing the plants demonstrated ability to sustain itself for as long as 20 years, and the resulting displacement (up to 50%) of some wetlands communities. Although no specific numbers are discussed in this context, "serious reductions in waterfowl and aquatic furbearer productivity have been observed," and some vertebrate endangered species are threatened by the effects on their habitat. The author closes the paragraph with the presentation (and qualification) of two approaches to the problem:

    a. Digging out the plants can temporarily halt the spread, but little is known about long-term control.

    b. Glyphosate has had success, but nothing is known about its impact on native plant communities.

Paragraph Two:

The author uses the brief final paragraph to conclude that the plant needs to be controlled. In the last sentence, the author asserts that the only way to cope with the weed is through early detection and local eradication with minimal damage to the native plant populations.

Passage Structure:

    Paragraph 1:   Introduce the purple loosestrife and characterize the plant as disastrous, discussing its ability to endure and displace local plant populations. Present two approaches to the problem, and the respective limitations of each.

    Paragraph 2:   Conclude that an integrative solution needs to be found, and present early eradication as the only way to cope with the problem.

Passage B

Paragraph One:

The introduction to this passage presents a rare instance of something approaching sarcasm from an LSAT author, who chooses very strong language from the outset ("tyrannical, life-destroying") to describe the purple loosestrife. While those who seek to control the weed say that they do so to save nature, the author tells us, perhaps they seek to control it. The author portrays the scientific community as "dutifully" focusing on possible threats to endangered species and biodiversity, closing the paragraph with another sarcastic exaggeration: "Purple loosestrife is a pollution…and all of nature suffers under its pervasive influence."

Paragraph Two:

The author opens the second paragraph implicitly questioning the seriousness of the effects of the "purple invader" (another shot at those who claim disaster). The "popular pollution ideologies" have spread to North American wetlands, and the author asserts the philosophical origin to be the desire to control nature. Concern for birds, particularly game and waterfowl, is characterized as "justification," and the author points out that only the canvasback is confirmed by literature to be endangered by the purple loosestrife. Although neither muskrat nor mink are endangered in North America, the effects on furbearing mammals are highlighted in literature, because of what the author believes to be the primary motivation behind the loosestrife concern to the U.S. and Canada: the millions of dollars in revenues that could be lost as a result of any decline in the furbearing population.

Passage Structure:

Paragraph 1: Present sarcastically exaggerated characterization of the purple loosestrife, suggest the concern about the plant as the intent to control nature.

Paragraph 2: Continue with the sarcastic characterizations of the "purple invader," and again suggest the intended desire to control nature. Assert the concern for birds to be merely a "justification," and economic considerations about furbearing mammals to be the true motivation behind efforts to control purple loosestrife.

8

Passage A Summary:

Purple loosestrife has spread across North America since it was brought to the continent in the early 1800s. The plant can sustain itself for twenty years or more, and can displace significant wetlands populations. Digging can work in the short term, but perhaps not for long-term control, and Glyphosate works but little is known about the herbicide's effects on other plants. While integrated control of the destructive year-round weed is needed, the only way to cope at present is through early detection and eradication to minimize collateral damage.

Passage B Summary:

The war on purple loosestrife is professed by its practitioners to be waged on behalf of nature, but this may be merely a justification, considering the fact that only one bird is documented to be at risk because of the purple weed. Although fur-bearing mammal populations are not currently threatened in North America, the concern may likely be based on prospective economic detriment to the U.S. and Canada.

Passage Similarities:

As is common among LSAT Comparative Reading passage sets, the two authors focus on the same topic, but from very different perspectives. Both passages focus on the purple loosestrife and some of the ramifications of the weed's spread, and both authors discuss the plant's ability to possibly reduce certain bird and furbearing mammal populations.

Passage Differences:

Both passages focus on the purple loosestrife and the effects of the weed's spread, but the authors' attitudes are diametrically opposed. The first author is clearly quite concerned about the environmental ramifications of the weed's displacement of some wetlands, while the second author sees such concerns as alarmist, and questions the real motivations of those who claim to be fighting for the environment. While the first author discusses various approaches to loosestrife control, the second author asserts that such approaches are efforts to control nature, and suggests that those fighting for loosestrife control may really be more concerned with financial considerations of the potential detriments to certain very profitable species.

Question #7: GR, Must. The correct answer choice is (A)

From the discussion of Passage Similarities above, we can prephrase some possible answers to this Must Be True question: both passages discuss the purple loosestrife and its spread, of course, and both authors point out detriment to some bird and furbearing mammal populations.

Answer choice (A): This is the correct answer choice. The author of passage A discusses aquatic furbearers (lines 11-12) and the author of passage B considers the threat to furbearing mammals as a likely cause for all of the concern about the weed. This discussion begins on line 55.

Answer choice (B): Only the author of passage A mentions this herbicide (line 21), or, for that matter, any particular approach to the control of the loosestrife.

Answer choice (C): The author of passage B presents this as a likely cause for the supposedly environmental concerns, but the economic threat is not referenced at all in passage A.

Answer choice (D): Only the author of passage B references these "pollution ideologies," on line 45.

Answer choice (E): While the author of passage A would likely be interested in such literature, it is only referenced in passage B (line 54).

Question #8: GR, Must. The correct answer choice is (E)

The answer to this question is difficult to prephrase, but must pass the Fact Test; both passages will provide sufficient information to answer only one of the questions presented in the answer choices.

Answer choice (A): The author of passage B does not discuss the history of the weed in North America, although the author of passage A answers this question on line 4.

Answer choice (B): Neither author discusses such literature or its abundance.

Answer choice (C): While we can infer that these two groups might agree on the need for control based on passage B, they are not mentioned by the author of passage A.

Answer choice (D): Although the author of passage A is clearly more concerned about the environmental impact of the spread of purple loosestrife, it is the author of passage B who mentions the canvasback, intended to point out the existence of only one known threat associated with the weed (according to the referenced literature).

Answer choice (E): This is the correct answer choice. Both authors point to the wetlands as affected terrain (lines 5 and 46).

8

Question #9: GR, Point at Issue. The correct answer choice is (B)

Based on the prior discussion of Passage Differences, we can create a general prephrase to answer this Point at Issue question: The main difference between the attitudes of the two authors is that while the first believes the weed to pose a serious environmental threat to North American wetlands, the author of passage B believes the threat to be overblown and the concern to be based on financial considerations.

Answer choice (A): While the author of passage A would agree with this statement (lines 15-18), the second author makes no reference to this comparison (additionally, there is no reason to infer that there would be any disagreement on this issue).

Answer choice (B): This is the correct answer choice, as prephrased above. The author of passage A believes the threat to be serious, and the author of passage B questions the seriousness of the environmental impact, pointing out that the furbearing mammals in question are not threatened in North America.

Answer choice (C): The author of passage A would most likely disagree with this bold claim, but we cannot assess the attitude of the second author regarding this group's sincerity; it is possible that even those primarily concerned with financial impact might still have concern for the environment.

Answer choice (D): This belief is not presented or alluded to in either passage.

Answer choice (E): Like incorrect answer choice (D) above, this is an issue that is not referenced by either author, so this can't be the right answer to this Point at Issue question.

8

Practice Passage I—October 2008 Passage #2 Answer Key

Question #10: GR, Must, AP. The correct answer choice is (E)

Like question #9 above, we can confidently attack this question armed with an understanding of the different attitudes of the two authors. The author of passage B has a cynical attitude reflected through use of exaggeration of the problem, and a questioning of the motivations of those who fight to control the loosestrife—people like the author of passage A.

Answer choice (A): This answer choice is clearly incorrect, since there is no such agreement relayed by the author of passage B.

Answer choice (B): Like incorrect answer choice (A) above, this choice includes the word "agreement," ruling it out as a contender.

Answer choice (C): The author of passage B is certainly not neutral, but rather outspoken in questioning the motives behind the efforts to control the loosestrife.

Answer choice (D): The author of passage B is neither purposely neutral (as suggested by answer choice (C) above), nor ambivalent—the second author displays a strongly skeptical attitude.

Answer choice (E): This is the correct answer choice, as prephrased above: the author of passage B is clearly skeptical about the seriousness of the purple loosestrife spread as characterized in passage A.

Question #11: CR, Point of Agreement, AP. The correct answer choice is (A)

Since there is not much agreement apparent between the two authors, we can prephrase the answer to this Point of Agreement question as well. They agree that the purple loosestrife can be detrimental to other populations, but they disagree as to the seriousness of ramifications and the basis of concern.

Answer choice (A): This is the correct answer choice. This is a major concern for the author of passage A, and even the author of passage B references some impact on certain species.

Answer choice (B): The author of passage A characterizes the weed's spread as disastrous, but the author of passage B would question this characterization.

Answer choice (C): Only the author of passage A even mentions herbicides, and merely points out that there is limited information regarding a certain herbicide's impact on other plants.

Answer choice (D): The first author believes the weed to be a major problem and would thus likely agree with this statement, but the second author would question whether bringing the plant to the continent was a "great ecological blunder."

Answer choice (E): Neither author references the weed's reaction to local elimination.

Practice Passage I—October 2008 Passage #2 Answer Key

Question #12: GR, Must. The correct answer choice is (C)

Although a precise prephrased answer to this general Passage Relationship question would be difficult to produce, the discussions of the passage similarities and differences above should be sufficient to locate the correct answer choice.

Answer choice (A): There is no such direct counter, and the authors don't necessarily disagree about the evidence presented—they disagree about the ramifications of noted effects.

Answer choice (B): Since the two authors would broadly disagree about the seriousness of the discussed phenomenon, this incorrect answer choice should be quickly eliminated.

Answer choice (C): This is the correct answer choice. The author of passage B specifically references and questions the professed concerns of environmentalists like the first author, but the first author makes no reference to the claim that financial considerations drive the concern about the loosestrife.

Answer choice (D): The author of passage B simply questions the seriousness of the purple loosestrife spread, advocating no specific policy.

Answer choice (E): This incorrect answer choice provides an Opposite Answer: it is actually passage B which downplays the seriousness of claims made in passage A.

Question #13: GR, Weaken/Strengthen. The correct answer choice is (A)

This Global Reference question presents a rare hybrid of a Weaken and Strengthen question. The correct answer choice will strengthen the conclusions in passage A (and the claim that the problem is serious) and weaken the dismissive assertions made in passage B.

Answer choice (A): This is the correct answer choice. If this is true, then even those species that are not currently threatened might eventually be endangered.

Answer choice (B): This is an Opposite Answer, supporting the second author's suggestion that financial considerations and the human desire to control nature have led to concern about the purple loosestrife.

Answer choice (C): Like answer choice (B) above, this choice would strengthen the argument in passage B, making concerns about the loosestrife more likely attributable to such effects.

Answer choice (D): This strengthens assertions found in passage B, not passage A.

Answer choice (E): This is another Opposite Answer which would certainly not strengthen the arguments made in passage A, but would bolster passage B's general assertion that the weed should not be the cause of serious concern.

Practice Passage II—September 2007 Passage #2 Answer Key

Passage A

Paragraph One:

The author begins this passage by pointing out that readers need to search for and find answers, but that there is little surprise in traditional academic history. Interestingly, this passage is written in first person (denoted with the use of "I", "we," etc.), and the author is apparently a teacher (or has taught at some point). The author's viewpoint is critical of the traditional, "historiographic" approach to teaching history, which requires students to read lifeless, formulaic, scholarly works that are aimed solely at the intellect, facilitating little emotional connection with the reader. In the course of explaining his or her viewpoint, the author also indicates that historians are the ones requiring students to read such lifeless texts, visiting upon the students that which was visited upon them.

Paragraph Two:

Here the author discusses the views of "some historians" (line 15). These historians have begun to rediscover storytelling as a method of teaching history. But the author criticizes these historians, giving the example of the American Historical Association conference, where the inclusion of a narrative component in the teaching of history gave evidence of a "fad" within the profession. Although the titles of several papers presented at the AHA conference did pay lip service to this idea, the author points out that they still exemplify historiography, intended solely for academics. The author's final conclusion is that historians still rarely elicit any real emotion in response to their accounts of history.

Passage A Summary:

The traditional, formulaic methods of teaching history fail to relay emotion, and academic required readings do not generally elicit any significant emotional connection with readers. One historical society included a narrative component in a recent convention, but the author believes that, with or without the word "narrative" in the title, much of this "historiography" is intended for academia, and still generally fails to bring any true emotional component to these accounts.

Passage Structure:

Paragraph 1:   Discuss problems with the traditional teaching approach (emotionless, scholarly history), identify author as a teacher through use of first person. Establish "historians" as a group with a different, inferior view of teaching history.

Paragraph 2:   Discuss the view of "some historians," who attempt to use a narrative component as one possible solution. Examine recent attempts to include this component, conclude that attaching the title "narrative"—without relaying to an audience any real emotion—does not solve the problems associated with the historiographic approach.

8

Passage B

Paragraph One:

In this introductory paragraph, the author, who clearly teaches law ("we who teach the law" line 30), discusses the standard approach to legal writing instruction, through specific courses as well as general writing constraints imposed throughout law school. Legal writing, we are told, is traditionally done predictably, in linear fashion, avoiding surprise, humor, and too much creativity.

Paragraph Two:

Because traditional legal writing style is perpetuated by lawyers, the author asserts that attorneys often write poorly. One factor that might influence writing quality is the attention to narrative on the part of legal educators. Although unsure of what role this might play in the law, the author points out that with traditional legal analysis, students tend to disregard the narrative content when considering the facts of a given case.

Paragraph Three:

In the final paragraph the author asserts that there might be some positive outcome from an increased attention to narrative (the author refers to such a movement as "potentially subversive," in order to underscore the very traditional nature of legal writing and associated aversion to change). While terminology associated with a greater focus on the narrative may at some point be reflected in the law curriculum, though, the author believes that this will not necessarily bring changes to the way legal writing is produced or taught. The author concludes that even a simple awareness of the value of the narrative, however, might lead to improvement.

Passage B Summary:

Throughout the law school curriculum students are taught to write without creativity or surprise. Lawyers do the same, and according to the author this often means poor writing. Perhaps legal educators could improve on this situation through greater attention to narrative (as traditional legal analysis tends to downplay narrative content). While this will not necessarily improve legal writing or how it is taught, the author concludes that even an appreciation for the value of a narrative component could help the situation.

Practice Passage II—September 2007 Passage #2 Answer Key

Passage Structure:

Paragraph 1:   Identify author as a teacher of law through use of first person perspective. Specify problems with traditional methods of teaching legal writing.

Paragraph 2:   Assert that the same problems are perpetuated by attorneys, many of whom are bad writers as a result. Introduce the notion of a greater focus on the narrative in legal education.

Paragraph 3:   Conclude that more attention to the narrative component might be somewhat helpful, even if it does not change the manner in which legal writing is taught.

Passage Similarities:

Both passages are written in the first person, and both authors are teachers. Both authors believe that their respective fields might be improved with a greater attention to narrative content, and neither one appears completely satisfied with the current level of such focus.

Passage Differences:

The author of passage A has apparently taught history at some point, and the author of passage B appears to be a legal professor. While the author in passage A seems completely unimpressed by the degree to which historians have actually applied the idea, the tone of passage B's author is more optimistic, as manifest in the conclusion that simple awareness can be somewhat curative.

8

Question #7: GR, Must. The correct answer choice is (D)

As with all Must Be True questions, the right answer to this question must pass the Fact Test.

Answer choice (A): The passages are not primarily discussions of what teaching methods would be most effective; rather, the authors discuss the possible value of introducing more narrative to their respective fields.

Answer choice (B): The authors do not show a concern about the representation of unfamiliar points of view—their concern is with the use of narrative (or lack thereof).

Answer choice (C): The word that makes this answer incorrect is cannot. The authors do not have a conviction that writing cannot be creatively crafted; they both believe that their respective discipline's writings might be improved with more attention to narrative.

Practice Passage II—September 2007 Passage #2 Answer Key

Answer choice (D): This is the correct answer choice. Both authors manifest the belief that their field's writing might derive benefit from increased attention to storytelling.

Answer choice (E): Neither author asserts the need for purging of either discipline, so this answer choice is incorrect.

Question #8: GR, Must. The correct answer choice is (B)

We can certainly prephrase the answer to this question. The authors of both passages appear to belong to the professions that they discuss.

Answer choice (A): Since this is exactly opposite our prephrase, this answer choice is incorrect.

Answer choice (B): This is the correct answer choice, and restates our prephrase; the first author is a history teacher, and the second author is involved in legal education.

Answer choice (C): Both authors are members of the professions they discuss.

Answer choice (D): The profession discussed in passage B is legal education, and since the author of passage A only discusses history, this answer choice is incorrect.

Answer choice (E): Again, each author is a member of the field discussed.

Question #9: CR, Must. The correct answer choice is (A)

Answer choice (A): This is the correct answer choice. Both authors mention the degree of abstraction in their fields. The author of passage A discusses the transformation of history into an abstract debate (line 10), and the author of passage B asserts that "legal analysis strips the human narrative content from the abstract, canonical legal form of the case" (lines 48-50).

Answer choice (B): Neither author discusses hyperbole (also known as extreme exaggeration).

Answer choice (C): The author of passage B refers to the narrative movement as "potentially subversive" (line 53) but does not assert that subversion is typical of legal writing. Additionally, subversion is not mentioned in passage A at all.

Answer choice (D): Both authors believe that more attention to narrative might provide benefit, but neither asserts that narrative is typical of the writing in their respective fields.

Answer choice (E): Neither author asserts that imagination is typical of the writing in either field, so this answer choice is incorrect on both counts.

Practice Passage II—September 2007 Passage #2 Answer Key

Question #10: GR, Must. The correct answer choice is (C)

This is an interesting question stem, because despite the presence of the words *NOT* and *parallel*, this is not a ParallelX question. Instead, this is actually a Must Be True question, since the correct answer choice must accurately describe how the passages *fail* to parallel one another.

Answer choice (A): Passage A does not present and reject an argument; rather, the author discusses recent focus on the narrative, but is somewhat unimpressed by the outcome.

Answer choice (B): Both passages provide evaluative claims, as both authors believe that their professions might benefit from the introduction of more narrative, so this answer choice is incorrect.

Answer choice (C): This is the correct answer choice. The author of passage A discusses several history presentations with the word "narrative" in their titles, but criticizes the lack of emotion in historiography regardless. As this answer choice correctly reflects, the author of passage B does not provide specific examples.

Answer choice (D): Both passages provide criticism, so this answer choice is incorrect.

Answer choice (E): Neither passage really outlines a theory—both just believe that more focus on narrative could bring benefits (if we consider this a theory, then this theory is offered in both passages—either way, this answer choice is incorrect.)

Question #11: SR, Must, P. The correct answer choice is (B)

The referenced quote is the author's assertion that historiography is dry and unemotional. If we are looking for a quote that plays the same role in passage B, we should seek the answer choice that presents legal writing in a similar light.

Answer choice (A): This quote does not present legal writing as dry or unemotional, so this answer choice is incorrect.

Answer choice (B): This is the correct answer choice. With this quote, it is clear that the author believes legal writing to be generally conformist and uninteresting, intended to lack humor, creativity, and individuality.

Answer choice (C): This quote deals with a facet of the self-perpetuating nature of legal writing style, but does not allude to the lack of creative or interesting presentation.

Answer choice (D): Unlike the referenced quote in the question stem, which criticized historiography as dry, the quote in this answer choice focuses on the other side—the emotional part of every legal case, so this answer choice is incorrect.

Practice Passage II—September 2007 Passage #2 Answer Key

Answer choice (E): This quote is the hopeful closing note of the second passage; it does not play a role that is anything like that of the quote in question, so this answer choice is incorrect.

Question #12: CR, Must, AP. The correct answer choice is (D)

Author B's perspective on most legal writing is quoted in the preceding question: "Conformity is a virtue, creativity suspect, humor forbidden, and voice mute."

Answer choice (A): The author of passage B does not claim that legal writing lacks explicit advice, or that all legal writing is poorly written—only that it will tend to lack creativity or individuality.

Answer choice (B): The author does not believe that such legal documents are generally crafted like a piece of fiction; in fact, the author asserts that legal writing could use more of a narrative component, so this answer choice is incorrect.

Answer choice (C): The author does not make the claim that legal writing is always concise or well-crafted, so this answer choice is not accurate.

Answer choice (D): This is the correct answer choice. The author believes that legal writing as it stands is likely to lack depth and emotion, although it may present accurate details.

Answer choice (E): The author does not make the argument that all legal writing fails to tie relevant legal doctrine to case facts, so this answer choice is incorrect.

8

Chapter Nine: Common Passage Themes

Chapter Nine: Common Passage Themes

Recurrent Themes

Our discussion of recurrent themes is partially built around passage topics. As discussed previously in this book, three passage types in particular—Humanities passages (often featuring Diversity), Science passages, and Law-Related passages—appear on virtually every LSAT, so a familiarity with these types is beneficial. And within these types there are certain themes that are used again and again, which we will review momentarily.

While we will examine the three most common topics of the LSAT Reading Comprehension section, we will not examine *every* topic that appears. Humanities passages, for example, appear quite frequently, but other than our discussion of diversity and law we will not examine Humanities passages as a separate entity. Why not? Because Humanities passages *as a whole* have no definable structure or theme. That is, there is no constant, predictable element that can be drawn from these passages and used to your advantage. In earlier chapters we have already discussed the tools of analysis that allow you to attack any Humanities passage, and there is no further information you need to be successful. This stands in sharp contrast to passages that feature diversity (and to a lesser degree science and law). In those passages, not only must you use the tools you already have, but you also need to further understand the aims of the test makers and the unique nature of how these particular passages function.

Diversity Passages

In Chapter Two it was noted that almost every LSAT contains a Humanities passage that features diversity elements. Diversity passages, as these are called, reflect a particularly interesting feature of the LSAT, and understanding how and why they appear can give you a significant advantage during the test. Before proceeding, however, we offer a disclaimer: please understand that the following discussion stems from an analysis of existing LSAT passages, and the views presented herein are those of the test makers or based on history. We back our conclusions using facts, and we are not making a value judgment about the existence of these passages. The truth is that these passages do exist, and understanding their nature helps you perform better on the LSAT.

It's also worth noting at the outset that LSATs of recent years are showing a tendency towards more subtle, nuanced presentations of the concepts discussed in this chapter, where, for instance, instead of a passage being *strict* Diversity and exhibiting the consistent, rigid form readers have come to expect, authors have softened their approach of late and may take a less absolute or predetermined stance on particular subjects. This in no way undermines the value of the ideas that follow; it simply suggests that you must be an attentive, considerate reader, and not rely on topic alone.

Diversity passages raise a sensitive topic. Prior to engaging in this discussion, we wish to reaffirm that we are not making a judgment about these passages or the motives of those who create them; we're just reporting the facts. To be a good test taker, you must have predictive knowledge of the actions of the test makers.

9

How Does Test Bias Play a Role in Test Content?

Test bias occurs when the questions innately favor one group over another, and the history of standardized testing is filled with accounts of biased questions and attitudes. In the early days of testing in the U.S., standardized tests were created by groups of predominantly Caucasian middle- to upper-class males, and questions from that era tend to represent their positions and values. Consider the following famous verbal analogy from the early days of the SAT:

RUNNER : MARATHON

(A) envoy : embassy
(B) martyr : massacre
(C) oarsman : regatta
(D) referee : tournament
(E) horse : stable

To learn more about the history of standardized testing in the U.S., we recommend Nicholas Lemann's fascinating book, "The Big Test."

The correct answer to this question is (C). The problem, as was later revealed by statistical analysis, was that various groups performed quite differently on this question (as opposed to a uniform distribution of performance, which is the goal of an unbiased test). Rowing, a sport popular with the wealthy, was a sport unknown to large segments of the testing population. Students from urban areas or students who grew up on the Western plains, for example, were unlikely to be familiar with the sport or its terminology.

Closer to home, the LSAT also saw test content changes based on bias concerns. One obvious example was the removal of Family Tree games from the Logic Games section. Family Tree games revolved around the relationships stemming from nuclear family structures (the traditional mother and father, brothers and sisters, aunts and uncles dynamic), and in today's society the nuclear family is not as prevalent, or even familiar, as it once was.

The LSAT is made in the U.S., and used by U.S., Canadian, and some Australian law schools for admission purposes. Thus, although many non-North American students take the LSAT, the results of the test are used primarily for admission to North American law schools.

Over time, as such biases were revealed and understood to be harmful to testing populations that were not from certain backgrounds, the test content began to change because the test makers recognized that particular questions were not a fair test of knowledge or abilities. As test makers came to recognize that the values of the test writer affected the scoring outcomes of various groups, they began to adjust the presentation and even the allowable content of the exam: in the quest to write questions that avoided even the perception of bias based on racial, cultural, and gender differences, certain topics became off-limits. For example, there are no questions about Christmas on a standardized test because not everyone celebrates Christmas (or Chanukah, or Kwanzaa, etc.). And, just as the makers of the exam do not want to create cultural confusion during the

9

exam, they also want to avoid emotional upset. Thus, the test makers avoid emotional or controversial topics such as abortion or torture. There are other proscriptions that the test makers follow, but the point is that they are aware of the history of bias in most exams, and the language you see on the LSAT is carefully chosen in an effort to remove bias.

So, in creating a widely-administered exam, the test makers seek to present an even, neutral, unbiased environment. However, the *history* of bias within testing remains, and in order to overcome accusations of possible bias against, or favoritism towards, any particular group, the test makers looked to expand the range of cultural, ethnic, and gender based topics on the exam. This is, of course, completely reasonable. The U.S. and Canada are societies that are comprised of a large number of different cultures, and individuals from many different social and ethnic backgrounds. Presenting a test that addresses and includes many different groups is not only understandable, it is desirable.

Take a moment to place yourself in the shoes of a test maker. On the one hand, you desire to create a fair and unbiased test that disadvantages no person or group. On the other hand, the history of standardized testing is fraught with accusations of the bias you dread. When choosing how to represent certain groups, then, would you not take care to present traditionally underrepresented groups in a generally favorable light? By doing so, you run no risk of biasing the test while also inoculating it against claims of prejudice. Without making a judgment about the value of taking this approach, an examination of the last 25-plus years of LSAT content shows undeniably that this is precisely the route taken by the test makers. The LSAT Reading Comprehension section tends to include at least one passage about a group (or member of a group) that has been traditionally viewed as underrepresented. As these passages contribute to the diversity of the test, we term them Diversity passages. As mentioned before, the mere presence of these passages is not surprising. What is most interesting about these passages, as we will see in a moment, is the striking consistency (and thus predictability) in the attitude that the test makers take towards different groups.

Before analyzing specific passages, we should take a moment to define underrepresented and overrepresented groups. For LSAT purposes, traditionally underrepresented groups typically focus on race and gender. Thus, there are a number of passages about African Americans, Women, Hispanic Americans, Asian Americans, and indigenous groups such as Native Americans and Native Canadians. Religious minorities and sexual orientation minorities, on the other hand, tend to be avoided because religion and sex are sensitive topics, and tests like the LSAT tend to avoid such topics except in the most general terms. The sole overrepresented group addressed on the LSAT is that of Caucasian males, typically those versed in Western thought.

The presence of diversity within standardized tests is not an accident. As noted in an ETS publication about testing guidelines, there are strict rules about test content:

"The ideal racial and ethnic balance in a test would reflect the diversity of the test-taking population. It is not feasible, however, to show members of every group in the test-taking population in every test. As a reasonable compromise, skills tests made for use primarily in the United States, strive to have about 20 percent of the items that mention people represent African American people, Asian American people, Latino American people, and/or Native American people."

9

The terms "underrepresented" and "overrepresented" reflect groups' law school attendance rates: the proportion of certain groups in law schools relative to their proportion in the North American population at large.

Groups comprising a larger portion of the general population than they do the law school population are considered to be under-represented, while a group whose population frequency matches or is lower than its law school attendance rate is overrepresented.

Let's now turn from our broader discussion of test bias to examine the three most common forms of Diversity passages on the LSAT: affirming underrepresented groups, undermining overrepresented groups, and mixed group passages.

1. Affirming Underrepresented Groups

Given the history of bias in standardized testing, it is no surprise that LSAC is very careful in how they present traditionally underrepresented groups. What is surprising is the consistency in the tone used by passage authors. In the dozens of passages addressing traditionally underrepresented groups that have appeared on the LSAT in the past 25-plus years, every single passage has addressed these groups in a positive manner. That is, in each instance, the attitude of the author toward the person or group under discussion has been positive or encouraging. This type of consistency goes beyond mere coincidence, and reveals one of the core attitudes of the test makers. Knowing how the test makers will approach a traditionally underrepresented group then allows you to predict the general direction of certain answer choices. Examine the following question, with the preface that the passage was about Miles Davis, the prominent African American jazz musician. Consider the answer choices based on that, and choose the one you feel is most likely correct:

4.   Which one of the following best describes the author's attitude toward Miles Davis's music?

   (A)   uneasy ambivalence
   (B)   cautious neutrality
   (C)   grudging respect
   (D)   moderate commendation
   (E)   appreciative advocacy

Without reading the passage, but knowing the consistent attitude held by the test makers, most students can predict the correct answer, which is (E). This result is contrary to the general aims of testing, because most students should *not* be able to choose correct answers without having read the passage. The fact that they can shows the power of recognizing in advance the views of the test makers! Of course, your job as a test taker is not to overly worry about the methods or aims of the test makers; your job is to simply understand that the test makers exhibit certain patterns, and then to capitalize on those patterns whenever possible.

With that in mind, let's examine how this knowledge applies to an entire passage. Please take approximately 2 to 3 minutes to read the following passage. As you read, keep the discussion above in mind.

9

October 1996—Passage #1

The career of trumpeter Miles Davis was one of the most astonishingly productive that jazz music has ever seen. Yet his genius has never received its due. The impatience and artistic restlessness that (5) characterized his work spawned one stylistic turn after another and made Davis anathema to many critics, who deplored his abandonment first of bebop and then of "cool" acoustic jazz for ever more innovative sounds.

(10) Having begun his career studying bebop, Davis pulled the first of many stylistic surprises when, in 1948, he became a member of an impromptu musical think tank that gathered in a New York City apartment. The work of this group not only (15) slowed down tempos and featured ensemble playing as much as or even more than solos—in direct reaction to bebop—it also became the seedbed for the "West Coast cool" jazz style.

In what would become a characteristic zigzag, (20) Davis didn't follow up on these innovations himself. Instead, in the late 1950s he formed a new band that broke free from jazz's restrictive pattern of chord changes. Soloists could determine the shapes of their melodies without referring back to (25) the same unvarying repetition of chords. In this period, Davis attempted to join jazz phrasings, harmonies, and tonal qualities with a unified and integrated sound similar to that of a classical orchestral piece: in his recordings the rhythms, no (30) matter how jazzlike, are always understated, and the instrumental voicings seem muted.

Davis's recordings from the late 1960s signal that, once again, his direction was changing. On *Filles de Kilimanjaro*, Davis's request that (35) keyboardist Herbie Hancock play electric rather than acoustic piano caused consternation among jazz purists of the time. Other albums featured rock-style beats, heavily electronic instrumentation, a loose improvisational attack and a growing use of (40) studio editing to create jagged soundscapes. By 1969 Davis's typical studio procedure was to have musicians improvise from a base script of material and then to build finished pieces out of tape, like a movie director. Rock groups had pioneered the (45) process; to jazz lovers, raised on the ideal of live improvisation, that approach was a violation of the premise that recordings should simply document the musicians' thought processes in real time. Davis again became the target of fierce polemics by purist (50) jazz critics, who have continued to belittle his contributions to jazz.

What probably underlies the intensity of the reactions against Davis is fear of the broadening of possibilities that he exemplified. Ironically, he was (55) simply doing what jazz explorers have always done: reaching for something new that was his own. But because his career endured, because he didn't die young or record only sporadically, and because he refused to dwell in whatever niche he had (60) previously carved out, critics find it difficult to definitively rank Davis in the aesthetic hierarchy to which they cling.

9

For the purposes of this discussion, we will dispense with the normal VIEWSTAMP analysis of the passage and simply note that the main viewpoints expressed are those of the author, an obvious admirer of Davis', and the critics mentioned throughout, who routinely fail to appreciate Davis' creative and artistic genius.

Paragraph One:

This passage begins with its main point, and clearly relays the author's attitude toward the subject: Miles Davis, despite his musical genius, has been critically disregarded or misunderstood. In the final sentence the author restates this idea, asserting that Davis has been overlooked because of work too innovative for critics to appreciate.

Paragraph Two:

Here we are provided with the first date along a timeline of Davis' artistic surprises: he began in bebop, but in 1948 moved on to a new style called "West Coast cool" (ironically started in New York City) with facets (slow tempos, ensemble play) that countered bebop's approach.

Paragraph Three:

In this paragraph the author provides another date for the timeline (the late 1950's), and another shift in Davis' musical approach. His new band "broke free from jazz's restrictive pattern," allowing band members to shape their own melodies, then weaving these pieces into a unified sound with understated rhythms and muted instrumentation.

Paragraph Four:

The author's attitude has been established, and the structure of this passage becomes increasingly clear at the start of the fourth paragraph: a discussion of further stylistic shifts, and yet another date. During the late 60's, Davis made several major changes, provided nearly in list form: electric piano, rock style beats, electronic instrumentation and studio editing. The author then provides an extensive description of Davis' studio process (provide basic structure, then edit together the improvised parts), and then revisits the theme of changes misunderstood by "purist" critics who belittled Davis' contribution.

9

The author uses the final paragraph to reassert the attitude that Davis was a great innovator, and that this was the basis of the critics' lack of understanding: his career lasted long enough for a lot of innovations, and the many shifts in direction led to the critics' inability to understand the jazz great or give him the credit he deserved.

Although the exact course of a passage cannot be determined before reading the text, the topic sometimes allows you to predict the *general* path that a passage will follow. This conveys an immense advantage upon you as a test taker because if you have some forewarning of the direction the author is about to take, then you can read faster and process information more quickly.

2. Undermining Overrepresented Groups

But what about the other side of the Diversity coin? If the test makers consistently take a positive attitude towards traditionally underrepresented groups, then what attitude would you expect them to take towards traditionally overrepresented groups? As you might expect, the attitude is often critical—if not wholly, then at least partially. This does make some sense, of course. If a test has historically been accused of prejudice in favor of a certain group, one method to counter such a view is to present a greater number of passages critical of that group. On the LSAT, this criticism most frequently appears in passages devoted to assessing the work of scholars, who, under the description of the overrepresented group we used earlier, are typically Caucasian males versed in Western thinking.

While this assertion may seem surprising, an analysis of every released LSAT from the modern era (1991 to the present) shows that usually when the test makers critique an individual or viewpoint, that person or perspective belongs to a historically well-represented group, that of Caucasian male authors.

Please read the passage on the following page with the discussion above in mind.

9

Fairy tales address themselves to two communities, each with its own interests and each in periodic conflict with the other: parents and children. Nearly every study of fairy tales has taken the perspective of the
(5) parent, constructing the meaning of the tales by using the reading strategies of an adult bent on identifying universally valid tenets of moral instruction for children.

For example, the plot of "Hansel and Gretel" is set
(10) in motion by hard-hearted parents who abandon their children in the woods, but for psychologist Bruno Bettelheim the tale is really about children who learn to give up their unhealthy dependency on their parents. According to Bettelheim, this story—in which the
(15) children ultimately overpower a witch who has taken them prisoner for the crime of attempting to eat the witch's gingerbread house—forces its young audience to recognize the dangers of unrestrained greed. As dependent children, Bettelheim argues, Hansel and
(20) Gretel had been a burden to their parents, but on their return home with the witch's jewels, they become the family's support. Thus, says Bettelheim, does the story train its young listeners to become "mature children."

There are two ways of interpreting a story: one is a
(25) "superficial" reading that focuses on the tale's manifest content, and the other is a "deeper" reading that looks for latent meanings. Many adults who read fairy tales are drawn to this second kind of interpretation in order to avoid facing the unpleasant truths that can emerge
(30) from the tales when adults—even parents—are portrayed as capable of acting out of selfish motives themselves. What makes fairy tales attractive to Bettelheim and other psychologists is that they can be used as scenarios that position the child as a
(35) transgressor whose deserved punishment provides a lesson for unruly children. Stories that run counter to such orthodoxies about child-rearing are, to a large extent, suppressed by Bettelheim or "rewritten" through reinterpretation. Once we examine his
(40) interpretations closely, we see that his readings produce meanings that are very different from those constructed by readers with different cultural assumptions and expectations, who, unlike Bettelheim, do not find inflexible tenets of moral instruction in the
(45) tales.

Bettelheim interprets all fairy tales as driven by children's fantasies of desire and revenge, and in doing so suppresses the true nature of parental behavior ranging from abuse to indulgence. Fortunately, these
(50) characterizations of selfish children and innocent adults have been discredited to some extent by recent psychoanalytic literature. The need to deny adult evil has been a pervasive feature of our society, leading us to position children not only as the sole agents of evil
(55) but also as the objects of unending moral instruction, hence the idea that a literature targeted for them must stand in the service of pragmatic instrumentality rather than foster an unproductive form of playful pleasure.

9

Again, for the purposes of discussion, we will dispense with the VIEWSTAMP analysis and focus primarily on the diversity elements within the passage.

Paragraph One:

This paragraph offers no indication that this passage will eventually contain diversity elements. Instead, the passage initially appears to be a discussion about the meaning of fairy tales.

Paragraph Two:

The second paragraph begins with an example about Hansel and Gretel, but the author quickly pivots the discussion and introduces the views of psychologist Bruno Bettelheim (line 11). The remainder of the paragraph discusses Bettelheim's views.

Paragraph Three:

The author begins this paragraph with discussion of two approaches to the interpretation of a story: a superficial consideration of the basic content, and a deeper examination of the work for hidden "latent meanings." The author uses the second half of this paragraph to criticize Bettleheim, characterizing the psychologist as an inflexible writer who chose to suppress or reinterpret those stories which failed to provide the standard lessons warning children against transgression.

You also should not overlook the importance of understanding the subtext of lines 39-45. Note the nature of the attack in this section: Bettelheim has certain cultural views that he cannot put aside, and his intellectual views are biased by those notions. This type of ethnocentrism has been frequently attacked by the makers of the LSAT. Ironic, since it was this type of ethnocentrism that led to the early bias in standardized tests discussed at the start of this section!

Paragraph Four:

The start of the last paragraph continues the attack, noting somewhat dismissively that Bettelheim's suppressive views have been discredited to some extent in recent psychoanalytic literature.

The final lines serve as an attempt to draw the passage back to the ideas of the first paragraph, and are, quite likely, also an attempt by the test makers to draw some attention away from Bettelheim.

Of course, understanding the underlying intent of the test makers does not answer all of the questions for you. Some of the questions will inevitably address details of the passage, or specific viewpoint elements. However, some of the questions will be made easier with knowledge of the test makers' viewpoint. Consider, for example, the following question:

Which one of the following most accurately states the main idea of the passage?

While the context of the discussion is fairy tales, the main idea is that Bettelheim's view is incorrect. Now consider the answer choices:

9. Which one of the following most accurately states the main idea of the passage?

   (A) While originally written for children, fairy tales also contain a deeper significance for adults that psychologists such as Bettelheim have shown to be their true meaning.
   (B) The "superficial" reading of a fairy tale, which deals only with the tale's content, is actually more enlightening for children than the "deeper" reading preferred by psychologists such as Bettelheim.
   (C) Because the content of fairy tales has historically run counter to prevailing orthodoxies about child-rearing, psychologists such as Bettelheim sometimes reinterpret them to suit their own pedagogical needs.
   (D) The pervasive need to deny adult evil has led psychologists such as Bettelheim to erroneously view fairy tales solely as instruments of moral instruction for children.
   (E) Although dismissed as unproductive by psychologists such as Bettelheim, fairy tales offer children imaginative experiences that help them grow into morally responsible adults.

As we know, the correct answer must attack Bettelheim. Answer choices (A), (B), (C), and (E) fail to attack Bettelheim, either sufficiently or at all. Only answer choice (D) directly attacks Bettelheim, by stating that "Bettelheim... erroneously view fairy tales..." Thus, answer choice (D) is correct. Statistically, this is a question that only about 60% of students answer correctly, yet, when placed against the background of our discussion of undermining overrepresented groups, answer choice (D) should jump off the page at you. This is how to improve your performance on the LSAT—when you can take advantage of any situation, either through well-founded expectation or in-the-moment understanding, do so with authority!

3. Mixed Group Passages

Thus far, we have examined passages based primarily on single groups, both traditionally underrepresented and traditionally overrepresented. What happens, though, when a passage contains both groups? How do the test makers handle a situation, for example, when one of the members from the overrepresented group addresses one of the traditionally underrepresented groups, or vice versa? Below we briefly discuss each scenario:

1. Member of an underrepresented group addresses a member of an overrepresented group.

   These scenarios occur relatively rarely, and thus they are not the focus of this section. When they do occur, it is normally because the member of the overrepresented group was initially critical of the member of the underrepresented group, and then the member of the underrepresented group typically responds somewhat dismissively to the member of the overrepresented group (which is quite reasonable—who wouldn't be dismissive toward someone who criticized them?).

2. Member of an overrepresented group addresses a member of an underrepresented group.

   Although there are passages where members of an overrepresented group criticize members of an underrepresented group (as outlined in point 1 above), the response in those passages is predictable: that initial, critical group or individual is then attacked. More interesting—and the focus of this section—are passages where members of an overrepresented group praise or commend members of an underrepresented group. For example, how would you expect the test takers to treat a Western Caucasian male scholar who wrote a study about the positive developments within a native culture? Such a scenario presents a bit of a dilemma for the test makers. Because the scholar is writing in a positive manner about a traditionally underrepresented group, the test makers endorse that position. But, perhaps because of the source of the commentary, the test makers usually also insert at least some mild criticism of the scholar. Thus, passages of this type, which we term "Assessing the Scholars," contain a fascinating display of the competing values of the test makers.

   Take a few minutes to consider the following passage, which falls into this category.

9

Most studies of recent Southeast Asian immigrants to the United States have focused on their adjustment to life in their adopted country and on the effects of leaving their homelands. James
(5) Tollefson's *Alien Winds* examines the resettlement process from a different perspective by investigating the educational programs offered in immigrant processing centers. Based on interviews, transcripts from classes, essays by immigrants, personal visits
(10) to a teacher-training unit, and official government documents, Tollefson relies on an impressive amount and variety of documentation in making his arguments about processing centers' educational programs.
(15) Tollefson's main contention is that the emphasis placed on immediate employment and on teaching the values, attitudes, and behaviors that the training personnel think will help the immigrants adjust more easily to life in the United States is often
(20) counterproductive and demoralizing. Because of concerns that the immigrants be self-supporting as soon as possible, they are trained almost exclusively for low-level jobs that do not require English proficiency. In this respect, Tollefson claims, the
(25) processing centers suit the needs of employers more than they suit the long-term needs of the immigrant community. Tollefson also detects a fundamental flaw in the attempts by program educators to instill in the immigrants the traditionally Western
(30) principles of self-sufficiency and individual success. These efforts often have the effect of undermining the immigrants' sense of community and, in doing so, sometimes isolate them from the moral support and even from business opportunities afforded by
(35) the immigrant community. The programs also encourage the immigrants to shed their cultural traditions and ethnic identity and adopt the lifestyles, beliefs, and characteristics of their adopted country if they wish to enter fully into the
(40) national life.
Tollefson notes that the ideological nature of these educational programs has roots in the turn-of-the-century educational programs designed to assimilate European immigrants into United
(45) States society. Tollefson provides a concise history of the assimilationist movement in immigrant education, in which European immigrants were encouraged to leave behind the ways of the Old World and to adopt instead the principles and
(50) practices of the New World.
Tollefson ably shows that the issues demanding real attention in the educational programs for Southeast Asian immigrants are not merely employment rates and government funding, but also
(55) the assumptions underpinning the educational values

in the programs. He recommends many improvements for the programs, including giving the immigrants a stronger voice in determining their needs and how to meet them, redesigning the
(60) curricula, and emphasizing long-term language education and job training over immediate employment and the avoiding of public assistance. Unfortunately, though, Tollefson does not offer enough concrete solutions as to how these reforms
(65) could be carried out, despite his own descriptions of the complicated bureaucratic nature of the programs.

9

From a quick reading of the first sentence, this passage would appear to be a standard Affirming Underrepresented Groups passage. If so, we would expect a discussion that praises or supports some aspect of the Southeast Asian immigrant experience. However, as the first paragraph continues, the text makes clear that the discussion will focus on James Tollefson's *Alien Winds*, a book about the immigrant educational programs offered in immigrant processing centers. If Tollefson's book were about a different topic, we would then expect this passage to fall into the Undermining Overrepresented Groups category, and that Tollefson's views would be undermined within the passage. But, because Tollefson's book discusses an underrepresented group in a positive manner, the passage takes an entirely different approach to him.

Specifically, Tollefson has blamed the educational programs offered at the processing centers for causing certain difficulties encountered by immigrants, instead of blaming the immigrants themselves. This viewpoint is considered a positive assessment of the situation, as opposed to the normal critical position taken by many authors who are unable to look beyond the assumptions of their own culture and upbringing. Hence, the test makers will generally praise Tollefson, but because he is a member of an overrepresented group, they are likely to criticize him in some small way as well.

Let us take a moment to review the passage, again focusing on the diversity elements and bypassing our VIEWSTAMP analysis:

> In the introductory paragraph of the passage, the author indicates that James Tollefson's work is distinct from most studies of southeast Asian immigrants (line 4-6). Unlike the majority of such inquiries, which tend to focus on immigrants' adaptation to change, Tollefson's work, *Alien Winds*, is a study of immigrant processing center educational programs, and is based on many sources, which the author calls "impressive" in amount and variety (line 11). This description is the first tangible sign that Tollefson is going to receive more lenient treatment than you would otherwise expect.
>
> The second paragraph begins with a review of Tollefson's main contention that the emphasis on immediate employment and on teaching employable qualities in the educational programs leads to problems for immigrants. The paragraph continues on to discuss the various supporting facts and theories advanced by Tollefson. The paragraph itself is quite dense and contains a number of disparate facts. Other than noting that Tollefson "detects a fundamental flaw" in the programs, the focus of the discussion in this paragraph is not on the diversity elements, but rather creating a section of text that can be used to generate questions for the problem set.

9

In the third paragraph, the author discusses the foundations of the educational programs that are the focus of the first two paragraphs of the passage. Aside from describing Tollefson's history as "concise," this paragraph does not touch on the author's attitude towards the groups under discussion.

Up to this point, the author has favorably reviewed Tollefson's approach in his book. Among other things, his work has been called "impressive" and "concise," and at the start of this paragraph the author mentions that Tollefson "ably shows" the real issues (line 51). Given that Tollefson is addressing an underrepresented group in a positive manner, this is not surprising. But, because Tollefson is also a member of an overrepresented group, the test makers typically feel some need to criticize. Consequently, in the final paragraph, starting at line 63, the author provides a light critique of *Alien Winds* as a closing note: the work presents good ideas but lacks sufficient suggestions for the implementation of the suggested reforms.

So, even though Tollefson is a member of an overrepresented group, there is a considerable reduction in the force of the criticism directed his way. This is likely because the general theme of diversity is dominant, and thus the test makers prefer to direct positive attention towards the underrepresented group.

Because such attitudes are central to the passage, there will often be a question about the author's opinion of the critiqued work. This passage is no exception:

> Which one of the following best describes the opinion
> of the author of the passage with respect to Tollefson's work?

The answer to this question is one that we should prephrase. Again, the general tone of the passage is positive with regard to the examined work, but of course it is vital that we recognize both sides of the author's mixed review of *Alien Winds*: the author is impressed with Tollefson's subject matter, sources, and basic assertions regarding immigrant education and necessary changes, but does not feel that Tollefson provides specific direction for the application of these changes.

9

Consider then, the entire question:

24. Which one of the following best describes the opinion of the author of the passage with respect to Tollefson's work?

   (A)   thorough but misguided
   (B)   innovative but incomplete
   (C)   novel but contradictory
   (D)   illuminating but unappreciated
   (E)   well documented but unoriginal

In this question, the first word in each answer choice could apply to the author's view of Tollefson's work. Thus, the last word must provide the principal basis for selecting the correct answer choice. Answer choice (B), "incomplete" is directly supported by lines 63-67 and is thus correct. Note that the last word in answer choice (D) is the most benign of the five choices, as the other four all reflect a more actively critical opinion.

As an aside, this particular format, where each answer choice contains one or two descriptive words, generally requires less time to complete than other questions. With that in mind, if you find yourself running out of time on a Reading Comprehension passage, it is recommended that you skip ahead to questions such as this one. You may be able to complete an extra question or two in the remaining time by answering easier question types.

The ultimate lesson here is that in passages that mix underrepresented and overrepresented groups, you must carefully examine the statements of each group. The test makers will direct the passage in various directions depending on the nature of what is being said, but, as we have seen throughout our discussion, those directions are generally predictable.

9

Common Diversity Passage Themes ■

Thus far in this section we have discussed how the test makers treat certain groups, and we have discovered that the test makers have consistent and predictable attitudes towards those groups. We can go a step further however, as there are also some recurrent themes *within* these types of passages that the test makers use to communicate the attitudes they hold.

Here we'll examine two major Diversity themes, each of which addresses underrepresented groups:

1. The Blending of the Old and New

At one point, the first passage from five LSATs in a row was a Diversity passage featuring a blending of the old and new. These were the five passages that appeared from September 2006 to December 2007.

Of course, there are many more examples; these five were unique because they occurred consecutively as passage 1.

These passages feature individuals or groups that adopt old approaches or ideas—some "tradition" or past cultural convention, typically—and marry them in some fashion to newer, more modern practices, thereby creating something unique and powerful. This "blended" approach bridges the gap between old and new by keeping some elements of the original custom while also adopting elements of the newer approach. The result is a synthesis of the two, producing a new form to be admired. In all cases, the person or group who does the blending is praised as innovative and inspired.

Why is this theme used frequently in Diversity passages? Because the ability to adapt and synthesize information and ideas is an extremely advanced and beneficial skill, and to attribute such a skill to any group is seen as a compliment (which is why in almost all instances the ability to blend elements is praised).

In a later passage we will see this theme at work, and if you wish to review additional examples of this theme in actual LSAT Reading Comprehension passages, here are a few excellent illustrations:

October 2013, Passage #2—Katherine Dunham

December 2011, Passage #1—U.S. Latina Autobiographies

June 2011, Passage #2—Kate Chopin

October 2010, Passage #4—Williams and DuBois

December 2008, Passage #1—Amos Tutuola

2. Defiance of Classification

A number of LSAT passages discuss persons or groups that in some way cannot be classified or judged by conventional means: they confound their critics, or are underappreciated in their time. The message of these passages is that the person or subject under discussion is too unique or pioneering to be appropriately assessed, or is so progressive (ahead of their time, typically) that their contemporaries could not understand the full merit of their work.

The Miles Davis passage discussed earlier perfectly exemplifies the concept of "Defiance of Classification," and these same basic ideas show up with surprising regularity.

Final Note ▆▆▆▆▆▆▆▆▆▆

The message of this section is that the makers of the test have certain goals that they prioritize quite highly, and that the checkered history of standardized testing—particularly the notions of fairness and equal representation—has played a role in shaping the test makers' approach to achieving those goals. When the makers of a test have a well-defined agenda, their views and intentions permeate the very fabric of the test's construction, leading to the emergence of identifiable, predictable patterns. And it's this general predictability that conveys an advantage to those aware of it and ready to capitalize!

While the test makers are not constrained to always follow the exact route they have taken in the past, the overwhelming evidence suggests that more often than not they will continue to do so.

The next section presents two Diversity practice passages, and thereafter we move on to discuss Law-Related and Science passages.

9

Two Diversity Practice Passages

Diversity Practice Passage I—December 2007 Passage #1

Asian American poetry from Hawaii, the Pacific island state of the United States, is generally characterizable in one of two ways: either as portraying a model multicultural paradise, or as
(5) exemplifying familiar Asian American literary themes such as generational conflict. In this light, the recent work of Wing Tek Lum in *Expounding the Doubtful Points* is striking for its demand to be understood on its own terms. Lum offers no romanticized notions of
(10) multicultural life in Hawaii, and while he does explore themes of family, identity, history, and literary tradition, he does not do so at the expense of attempting to discover and retain a local sensibility. For Lum such a sensibility is informed by the fact
(15) that Hawaii's population, unlike that of the continental U.S., has historically consisted predominantly of people of Asian and Pacific island descent, making the experience of its Asian Americans somewhat different than that of mainland
(20) Asian Americans.

In one poem, Lum meditates on the ways in which a traditional Chinese lunar celebration he is attending at a local beach both connects him to and separates him from the past. In the company of new
(25) Chinese immigrants, the speaker realizes that while ties to the homeland are comforting and necessary, it is equally important to have "a sense of new family" in this new land of Hawaii, and hence a new identity-one that is sensitive to its new environment.
(30) The role of immigrants in this poem is significant in that, through their presence, Lum is able to refer both to the traditional culture of his ancestral homeland as well as to the flux within Hawaiian society that has been integral to its heterogeneity. Even in a laudatory
(35) poem to famous Chinese poet Li Po (701-762 A.D.), which partly serves to place Lum's work within a distinguished literary tradition, Lum refuses to offer a stereotypical nostalgia for the past, instead pointing out the often elitist tendencies inherent in the work of
(40) some traditionally acclaimed Chinese poets.

Lum closes his volume with a poem that further points to the complex relationships between heritage and local culture in determining one's identity. Pulling together images and figures as vastly
(45) disparate as a famous Chinese American literary character and an old woman selling bread, Lum avoids an excessively romantic vision of U.S. culture, while simultaneously acknowledging the dream of this culture held by many newly arrived immigrants.
(50) The central image of a communal pot where each person chooses what she or he wishes to eat but shares with others the "sweet soup / spooned out at the end of the meal" is a hopeful one; however, it also appears to caution that the strong cultural
(55) emphasis in the U.S. on individual drive and success that makes retaining a sense of homeland tradition difficult should be identified and responded to in ways that allow for a healthy new sense of identity to be formed.

1. Which one of the following most accurately expresses the main point of the passage?

   (A) The poetry of Lum departs from other Asian American poetry from Hawaii in that it acknowledges its author's heritage but also expresses the poet's search for a new local identity.

   (B) Lum's poetry is in part an expression of the conflict between a desire to participate in a community with shared traditions and values and a desire for individual success.

   (C) Lum writes poetry that not only rejects features of the older literary tradition in which he participates but also rejects the popular literary traditions of Hawaiian writers.

   (D) The poetry of Lum illustrates the extent to which Asian American writers living in Hawaii have a different cultural perspective than those living in the continental U.S.

   (E) Lum's poetry is an unsuccessful attempt to manage the psychological burdens of reconciling a sense of tradition with a healthy sense of individual identity.

2. Given the information in the passage, which one of the following is Lum most likely to believe?

   (A) Images in a poem should be explained in that poem so that their meaning will be widely understood.

   (B) The experience of living away from one's homeland is necessary for developing a healthy perspective on one's cultural traditions.

   (C) It is important to reconcile the values of individual achievement and enterprise with the desire to retain one's cultural traditions.

   (D) One's identity is continually in transition and poetry is a way of developing a static identity.

   (E) One cannot both seek a new identity and remain connected to one's cultural traditions.

3. The author of the passage uses the phrase "the flux within Hawaiian society" (line 33) primarily in order to

    (A) describe the social tension created by the mix of attitudes exhibited by citizens of Hawaii
    (B) deny that Hawaiian society is culturally distinct from that of the continental U.S.
    (C) identify the process by which immigrants learn to adapt to their new communities
    (D) refer to the constant change to which the culture in Hawaii is subject due to its diverse population
    (E) emphasize the changing attitudes of many immigrants to Hawaii toward their traditional cultural norms

4. According to the passage, some Asian American literature from Hawaii has been characterized as which one of the following?

    (A) inimical to the process of developing a local sensibility
    (B) centered on the individual's drive to succeed
    (C) concerned with conflicts between different age groups
    (D) focused primarily on retaining ties to one's homeland
    (E) tied to a search for a new sense of family in a new land

5. The author of the passage describes *Expounding the Doubtful Points* as "striking" (lines 7-8) primarily in order to

    (A) underscore the forceful and contentious tone of the work
    (B) indicate that the work has not been properly analyzed by literary critics
    (C) stress the radical difference between this work and Lum's earlier work
    (D) emphasize the differences between this work and that of other Asian American poets from Hawaii
    (E) highlight the innovative nature of Lum's experiments with poetic form

6. With which one of the following statements regarding Lum's poetry would the author of the passage be most likely to agree?

    (A) It cannot be used to support any specific political ideology.
    (B) It is an elegant demonstration of the poet's appreciation of the stylistic contributions of his literary forebears.
    (C) It is most fruitfully understood as a meditation on the choice between new and old that confronts any human being in any culture.
    (D) It conveys thoughtful assessments of both his ancestral homeland tradition and the culture in which he is attempting to build a new identity.
    (E) It conveys Lum's antipathy toward tradition by juxtaposing traditional and nontraditional images.

9

Diversity Practice Passage II—October 2004 Passage #2

In the field of historiography—the writing of history based on a critical examination of authentic primary information sources—one area that has recently attracted attention focuses on the responses
(5) of explorers and settlers to new landscapes in order to provide insights into the transformations the landscape itself has undergone as a result of settlement. In this endeavor historiographers examining the history of the Pacific Coast of the
(10) United States have traditionally depended on the records left by European American explorers of the nineteenth century who, as commissioned agents of the U.S. government, were instructed to report thoroughly their findings in writing.

(15) But in furthering this investigation some historiographers have recently recognized the need to expand their definition of what a source is. They maintain that the sources traditionally accepted as documenting the history of the Pacific Coast have too
(20) often omitted the response of Asian settlers to this territory. In part this is due to the dearth of written records left by Asian settlers; in contrast to the commissioned agents, most of the people who first came to western North America from Asia during this
(25) same period did not focus on developing a self-conscious written record of their involvement with the landscape. But because a full study of a culture's historical relationship to its land cannot confine itself to a narrow record of experience, these
(30) historiographers have begun to recognize the value of other kinds of evidence, such as the actions of Asian settlers.

As a case in point, the role of Chinese settlers in expanding agriculture throughout the Pacific Coast
(35) territory is integral to the history of the region. Without access to the better land, Chinese settlers looked for agricultural potential in this generally arid region where other settlers did not. For example, where settlers of European descent looked at willows
(40) and saw only useless, untillable swamp, Chinese settlers saw fresh water, fertile soil, and the potential for bringing water to more arid areas via irrigation. Where other settlers who looked at certain weeds, such as wild mustard, generally saw a nuisance,
(45) Chinese settlers saw abundant raw material for valuable spices from a plant naturally suited to the local soil and climate.

Given their role in the labor force shaping this territory in the nineteenth century, the Chinese settlers
(50) offered more than just a new view of the land. Their vision was reinforced by specialized skills involving swamp reclamation and irrigation systems, which helped lay the foundation for the now well-known and prosperous agribusiness of the region. That
(55) 80 percent of the area's cropland is now irrigated and that the region is currently the top producer of many specialty crops cannot be fully understood by historiographers without attention to the input of Chinese settlers as reconstructed from their
(60) interactions with that landscape.

8. Which one of the following most accurately states the main point of the passage?

(A) The history of settlement along the Pacific Coast of the U.S., as understood by most historiographers, is confirmed by evidence reconstructed from the actions of Asian settlers.

(B) Asian settlers on the Pacific Coast of the U.S. left a record of their experiences that traditional historiographers believed to be irrelevant.

(C) To understand Asian settlers' impact on the history of the Pacific Coast of the U.S., historiographers have had to recognize the value of nontraditional kinds of historiographic evidence.

(D) Spurred by new findings regarding Asian settlement on the Pacific Coast of the U.S. historiographers have begun to debate the methodological foundations of historiography.

(E) By examining only written information, historiography as it is traditionally practiced has produced inaccurate historical accounts.

9. Which one of the following most accurately describes the author's primary purpose in discussing Chinese settlers in the third paragraph?

(A) to suggest that Chinese settlers followed typical settlement patterns in this region during the nineteenth century

(B) to argue that little written evidence of Chinese settlers' practices survives

(C) to provide examples illustrating the unique view Asian settlers had of the land

(D) to demonstrate that the history of settlement in the region has become a point of contention among historiographers

(E) to claim that the historical record provided by the actions of Asian settlers is inconsistent with history as derived from traditional sources

10. The passage states that the primary traditional historiographic sources of information about the history of the Pacific Coast of the U.S. have which one of the following characteristics?

(A) They were written both before and after Asian settlers arrived in the area.

(B) They include accounts by Native Americans in the area.

(C) They are primarily concerned with potential agricultural uses of the land.

(D) They focus primarily on the presence of water sources in the region.

(E) They are accounts left by European American explorers.

9

11. The author would most likely disagree with which one of the following statements?

(A) Examining the actions not only of Asian settlers but of other cultural groups of the Pacific Coast of the U.S. is necessary to a full understanding of the impact of settlement on the landscape there.

(B) The significance of certain actions to the writing of history may be recognized by one group of historiographers but not another.

(C) Recognizing the actions of Asian settlers adds to but does not complete the writing of the history of the Pacific Coast of the U.S.

(D) By recognizing as evidence the actions of people, historiographers expand the definition of what a source is.

(E) The expanded definition of a source will probably not be relevant to studies of regions that have no significant immigration of non-Europeans.

12. According to the passage, each of the following was an aspect of Chinese settlers' initial interactions with the landscape of the Pacific Coast of the U.S. EXCEPT:

(A) new ideas for utilizing local plants
(B) a new view of the land
(C) specialized agricultural skills
(D) knowledge of agribusiness practices
(E) knowledge of irrigation systems

13. Which one of the following can most reasonably be inferred from the passage?

(A) Most Chinese settlers came to the Pacific Coast of the U.S. because the climate was similar to that with which they were familiar.

(B) Chinese agricultural methods in the nineteenth century included knowledge of swamp reclamation.

(C) Settlers of European descent used wild mustard seed as a spice.

(D) Because of the abundance of written sources available, it is not worthwhile to examine the actions of European settlers.

(E) What written records were left by Asian settlers were neglected and consequently lost to scholarly research.

14. Which one of the following, if true, would most help to strengthen the author's main claim in the last sentence of the passage?

(A) Market research of agribusinesses owned by descendants of Chinese settlers shows that the market for the region's specialty crops has grown substantially faster than the market for any other crops in the last decade.

(B) Nineteenth-century surveying records indicate that the lands now cultivated by specialty crop businesses owned by descendants of Chinese settlers were formerly swamp lands.

(C) Research by university agricultural science departments proves that the formerly arid lands now cultivated by large agribusinesses contain extremely fertile soil when they are sufficiently irrigated.

(D) A technological history tracing the development of irrigation systems in the region reveals that their efficiency has increased steadily since the nineteenth century.

(E) Weather records compiled over the previous century demonstrate that the weather patterns in the region are well-suited to growing certain specialty crops as long as they are irrigated.

9

Diversity Practice Passage I—December 2007 Passage #1 Answer Key

Paragraph One:

This passage focuses on Wing Tek Lum, a member of a traditionally underrepresented group. Aside from falling into the Affirming Underrepresented Groups category, this passage also exemplifies the Defiance of Classification that is an underlying theme in many Diversity passages. It is also common for an LSAT author to begin a passage by introducing traditional viewpoints, in order to then present a contrasting perspective. In this passage, the author starts with an introduction to the traditional viewpoints of Asian American poets from Hawaii: generally their work reflects either a multicultural utopia, or traditional themes found in Asian American literature (the example provided is that of generational conflict). The author presents these traditional perspectives in order to immediately distinguish the work of Wing Tek Lum from most examples of Hawaiian Asian American writings. Lum's work, *Expounding the Doubtful Points*, is very distinct (*striking*ly so, according to the author of the passage) in that the work does not portray Hawaii as a multicultural paradise, and even familiar themes are explored with the understanding that the experiences of Hawaiian Asian Americans is different from that of Asian Americans on the mainland.

This introductory paragraph provides vital information; the author introduces traditional viewpoints of Asian American poetry from Hawaii, and distinguishes the work of Wing Tek Lum. The passage to this point reflects the author's viewpoint, which takes on an extremely positive tone with regard to Lum and the work under review.

Paragraph Two:

In the second paragraph we see another theme common among Diversity passages: The Blending of Old and New. The author begins the paragraph discussing a poem about a Chinese lunar celebration. Lum appreciates the homeland connection provided by the traditional celebration, as well as the identity that comes with "a sense of new family." The recent Chinese immigrants in attendance provide Lum with a reference to the dynamic and multifaceted Hawaiian society, which the poet blends with reference to the beach celebration which reflects his ancestral tradition.

This paragraph ends with the author providing another example of Lum's Defiance of Classification: in a poem which praises Li Po, a Chinese poet from the eighth century, Lum chooses to underscore the elitism of some traditional Chinese poetry, rather than taking the more standard nostalgic perspective that might be expected in such a poem.

This second paragraph continues the positive tone from the introduction—the author's viewpoint: Lum is not like the rest; the poet blends the old with the new and provides a perspective which is distinct from the traditional.

Diversity Practice Passage I—December 2007 Passage #1 Answer Key

Paragraph Three:

It is now clear that the entire passage presents the viewpoint of the author, who is very impressed with Lum. In this third paragraph, the author continues the positive tone with a discussion of the final poem from *Expounding the Doubtful Points*. By striking up the image of a famous Chinese American character alongside that of an old woman selling bread, Lum pays homage to the new immigrants' dreams without portraying an overly romantic notion of U.S. culture. As a closing note, the author of the passage references a Lum quote which is optimistic but cautionary: the American focus on drive and success might make it difficult for an immigrant to hold onto the homeland culture, but with the proper response, a "healthy new sense of identity" can emerge (this closing note provides another great example of the emphasis on Blending the Old and New).

VIEWSTAMP Analysis:

The entire passage is written from the **Viewpoint** of the author, who is very impressed with Lum's distinct approach to Asian American poetry.

The author's **Tone** is clearly positive with regard to Lum, and respectful of the poet's focus on both tradition and "a sense of new family."

The **Argument** in the passage is the author's assertion that Lum's work defies the traditional characterizations, blending the old and the new to present a distinct perspective.

The author's **Main Point** is that Lum's poetry represents a departure from the norm, reflecting both a respect for tradition and an understanding of the importance of developing a new immigrant identity.

The **Structure** of the passage is as follows:

> Paragraph One: Introduce the general topic of Asian American poetry from Hawaii, Lum's *Expounding the Doubtful Points*, and the work's "demand to be understood on its own terms."
>
> Paragraph Two: Discuss one of Lum's poems in which the poet Blends the Old and New, and another which distinguishes Lum's poetry from the traditional Chinese poetry.
>
> Paragraph Three: Discuss another poem which Blends Old and New, and show Lum's attitude to be optimistic but cautionary.

9

Diversity Practice Passage I—December 2007 Passage #1 Answer Key

Question #1: GR, Main Point. The correct answer choice is (A)

Answer choice (A): This is the correct answer choice, as it restates the author's Main Point, discussed above; Lum is distinctive in that he focuses on both tradition and the importance of a new identity.

Answer choice (B): Although the poem discussed in the last paragraph does reference the conflict between homeland tradition and the American emphasis on success, this does not represent the main point of the passage.

Answer choice (C): Lum does highlight the elitist tendencies of some traditional Chinese poetry in lines 39-40, although this does not necessarily amount to rejection. And while the author does believe that Lum's work is distinct from other Asian American poetry from Hawaii, this is certainly not the same as rejecting popular literary traditions of Hawaii.

Answer choice (D): At the end of the first paragraph the author points out Lum's understanding that the Hawaiian Asian Americans' perspective differs from that of mainland Asian Americans (not referring solely to *writers*, however). In any case, this is certainly not the main point of the passage, so this answer choice is incorrect.

Answer choice (E): If we have an understanding of the tone of this passage, we can recognize that this answer choice is incorrect when we get to the phrase "unsuccessful attempt." The author of the passage is clearly a fan of Lum's, and believes that Lum is successful in his efforts to blend tradition with a new sense of identity.

Question #2: GR, Must, SP. The correct answer choice is (C)

With regard to Subject Perspective questions, it is always important to understand what the author has relayed about the subject in question. In this case, we know that the author is impressed with Lum's perspective, since the poet considers the importance of both the old and the new in the development of an identity.

Answer choice (A): The author of this passage never discusses Lum's focus on widespread understanding; there is a reference to the disparate imagery in Lum's poetry, but this is very different from a focus on making the work widely understandable.

Answer choice (B): Lum believes that it is possible to develop a healthy perspective on one's culture while living away from the homeland, but nothing in the passage suggests that leaving one's homeland is necessary for this sort of development.

Answer choice (C): This is the correct answer choice. This answer passes the Fact Test; we can confirm this choice with the information from the cautionary note in the last sentence of the passage. Lum believes that it is important to respond to the American drive for success in a way that allows for retention of one's homeland culture; this is an important reconciliation between traditional culture and one particular emphasis of the new culture.

9

Diversity Practice Passage I—December 2007 Passage #1 Answer Key

Answer choice (D): The passage does not refer to poetry as a way to fight change; on the contrary, the author praises Lum's recognition of the "flux within Hawaiian society that has been integral to its heterogeneity." (lines 33-34)

Answer choice (E): This is an Opposite Answer choice: it is completely contrary to the passage, in which the author praises Lum for his ability to remain connected to his homeland culture while understanding the importance of developing a new sense of identity.

Question #3: SR, Must. The correct answer choice is (D)

In responding to Specific Reference questions such as this one, it is advisable to examine the referenced quote in context. In this case, the author praises Lum for being "able to refer both to the traditional culture…as well as to the flux within Hawaiian society that has been integral to its heterogeneity." So, Lum references tradition, and the quote referenced in the question regards the dynamic nature that has been integral to the society's multi-faceted culture.

Answer choice (A): The author sees the flux as positive, and integral to the heterogeneity of the society; there is no discussion of social tension.

Answer choice (B): Since the author (and Lum) clearly believe that there are cultural distinctions between Hawaiian society and that of the mainland, this answer choice is incorrect.

Answer choice (C): The referenced quote is intended to describe an attribute of the Hawaiian society, not to identify specific adaptation processes.

Answer choice (D): This is the correct answer choice. As prephrased above, the quote refers to the changes that come with Hawaii's cultural diversity.

Answer choice (E): In context, "flux" references the changing nature of the society, not the changing attitudes of immigrants toward their cultural norms.

Question #4: GR, Must. The correct answer choice is (C)

There are references to other Asian American literature (not by Lum) in the first and second paragraphs of the passage. In the first paragraph, the author tells us that generally Asian American poetry characterized Hawaii as a multicultural paradise, or explores familiar themes such as generational conflict. At the end of the second paragraph, the author refers to Lum's assertion of elitism in some traditional Chinese poetry.

Answer choice (A): "Inimical" basically means adverse, or harmful, and the author does not characterize Asian American poetry as adverse to the process of developing a local sensibility. Note: if unsure of the meaning of a word such as "inimical," it is advisable to skip the answer while assessing the other choices.

9

Diversity Practice Passage I—December 2007 Passage #1 Answer Key

Answer choice (B): The passage does not characterize Asian American literature as focused on the individual's drive to succeed—it is United States culture that maintains this focus, according to the final paragraph of the passage.

Answer choice (C): This is the correct answer choice. This conflict is described as an attribute of some Asian American poetry in the first paragraph; the author provides generational conflict as an example of a familiar theme in Asian American literature.

Answer choice (D): In the second paragraph of the passage the author discusses the comfort and necessity of retaining ties to one's homeland, but this is not presented as a *primary* focus of some Asian American literature.

Answer choice (E): Again, the search for a new sense of family in a new land is discussed with regard to Lum, but is not presented as a primary focus of some Asian American literature, so this answer choice is incorrect.

Question #5: SR, Must. The correct answer choice is (D)

Again, with specific reference questions we should always be sure to have the proper context associated with a referenced word or phrase. In this case, the author describes *Expounding the Doubtful Points* as "striking for its demand to be understood on its own terms." *Striking* is a rather strong term, intended to strongly distinguish Lum's work from much other Asian American poetry.

Answer choice (A): Lum's work is described by the author as neither forceful nor contentious, so this answer choice is incorrect.

Answer choice (B): Since there is no reference to the other critics' analysis of Lum's work, this answer choice cannot be correct.

Answer choice (C): The quote in this question does reference a radical difference—the difference between Lum's poetry and the work of *other* poets, not between Lum's recent and past work.

Answer choice (D): This is the correct answer choice. Unlike other examples of Asian American poetry from Hawaii, the author provides, Lum's work is strikingly distinct.

Answer choice (E): The term *striking* is used to describe the distinction between Lum's poetry and the work of others, with regard to Lum's characterizations of the culture in Hawaii, not with regard to his experimental poetic form.

9

Question #6: GR, Must, AP. The correct answer choice is (D)

Since this is an Author's Perspective question we should be sure to identify the tone reflected in the passage. In this case, the author's tone is very positive with respect to Lum's poetry; in particular the author is impressed with the poet's focus on the importance to immigrants of retaining a sense of homeland culture, coupled with the value of developing a new sense of identity and culture.

Answer choice (A): The passage contains no reference to the poetry's prospective use in support of political ideology, so this answer choice is incorrect.

Answer choice (B): At the end of the second paragraph, the author does refer to one of Lum's poems as "laudatory," but there is no specific reference to the poet's appreciation for the stylistic contributions of his literary forebears.

Answer choice (C): The author does not perceive Lum's poetry as choosing sides; rather, the author is impressed with the way the poet blends themes which reference the Old and the New.

Answer choice (D): This is the correct answer choice, and reflects the same theme as our prephrase: the author is impressed with Lum's references to the importance of both the homeland culture and a new sense of identity.

Answer choice (E): The use of the term *antipathy* (meaning distaste or aversion; roughly the opposite of sympathy) should tell us that this answer choice doesn't reflect the tone of the passage. Lum is not characterized by the passage as having an *aversion* to tradition; rather, Lum sees the importance of both tradition and a new sense of identity.

9

Diversity Practice Passage II—October 2004 Passage #2 Answer Key

This passage, in which the author discusses how Chinese settlers influenced the Pacific Coast landscape, and the value of studying this influence, reflects two common themes discussed earlier in this chapter. First, this is a Diversity passage in which a traditionally underrepresented group is praised for its positive impact; second, the value of studying this influence represents the application of a new perspective to an old line of inquiry.

Paragraph One:

The author starts the passage by providing the definition of Historiography—the writing of history based on certain authentic sources. The author points to an area that has recently attracted attention. The focus on how explorers and settlers responded to their newfound landscapes can provide insight into the land's transformations during that era. Previously, settlers' accounts have been used as the primary source of information about the settling of the United States Pacific Coast; European American explorers have been the traditional sources of such accounts, as they were commissioned by the U.S. government to keep detailed written records of their findings.

Paragraph Two:

Now that we have some background, the author turns to historiographers' recent recognition of the need to expand their definition of a source. Historical accounts have often omitted the perspectives of Asian settlers, in part because these people were less focused on documentation of such matters and therefore left less written records. The point here is to emphasize the importance of the Asian in the development of the landscape. This provides the author with the opportunity to praise a traditionally underrepresented group, and to point out that ignoring the influence of the Asian would leave a cultural study incomplete. This is why historiographers have come to rely on other sources of historical data. Note that reliance on new sources of data reflects the application of a new approach or perspective to old inquiries regarding the development of the U.S. Pacific Coast landscape.

Paragraph Three:

The third paragraph offers examples of the actions of the early Chinese settlers, showing how such evidence is relevant to the creation of a more complete cultural history of the area: with less access to more fertile soil, the Chinese found potential where the Europeans had not, using irrigation and taking advantage of some of the area's natural harvests, such as wild mustard, which had previously been seen only as a nuisance.

Paragraph Four:

In the last paragraph, the author again emphasizes the importance of the Chinese settlers in shaping this territory, given their vision and expertise in irrigation and swamp reclamation. In the final sentence, the author argues that historiographers should pay attention to the Chinese influence on this region's settlement, considering its modern day irrigated farmlands and various specialty crops.

Diversity Practice Passage II—October 2004 Passage #2 Answer Key

<u>VIEWSTAMP</u> Analysis:

This passage presents the **Viewpoint** of the author, who believes that historiography can benefit from studying the effects of the early settlers on the U.S. Pacific Coast landscape.

The **Tone** of the passage is positive with respect to the settlers, and supportive of the appropriate addition of relevant sources to the field of historiography

The primary **Argument** of the passage is that of the author, whose primary assertion is that the early Chinese settlers had a significant effect on the Pacific Coast landscape, and that this effect should be considered to develop a broader view of historiography.

The author's **Main Point** is to introduce the concept of historiography, and to point out the importance of non-traditional information sources, especially with respect to the actions of the Chinese settlers, in understanding the development of the Pacific Coast landscape.

The **Structure** of the passage is as follows:

> Paragraph One: Introduce historiography, and its traditional sources of evidence.

> Paragraph Two: Discuss the recent recognition of the need to expand on sources used, to include consideration of the actions of Asian settlers.

> Paragraph Three: List specific influences of the Chinese settlers.

> Paragraph Four: Restate the importance of considering the effects of these settlers on the landscape that developed.

Question #8: GR, Main Point. The correct answer choice is (C)

Since this is a Main Point question, we should attempt to form a prephrase before beginning to assess the answer choices. The main point of this passage, roughly, is to introduce historiography and discuss the need to include early Chinese settlers' actions as a source of historical information.

Answer choice (A): Part of the point of this passage is that historiographers need to expand their definition of a source if they are to have a complete understanding of the development of the landscape. If historiographers need to pay attention to non-written evidence made by Chinese settlers, it must be that this new evidence would offer some insight, so it seems highly unlikely that such new sources might simply confirm what historians already knew.

Answer choice (B): The passage suggested that the attention to the influence of Chinese settlers is recent, but that doesn't mean that historiographers have traditionally assumed that such evidence is irrelevant. They might simply have failed to see the existence of such evidence.

9

Diversity Practice Passage II—October 2004 Passage #2 Answer Key

Answer choice (C): This is the correct answer choice, as it sums up the author's main point in writing this passage. The author states in lines 15-17 that historiographers have recognized a need to expand their definition of a source, and in lines 54-60 the author states that historiographers cannot understand the development of the U.S. Pacific Coast without considering the actions of Chinese settlers.

Answer choice (D): Since the passage never suggests that Pacific Coast historiographers are divided over whether to pay attention to new types of evidence, this answer choice is unfounded. Furthermore, since historiographers recognize the need for new types of evidence, there appears to be some consensus. Finally, adding a new type of evidence is not the same as challenging a methodological foundation.

Answer choice (E): The author's point is not that older accounts have been inaccurate, but rather that they have been incomplete. Further, since the author explicitly confines the discussion to the historiography of the U.S. Pacific Coast, we cannot justifiably select a response that refers to the whole of historiography.

Question #9: SR, P. The correct answer choice is (C)

Since this question specifically refers to the third paragraph, it is once again advantageous to have an understanding of the structure of the passage. The third paragraph provides examples of the integral role of the Chinese settlers on the landscape, which is what we should prephrase before moving on to the answer choices.

Answer choice (A): The examples in the third paragraph illustrate that Chinese settlers were atypical, and the author doesn't examine their settlement patterns.

Answer choice (B): It seems true that there is little written evidence of the practices of the Chinese settlers. But this is not because such records didn't survive, but because the Chinese settlers simply didn't leave "a self-conscious written record" (lines 21-27).
Further, since the question is about the function of the third paragraph, we can confidently eliminate this incorrect answer choice.

Answer choice (C): This is the correct answer choice. The author argues that considering the Chinese perspective on the landscape is critical to understanding the transformation of the U.S. Pacific Coast. The third paragraph develops that argument by showing how the Chinese perspective was distinctive from the European perspective.

Answer choice (D): This answer choice is incorrect, since no debate among the historiographers is even alluded to in the passage. On the contrary, there appears to be a consensus among historiographers that new sources must be considered to have a more complete perspective on the development of the region.

Answer choice (E): The author's claim is not that the new sources of evidence are inconsistent with traditional accounts, but rather that information about the actions of the Chinese settlers would complement the sources already considered. The new sources, when considered along with the traditional, would offer a more complete historiography.

Diversity Practice Passage II—October 2004 Passage #2 Answer Key

Question #10: CR, Must. The correct answer choice is (E)

Since this question concerns the traditional sources of information for historiographers, the relevant reference point, considering the organization of the passage, would be the first paragraph.

Answer choice (A): Since the passage offers no information as to the timing of the Chinese settlement relative to the writing of the traditional sources of historiography, this answer choice is incorrect.

Answer choice (B): No mention is made in the passage concerning Native American accounts, so we cannot confidently confirm or deny this assertion.

Answer choice (C): While it does seem likely that traditional sources are concerned with potential agricultural uses of the land, the author never specifies this, and certainly does not assert that this was a primary concern.

Answer choice (D): Once again, the author does not indicate precisely an American-European explorer's focus. The passage explicitly states that the Chinese were concerned with water sources, which should not be confused with American-European concern. Furthermore, once again there is no evidence as to the primary concern of any of the parties in the passage.

Answer choice (E): This is the correct answer choice, as it references the author's explicit statements in lines 8-14. Since historiographers have traditionally depended on the written records of European American explorers, it makes sense that, traditionally, the primary sources have been the accounts of those explorers.

Question #11: GR, Must, AP. The correct answer choice is (E)

Since this question asks for the response that the author would most likely disagree with, we should look for the answer choice that cannot be true based on the information provided in the stimulus.

Answer choice (A): Since the author acknowledges that a specific new source is likely to be valuable to the formation of a complete cultural perspective, this answer choice provides an assertion with which the author would likely agree.

Answer choice (B): Since there has been a change in what historiographers of the U.S. Pacific Coast view as a source, some time might lapse before every historiographer knows of these new sources to be considered, so the author might agree with this assertion. In any case, there is no reason to assume that the author would disagree, so this answer choice is incorrect.

Answer choice (C): The author asserts that the historiography was incomplete without consideration of the acts of early Chinese settlers, so the same might be said for other sources not previously considered. Since the author would be likely to agree with this statement, this answer choice is incorrect.

9

Answer choice (D): Since this answer basically paraphrases the claims found in lines 15-17, this assertion is not one with which the author would disagree, so this answer is incorrect.

Answer choice (E): This is the correct answer choice. The author's arguments relay the idea that, wherever written evidence neglects an important, contributing population, historiographers should investigate this new source of information. This assertion is based not on the fact that the settlers were non-European, but rather that they made important contributions. Thus the author would disagree with this answer choice, which asserts non-European participation is required to expand the definition of a source.

Question #12: GR, MustX. The correct answer choice is (D)

This is another example of a question which becomes much easier when one considers passage organization. Since this question concerns early Chinese settlers' interactions with the landscape, it seems that the relevant reference point would be the third paragraph, which deals almost exclusively with Chinese influences on the initial development of the region.

Answer choice (A): The new utilizations of local plants are discussed in lines 43-47, which describe the Chinese use of the wild mustard plant. Because this is an Except question, this answer choice, which accurately reflects information in the passage, should be eliminated.

Answer choice (B): The author specifically discusses the Chinese view of the land in lines 36-42, so this response provides an aspect discussed in the passage, and is therefore incorrect.

Answer choice (C): The discussion of Chinese ability to find unexpected agricultural potential in new areas and new plants, and use irrigation, as described in the third paragraph, is evidence that the Chinese had specialized agricultural skills. Since this is discussed in the passage, this answer choice is incorrect.

Answer choice (D): This is the correct answer choice, because the author makes no mention of initial Chinese knowledge of agribusiness practices. The Chinese settlers helped lay the foundations for what is now the well-known, prosperous agribusiness of the region (lines 50-54). Since the question asked about the settlers' initial interactions, and the passage discusses the agribusiness of a later era, this choice is the only answer that is unsupported, and it is therefore the correct response to this EXCEPT question.

Answer choice (E): Since the passage explicitly states in lines 48-54 that the Chinese settlers had knowledge of irrigation systems, this choice is supported, and incorrect.

9

Diversity Practice Passage II—October 2004 Passage #2 Answer Key

Question #13: GR, Must. The correct answer choice is (B)

This question asks for the response that can be most reasonably inferred from the passage, so we must find the answer choice that is consistent with the author's reasoning. Often the most efficient approach to this sort of question is to review the choices and quickly eliminate any that are inconsistent with the passage, and then examine the remaining responses more closely.

Answer choice (A): While the early Chinese settlers did have important, transferable skills, there is no reason to presume that these were the result of having come from similar climates, and the passage offers no insight into whether the climate was the reason for their migration.

Answer choice (B): This is the correct answer choice, based on the fact that Chinese settlers brought these swamp reclamation skills to the Pacific Coast (lines 50-54). As for the fact that these methods were used in the 19th century, this is confirmed by the fact that the historiographers of the U.S. Pacific Coast region have, as explicitly stated, traditionally used nineteenth-century European-American accounts (lines 8-14), and the Chinese settlers discussed fall in the same period (lines 21-27).

Answer choice (C): According to the passage, it was the Chinese settlers who used the wild mustard seeds, while the European settlers generally viewed the plants as weeds (lines 43-47).

Answer choice (D): It is valuable to study the actions of the Chinese settlers because there was little recorded by them. The actions of the European settlers have presumably already been considered by the historiographers, and this is because of the abundance of written sources available.

Answer choice (E): Since the author explicitly states in lines 21-22 that written records never existed in many cases, this choice, which suggests that such written records did exist at one time, is unsupported.

Diversity Practice Passage II—October 2004 Passage #2 Answer Key

Question #14: SR, Strengthen. The correct answer choice is (B)

This question asks which answer choice most effectively strengthens the author's claim in the last sentence, which basically states the main point of the passage: a complete historiography requires consideration of the actions of the early Chinese settlers. The correct answer choice will bolster this argument.

Answer choice (A): Since this response implies nothing directly about Chinese involvement in transforming the landscape, this answer is incorrect. Things change with time, and knowing what occurred during the past decade does not prove what occurred over a century ago. Further, the speed of the growth of the specialty crops relative to that of other crops has no clear relevance.

Answer choice (B): This is the correct answer choice, as this response would lend credibility to the claim that it was Chinese ancestors who converted the swamplands to grow the specialty crops currently cultivated by their Chinese-American descendants.

Answer choice (C): While this answer choice does provide evidence that irrigation is beneficial to agribusiness, it does nothing to provide support for the assertion that this benefit is attributable to early Chinese influence. Since this answer does not strengthen the claim from the last sentence in the passage, this choice is incorrect.

Answer choice (D): A steady increase in the efficiency of irrigation systems does not offer insight into their original source in the region. While this answer choice does appear to support the claim that irrigation improvements began in the nineteenth century, it does little to strengthen the claim that the early Chinese influence must be considered to form a more complete historiography.

Answer choice (E): Since we already know, given the passage, that agribusiness in the U.S. Pacific Coast region is thriving, it does not strengthen the author's argument to add reasons to believe that vegetation can grow well in that area. Although this response might make it more likely that irrigation is a good idea, it has nothing to do with whether such irrigation is attributable to early Chinese influence.

9

Law-Related Passages

As we discussed in Chapter Two, the LSAT Reading Comprehension section usually features one passage based on a law-related issue. Therefore, a brief examination of Law-Related passages is helpful to understanding the full scope of topics you will likely encounter.

Many students assume that because the LSAT is a test to gain admission to law school, the makers of the test must defend the legal system at every turn in the passages they present. This assumption is incorrect. Instead, the test makers treat the Law as a positive, benevolent, dynamic, and at times flawed construct.

Seeing the legal system as having faults is not unreasonable: a system as complex as law is bound to have areas where confusion, uncertainty, or change arises. This uncertainty within law can come from the rules, the witnesses, the attorneys, and even the judges. The test makers are happy to engage in frank discussions of the issues related to improving any aspect of the judicial system, and passages have done so regarding the following issues:

> Overinclusive laws
>
> Blackmail
>
> Deterrence of deliberate crimes
>
> Custom medical illustrations as evidence
>
> Statutory law training

If you encounter any unknown legal terminology while reading a Law-Related passage, do not be concerned. Any legal terms will be explained in the text.

The above is just a small sampling of issues that the LSAT has presented regarding the legal system.

On the other hand, the test makers show no hesitation in discussing the law as a positive force, and as a remedy to right social injustice. For example, passages have touched on the following topics where the law is used as a remedy or an aid:

> Exemptions for "traditional" activities in Alaska
>
> The Universal Declaration of Human Rights
>
> The Law Reform Commission of Western Australia

9

There are also a number of passages that deal with legal theory, and "big picture" issues related to the legal system. Various passages have addressed how to interpret law, how to model legal reasoning on computers, and the basis for punishment within the legal system. These passages tend to be more theoretical in nature—and thus occasionally more difficult—and focus less on real world examples.

The makers of the test also do not limit themselves to just the U.S. system of law. A number of previous passages have focused on the legal systems of Canada, England, and even South Africa.

In short, the law is treated as the complicated, powerful system it is, and the test makers examine both the faults and benefits of it, as well as the theoretical underpinnings.

Two Special Topics

There are two topics that appear within Law-Related passages that bear further examination, since in each case the viewpoint taken by the makers of the test tends to be consistent, and thus predictable. As we saw with Diversity passages, you can then use this information to inform your expectations and move more quickly within the passage.

1. Regulation

The legal system is used to prevent and remedy possible damages, and to regulate actions and industries. On the LSAT, passages occasionally appear that address the legal regulation of marketplaces and borders, and in almost every instance the viewpoint presented by the authors is the same: regulation is either needed or should be expanded if already in place. Given that LSAC is an organization that ultimately assists in producing lawyers, and it is the law which regulates our society, the consistency of this pro-regulation viewpoint should come as no surprise.

2. Diversity

We have already discussed passages that contain Diversity ideas and the consistency of the viewpoints given therein. When passages concerning Law-Related issues include Diversity elements, that consistency is of course maintained: in almost all cases, the test makers advocate legal remedies and relief for underrepresented groups.

A Law-Related Passage Analyzed ■■■

Now that we have discussed some of the different ways Law-Related passages are presented, it's time to examine a Law-Related passage, and then discuss some of its notable elements. As you read the passage on the following page, attempt to complete it (with notations) in under three minutes, but continue on with more time as needed to finish.

9

Individual family members have been assisted in resolving disputes arising from divorce or separation, property division, or financial arrangements, through court-connected family mediation programs, which
(5) differ significantly from court adjudication. When courts use their authority to resolve disputes by adjudicating matters in litigation, judges' decisions are binding, subject only to appeal. Formal rules govern the procedure followed, and the hearings are
(10) generally open to the public. In contrast, family mediation is usually conducted in private, the process is less formal, and mediators do not make binding decisions. Mediators help disputing parties arrive at a solution themselves through communication and
(15) cooperation by facilitating the process of negotiation that leads to agreement by the parties.

Supporters of court adjudication in resolving family disputes claim that it has numerous advantages over family mediation, and there is some validity to
(20) this claim. Judges' decisions, they argue, explicate and interpret the broader social values involved in family disputes, and family mediation can neglect those values. Advocates of court adjudication also argue that since the dynamics of power in disputes
(25) are not always well understood, mediation, which is based on the notion of relatively equal parties, would be inappropriate in many situations. The court system, on the other hand, attempts to protect those at a disadvantage because of imbalances in bargaining
(30) power. Family mediation does not guarantee the full protection of an individual's rights, whereas a goal of the court system is to ensure that lawyers can secure all that the law promises to their clients. Family mediation also does not provide a formal record of
(35) the facts and principles that influence the settlement of a dispute, so if a party to a mediated agreement subsequently seeks modification of the judgment, the task of reconstructing the mediation process is especially difficult. Finally, mediated settlements
(40) divert cases from judicial consideration, thus eliminating the opportunity for such cases to refine the law through the ongoing development of legal precedent.

But in the final analysis, family mediation is
(45) better suited to the unique needs of family law than is the traditional court system. Proponents of family mediation point out that it constitutes a more efficient and less damaging process than litigation. By working together in the mediation process, family members
(50) can enhance their personal autonomy and reduce government intervention, develop skills to resolve future disputes, and create a spirit of cooperation that can lead to greater compliance with their agreement. The family mediation process can assist in resolving
(55) emotional as well as legal issues and thus may reduce

stress in the long term. Studies of family mediation programs in several countries report that the majority of participants reach a full or partial agreement and express positive feelings about the process, perceiving
(60) it to be more rational and humane than the court system.

9

Law-Related Passage Analysis—October 2005 Passage #3

The passage concerns the value of family mediation programs versus the formalized process of court adjudication. Not unsurprisingly for a Law-Related passage, the author provides a frank discussion of the issue at hand, showing both positives and negatives of each option before concluding that the non-court solution is better for the needs of this particular situation.

Paragraph One:

The passage opens by explaining that family members can be assisted in dispute resolution in a variety of instances with family mediation programs, which are court-connected but significantly different from court adjudication. Whereas court decisions use formal rules in public hearings to produce binding results, family mediation is less formal, private, and not binding, and aimed at finding a mutually agreeable resolution.

Paragraph Two:

The second paragraph is dedicated to a discussion of the value of court adjudication of family disputes. The paragraph opens with the viewpoint of the supporters of court adjudication, and the author separately weighs in with the view that the supporters have some valid claims. Specifically, the supporters of the court make four claims:

1. Judges' decisions explain and interpret the broader social values present in family disputes, something that family mediation can neglect.

2. The court system protects the disadvantaged and ensures full protection of an individual's rights, whereas mediation does not guarantee full protection of rights and can be inappropriate in many instances because it is based on the notion of relatively equal parties.

3. Family mediation does not provide a formal record of the facts in a case, and thus modifying an agreement can be difficult.

4. Mediated settlements are not part of the formal system, and thus they eliminate opportunities for such cases to contribute to the development of the law and legal precedent.

9

Law-Related Passage Analysis—October 2005 Passage #3

Paragraph Three:

In the last paragraph, the author states the main point of the passage, namely that family mediation is a better choice for resolving family disputes than the traditional court system. The author then provides the viewpoint of the proponents of family mediation, who state that mediation is more efficient and less damaging than litigation. As an aside, note how the passage uses the terms "court adjudication," "judge's decisions," "court system," and "litigation" to all refer to the generally same idea. The use of interchangeable names is not an accident; one of the goals of the test makers is to test your ability to track related ideas within sections of text, and using this technique gives them that opportunity. Returning to the passage, the paragraph closes with a recitation of the benefits of the family mediation process.

VIEWSTAMP Analysis:

The passage contains a viewpoint neutral section and then three distinct **Viewpoints:**

The first paragraph is viewpoint neutral.

The view of the supporters of court adjudication (line 17).

The view of the author, who believes that family mediation programs are better than court adjudication in cases of family disputes (line 44), even though the court adjudication process has merit (line 19).

The view of the proponents of family mediation (line 46).

The author's **Tone** is positive towards family mediation, but also acknowledges the benefits of court adjudication. This is more a case of mediation being better suited for this particular task than court adjudication being entirely unsuitable.

The **Arguments** in the passage are mainly a set of benefits proposed by each side, with the author making the judgment that the family mediation benefits outweigh the court adjudication benefits.

The author's **Main Point** is family mediation is a better solution for resolving family disputes than is court adjudication.

Law-Related Passage Analysis—October 2005 Passage #3

The **Structure** of the passage is as follows:

Paragraph One: Compare and contrast family mediation with court adjudication.

Paragraph Two: Discuss four points raised by the supporters of court adjudication.

Paragraph Three: State the Main Point and then outline the view of the proponents of family mediation, views that the author agrees with.

The clear structure of this passage, along with the well-defined viewpoints, places you in an excellent position to answer the questions.

Two of the questions relate to the Global direction of the passage; one is a Main Point question and the other is a Global Purpose question. These two questions are easily answered by understanding the author's view that family mediation is a better solution for resolving family disputes than is court adjudication. Three other questions also relate directly to viewpoints: one involves the author, one involves the supporters of court adjudication, and one involves the proponents of family mediation. With the clear structure of the passage, these questions are also easy to answer. Here is one of the questions:

17. According to the passage, proponents of court adjudication of family disputes would be most likely to agree with which one of the following?

(A)   Court adjudication of family disputes usually produces a decision that satisfies all parties to the dispute equally.

(B)   Family mediation fails to address the underlying emotional issues in family disputes.

(C)   Settlements of disputes reached through family mediation are not likely to guide the resolution of similar future disputes among other parties.

(D)   Court adjudication presumes that the parties to a dispute have relatively equal bargaining power.

(E)   Court adjudication hearings for family disputes should always be open to the public.

Law-Related Passage Analysis—October 2005 Passage #3

In this Subject Perspective question stem, note how the test makers decide to suddenly use the term "proponents of court adjudication" instead of "supporters of court adjudication," which they had used previously. This switch is made because "proponents" was previously used in relation to family mediation, and the test makers are hoping that the careless or hurried test taker will misunderstand which group the question refers to. A student could see "proponent" and easily make the mistake of thinking the question referred to the proponents of family mediation when in fact the question refers to the supporters of court adjudication (especially when "family disputes" appears shortly thereafter). This type of test making trick is not uncommon, and this is one reason why you must always read very carefully.

Because the question is about the supporters of court adjudication, you should know that the correct answer will likely be generated by the information in the second paragraph. There were four reasons given in that paragraph, so you should seek an answer that matches one or more of those four. The correct answer choice is (C), which is based on the final reason given in the second paragraph (lines 39-43). Note how some of the wrong answer choices mix up the viewpoints in an attempt to lure you in: answer choice (B) is an answer better attributed to the proponents of family mediation, and answer choice (D) ascribes the wrong view to court adjudication. Answer choice (E) is incorrect because the passage states that hearings are *generally* open to the public, not always open to the public (lines 9-10), and, more importantly, because no comment is made about how the supporters of court adjudication view the subject.

Law-Related passages, like all Reading Comprehension passages, are tailor-made for the VIEWSTAMP approach we advocate in this book. You will likely see a Law-Related passage on the LSAT you take, but there is no specific viewpoint that the passage will take unless it addresses Regulation or Diversity. Simply focus on the VIEWSTAMP elements and you will be able to effectively navigate any Law passage.

9

Two Law-Related Practice Passages ■

The next four pages contain two actual LSAT Law-Related passage sets. After the two passages, a complete analysis of each passage and all of the corresponding questions is presented.

To most effectively benefit from this section, time yourself on the first passage. Attempt to finish the passage in 8 minutes and 45 seconds, but if you cannot, continue working until you complete all of the questions and then note your time. Then, read the entire explanation section for the first passage. Afterwards, move to the second passage and repeat the process.

9

In many Western societies, modern bankruptcy
laws have undergone a shift away from a focus on
punishment and toward a focus on bankruptcy as a
remedy for individuals and corporations in financial
(5) trouble—and, perhaps unexpectedly, for their
creditors. This shift has coincided with an ever-
increasing reliance on declarations of bankruptcy by
individuals and corporations with excessive debt, a
trend that has drawn widespread criticism. However,
(10) any measure seeking to make bankruptcy protection
less available would run the risk of preventing
continued economic activity of financially troubled
individuals and institutions. It is for this reason that
the temptation to return to a focus on punishment of
(15) individuals or corporations that become insolvent
must be resisted. Modern bankruptcy laws, in serving
the needs of an interdependent society, serve the
varied interests of the greatest number of citizens.
    The harsh punishment for insolvency in centuries
(20) past included imprisonment of individuals and
dissolution of enterprises, and reflected societies'
beliefs that the accumulation of excessive debt
resulted either from debtors' unwillingness to meet
obligations or from their negligence. Insolvent debtors
(25) were thought to be breaking sacrosanct social
contracts; placing debtors in prison was considered
necessary in order to remove from society those who
would violate such contracts and thereby defraud
creditors. But creditors derive little benefit from
(30) imprisoned debtors unable to repay even a portion of
their debt. And if the entity to be punished is a large
enterprise, for example, an auto manufacturer, its
dissolution would cause significant unemployment
and the disruption of much-needed services.
(35)   Modern bankruptcy law has attempted to address
the shortcomings of the punitive approach. Two
beliefs underlie this shift: that the public good ought
to be paramount in considering the financial
insolvency of individuals and corporations; and that
(40) the public good is better served by allowing
debt-heavy corporations to continue to operate, and
indebted individuals to continue to earn wages,
than by disabling insolvent economic entities. The
mechanism for executing these goals is usually a
(45) court-directed reorganization of debtors' obligations to
creditors. Such reorganizations typically comprise
debt relief and plans for court-directed transfers of
certain assets from debtor to creditor. Certain
strictures connected to bankruptcy—such as the fact
(50) that bankruptcies become matters of public record
and are reported to credit bureaus for a number of
years—may still serve a punitive function, but not by
denying absolution of debts or financial
reorganization. Through these mechanisms, today's
(55) bankruptcy laws are designed primarily to assure
continued engagement in productive economic
activity, with the ultimate goal of restoring businesses
and individuals to a degree of economic health and
providing creditors with the best hope of collecting.

6. Which one of the following most accurately expresses
    the main point of the passage?

    (A) The modern trend in bankruptcy law away from
         punishment and toward the maintenance of
         economic activity serves the best interests of
         society and should not be abandoned.
    (B) Bankruptcy laws have evolved in order to meet
         the needs of creditors, who depend on the
         continued productive activity of private citizens
         and profit-making enterprises.
    (C) Modern bankruptcy laws are justified on
         humanitarian grounds, even though the earlier
         punitive approach was more economically
         efficient.
    (D) Punishment for debt no longer holds deterrent
         value for debtors and is therefore a concept that
         has been largely abandoned as ineffective.
    (E) Greater economic interdependence has triggered
         the formation of bankruptcy laws that reflect
         a convergence of the interests of debtors and
         creditors.

7. In stating that bankruptcy laws have evolved "perhaps
    unexpectedly" (line 5) as a remedy for creditors, the
    author implies that creditors

    (A) are often surprised to receive compensation in
         bankruptcy courts
    (B) have unintentionally become the chief
         beneficiaries of bankruptcy laws
    (C) were a consideration, though not a primary one,
         in the formulation of bankruptcy laws
    (D) are better served than is immediately apparent by
         laws designed in the first instance to provide a
         remedy for debtors
    (E) were themselves active in the formulation of
         modern bankruptcy laws

8. The author's attitude toward the evolution of bankruptcy
    law can most accurately be described as

    (A) approval of changes that have been made to
         inefficient laws
    (B) confidence that further changes to today's laws
         will be unnecessary
    (C) neutrality toward laws that, while helpful to
         many, remain open to abuse
    (D) skepticism regarding the possibility of solutions
         to the problem of insolvency
    (E) concern that inefficient laws may have been
         replaced by legislation too lenient to debtors

9

9. The primary purpose of the passage is to

(A) offer a critique of both past and present approaches to insolvency

(B) compare the practices of bankruptcy courts of the past with those of bankruptcy courts of the present

(C) criticize those who would change the bankruptcy laws of today

(D) reexamine today's bankruptcy laws in an effort to point to further improvements

(E) explain and defend contemporary bankruptcy laws

10. Which one of the following claims would a defender of the punitive theory of bankruptcy legislation be most likely to have made?

(A) Debt that has become so great that repayment is impossible is ultimately a moral failing and thus a matter for which the law should provide punitive sanctions.

(B) Because insolvency ultimately harms the entire economy, the law should provide a punitive deterrent to insolvency.

(C) The insolvency of companies or individuals is tolerable if the debt is the result of risk-taking, profit-seeking ventures that might create considerable economic growth in the long run.

(D) The dissolution of a large enterprise is costly to the economy as a whole and should not be allowed, even when that enterprise's insolvency is the result of its own fiscal irresponsibility.

(E) The employees of a large bankrupt enterprise should be considered just as negligent as the owner of a bankrupt sole proprietorship.

11. Which one of the following sentences could most logically be appended to the end of the last paragraph of the passage?

(A) Only when today's bankruptcy laws are ultimately seen as inadequate on a large scale will bankruptcy legislation return to its original intent.

(B) Punishment is no longer the primary goal of bankruptcy law, even if some of its side effects still function punitively.

(C) Since leniency serves the public interest in bankruptcy law, it is likely to do so in criminal law as well.

(D) Future bankruptcy legislation could include punitive measures, but only if such measures ultimately benefit creditors.

(E) Today's bankruptcy laws place the burden of insolvency squarely on the shoulders of creditors, in marked contrast to the antiquated laws that weighed heavily on debtors.

12. The information in the passage most strongly suggests which one of the following about changes in bankruptcy laws?

(A) Bankruptcy laws always result from gradual changes in philosophy followed by sudden shifts in policy.

(B) Changes in bankruptcy law were initiated by the courts and only grudgingly adopted by legislators.

(C) The adjustment of bankruptcy laws away from a punitive focus was at first bitterly opposed by creditors.

(D) Bankruptcy laws underwent change because the traditional approach proved inadequate and contrary to the needs of society.

(E) The shift away from a punitive approach to insolvency was part of a more general trend in society toward rehabilitation and away from retribution.

13. Which one of the following, if true, would most weaken the author's argument against harsh punishment for debtors?

(A) Extensive study of the economic and legal history of many countries has shown that most individuals who served prison time for bankruptcy subsequently exhibited greater economic responsibility.

(B) The bankruptcy of a certain large company has had a significant negative impact on the local economy even though virtually all of the affected employees were able to obtain similar jobs within the community.

(C) Once imprisonment was no longer a consequence of insolvency, bankruptcy filings increased dramatically, then leveled off before increasing again during the 1930s.

(D) The court-ordered liquidation of a large and insolvent company's assets threw hundreds of people out of work, but the local economy nevertheless demonstrated robust growth in the immediate aftermath.

(E) Countries that continue to imprison debtors enjoy greater economic health than do comparable countries that have ceased to do so.

9

Law-Related Practice Passage II—December 2006 Passage #4

Computers have long been utilized in the sphere of law in the form of word processors, spreadsheets, legal research systems, and practice management systems. Most exciting, however, has been the
(5) prospect of using artificial intelligence techniques to create so-called legal reasoning systems—computer programs that can help to resolve legal disputes by reasoning from and applying the law. But the practical benefits of such automated reasoning
(10) systems have fallen short of optimistic early predictions and have not resulted in computer systems that can independently provide expert advice about substantive law. This is not surprising in light of the difficulty in resolving problems involving the
(15) meaning and applicability of rules set out in a legal text.

Early attempts at automated legal reasoning focused on the doctrinal nature of law. They viewed law as a set of rules, and the resulting computer
(20) systems were engineered to make legal decisions by determining the consequences that followed when its stored set of legal rules was applied to a collection of evidentiary data. Such systems underestimated the problems of interpretation that can arise at every
(25) stage of a legal argument. Examples abound of situations that are open to differing interpretations: whether a mobile home in a trailer park is a house or a motor vehicle, whether a couple can be regarded as married in the absence of a formal legal ceremony,
(30) and so on. Indeed, many notions invoked in the text of a statute may be deliberately left undefined so as to allow the law to be adapted to unforeseen circumstances. But in order to be able to apply legal rules to novel situations, systems have to be equipped
(35) with a kind of comprehensive knowledge of the world that is far beyond their capabilities at present or in the foreseeable future.

Proponents of legal reasoning systems now argue that accommodating reference to, and reasoning from,
(40) cases improves the chances of producing a successful system. By focusing on the practice of reasoning from precedents, researchers have designed systems called case-based reasoners, which store individual example cases in their knowledge bases. In contrast
(45) to a system that models legal knowledge based on a set of rules, a case-based reasoner, when given a concrete problem, manipulates the cases in its knowledge base to reach a conclusion based on a similar case. Unfortunately, in the case-based systems
(50) currently in development, the criteria for similarity among cases are system dependent and fixed by the designer, so that similarity is found only by testing for the presence or absence of predefined factors. This simply postpones the apparently intractable
(55) problem of developing a system that can discover for itself the factors that make cases similar in relevant ways.

21. Which one of the following most accurately expresses the main point of the passage?

(A) Attempts to model legal reasoning through computer programs have not been successful because of problems of interpreting legal discourse and identifying appropriate precedents.

(B) Despite signs of early promise, it is now apparent that computer programs have little value for legal professionals in their work.

(C) Case-based computer systems are vastly superior to those computer systems based upon the doctrinal nature of the law.

(D) Computers applying artificial intelligence techniques show promise for revolutionizing the process of legal interpretation in the relatively near future.

(E) Using computers can expedite legal research, facilitate the matching of a particular case to a specific legal principle, and even provide insights into possible flaws involving legal reasoning.

22. The logical relationship of lines 8-13 of the passage to lines 23-25 and 49-53 of the passage is most accurately described as

(A) a general assertion supported by two specific observations

(B) a general assertion followed by two arguments, one of which supports and one of which refutes the general assertion

(C) a general assertion that entails two more specific assertions

(D) a theoretical assumption refuted by two specific observations

(E) a specific observation that suggests two incompatible generalizations

23. In the passage as a whole, the author is primarily concerned with

(A) arguing that computers can fundamentally change how the processes of legal interpretation and reasoning are conducted in the future

(B) indicating that the law has subtle nuances that are not readily dealt with by computerized legal reasoning programs

(C) demonstrating that computers are approaching the point where they can apply legal precedents to current cases

(D) suggesting that, because the law is made by humans, computer programmers must also apply their human intuition when designing legal reasoning systems

(E) defending the use of computers as essential and indispensable components of the modem legal profession

24. The passage suggests that the author would be most likely to agree with which one of the following statements about computerized automated legal reasoning systems?

(A) These systems have met the original expectations of computer specialists but have fallen short of the needs of legal practitioners.

(B) Progress in research on these systems has been hindered, more because not enough legal documents are accessible by computer than because theoretical problems remain unsolved.

(C) These systems will most likely be used as legal research tools rather than as aids in legal analysis.

(D) Rule systems will likely replace case-based systems over time.

(E) Developing adequate legal reasoning systems would require research breakthroughs by computer specialists.

25. It can be most reasonably inferred from the passage's discussion of requirements for developing effective automated legal reasoning systems that the author would agree with which one of the following statements?

(A) Focusing on the doctrinal nature of law is the fundamental error made by developers of automated legal systems.

(B) Contemporary computers do not have the required memory capability to store enough data to be effective legal reasoning systems.

(C) Questions of interpretation in rule-based legal reasoning systems must be settled by programming more legal rules into the systems.

(D) Legal statutes and reasoning may involve innovative applications that cannot be modeled by a fixed set of rules, cases, or criteria.

(E) As professionals continue to use computers in the sphere of law they will develop the competence to use legal reasoning systems effectively.

26. Based on the passage, which one of the following can be most reasonably inferred concerning case-based reasoners?

(A) The major problem in the development of these systems is how to store enough cases in their knowledge bases.

(B) These systems are more useful than rule systems because case-based reasoners are based on a simpler view of legal reasoning.

(C) Adding specific criteria for similarity among cases to existing systems would not overcome an important shortcoming of these systems.

(D) These systems can independently provide expert advice about legal rights and duties in a wide range of cases.

(E) These systems are being designed to attain a much more ambitious goal than had been set for rule systems.

27. Which one of the following is mentioned in the passage as an important characteristic of many statutes that frustrates the application of computerized legal reasoning systems?

(A) complexity of syntax
(B) unavailability of relevant precedents
(C) intentional vagueness and adaptability
(D) overly narrow intent
(E) incompatibility with previous statutes

28. The examples of situations that are open to differing interpretations (lines 25-30) function in the passage to

(A) substantiate the usefulness of computers in the sphere of law

(B) illustrate a vulnerability of rule systems in computerized legal reasoning

(C) isolate issues that computer systems are in principle incapable of handling

(D) explain how legal rules have been adapted to novel situations

(E) question the value of reasoning from precedents in interpreting legal rules

9

Law-Related Practice Passage I—September 2006 Passage #2 Answer Key

Paragraph One:

The author begins this passage discussing the shift in Western bankruptcy laws away from an emphasis on punishment and toward a focus on bankruptcy as a remedy. This approach has drawn criticism as declarations of bankruptcy have increased.

Following a viewpoint-neutral introduction, the author's viewpoint is presented: we should resist the temptation to make bankruptcy protection less available, because this protection helps to ensure continued economic activity. Modern bankruptcy laws, the author argues, recognize interdependence and serve the interests of the greatest number of citizens.

Paragraph Two:

In the second paragraph the author presents the historical (from past centuries) viewpoint on bankruptcy, when harsh punishments were imposed based on the belief that excessive debt came from negligence or unwillingness to pay. Those who broke sacred social payment contracts were removed from society through imprisonment.

Having presented the old way of dealing with debtors, the author points out two disadvantages of the historical approach: a focus on separation and punishment does not repay creditors, and under the old approach large entities' bankruptcies can lead to further detriment for society.

Paragraph Three:

At this point in the passage, the author has discussed the old approach to bankruptcy, and why we should avoid a similar approach. In this paragraph, the author examines modern bankruptcy law, which is based on a primary concern for public good in consideration of bankruptcy issues. The public good is better served by continued economic activity than by the presence of disabled, insolvent entities. Modern bankruptcy involves reorganization, court transfers of assets, and some debt relief, and these reorganizations are made public and have credit bureau ramifications, so there is some punitive aspect. But providing these individuals and corporations with bankruptcy protection helps to ensure continued productivity and provides creditors with the best chance of collecting their debts.

VIEWSTAMP Analysis:

The **Viewpoints** presented in this passage are those of the historical view (from "centuries past"), and those of the more modern perspective, which are shared by the author. The historical view on bankruptcy in Western societies maintained a focus on punishment, while the more modern perspective (and the one to which the author subscribes) approaches the issue with a view toward continued productivity.

9

Law-Related Practice Passage I—September 2006 Passage #2 Answer Key

The **Tone** of the passage is quite positive with respect to modern bankruptcy law, and negative with regard to the historical view on bankruptcy. The author clearly believes that modern laws provide a more practical approach to helping all parties involved.

The author's main **Argument** is that modern bankruptcy law is preferable to laws from past centuries, and that we should not be tempted to go back to the traditional perspective.

The **Main Point** of the passage is that the changes to bankruptcy laws that have taken place are for the best, so we should avoid the old approach and focus more on productivity and the greater good than on punishment.

The **Structure** of the passage is as follows:

Paragraph One: Introduce shift in bankruptcy in Western societies, from focus on punishment to focus on continued productivity. Shift from viewpoint-neutral discussion to the author's viewpoint, author asserts that bankruptcy protection should continue to be available in the interest of the common good.

Paragraph Two: Present historical perspective on insolvent debtors; point out that the old debtors' prison approach provides little benefit for the creditor, and slowing or stopping individual or corporate productivity can yield negative results.

Paragraph Three: Discuss modern bankruptcy law, and the beliefs that have driven changes from the old ways (public good, continued productivity should be the main considerations). Present specific mechanisms, and restate the goal of modern bankruptcy law, to help those in debt while also trying to provide creditors with the best chance to collect.

9

Law-Related Practice Passage I—September 2006 Passage #2 Answer Key

Question #6: GR, Main Point. The correct answer choice is (A)

Before looking at the choices, you should be sure to prephrase the answer to any Main Point question. In this case, the Main Point is that bankruptcy laws in Western societies have changed to better serve the interests of the greater good.

Answer choice (A): This is the correct answer choice, as it provides a basic restatement of our prephrase above. The author believes that bankruptcy laws have changed, and we should not go back to a system that focuses on punishment rather than on the greater good of society.

Answer choice (B): Although the author points out that modern bankruptcy laws do help creditors, the author does not claim that creditors' needs caused the evolution of these laws, so this answer choice is incorrect.

Answer choice (C): Modern bankruptcy laws are based in part on humanitarian concerns, but the author does not assert that the earlier approach was more efficient. In fact, the passage specifically points out that the imprisonment of debtors could not benefit creditors (line 29).

Answer choice (D): According to the passage, the old approach was focused on punishment and was an inefficient means of dealing with insolvency. The author does not discuss the issue of deterrence, and does not assert that a lack of deterrence caused the discussed changes in the laws.

Answer choice (E): Economic interdependence allows for the interests of debtors and creditors to be aligned, but the author does not claim that increased interdependence has triggered current laws, so this answer choice is incorrect.

Question #7: SR, Must. The correct answer choice is (D)

The "unexpected remedy" implies that the creditors may not have expected to gain from laws meant to help debtors.

Answer choice (A): The author does not imply that creditors are surprised to get any compensation in bankruptcy court, so this answer should be eliminated.

Answer choice (B): There is no implication that the creditors would be the chief beneficiaries, only that they might benefit.

Answer choice (C): This is a potentially tricky wrong answer choice. The referenced implication is that the creditors might unexpectedly benefit from laws that serve an interdependent society, but the author does not discuss whether the creditors were considered when the bankruptcy laws were formulated.

9

Answer choice (D): This is the correct answer choice. The implication, as prephrased, is that creditors may, surprisingly, benefit from laws intended to help debtors.

Answer choice (E): There is no implication that the creditors were involved in formulating modern bankruptcy laws. Further, the author implies that the creditors were surprised to benefit from the laws, so it seems unlikely that they were involved in their formulation.

Question #8: GR, AP. The correct answer choice is (A)

The author's attitude is that the old laws were counterproductive and detrimental, and the modern approach to bankruptcy makes more sense for all parties involved.

Answer choice (A): This is the correct answer choice, and reflects our prephrase above. The author approves of the modern approach as more reasonable and effective than the historical approach.

Answer choice (B): This answer goes too far. The author agrees with the changes that have taken place, but does not go so far as to claim that no further changes to the laws will ever be necessary.

Answer choice (C): The author's attitude is not neutral; it is supportive of the changes that have taken place, so this answer choice is incorrect.

Answer choice (D): The author is not skeptical, but supportive of the idea that bankruptcy under the modern approach can serve the interests of both debtors and creditors.

Answer choice (E): The author supports modern legislation, and never suggests that newer laws are too lenient, so this answer choice should be eliminated.

9

Law-Related Practice Passage I—September 2006 Passage #2 Answer Key

Question #9: GR, P. The correct answer choice is (E)

The author's main purpose is to discuss the old and new approaches to bankruptcy, and explain why the modern approach is preferable.

Answer choice (A): The passage does discuss both past and present approaches, but the purpose is more than to provide a critique of each. The author clearly wants to support the modern approach and warn against going back to the historical approach.

Answer choice (B): The author does compare the old approach to the new approach, but this is not the primary purpose, which is to lend support to the modern perspective on bankruptcy.

Answer choice (C): The author does not seek to criticize currently proposed changes, but to warn against the historical, punishment-based perspective.

Answer choice (D): The author supports the modern perspective on bankruptcy, and does not discuss further improvements.

Answer choice (E): This is the correct answer choice. The author discusses the basis of the modern approach, and provides several points in support of this perspective.

Question #10: GR, SP. The correct answer choice is (A)

To prephrase the answer to this question, we should consider what drove the historical perspective. This comes from the discussion in the second paragraph, in which the author explains that insolvent debtors were seen as negligent or unwilling to pay, and it was necessary to punish and remove these contract breakers from society.

Answer choice (A): This is the correct answer choice. The historical perspective saw the insolvent as deserving of punishment. Punishment was a primary focus of the old perspective, so a proponent of this perspective would likely call for punitive sanctions.

Answer choice (B): This is a popular wrong answer, as it seems a reasonable defense of a punitive approach. The passage does not present *deterrence* as a driving justification for the historical approach, however, so this answer choice is incorrect.

Answer choice (C): A proponent of the historical perspective would likely have little tolerance for insolvency, regardless of the long term prospects.

Answer choice (D): This answer choice represents the modern perspective, and that of the author, rather than the viewpoint associated with the historical approach to bankruptcy.

Law-Related Practice Passage I—September 2006 Passage #2 Answer Key

Answer choice (E): There is no reference or implication regarding this specific assignment of negligence, so we cannot be sure of the historical perspective on this issue.

Question #11: SR, E. The correct answer choice is (B)

If we are to prephrase an answer to this passage expansion question, it is valuable to consider how the passage ended. In this case the closing point was that modern bankruptcy laws may be punitive on some level, but they are intended to promote economic activity and help all parties involved. The right answer choice will likely either continue this general theme, or reference the passage in general.

Answer choice (A): This response would make no sense at the end of this passage. The author is a fan of today's bankruptcy laws, and would not have such a positive tone with regard to original intent.

Answer choice (B): This is the correct answer choice, as this response logically restates the point with which the author ends the passage.

Answer choice (C): There is no reference to criminal law in the passage, so this answer choice would not logically follow.

Answer choice (D): The author mentions the punitive facet of current bankruptcy law, but never references prospective punitive measures in the future, so this answer choice should be eliminated.

Answer choice (E): The author believes that modern law favors all parties concerned/involved, in stark contrast to this answer choice.

Question #12: GR, Must. The correct answer choice is (D)

As with all Must questions, the correct answer choice must pass the Fact Test.

Answer choice (A): We can rule out this answer choice based on the word "always," since the author makes no such absolute claims. Further, in the one example discussed, it seems that a change in policy was followed by a gradual change in philosophy among creditors.

Answer choice (B): There is no reference or implication that the courts led the way, so this answer choice is incorrect.

Answer choice (C): The author implied that benefit to creditors may have been unexpected, but this is not the same as claiming a bitter opposition on the part of the creditors.

Law-Related Practice Passage I—September 2006 Passage #2 Answer Key

Answer choice (D): This is the correct answer choice. The author discusses several points of inadequacy of the historical approach, and asserts that the new laws are an improvement, so we can assume that the changes were a result of these inadequacies.

Answer choice (E): Since there are no discussions or implications of such broad societal trends, this cannot be the right answer choice.

Question #13: CR, Weaken. The correct answer choice is (E)

The author's argument *against* harsh punishment for debtors is that this treatment is economically counterproductive. The correct answer choice will somehow weaken or cast doubt on this point.

Answer choice (A): This answer choice does not weaken the basic argument that bankrupt individuals cannot be productive while in prison.

Answer choice (B): This choice supports the author's argument against harsh punishment.

Answer choice (C): This answer choice would not weaken the general claims about non-productivity, only that there may have been many who needed bankruptcy but had been afraid to make a claim.

Answer choice (D): A single example of immediate growth does not disprove the author's more general claims about bankruptcy, so this answer choice is incorrect.

Answer choice (E): This is the correct answer choice, as it strengthens the assertion that harsh debtor punishment is good for an economy.

9

Law-Related Practice Passage II—December 2006 Passage #4 Answer Key

Paragraph One:

The author begins this passage by stating that computers have been commonly used for basic functions in law, with interesting prospects in the area of "legal reasoning systems." These are defined as "computer programs that can help to resolve legal disputes by reasoning from and applying the law." Early efforts to use artificial intelligence in this way have been unable to produce expert legal advice. According to the author this is to be expected, considering the complexity of any system of legal rules. The final sentence in the paragraph provides the first bit of tone in the passage, reflecting the author's skepticism regarding the prospects for computer legal reasoning.

Paragraph Two:

Here the author discusses early efforts to create legal reasoning systems, which began with programs based on sets of rules, or doctrine. These were found ineffective because of the legal interpretations required at every level. Since many laws are written vaguely and require some degree of interpretation, access to the vast information required for this interpretation is beyond computer capability now or in the near future. Note that while the first paragraph closed with the author's skeptical viewpoint, this paragraph is generally informational, and viewpoint-neutral.

Paragraph Three:

In the final paragraph the author presents current thoughts on the creation of legal reasoning systems. Here, the author introduces the perspective of proponents, who say that basing decisions on past similar cases might improve prospects for a working system. The problem is that the case-based reasoning program would have to recognize similar cases and issues, and criteria for this similarity would have to be predetermined within the program. Here we see another manifestation of the author's skeptical tone: this new approach, the author points out, is sure to have serious challenges as well, because at some point it will be necessary to enable the program to determine relevant precedent.

VIEWSTAMP Analysis:

The **Viewpoints** presented in this passage are those of the proponents of legal systems, who believe in the prospects of case-based legal systems, and of the author, who is skeptical about the possibility of finding a solution to this very complex problem.

9

Law-Related Practice Passage II—December 2006 Passage #4 Answer Key

The author's **Tone** is skeptical regarding the possibility of creating a fully functional legal reasoning system that is capable of determining relevant precedent or dispensing expert legal advice.

The **Arguments** in the passage are those of the legal reasoning proponents, who assert that the chances of developing such a system are improved with the use of precedent-based reasoning, and of the author, who is skeptical about the prospects.

The **Main Point** of this passage is to discuss attempts at reasoning systems, and the challenges of developing programs with comprehensive legal knowledge or understanding of relevant precedents.

The **Structure** of the passage is as follows:

Paragraph One: Introduce the concept of legal reasoning systems, and discuss how early attempts have been unable to automate legal reasoning.

Paragraph Two: Discuss early attempts to base legal reasoning systems on sets of legal rules; this doctrinal approach required interpretations at each level. Point out that computers are currently not capable of storing the comprehensive knowledge required to create a rule-based automated system.

Paragraph Three: Introduce another approach suggested by legal reasoning systems proponents—case-based reasoners attempt to reach conclusions based on similar case precedents. Assert that there still exists the underlying problem of creating a program that can assess legally relevant similarities.

9

Law-Related Practice Passage II—December 2006 Passage #4 Answer Key

Question #21: GR, Main Point. The correct answer choice is (A)

The question stem asks for the main point of the passage, which is to introduce the concept of legal reasoning systems and the challenges associated with the development of artificial intelligence-based legal reasoning systems.

Answer choice (A): This is the correct answer choice, discussing the same points emphasized in our prephrased answer above.

Answer choice (B): This answer choice is incorrect, because computer programs are presently used in law, as discussed in the first sentence of the passage.

Answer choice (C): While earlier, doctrinal approaches apparently were not successful, and case-based programs represent the latest effort to develop legal reasoning systems, it is still unclear whether they will be able to provide a better solution, so this answer choice is incorrect.

Answer choice (D): While there is promise, the author highlights the challenges involved going forward, and never makes the assertion that revolutionary results will be achieved in the near future.

Answer choice (E): While this may be true, the main point of the passage involves the challenges associated with developing legal reasoning systems, so this answer choice is incorrect.

Question #22: SR, O. The correct answer choice is (A)

With specific reference, passage organization questions such as this one, we need to understand the organization and specific context of the passage. In lines 8-13, the author is summarizing the main point: the benefits of legal reasoning systems have fallen short of predictions. In lines 23-25, the discussion focuses on how rule-based systems have proven inadequate because of the problems of interpretation. In lines 49-53, the discussion surrounds how case-based systems are limited. The first statement is a general statement: the benefits of legal reasoning systems have fallen short of expectations. The second statement is one example of how the first portion of the passage is true. The third statement is another example to support the first referenced assertion.

Answer choice (A): This is the correct answer choice. The first statement is the general assertion that legal reasoning systems have fallen short of predictions, and the other referenced statements are specific observations that lend support to the general assertion.

Answer choice (B): Since both later points support the first, this answer choice is incorrect.

Answer choice (C): The first reference is a general assertion, but the later two referenced excerpts are facts in support and not the author's *assertions*.

9

Law-Related Practice Passage II—December 2006 Passage #4 Answer Key

Answer choice (D): Since the two observations support the first assertion, this answer choice should be eliminated.

Answer choice (E): The first referenced quote is a general assertion, rather than a specific observation.

Question #23: GR, P. The correct answer choice is (B)

The question stem asks for the author's primary concern. Again, the author is primarily interested in discussing the concept of legal reasoning systems and the associated challenges.

Answer choice (A): Although the author does allude to the potential benefits of legal reasoning systems, this is not the primary concern.

Answer choice (B): This is the correct answer choice, as the author is interested in discussing the challenges of such systems—the subtleties of law that make interpretation and determinations of relevance difficult.

Answer choice (C): There is no such demonstration—the author focuses on the challenges that are sure to come with systems based on precedent, so this answer choice should be eliminated.

Answer choice (D): The passage provides no such suggestion, and while this may be true, it is not supported by the passage and certainly not the primary focus.

Answer choice (E): While the author could be a proponent of the use of computers in the law office, the primary concern is to note that legal reasoning systems are sure to bring challenges during development.

Question #24: GR, AP. The correct answer choice is (E)

This question regarding the author's perspective cannot be perfectly prephrased, but it is advisable to know the author's basic attitude, which is that computer reasoning systems are a good idea but have yet to be successfully implemented.

Answer choice (A): The passage specifically states in line 10 that these systems have fallen short of original predictions, so this choice is incorrect.

Answer choice (B): The hindrance to progress has come from difficulties in subtle interpretations, not lack of accessibility to legal documents.

Answer choice (C): The author highlights the challenges that will go along with developing a system for legal analysis, but is not so skeptical as to presume that such efforts will be futile.

Law-Related Practice Passage II—December 2006 Passage #4 Answer Key

Answer choice (D): Rule systems represented the early attempts at legal reasoning systems, while case-based systems are the latest approach.

Answer choice (E): This is the correct answer choice. In rule systems, the author notes that these systems would have to be equipped with knowledge "that is far beyond their capabilities at present or in the foreseeable future" (lines 34-37). For case-based systems, lines 50-57 state that the criteria for these systems are system dependent and fixed by their designers, and that there is a problem of developing a system that can determine relevant precedents.

Question #25: GR, AP. The correct answer choice is (D)

Since this is another author's perspective question, it is again helpful to note that there are various reasons presented which drive the author's uncertainty about whether computer-based reasoning can be implemented successfully.

Answer choice (A): With regard to the doctrinal model, the author discusses the challenges associated but does not suggest that the choice of this focus was a fundamental error. Rather, the challenges go along with the task itself, for which a solution has not yet been found.

Answer choice (B): The chief problem with legal reasoning systems is not memory but the limitations of the programming, so this answer choice is incorrect.

Answer choice (C): In the examples provided in the second paragraph of the passage, it is not rules programming that is the problem. Rather, it is an inability to equip the systems with the comprehensive knowledge required for expert interpretation that has resulted in difficulties.

Answer choice (D): This is the correct answer choice. The rule-based system appears to require more comprehensive legal knowledge than computers are currently capable of, and at the end of the passage (line 54) the author notes the "intractable problem of developing a system that can discover for itself the factors that make cases similar in relevant ways."

Answer choice (E): The incompetence of the legal practitioners is not the source of the problems with legal reasoning systems; the challenge lies in the creation of the programming.

9

Law-Related Practice Passage II—December 2006 Passage #4 Answer Key

Question #26: CR, Must. The correct answer choice is (C)

The question stem asks what can be inferred concerning case-based reasoning systems. Active readers with a good grasp of this passage's organization recognize that this discussion comes from the last paragraph of the passage.

Answer choice (A): In lines 49-57, the author notes that the major problem is the human limitations created by the programmers, not the lack of storage capacity. In fact, inadequate storage is not mentioned at all.

Answer choice (B): The author will likely agree that case-based systems currently appear to have more potential than rule-based systems, but this is not because they are based on a simpler view of legal reasoning.

Answer choice (C): This is the correct answer choice, rephrasing the author's assertion at the end of the passage that there remains the "intractable problem of developing a system that can discover for itself the factors that make cases similar in relevant ways." (54-57).

Answer choice (D): The author is focused on the challenges associated with developing a program that can independently provide such advice, but such programs have not yet been successfully developed, so this answer choice should be eliminated.

Answer choice (E): There is nothing in the passage to suggest that there is a more ambitious goal for case systems versus rule systems. Rather, the two models simply represent two different approaches to the same problem.

Question #27: GR, Must. The correct answer choice is (C)

An important characteristic of many statutes that frustrates the application of computerized legal reasoning systems is the vagueness that is often written into statutes to allow for (and require) flexible interpretation.

Answer choice (A): The complexity of the syntax is never mentioned, so this is incorrect.

Answer choice (B): It is not the unavailability of relevant precedents that is the problem, but rather the flexible determination of the relevance of various precedents, so this answer choice should be eliminated.

Answer choice (C): This is the correct answer choice, reflecting our prephrased answer above. This is noted in lines 31-33: "a statute may be deliberately left undefined so as to allow the law to be adapted to unforeseen circumstances."

9

Answer choice (D): The problem is not an overly narrow intent. It is the opposite—the built-in flexibility—that is mentioned as a challenging attribute.

Answer choice (E): There is no reference to statutes' incompatibility, so this answer choice cannot be correct.

Question #28: SR, P. The correct answer choice is (B)

This question stem asks what function is served by the examples of situations that are open to differing interpretations (lines 25-30). These are offered to show that rule-based systems underestimated the complexity of interpretation that can arise at each stage of a legal argument.

Answer choice (A): Given the fact that the author focuses on the inability thus far to create legal reasoning systems, this answer choice is incorrect.

Answer choice (B): This is the correct answer choice, consistent with our prephrase above.

Answer choice (C): Since the issues exemplify the challenges of rule based systems, this answer choice is incorrect.

Answer choice (D): The referenced examples show the difficulties of adapting to novel situations, so this answer choice should be eliminated.

Answer choice (E): The discussion of precedents is pertinent to case-based systems rather than rule-based systems, which is the context for the referenced examples, so this answer choice is incorrect.

9

Science Passages

The spectrum of topics covered in the Reading Comprehension section is quite broad, but one topic that consistently appears is Science. On average, each Reading Comprehension section contains one passage based on a scientific idea.

Types of Science Passages

Up until the October 1991 LSAT, all LSAT Reading Comprehension Science passages addressed the topic in a social science environment. For example, a passage would discuss the effects of technology on society, and examine the social implications of the new technology. Passages of this type, which we term Soft Science, still appear on the LSAT today. These passages are relatively easy because they focus more on social impact, or alternatively they address scientific ideas that the average person is somewhat familiar with, such as oil drilling or renewable energy resources.

Starting in October 1991 with the infamous Waterbugs passage, the makers of the LSAT began to introduce passages based on scientific topics that the average student had never previously encountered, or knew little about. These passages, which we term Hard Science, still exist on today's LSAT as well, and appear more frequently than Soft Science passages. The inclusion of a Hard Science passage often increases the difficulty of the section by introducing a broader variety of subject matter and a deeper level of complexity to the test.

Hard Science passages appear more frequently than Soft Science passages.

In a moment we will discuss how to attack all Science passages, but in the meantime, consider some of the Science topics that have appeared on the LSAT:

Creutzfeldt-Jakob Disease

Calvaria major

Floral balance restoration

Geology of the ocean floor

Lichenometry

To many students, those ideas appear at least a bit intimidating (and in most cases entirely foreign). However, you should not be overly concerned about any individual Science passage, as discussed next.

9

Why You Should Not Fear Science Passages

The makers of the LSAT state that question topics "reflect a broad range of academic disciplines and are intended to give no advantage to candidates from a particular background," but many LSAT students come from a humanities background and thus often worry about passages containing scientific elements. If the topic of science concerns you, please keep in mind these two points:

1. As discussed in Chapter Two, the topic of a passage does not affect the underlying logical relationship of the parts of the passage, or your approach to reading it. Thus, regardless of the topic, you can still use the VIEWSTAMP method and succeed.

2. One of the fears of test takers is encountering concepts that they do not know or that sound intimidating. Naturally, someone who encounters terms like "riddled basins of attraction" or "rubisco" is unlikely to have seen them before and would seemingly have a valid reason for worrying that they will be at a disadvantage if faced with a passage containing those ideas. However, you should not worry because the LSAT will *never* assume that you know anything about advanced technical or scientific ideas! Any term or idea beyond the domain of general public knowledge will be explained for you. Consider the following items:

   These points are also true for Logical Reasoning questions.

   A. Example: "But for decades cosmologists (scientists who study the universe) have attempted to account for..."

   In this example, the term "cosmologists" is immediately followed by a parenthetical definition that explains that cosmologists are scientists who study the universe. So, even if you do not know what a cosmologist is, the test makers provide you with the definition.

   B. Example: "among the more attractive candidates are neutrinos, elementary particles created as a by-product of nuclear fusion, radioactive decay, or catastrophic collisions between particles."

   In this example, the definition of "neutrinos" is set off by a comma, and the remainder of the sentence provides the explanation of the term.

9

C. Example: "This is because the boundary between one basin of attraction and another is riddled with fractal properties; in other words, the boundary is permeated by an extraordinarily high number of physical irregularities such as notches or zigzags."

In this example the definition of "fractal properties" is slightly separated from the term, but the definition is still relatively close by. Note that there is no rule that says that the definition has to immediately follow the term in question. If a definition is not in close proximity to the unfamiliar element, simply note the term and continue reading until you encounter the explanation.

D. Example: "Until recently, biologists were unable to explain the fact that pathogens—disease-causing parasites—have evolved to incapacitate, and often overwhelm, their hosts."

This example uses dashes to provide the definition of the term "pathogen." Once you know that a pathogen is simply a disease-causing parasite, the passage doesn't seem nearly as complex.

E. Example: "When genes are inserted into an individual's cells and tissues to treat a disease, this treatment is known as gene therapy."

While in the first four examples the definition followed the term, in this example the definition actually precedes the term. Although this arrangement occurs less frequently than the definition following the term, you should still be aware that the test makers have the option of placing the definition either before or after the concept being defined, and either in immediate proximity or several lines away.

The important point to draw from this discussion is that nothing you will encounter in a Science passage (or any other passage) will remain unexplained, and that you already have the methods in hand to attack Science passages effectively.

9

Remember, despite occasional passages that reference an ominous looking word or idea (whether Science or Law or any other subject matter), you will never be expected to know, or even *need* to know, anything more about those elements than what you are told by the test makers. When you read a science-based passage, focus on understanding the relationship of the ideas and do not be intimidated by the terminology used by the author.

Handling Scientific Elements

While we are fully confident that any student can handle the scientific concepts that exist in passages, there is value in revisiting how to diagram the elements that appear most frequently.

1. Handling Scientific Terminology

   When you encounter scientific terms or phrases, underline or highlight the phrase, or make note of the definition by marking the section with a "DEF" notation on your scratch paper. If necessary, you can also reduce the scientific term to an acronym.

If necessary, return to Chapter Five for a refresher in diagramming.

2. Handling Dense Sections of Scientific Explanation

   If you encounter an extended section of complex scientific terminology, at most highlight the section and do not worry too much about understanding every single idea within it. You can return to the highlighted area if you are asked to do so by a question, and focus on understanding the ideas at that point.

A Science Passage Analyzed

On the following page an actual LSAT Science passage is presented, along with a complete analysis of the passage and all of the corresponding questions.

To most effectively benefit from this section, time yourself on the passage. Attempt to finish the passage in 8 minutes and 45 seconds, but if you cannot, continue working until you complete all of the questions and note your time. While reading, remember to apply the VIEWSTAMP approach advocated throughout the book. Then, read the entire explanation section and consider what elements you missed, and what you need to do to improve.

9

Sometimes there is no more effective means of controlling an agricultural pest than giving free rein to its natural predators. A case in point is the cyclamen mite, a pest whose population can be
(5) effectively controlled by a predatory mite of the genus *Typhlodromus*. Cyclamen mites infest strawberry plants; they typically establish themselves in a strawberry field shortly after planting, but their populations do not reach significantly damaging
(10) levels until the plants' second year. *Typhlodromus* mites usually invade the strawberry fields during the second year, rapidly subdue the cyclamen mite populations, and keep them from reaching significantly damaging levels.
(15) *Typhlodromus* owes its effectiveness as a predator to several factors in addition to its voracious appetite. Its population can increase as rapidly as that of its prey. Both species reproduce by parthenogenesis-a mode of reproduction in which unfertilized eggs
(20) develop into fertile females. Cyclamen mites lay three eggs per day over the four or five days of their reproductive life span; *Typhlodromus* lay two or three eggs per day for eight to ten days. Seasonal synchrony of *Typhlodromus* reproduction with the
(25) growth of prey populations and ability to survive at low prey densities also contribute to the predatory efficiency of *Typhlodromus*. During winter, when cyclamen mite populations dwindle to a few individuals hidden in the crevices and folds of leaves
(30) in the crowns of the strawberry plants, the predatory mites subsist on the honeydew produced by aphids and white flies. They do not reproduce except when they are feeding on the cyclamen mites. These features, which make *Typhlodromus* well-suited for
(35) exploiting the seasonal rises and falls of its prey, are common among predators that control prey populations.
Greenhouse experiments have verified the importance of *Typhlodromus* predation for keeping
(40) cyclamen mites in check. One group of strawberry plants was stocked with both predator and prey mites; a second group was kept predator-free by regular application of parathion, an insecticide that kills the predatory species but does not affect the cyclamen
(45) mite. Throughout the study, populations of cyclamen mites remained low in plots shared with *Typhlodromus,* but their infestation attained significantly damaging proportions on predator-free plants.
(50) Applying parathion in this instance is a clear case in which using a pesticide would do far more harm than good to an agricultural enterprise. The results were similar in field plantings of strawberries, where cyclamen mites also reached damaging levels when
(55) predators were eliminated by parathion, but they did not attain such levels in untreated plots. When cyclamen mite populations began to increase in an untreated planting, the predator populations quickly responded to reduce the outbreak. On average,
(60) cyclamen mites were about 25 times more abundant in the absence of predators than in their presence.

20. Which one of the following most accurately expresses the main point of the passage?

(A) Control of agricultural pests is most effectively and safely accomplished without the use of pesticides, because these pesticides can kill predators that also control the pests.

(B) Experimental verification is essential in demonstrating the effectiveness of natural controls of agricultural pests.

(C) The relationship between *Typhlodromus* and cyclamen mites demonstrates how natural predation can keep a population of agricultural pests in check.

(D) Predation by *Typhlodromus* is essential for the control of cyclamen mite populations in strawberry fields.

(E) Similarity in mode and timing of reproduction is what enables *Typhlodromus* effectively to control populations of cyclamen mites in fields of strawberry plants.

21. Based on the passage, the author would probably hold that which one of the following principles is fundamental to long-term predatory control of agricultural pests?

(A) The reproduction of the predator population should be synchronized with that of the prey population, so that the number of predators surges just prior to a surge in prey numbers.

(B) The effectiveness of the predatory relationship should be experimentally demonstrable in greenhouse as well as field applications.

(C) The prey population should be able to survive in times of low crop productivity, so that the predator population will not decrease to very low levels.

(D) The predator population's level of consumption of the prey species should be responsive to variations in the size of the prey population.

(E) The predator population should be vulnerable only to pesticides to which the prey population is also vulnerable.

22. Which one of the following is mentioned in the passage as a factor contributing to the effectiveness of *Typhlodromus* as a predator?

(A) its ability to withstand most insecticides except parathion

(B) its lack of natural predators in strawberry fields

(C) its ability to live in different climates in different geographic regions

(D) its constant food supply in cyclamen mite populations

(E) its ability to survive when few prey are available

23. Suppose that pesticide X drastically slows the reproductive rate of cyclamen mites and has no other direct effect on cyclamen mites or *Typhlodromus*. Based on the information in the passage, which one of the following would most likely have occurred if, in the experiments mentioned in the passage, pesticide X had been used instead of parathion, with all other conditions affecting the experiments remaining the same?

(A) In both treated and untreated plots inhabited by both *Typhlodromus* and cyclamen mites, the latter would have been effectively controlled.

(B) Cyclamen mite populations in all treated plots from which *Typhlodromus* was absent would have been substantially lower than in untreated plots inhabited by both kinds of mites.

(C) In the treated plots, slowed reproduction in cyclamen mites would have led to a loss of reproductive synchrony between *Typhlodromus* and cyclamen mites.

(D) In the treated plots, *Typhlodromus* populations would have decreased temporarily and would have eventually increased.

(E) In the treated plots, cyclamen mite populations would have reached significantly damaging levels more slowly, but would have remained at those levels longer, than in untreated plots.

24. It can be inferred from the passage that the author would be most likely to agree with which one of the following statements about the use of predators to control pest populations?

(A) If the use of predators to control cyclamen mite populations fails, then parathion should be used to control these populations.

(B) Until the effects of the predators on beneficial insects that live in strawberry fields are assessed, such predators should be used with caution to control cyclamen mite populations.

(C) Insecticides should be used to control certain pest populations in fields of crops only if the use of natural predators has proven inadequate.

(D) If an insecticide can effectively control pest populations as well as predator populations, then it should be used instead of predators to control pest populations.

(E) Predators generally control pest populations more effectively than pesticides because they do not harm the crops that their prey feed on.

25. The author mentions the egg-laying ability of each kind of mite (lines 20-23) primarily in order to support which one of the following claims?

(A) Mites that reproduce by parthenogenesis do so at approximately equal rates.

(B) Predatory mites typically have a longer reproductive life span than do cyclamen mites.

(C) *Typhlodromus* can lay their eggs in synchrony with cyclamen mites.

(D) *Typhlodromus* can reproduce at least as quickly as cyclamen mites.

(E) The egg-laying rate of *Typhlodromus* is slower in the presence of cyclamen mites than it is in their absence.

26. Which one of the following would, if true, most strengthen the author's position regarding the practical applicability of the information about predatory mites presented in the passage?

(A) The individual *Typhlodromus* mites that have the longest reproductive life spans typically also lay the greatest number of eggs per day.

(B) The insecticides that are typically used for mite control on strawberry plants kill both predatory and nonpredatory species of mites.

(C) In areas in which strawberry plants become infested by cyclamen mites, winters tend to be short and relatively mild.

(D) *Typhlodromus* are sometimes preyed upon by another species of mites that is highly susceptible to parathion.

(E) *Typhlodromus* easily tolerate the same range of climatic conditions that strawberry plants do.

27. Information in the passage most strongly supports which one of the following statements?

(A) Strawberry crops can support populations of both cyclamen mites and *Typhlodromus* mites without significant damage to those crops.

(B) For control of cyclamen mites by another mite species to be effective, it is crucial that the two species have the same mode of reproduction.

(C) Factors that make *Typhlodromus* effective against cyclamen mites also make it effective against certain other pests of strawberry plants.

(D) When *Typhlodromus* is relied on to control cyclamen mites in strawberry crops, pesticides may be necessary to prevent significant damage during the first year.

(E) Strawberry growers have unintentionally caused cyclamen mites to become a serious crop pest by the indiscriminate use of parathion.

9

Science Passage Analysis—December 2007 Passage #4

This passage contains a classic structure, and one that has been used in Science passages before: the opening lines state a principle or belief, and then the remaining lines provide examples that illustrate the theory or belief. The passage, which appears to be solely about cyclamen mites, is actually about demonstrating the statement in the first sentence (using natural predation to control agricultural pests).

Paragraph One:

The passage opens with the assertion that will be shown throughout the passage: sometimes the most effective agent for controlling an agricultural pest is its natural predators (lines 1-3). The example that is used to discuss this statement is that of the cyclamen mites, who infest strawberry plants. Cyclamen mites can be controlled by another mite, that of the genus *Typhlodromus*. The remainder of the paragraph establishes a timeline: cyclamen mites infest strawberry fields shortly after planting but their levels do not become damaging until the second year (lines 6-10). In the second year, mites from the genus *Typhlodromus* appear and subdue the cyclamen mite population before damage occurs (lines 10-14).

Regarding the scientific terminology in this paragraph, you are not expected to know anything about mites, and certainly nothing about their specific names or genus. You simply need to know that there are two types of mites—cyclamen mites and mites from the genus *Typhlodromus*—and that *Typhlodromus* mites are predators of the cyclamen mites, which feed on strawberries.

Paragraph Two:

The second paragraph is devoted to a discussion of why *Typhlodromus* mites are effective predators, and three main reasons are presented. The first is their voracious appetite (line 16), the second is that their population can increase as rapidly as that of the cyclamen mites (line 17-18), and the third is that they have a population that seasonally matches the population of their prey (lines 23-27). The author closes the paragraph by noting that such features are common among predators that control prey populations (in other words, these features of *Typhlodromus* mites are not unique).

There are two scientific terms used in the paragraph. The first, "parthenogenesis," is immediately defined after the dash in line 18. The second term, "seasonal synchrony," is finally defined in line 35, more than 10 lines later. However, this term is relatively easy to figure out from context, and so most readers are able to move forward from line 23 without confusion.

Paragraphs Three and Four:

These paragraphs offer proof for the opening statement in the form of experimental results. As recounted in the third paragraph, using greenhouse experiments, researchers demonstrated the importance of the predator *Typhlodromus* mites. In the fourth paragraph, the results were similar when live field plantings were done.

9

The third paragraph also offers up another ominous looking term—"parathion"—but then immediately defines it as an insecticide that kills the *Typhlodromus* predator mites but not the cyclamen mites.

<u>VIEWSTAMP</u> Analysis:

The passage contains just a single **Viewpoint:**

> The view of the author, who believes that at times the best means of controlling an agricultural pest is giving free rein to its natural predators.

The author's **Tone** is confident in the stated principle, and positive that the example of the mites and corresponding experiment results provide proof of the principle.

The **Arguments** in the passage are mainly an explanation of how the example of the mites illustrates the assertion that opens the passage.

The author's **Main Point** is that at times the best means of controlling an agricultural pest is giving free rein to its natural predators, as exemplified by the relationship of the two mite types.

The **Structure** of the passage is as follows:

<u>Paragraph One:</u>   Assert a principle, begin explanation of an example.

<u>Paragraph Two:</u>   Discuss three advantages of the predator *Typhlodromus* mite.

<u>Paragraph Three:</u> Provide proof in the form of experimental results.

<u>Paragraph Four</u>   Provide further proof from field tests, which confirmed the greenhouse experiment results.

Overall, this passage looks forbidding at first glance. The passage appears to be filled with scientific terms and references, and many students may simply bail out after glancing at the text. While there are some sections that are a bit dense and will require re-examination during the questions (such as lines 23-37 and lines 52-59), the overall structure of the passage and the general message is clear.

Science Passage Analysis—December 2007 Passage #4

Question #20: GR, Main Point. The correct answer choice is (C)

This question should be easy, as long as you realize that the first sentence of the passage sets up a framework for the remaining discussion. If you did not realize this point, you may fall for an answer choice such as (D).

Answer choice (A): This answer choice is incorrect because of the phrase "most effectively." The author simply noted that predator control was "sometimes" the most effective method, not that pesticides were never the most effective method. Pesticides just were not the most effective method in this situation.

Answer choice (B): The phrase, "Experimental verification is essential" is problematic. The author neither states this point nor would it be the main point even if stated in the passage.

Answer choice (C): This is the correct answer choice, as indicated in the passage analysis.

Answer choice (D): This answer choice focuses on the cyclamen mite example but never references the first sentence of the passage, and so it is incorrect. Remember, examples are never the main point of the passage; the principle that the examples explain is usually the main point.

Aside from the fact that this point—even if it were true—is not the main point, the author never states this point in the passage. The author instead states that the *Typhlodromus* mite is effective in controlling cyclamen mites (lines 3-6), and important to keeping the cyclamen mites in check (lines 38-40), but not *essential*.

Answer choice (E): This answer addresses a minor point within the passage, not the broad overall theme of the passage.

Question #21: GR, Must, AP, PR. The correct answer choice is (D)

This question asks you to identify the author's perspective regarding a principle of long-term predatory control of pests. Aside from knowing that the author believes that it can be an effective method, we also know that the author believes the *Typhlodromus* mite has several features that make it an effective predator (as related in the second paragraph).

Answer choice (A): This answer choice is incorrect because of the phrase "just prior." In lines 17-18, the author states that "Its population can increase *as rapidly as* that of its prey" (italics added for emphasis). The *Typhlodromus* mite is effective because it matches or responds to the cyclamen mite, not because it anticipates the cyclamen mite.

Answer choice (B): This answer choice does not address the principle of predatory *control*, just a principle of theory viability.

9

Answer choice (C): The author does not offer any opinions on whether the *prey* population should be able to survive.

Answer choice (D): This is the correct answer choice. Lines 23-33 support this statement as a principle the author believes in.

Answer choice (E): The reference to the use of pesticides and their effect on the predator population was part of the discussion of experimental results. The author was not implying that the predators should be vulnerable only to pesticides that also affect the prey.

Question #22: GR, Must. The correct answer choice is (E)

This question asks you to identify the advantages of the *Typhlodromus* mite, and you should immediately refer to the second paragraph for more information.

Answer choice (A): This is not mentioned as a factor contributing to the effectiveness of the *Typhlodromus* mite.

Answer choice (B): This is not mentioned in the passage.

Answer choice (C): Although the *Typhlodromus* mite can live during different seasons (lines 23-28), no mention is made of the *Typhlodromus* mite living in different geographic regions.

Answer choice (D): This is not given as a factor in why the *Typhlodromus* mite is an *effective* predator.

Answer choice (E): This is the correct answer choice. As mentioned in lines 27-32, this is an advantage of the *Typhlodromus* mite.

Question #23: CR, Must. The correct answer choice is (A)

The question stem supposes a situation wherein the *Typhlodromus* mite is unaffected by a particular pesticide, but the cyclamen mite has its reproductive rate slowed. Although pesticides are discussed in the third paragraph, the issue of reproductive rates is one that appears in the second paragraph. Hence, you should refer to the second paragraph for more information. From that paragraph, we know that the *Typhlodromus* mite can already keep up with the cyclamen mite, so if the cyclamen mite reproductive rate slowed, the effect would be that there would be less food for the *Typhlodromus* mite. The question stem also references the experiments discussed in the passage, so that reference takes you to the third and fourth paragraphs. Because those paragraphs reference greenhouse and field tests, the conclusion is that there is likely to be no change in how cyclamen mites are affected by the *Typhlodromus* mite, and the only impact would be on the food supply of the *Typhlodromus* mite.

Science Passage Analysis—December 2007 Passage #4

Answer choice (A): This is the correct answer choice. In both experiments, the cyclamen mite would still be controlled.

Answer choice (B): You cannot make a comparison between these two populations; given that cyclamen mites were 25 times more prevalent in the absence of predators (lines 59-61), they may have had a higher population even with the pesticide than when the *Typhlodromus* mite was present without pesticides.

Answer choice (C): Given the meaning of seasonal synchrony, it is unlikely that it would be lost just because the cyclamen mite population was lower than normal. The likely scenario is that the *Typhlodromus* mite would simply respond with lower numbers.

Answer choice (D): Although the first half of this answer sounds valid, the second half is unknown. Therefore, this answer choice is incorrect.

Answer choice (E): There is no way to draw this conclusion based on the information in the question stem or passage.

Question #24: GR, Must, Author's Perspective. The correct answer choice is (C)

We know from our initial analysis that the author believes at times the best means of controlling an agricultural pest is giving free rein to its natural predators.

Answer choice (A): Parathion was just the pesticide used in the experiments discussed in the passage, and it was a pesticide used to control *Typhlodromus* mites, not cyclamen mites.

Answer choice (B): No, the author would disagree with this statement. He or she has already stated that at times the best means of controlling an agricultural pest is giving free rein to its natural predators.

Answer choice (C): This is the correct answer choice. This conditional answer choice indicates that insecticides should be used only if natural predators could not do the job. The contrapositive, which states that if natural predators can do the job then insecticides should not be used, is a statement that the author would agree with based on the statements in the passage. Thus, this answer choice is correct.

Answer choice (D): No, this answer choice is incorrect, in part because the passage is not about controlling *predator* populations. Plus, the author is pro-predator control, not anti-predator control.

Answer choice (E): The passage is about the effectiveness of control (lines 1-3), and harm to the crops does not play a role.

9

Science Passage Analysis—December 2007 Passage #4

Question #25: SR, Purpose. The correct answer choice is (D)

The question stem refers you to lines 20-23, so return to line 15 to gain context for what is presented in lines 20-23. The overall message of this paragraph is the effectiveness of the *Typhlodromus* mites, and the point made specifically in lines 17-18 is in reference to the ability of the *Typhlodromus* mites to increase population as rapidly as cyclamen mites. Hence, answer choice (D) is correct.

Answer choice (A): The information in lines 20-23 seems to suggest that this answer choice is incorrect.

Answer choice (B): While this statement appears to be true for *Typhlodromus* mites in relation to cyclamen mites, the passage does not address all predatory mites (as does this answer). In addition, even if this statement were true, making that point still would not be the purpose of the author in lines 20-23.

Answer choice (C): The synchrony discussed in the passage is based on seasonal populations, not reproductive rates.

Answer choice (D): This is the correct answer choice.

Answer choice (E): There is no mention made of differences in *Typhlodromus* mite reproductive rates in the presence or absence of cyclamen mites.

Question #26: GR, Strengthen. The correct answer choice is (E)

In this question, you are asked to select an answer choice that supports the author's overall contention about the applicability of predatory mites. To prephrase this question is somewhat difficult because there is no way to know what aspect of the author's position the test makers will choose to support.

Answer choice (A): The passage is about the mites as a whole, not individual mites. This information does not support the author.

Answer choice (B): This answer indicates that the pesticides typically used for mite control kill all mites. This information has no material effect on the applicability of predatory mites.

Answer choice (C): The severity of winter was not a germane issue to the argument made by the author. The author simply stated that *Typhlodromus* mites could survive the winter (lines 27-32).

Answer choice (D): This answer indicates that in a field sprayed with parathion, the predators of the *Typhlodromus* mites would also be affected. However, because parathion affects the *Typhlodromus* mites as well, this information is not helpful.

Answer choice (E): This is the correct answer choice. This answer shows that the *Typhlodromus* mites can survive in the habitats of the cyclamen mites, and thus would be able to prey upon them.

Question #27: GR, Must. The correct answer choice is (A)

In a Global Must Be true question, do not worry about prephrasing an answer because there are too many options. Simply move from the question stem directly to the answer choices.

Answer choice (A): This is the correct answer choice. This answer choice is supported by lines 10-14.

Answer choice (B): Although the passage states that *Typhlodromus* mites and cyclamen mites have the same mode of reproduction (line 18), the passage does not suggest that this is a necessary element for effective predatory control.

Answer choice (C): The example in the passage just discusses how *Typhlodromus* mites can control cyclamen mites; the effectiveness of *Typhlodromus* mites against other strawberry plant pests is not addressed.

Answer choice (D): This answer choice is incorrect. As stated in lines 6-10, during the first year of a cyclamen mite infestation, the population does not reach a significantly damaging level. Hence, it is unlikely that pesticides would be needed.

Answer choice (E): Although certain experiments seem to suggest that the indiscriminate application of parathion could create the situation described in this answer choice, nowhere does the passage suggest that this is an actual problem.

9

Two Science Practice Passages ▮▮▮

The next several pages contain two actual LSAT Science passage sets. After the two passages, a complete analysis of each passage and all of the corresponding questions is presented.

To most effectively benefit from this section, time yourself on the first passage. Attempt to finish the passage in 8 minutes and 45 seconds, but if you cannot, continue working until you complete all of the questions and then note your time. Then, read the entire explanation section for the first passage. Afterwards, move to the second passage and repeat the process.

9

The pronghorn, an antelope-like mammal that lives on the western plains of North America, is the continent's fastest land animal, capable of running 90 kilometers per hour and of doing so for several
(5) kilometers. Because no North American predator is nearly fast enough to chase it down, biologists have had difficulty explaining why the pronghorn developed its running prowess. One biologist, however, has recently claimed that pronghorns run as
(10) fast as they do because of adaptation to predators known from fossil records to have been extinct for 10,000 years, such as American cheetahs and long-legged hyenas, either of which, it is believed, were fast enough to run down the pronghorn.
(15) Like all explanations that posit what is called a relict behavior—a behavior that persists though its only evolutionary impetus comes from long-extinct environmental conditions—this one is likely to meet with skepticism. Most biologists distrust explanations positing relict
(20) behaviors, in part because testing these hypotheses is so difficult due to the extinction of a principal component. They typically consider such historical explanations only when a lack of alternatives forces them to do so. But present-day observations sometimes yield
(25) evidence that supports relict behavior hypotheses.
In the case of the pronghorn, researchers have identified much supporting evidence, as several aspects of pronghorn behavior appear to have been shaped by enemies that no longer exist. For example,
(30) pronghorns—like many other grazing animals—roam in herds, which allows more eyes to watch for predators and diminishes the chances of any particular animal being attacked but can also result in overcrowding and increased competition for food. But, since
(35) pronghorns have nothing to fear from present-day carnivores and thus have nothing to gain from herding, their herding behavior appears to be another adaptation to extinct threats. Similarly, if speed and endurance were once essential to survival, researchers would
(40) expect pronghorns to choose mates based on these athletic abilities, which they do—with female pronghorns, for example, choosing the victor after male pronghorns challenge each other in sprints and chases.
Relict behaviors appear to occur in other animals
(45) as well, increasing the general plausibility of such a theory. For example, one study reports relict behavior in stickleback fish belonging to populations that have long been free of a dangerous predator, the sculpin. In the study, when presented with sculpin, these
(50) stickleback fish immediately engaged in stereotypical antisculpin behavior, avoiding its mouth and swimming behind to bite it. Another study found that ground squirrels from populations that have been free from snakes for 70,000 to 300,000 years still clearly recognize
(55) rattlesnakes, displaying stereotypical antirattlesnake behavior in the presence of the snake. Such fear, however, apparently does not persist interminably. Arctic ground squirrels, free of snakes for about 3 million years, appear to be unable to recognize the

(60) threat of a rattlesnake, exhibiting only disorganized caution even after being bitten repeatedly.

16. Which one of the following most accurately states the main point of the passage?

(A) Evidence from present-day animal behaviors, together with the fossil record, supports the hypothesis that the pronghorn's ability to far outrun any predator currently on the North American continent is an adaptation to predators long extinct.

(B) Although some biologists believe that certain animal characteristics, such as the speed of the pronghorn, are explained by environmental conditions that have not existed for many years, recent data concerning arctic ground squirrels make this hypothesis doubtful.

(C) Research into animal behavior, particularly into that of the pronghorn, provides strong evidence that most present-day characteristics of animals are explained by environmental conditions that have not existed for many years.

(D) Even in those cases in which an animal species displays characteristics clearly explained by long-vanished environmental conditions, evidence concerning arctic ground squirrels suggests that those characteristics will eventually disappear.

(E) Although biologists are suspicious of hypotheses that are difficult to test, there is now widespread agreement among biologists that many types of animal characteristics are best explained as adaptations to long-extinct predators.

17. Based on the passage, the term "principal component" (line 21) most clearly refers to which one of the following?

(A) behavior that persists even though the conditions that provided its evolutionary impetus are extinct

(B) the original organism whose descendants' behavior is being investigated as relict behavior

(C) the pronghorn's ability to run 90 kilometers per hour over long distances

(D) the environmental conditions in response to which relict behaviors are thought to have developed

(E) an original behavior of an animal of which certain present-day behaviors are thought to be modifications

18. The last paragraph most strongly supports which one of the following statements?

   (A) An absence of predators in an animal's environment can constitute just as much of a threat to the well-being of that animal as the presence of predators.

   (B) Relict behaviors are found in most wild animals living today.

   (C) If a behavior is an adaptation to environmental conditions, it may eventually disappear in the absence of those or similar conditions.

   (D) Behavior patterns that originated as a way of protecting an organism against predators will persist interminably if they are periodically reinforced.

   (E) Behavior patterns invariably take longer to develop than they do to disappear.

19. Which one of the following describes a benefit mentioned in the passage that grazing animals derive from roaming in herds?

   (A) The greater density of animals tends to intimidate potential predators.

   (B) The larger number of adults in a herd makes protection of the younger animals from predators much easier.

   (C) With many animals searching it is easier for the herd to find food and water.

   (D) The likelihood that any given individual will be attacked by a predator decreases.

   (E) The most defenseless animals can achieve greater safety by remaining in the center of the herd.

20. The passage mentions each of the following as support for the explanation of the pronghorn's speed proposed by the biologist referred to in line 8 EXCEPT:

   (A) fossils of extinct animals believed to have been able to run down a pronghorn

   (B) the absence of carnivores in the pronghorn's present-day environment

   (C) the present-day preference of pronghorns for athletic mates

   (D) the apparent need for a similar explanation to account for the herding behavior pronghorns now display

   (E) the occurrence of relict behavior in other species

21. The third paragraph of the passage provides the most support for which one of the following inferences?

   (A) Predators do not attack grazing animals that are assembled into herds.

   (B) Pronghorns tend to graze in herds only when they sense a threat from predators close by.

   (C) If animals do not graze for their food, they do not roam in herds.

   (D) Female pronghorns mate only with the fastest male pronghorn in the herd.

   (E) If pronghorns did not herd, they would not face significantly greater danger from present-day carnivores.

The survival of nerve cells, as well as their performance of some specialized functions, is regulated by chemicals known as neurotrophic factors, which are produced in the bodies of animals,
(5) including humans. Rita Levi-Montalcini's discovery in the 1950s of the first of these agents, a hormonelike substance now known as NGF, was a crucial development in the history of biochemistry, which led to Levi-Montalcini sharing the Nobel Prize
(10) for medicine in 1986.

In the mid-1940s, Levi-Montalcini had begun by hypothesizing that many of the immature nerve cells produced in the development of an organism are normally programmed to die. In order to confirm this
(15) theory, she conducted research that in 1949 found that, when embryos are in the process of forming their nervous systems, they produce many more nerve cells than are finally required, the number that survives eventually adjusting itself to the volume of
(20) tissue to be supplied with nerves. A further phase of the experimentation, which led to Levi-Montalcini's identification of the substance that controls this process, began with her observation that the development of nerves in chick embryos could be
(25) stimulated by implanting a certain variety of mouse tumor in the embryos. She theorized that a chemical produced by the tumors was responsible for the observed nerve growth. To investigate this hypothesis, she used the then new technique of tissue culture, by
(30) which specific types of body cells can be made to grow outside the organism from which they are derived. Within twenty-four hours, her tissue cultures of chick embryo extracts developed dense halos of nerve tissue near the places in the culture where she
(35) had added the mouse tumor. Further research identified a specific substance contributed by the mouse tumors that was responsible for the effects Levi-Montalcini had observed: a protein that she named "nerve growth factor" (NGF).
(40) NGF was the first of many cell-growth factors to be found in the bodies of animals. Through Levi-Montalcini's work and other subsequent research, it has been determined that this substance is present in many tissues and biological fluids, and that it is
(45) especially concentrated in some organs. In developing organisms, nerve cells apparently receive this growth factor locally from the cells of muscles or other organs to which they will form connections for transmission of nerve impulses, and sometimes from
(50) supporting cells intermingled with the nerve tissue. NGF seems to play two roles, serving initially to direct the developing nerve processes toward the correct, specific "target" cells with which they must connect, and later being necessary for the continued
(55) survival of those nerve cells. During some periods of their development, the types of nerve cells that are affected by NGF—primarily cells outside the brain and spinal cord—die if the factor is not present or if they encounter anti-NGF antibodies.

15. Which one of the following most accurately expresses the main point of the passage?

(A) Levi-Montalcini's discovery of neurotrophic factors as a result of research carried out in the 1940s was a major contribution to our understanding of the role of naturally occurring chemicals, especially NGF, in the development of chick embryos.

(B) Levi-Montalcini's discovery of NGF, a neurotrophic factor that stimulates the development of some types of nerve tissue and whose presence or absence in surrounding cells helps determine whether particular nerve cells will survive, was a pivotal development in biochemistry.

(C) NGF, which is necessary for the survival and proper functioning of nerve cells, was discovered by Levi-Montalcini in a series of experiments using the technique of tissue culture, which she devised in the 1940s.

(D) Partly as a result of Levi-Montalcini's research, it has been found that NGF and other neurotrophic factors are produced only by tissues to which nerves are already connected and that the presence of these factors is necessary for the health and proper functioning of nervous systems.

(E) NGF, a chemical that was discovered by Levi-Montalcini, directs the growth of nerve cells toward the cells with which they must connect and ensures the survival of those nerve cells throughout the life of the organism except when the organism produces anti-NGF antibodies.

16. Based on the passage, the author would be most likely to believe that Levi-Montalcini's discovery of NGF is noteworthy primarily because it

(A) paved the way for more specific knowledge of the processes governing the development of the nervous system

(B) demonstrated that a then new laboratory technique could yield important and unanticipated experimental results

(C) confirmed the hypothesis that many of a developing organism's immature nerve cells are normally programmed to die

(D) indicated that this substance stimulates observable biochemical reactions in the tissues of different species

(E) identified a specific substance, produced by mouse tumors, that can be used to stimulate nerve cell growth

9

17. The primary function of the third paragraph of the passage in relation to the second paragraph is to

    (A)   indicate that conclusions referred to in the second paragraph, though essentially correct, require further verification
    (B)   indicate that conclusions referred to in the second paragraph have been undermined by subsequently obtained evidence
    (C)   indicate ways in which conclusions referred to in the second paragraph have been further corroborated and refined
    (D)   describe subsequent discoveries of substances analogous to the substance discussed in the second paragraph
    (E)   indicate that experimental procedures discussed in the second paragraph have been supplanted by more precise techniques described in the third paragraph

18. Information in the passage most strongly supports which one of the following?

    (A)   Nerve cells in excess of those that are needed by the organism in which they develop eventually produce anti-NGF antibodies to suppress the effects of NGF.
    (B)   Nerve cells that grow in the absence of NGF are less numerous than, but qualitatively identical to, those that grow in the presence of NGF.
    (C)   Few of the nerve cells that connect with target cells toward which NGF directs them are needed by the organism in which they develop.
    (D)   Some of the nerve cells that grow in the presence of NGF are eventually converted to other types of living tissue by neurotrophic factors.
    (E)   Some of the nerve cells that grow in an embryo do not connect with any particular target cells.

19. The passage describes a specific experiment that tested which one of the following hypotheses?

    (A)   A certain kind of mouse tumor produces a chemical that stimulates the growth of nerve cells.
    (B)   Developing embryos initially grow many more nerve cells than they will eventually require.
    (C)   In addition to NGF, there are several other important neurotrophic factors regulating cell survival and function.
    (D)   Certain organs contain NGF in concentrations much higher than in the surrounding tissue.
    (E)   Certain nerve cells are supplied with NGF by the muscle cells to which they are connected.

20. Which one of the following is most strongly supported by the information in the passage?

    (A)   Some of the effects that the author describes as occurring in Levi-Montalcini's culture of chick embryo extract were due to neurotrophic factors other than NGF.
    (B)   Although NGF was the first neurotrophic factor to be identified, some other such factors are now more thoroughly understood.
    (C)   In her research in the 1940s and 1950s, Levi-Montalcini identified other neurotrophic factors in addition to NGF.
    (D)   Some neurotrophic factors other than NGF perform functions that are not specifically identified in the passage.
    (E)   The effects of NGF that Levi-Montalcini noted in her chick embryo experiment are also caused by other neurotrophic factors not discussed in the passage.

9

Science Practice Passage I—June 2005 Passage #3 Answer Key

Paragraph One:

In this scientific passage, the author begins with a brief discussion of the 90 kilometers North American pronghorn and the interesting question of why it is able to run so much faster than any of its predators. The introduction is viewpoint neutral, and in line 8 the author introduces the viewpoint of "one biologist," who claims that the speed was developed to escape from some predators before extinction over 10,000 years ago. The author provides two examples of such predators: the American cheetah and the long-legged hyena.

Paragraph Two:

In this paragraph the author expands upon the explanation begun in the introduction and continues the passage in a neutral, academic tone, basically reporting the facts. "Relict behavior" is currently exhibited behavior that was developed in response to conditions that no longer exist. This theory generally draws skepticism since it cannot be tested, and is usually a last resort for scientists, but seems to be supported in some cases by present-day evidence.

Paragraph Three:

Here the author introduces current evidence to support the idea of relict behavior: pronghorns herd even though they have no predators to fear and herding can result in overcrowding, and pronghorns choose mates based on physical prowess.

Paragraph Four:

The author ends the passage with further examples that strengthen the claim of the existence of relict behavior, and discusses the lengths of time that relict behaviors seem to persist (and eventually disappear).

VIEWSTAMP Analysis:

This passage is fairly **Viewpoint** neutral, discussing the possible existence of relict behavior and presenting evidence in its favor.

The author's **Tone** is academic and viewpoint neutral, as often occurs in Science passages.

This is a basic Science passage with little real argumentation. The only real **Argument** is that of the author, who believes that relict behavior likely exists.

The **Main Point** of the passage is that the pronghorn's relative speed may be a relict behavior based on the need to escape predators that no longer exist.

Science Practice Passage I—June 2005 Passage #3 Answer Key

The **Structure** of the passage is as follows:

Paragraph One: Introduce the pronghorn, the possibility of behavior based on outdated necessity, and two examples of extinct predators of the pronghorn.

Paragraph Two: Introduce the concept of relict behavior, and that the theory elicits skepticism but is supported by modern day evidence.

Paragraph Three: Introduce specific examples of modern evidence supporting the existence of relict behavior.

Paragraph Four: Provide further examples of possible relict behavior, and one example of lost relict behavior.

Question #16: GR, Main Point. The correct answer choice is (A)

The main point of the passage, as prephrased above, is to introduce the pronghorn, and to introduce and provide evidence to support the notion of relict behavior.

Answer choice (A): This is the correct answer choice, as it reflects the same basic information discussed above.

Answer choice (B): The example of the squirrel serves to show that at some point relict behavior dissipates, but it does not weaken the argument for the existence of relict behavior.

Answer choice (C): The author does not suggest that most behavior is relict, only that relict behavior does appear to exist.

Answer choice (D): The ground squirrel is one case and does not provide enough evidence to draw such a broad conclusion regarding all relict behavior.

Answer choice (E): The author discusses the logical skepticism of a theory that is difficult to test, but does not assert that there is widespread agreement about the existence of relict behavior.

9

Question #17: SR, Must. The correct answer choice is (D)

For this Specific Reference question, we should be sure that we know the context of the reference: There is skepticism about the theory of relict behavior, partly because it is so difficult to test due to the absence of a principal component. In the case of the pronghorn, this refers to the long extinct predators that may have led to the pronghorn's speed and other relict behavior.

Answer choice (A): Since the behavior that persists is not absent, we can rule out this choice.

Answer choice (B): The principal component does not refer to the ancestor of the pronghorn, so this answer choice is incorrect.

Answer choice (C): This ability is not absent, so this answer choice must be wrong.

Answer choice (D): This is the correct answer choice, aligned with our prephrase. In the case of the pronghorn, the referenced environmental condition would be the extinct predators.

Answer choice (E): The passage does not talk about original behavior that is different from modern day behavior, so this answer choice should be eliminated.

Question #18: SR, Must. The correct answer choice is (C)

Since this passage references the last paragraph, we should consider what information was provided there. There are other examples that appear evidentiary of relict behavior, and there is one example when relict behavior has apparently ended.

Answer choice (A): There is no reference to any detriment associated with the absence of predators, so this answer choice can be safely eliminated.

Answer choice (B): The word that makes this answer choice a definite loser is "most"—the author would not claim that most animals display relict behavior.

Answer choice (C): This is the correct answer choice, as it refers to the end of the paragraph, and the example of the squirrel whose relict behavior apparently no longer exists.

Answer choice (D): There is no such claim in the passage, so this answer choice is incorrect.

Answer choice (E): The author of this passage never makes any such comparison, so this answer choice is incorrect.

9

Science Practice Passage I—June 2005 Passage #3 Answer Key

Question #19: CR, Must. The correct answer choice is (D)

The answer to this Concept Reference question should be prephrased: the benefits of the herd, discussed in the third paragraph, are the greater number of eyes watching out, and the lower likelihood that any one animal will be attacked.

Answer choice (A): The author does not discuss density in the passage, so although this may sound like reasonable speculation, it must be eliminated because it cannot be confirmed by the information provided.

Answer choice (B): This is another choice that seems like it could be true, but since it is not discussed in the passage, this answer choice must be incorrect.

Answer choice (C): This answer choice seems reasonable enough, but since it is not discussed in the passage, it cannot be correct.

Answer choice (D): This is the correct answer choice, as it presents one of the two benefits listed in our prephrase.

Answer choice (E): This answer choice seems like it could be true, but it is not offered specifically as a benefit, so it must not be correct.

Question #20: SR, MustX. The correct answer choice is (B)

Since this is an Except question, the four incorrect answer choices will support the biologist's explanation, and the correct answer will not.

Answer choice (A): This evidence is mentioned, so this choice is one of the four wrong answers that is mentioned in the passage.

Answer choice (B): This is the correct answer choice. There is no discussion of the absence of "carnivores," only the absence of predators.

Answer choice (C): This is discussed in the third paragraph, so this answer choice should be eliminated.

Answer choice (D): This is alluded to in the third paragraph, so we can safely eliminate this choice from contention as well.

Answer choice (E): This evidence is presented in the final paragraph, so this answer choice must be incorrect.

Question #21: SR, Must. The correct answer choice is (E)

In the third paragraph of the passage the author discusses the various behaviors of the pronghorn that may be explained as relict behavior.

Answer choice (A): This choice is far more absolute than provided for by the author, who only says that herding is beneficial, not that herding grazers never get attacked.

Answer choice (B): The point is that they do not need to graze in herds, but they still do, so it must have something to do with past stimuli.

Answer choice (C): There is nothing mentioned in the passage that allows this conditional relationship to be drawn, so this answer choice should be eliminated.

Answer choice (D): While the third paragraph does refer to a preference for athletic prowess, there is no assertion that only the fastest is chosen to mate.

Answer choice (E): This is the correct answer choice. Again, since the point is that they herd without the necessity for herding protection, this answer choice must be true.

9

Science Practice Passage II—October 2004 Passage #3 Answer Key

In this passage, the author discusses some of the specific research that led to Rita Levi-Montalcini's Nobel Prize winning discovery of NGF, or "Nerve Growth Factor," and the broad ramifications of this and subsequent discoveries regarding neurotrophic factors.

Paragraph One:

The author begins this passage with an introduction to the concept of neurotrophic factors: Chemicals which regulate the survival of nerve cells in animals. The first of these agents, known as NGF, was discovered in the 1950s by Rita Levi-Montalcini, who in 1986 shared the Nobel Prize for this discovery. As is common in Science passages such as this one, the tone of the author is somewhat academic and the passage to this point is fairly viewpoint neutral.

Paragraph Two:

In the second paragraph, the author continues this viewpoint-neutral, factual account, taking us back in time, to the mid-1940s, at which point Levi-Montalcini had hypothesized that many immature nerve cells are normally programmed to die. She did research to confirm this study, and in 1949 found that embryos produce many more nerve cells than are needed, adjusting downward to suit the tissue's necessity. A later phase of the research dealt with chick embryos, whose nerve development could be stimulated with tumor implantation. Levi-Montalcini hypothesized this to be caused by a chemical produced by tumors. The technique of tissue culture, which grows cells outside an organism, was used to investigate and then prove her hypothesis. Further research identified the tumor substance responsible for the observed effects, and Levi-Montalcini called it NGF, which stands for "nerve growth factor."

Paragraph Three:

The third paragraph continues in the same neutral, scientific tone, discussing that NGF was the first of many cell-growth factors found in animals. Levi-Montalcini's work, supplemented by later research, led to the determination that NGF is present in many tissues and fluids, and in heavy concentrations in some organs. This growth factor appears to be supplied by muscle cells, by organs over which nerve impulses will be transmitted, or sometimes by cells that are interspersed within the nerve tissues. The cells affected by NGF, generally those outside the brain and spinal cord, die if NGF is absent, or if anti-NGF antibodies are present.

9

VIEWSTAMP Analysis:

This passage, like many (but not all) Science passages, is fairly **Viewpoint-neutral**. The author does believe that Levi-Montalcini played an important role, but this assertion appears to be well-founded and factual.

Science Practice Passage II—October 2004 Passage #3 Answer Key

The author's **Tone** is academic and viewpoint neutral.

There are no real **Arguments** advanced in this passage, as is not uncommon in Science passages.

The author's **Main Point** is that Levi-Montalcini's discovery of NGF was based on significant research and yielded important results in the history of biochemistry.

The **Structure** of the passage is as follows:

> Paragraph One: Introduce NGF, its function, and its Nobel Prize winning discoverer.
>
> Paragraph Two: Provide background on the hypothesis, research that led to discovery.
>
> Paragraph Three: Provide further information about subsequent research which shed light on sources of NGF within an organism.

Question #15: GR, Main Point. The correct answer choice is (B)

Again, with Main Point questions we should always try to prephrase an answer before looking at the choices provided. In this case, the main point of this passage is to introduce the reader to the important scientific discovery of NGF, as well as the steps taken by the scientist in confirming early hypotheses, and further details about NGF uncovered through subsequent research.

Answer choice (A): The first half of this answer choice looks good, but the importance of the scientist's discovery was not to simply increase our understanding of chick embryos. Since the ramifications of Levi-Montalcini's discovery were further-reaching, this choice is wrong.

Answer choice (B): This is the correct answer choice. Most importantly, this response concludes that the discovery of NGF was pivotal to biochemistry, a fact reflected in the first paragraph.

Answer choice (C): This answer choice is relevant only to the second paragraph. Since the question asks for the main point of the passage, this answer should be eliminated. Furthermore, the passage states that Levi-Montalcini used the tissue-culture technique, not that she *devised* it.

Answer choice (D): This response confines its observations to the last paragraph, and does not reflect the main point of the passage. Furthermore, the passage actually stated that NGF is produced by tissues *to which the nerve cells will connect*, and this choice contrarily claims that NGF is produced only when nerve cells have already connected.

Answer choice (E): Once again, this response should be immediately eliminated simply because it is relevant only to the last paragraph. Furthermore, this choice is false given the passage, because it leaves out the possibility that nerve cells die if NGF is simply removed.

9

Question #16: GR, AP. The correct answer choice is (A)

This question asks why the discovery of NGF is important, from the perspective of the author. Since the author referenced the Nobel Prize and the importance of this discovery to biochemistry in general, and because an entire paragraph is dedicated to the discoveries that Levi-Montalcini's findings made possible, we should look for an answer that underscores the significance of this contribution.

Answer choice (A): This is the correct answer choice. The last paragraph describes the more specific understanding that subsequent research led to, and the first paragraph describes the contribution to biochemistry as "crucial," and indicates that the contribution led to Levi-Montalcini's eventually winning the Nobel Prize.

Answer choice (B): Since Levi-Montalcini actually expected many of the results that she eventually observed, there is no support for the idea that the author believes anything about "unanticipated" results.

Answer choice (C): It seems that the discoveries in the last paragraph have been the most important from the author's perspective, rather than this particular confirmation. The author refers to the development as "crucial" to biochemistry, and it is advisable to look for a choice that explains the crucial nature of the development.

Answer choice (D): Levi-Montalcini's experiments did show observable reactions in the tissues of different species; however, the ultimate significance in these experiments lies in the fact that they led to the expansion of knowledge of how the nervous system develops and functions.

Answer choice (E): The experiments did identify a substance, produced by mouse tumors, that stimulates nerve growth. However, that was not the ultimate finding of this important scientific discovery, so this choice is wrong.

9

Science Practice Passage II—October 2004 Passage #3 Answer Key

Question #17: SR, O. The correct answer choice is (C)

This question exemplifies the value of understanding passage organization. Again, the second paragraph describes the experiments, and the third paragraph describes subsequent developments, so the correct response should reflect such a relationship. In reviewing the answer choices, it is advisable to eliminate any response that is not aligned with this description, and verify or rule out the remaining choices based on the information in the passage.

Answer choice (A): The third paragraph offers no indication that Levi-Montalcini's conclusions required further confirmation. In fact, the third paragraph deals with some of the findings that are built on discoveries dealt with in the second paragraph.

Answer choice (B): In the third paragraph, the author discusses how science has built upon Levi-Montalcini's conclusions, which is rather contrary to the idea that science has undermined those conclusions.

Answer choice (C): This is the correct answer choice, as the third paragraph deals with further scientific developments based on discoveries discussed in the second paragraph.

Answer choice (D): In the third paragraph the author does not introduce any new, analogous substances, so this answer is incorrect.

Answer choice (E): Since the third paragraph discusses no experimental techniques, this response cannot be a description of its function.

Question #18: GR, Must. The correct answer choice is (E)

In approaching this Must Be True question, we should eliminate responses that are contrary to facts and inferences within the passage.

Answer choice (A): This answer choice states that nerve cells produce anti-NGF, and is therefore unsupported by the passage, which never indicates precisely where anti-NGF is produced.

Answer choice (B): This choice asserts that cells not affected by NGF are less numerous than those affected by NGF, and that the different cells have the same qualities. While the passage does support the idea that there are different types of cells, not all of which are affected by NGF, no further detail is offered as to similarities or quantitative comparisons.

Answer choice (C): The passage does suggest that a significant number of nerve cells probably die off in the process of an organism's development. However, since the passage never offers any information about the relative number of surviving cells, the conclusion that "few" cells are needed is unsupported.

Answer choice (D): Nothing in the passage indicates that some nerve cells have the capacity to change into other types of living tissue, so this answer choice is incorrect.

Answer choice (E): This is the correct answer choice, as it is supported by the discussion in the second paragraph. The passage states that an embryo initially produces more nerve cells than needed, and that the extra cells die off, which already supports the idea that the embryo produces nerve cells that do not end up connecting to anything. Furthermore, the second paragraph indicates that NGF governs the process by which some nerve cells develop and others die off (lines 14-26), and the third paragraph explains, in detail, that NGF is the causal factor that helps direct nerve cells toward target cells. It is reasonable to conclude that since some nerve cells will die off, they do not receive NGF, and do not connect with target cells.

Question #19: CR, Must. The correct answer choice is (A)

There is only one specifically described experiment, and that is the one that tests Levi-Montalcini's hypothesis that a chemical produced by mouse tumors stimulated nerve growth.

Answer choice (A): This is the correct answer choice. Lines 20-28 deal with Levi-Montalcini's hypothesis that a mouse tumor produces a chemical that stimulates nerve growth, and lines 28-39 provide a description of the experiment.

Answer choice (B): This choice contains true information; in lines 14-20, the passage informs us that Levi-Montalcini actually did test the hypothesis that many nerve cells are pre-programmed to die. However, the passage does not *describe* that experiment, offering no details about the *process* of the experiment.

Answer choice (C): The author indicates in the first paragraph that NGF is not the only neurotrophic factor, and mentions anti-NGF antibodies in the last paragraph; however, the author never provides the particulars of experiments that tested any such hypothesis or produced these results.

Answer choice (D): The information in this answer choice may be true, given the fact that NGF is "especially concentrated in some organs." However, the passage does not deal with organs' NGF concentration relative to that of surrounding tissue. Further, this is not the hypothesis that the passage described the *testing experiment* for, so this answer choice is incorrect.

Answer choice (E): While this is apparently the case, given the information in the third paragraph, the passage never deals with any specific experiment that confirmed this hypothesis.

Question #20: GR, Must. The correct answer choice is (D)

Once again, for Must Be True questions, we should seek to eliminate all answer choices that are unconfirmed by, or clearly contrary to the information within the passage.

Answer choice (A): Since the author never discusses neurotrophic factors other than NGF, this response is unsupported.

Answer choice (B): This answer choice is only partially accurate, and therefore incorrect. It is true that NGF was the first neurotrophic factor to be identified, and that other such substances have since been found. However, the passage never offers any information about the relative degree to which these various factors are currently understood, so this answer is incorrect.

Answer choice (C): The passage only deals with the scientist's discovery of NGF. While there is discussion of other such factors, there is no reference to her having discovered them. This answer choice is thus unsupported and incorrect.

Answer choice (D): This is the correct answer choice. In the first paragraph, the author describes NGF as the *first* such agent discovered, and that neurotrophic factors regulate nerve cell survival as well as "some specialized functions." Since these further functions are not specified within the passage, and the role of NGF as discussed seems to be relevant only to growth and survival, the assertion in this answer choice seems quite likely.

Answer choice (E): Since the experiments discussed in the passage only concern NGF with respect to nerve growth, there is no reason to assume that the observed effects were caused by other neurotrophic factors. Other factors certainly *might have* come into play, but we cannot assume that this was the case.

9

Chapter Ten: Section Strategy and Management

Chapter Ten: Section Strategy and Management

Approaching the Section Strategically

To this point we have outlined a powerful, all-encompassing system to attack and conquer LSAT Reading Comprehension. Following the methodology presented thus far, the majority of test takers find that they are able to reach, and often exceed, their RC goals. If you count yourself among this group, congratulations! Keep practicing, of course, but consider the pages ahead more as bonus content than required reading.

However, for students still chasing those final few points before test day, it may be time for a strategy adjustment to maximize your potential. This chapter provides a number of suggestions to help you do just that.

Similarly, how you ultimately choose to approach the section depends in large part on your intended outcome: if anything less than competent completion of all passage sets means failure to you—if you'll stop at nothing short of perfection—then certain portions of this chapter can be disregarded; on the other hand, if you continue to struggle with Reading Comp even after diligently working with the techniques presented previously, then the following advice is designed with you in mind.

Regardless, thinking strategically about Reading Comprehension, and drilling to target and resolve areas of weakness, are of value to everyone, as we will demonstrate in the pages remaining to us.

Section Structure

Many students believe that the passages in the Reading Comprehension section are presented in order of difficulty, and that each passage set is more difficult than the one prior. As we noted in Chapter Four, this is false. The difficulty of individual passages varies greatly, and the last passage in a section may be easier than, say, the second passage or the first.

Passages are NOT presented in order of difficulty.

Questions are also not presented in order of difficulty, and you cannot tell beforehand which question(s) in a set will be the most difficult. However, there are two statistics that are helpful when considering the task at hand:

1. Over 90% of the questions in Reading Comprehension are Must Be True-type questions. Because these are based directly on what you have read, you should never be intimidated by any individual question—the information needed to answer everything you're asked is always right there in the passage.

2. In over 80% of passages, the first question is a Main Point question. As we know from Chapter Three, you must always seek to identify the main point, and when you do so, most of the time you will be immediately repaid in the questions.

10

Time Management: The Nexus of Speed and Accuracy

All passage set completion times listed are averages. However, you should expect to move more quickly or more slowly depending on the difficulty of each passage and the number of questions.

Time management is critical to your success on this section. Each section of the LSAT is 35 minutes in length, and since there are always four passage sets per section, you have on *average* 8 minutes and 45 seconds to complete each passage set. However, this assumes you will complete all four passage sets and work with machine-like efficiency. For a number of students that is not possible or advisable! In a moment we will discuss a variable timing strategy, but first let's consider the broad effects that time has on the section.

Strong performance on the LSAT depends on two factors: speed and accuracy. If you rush to complete every question but miss most of them, you will not receive a high score. On the other hand, if, by slowing down, you dramatically increase your accuracy, you may be able to improve your score despite doing fewer questions. Consider the following comparison:

	Student #1	Student #2	Student #3
Questions completed in section	28	24	20
Accuracy Rate	50%	75%	100%
Total Correct Answers	14	18	20

Of course our preference is to have you complete each question and answer them all correctly. That should always be your goal. But as you practice with the techniques, you will naturally find a level of comfort. That may be doing all four passages, or it may involve doing fewer passages.

Obviously, actual performance in a section depends on a variety of factors, and each student must assess their own strengths and weaknesses. Regardless, the message is the same: you *might* benefit from slowing down and attempting fewer passages. The following table displays the average amount of time that would be allotted to each passage set, depending on how many are attempted:

Number of Passages Attempted	Time per Passage Attempted
2	17 minutes, 30 seconds
3	11 minutes, 40 seconds
4	8 minutes, 45 seconds

10

If you rush through the four passages and only get 14 correct, then perhaps a better choice would be to attack only three passages, spend more time on each, and aim for a higher accuracy rate. Practice will dictate which strategy is best for you, but do keep in mind that there is a point of diminishing returns: spending 35 minutes on one passage, even if your accuracy is 100% and you answer all seven questions correctly, will not lead to a very high LSAT score!

Instead, you must seek the level that provides you with the best combination of speed and accuracy. We strongly believe that you should attempt *at least* three passages unless there is a compelling reason to do otherwise.

Doing Fewer Passages

Prior to the test, if practice has proven that you should attempt three passages or less, it would make sense to select the passages according to your test-taking strengths. This requires two steps:

1. Know your personal strengths and weaknesses in the Reading Comprehension section. Determine which kinds of passages you prefer, and be detailed in your assessment. For example, do you like passages about Law? Or Comparative Reading passage sets? Do you like Science passages but dislike passages about History?

2. Choose the best passages to work on as soon as you begin the section. As the section starts, look for the passage types you prefer. Usually a quick reading of the first few lines reveals whether you will like a passage or not. Know that sometimes the test makers use "easy" topics in difficult passages (we covered that in Chapter Four), so your selections will not be infallible. But with practice they'll help.

So at the beginning of each Reading Comprehension section, you should quickly scan the first few lines of the passage 1. If it looks like a passage you would like to do or one that seems easy to you, start with that passage. If, on the other hand, the first passage appears hard or is of a type you dislike, immediately move to the second passage and scan its first few lines. Complete the same analysis to decide if you want to do the passage.

One factor to keep in mind when analyzing a passage set is the number of questions it contains. Suppose two passages appear equally attractive to you. In this case you should do the passage set with the greater number of questions, the theory being you get "more for your money" when there are more questions: the reading time is roughly the same in each but one

> Apply this strategy after you have determined that you cannot complete four passages with sufficient accuracy.

> All else being equal, do the passage with more questions.

passage offers a greater opportunity for points (and you can easily see the number of questions in each passage by glancing at the navigation bar at the bottom of the screen).

Your actions within each passage set are also important, and you can never let a single question consume too much time. You must keep focused, and if you do not see a clear path to solving the question, move on.

If you do decide to do only three passages but you find yourself with an extra minute or two at the end of the section, use one of the approaches discussed under Limited Time Strategies later in this chapter.

The "Plus 2" Timing Formula

The idea of working with metronomic efficiency through a Reading Comprehension section is appealing but also nearly unattainable. If you plan to attempt all four passages, you must recognize that the number of questions has a direct effect on the amount of time needed to complete each passage and adjust your pacing accordingly. One simple approach is the Plus 2 Timing Formula, which takes the number of questions in the passage set and adds "2" to it, resulting in the total number of minutes you have to complete that passage:

Time per Passage in Minutes = # of Questions in the Passage + 2

With this formula, you have a simple way to account for the time variability caused by the changing number of questions per passage:

Number of Questions in the Passage	+2	Total Time Allotted to the Passage
5	2	7 minutes
6	2	8 minutes
7	2	9 minutes
8	2	10 minutes

This is a simple yet effective strategy for gauging your intended pace, and one that gives you extra breathing room during passages that have a greater number of questions.

10

Using a Timer

The LSAT itself has a built-in timer on the tablet and timing is done automatically, and so practicing under timed conditions is critically important. PowerScore has online tools that allow you to experience the digital environment while practicing, but you will also likely use different paper resources while you are preparing. In those cases, one of the most important tools for preparation success is a timer. When not working online, your timer should be a constant companion during your LSAT preparation, and, as will be discussed in the next section, you should use your timer to help construct an accurate Pacing Guideline.

Although not all of your practice efforts should be timed, you should attempt to do as many questions as possible under timed conditions in order to acquaint yourself with the difficulties of the test. After all, if the LSAT was a take-home test, no one would be too worried about it.

A timer is invaluable because it acts as an odometer for the section. With sufficient practice you will begin to establish a comfortably aggressive test-taking speed and your timer helps confirm you are maintaining or improving it, passage to passage, day to day. If you find you are moving too quickly or too slowly during the test, you can then make instant adjustments, just as you've done in practice.

Practice doing as many passages as possible with your timer so that you can develop a comfortable and familiar pace.

The following time-markers occur in connection with the *average* time per passage:

Number of Passages Attempted	Average Timing Marking Points (counting DOWN from 35:00 to 0:00 minutes)
2	Move to passage #2 at 17 minutes and 30 seconds
3	Move to passage #2 at 23 minutes and 20 seconds; Move to passage #3 at 11 minutes and 40 seconds
4	Move to passage #2 at 26 minutes and 15 seconds; Move to passage #3 at 17 minutes and 30 seconds; Move to passage #4 at 8 minutes and 45 seconds

10

The table just seen assumes that each passage is done in exactly the average allotted time, which in reality never occurs. Nonetheless, it's interesting to look at the table and understand what happens as you vary the number of passages attempted. If you spend more time on one of the passages, you must make up that time in another passage to stay on pace. If you do one of the passages more quickly, that gives you the luxury of spending more time on a later passage. Expect to see some variation in your timing due to the inherent difficulty of each passage and the number of questions, and account for that accordingly.

If you use the Plus 2 Timing Formula, your approach is somewhat easier: simply add up the allotted minutes per passage as you move through the section.

For example, if in a section you completed passages with 7, 8, 5, and 7 questions, then your Timing Marking Points would appear as follows:

Passage 1 = 9 minutes (7 + 2 = 9)

Move to passage #2 at 26 minutes

Passage 2 = 10 minutes (8 + 2 = 10)

Move to passage #3 at 16 minutes

Passage 3 = 7 minutes (5 + 2 = 7)

Move to passage #4 at 9 minutes

Passage 4 = 9 minutes (7 + 2 = 9)

10

Or, if in a section you completed passages with 6, 7, 6, and 7 questions, then your Timing Marking Points would be:

Passage 1 = 8 minutes (6 + 2 = 8)

> Move to passage #2 at 27 minutes

Passage 2 = 9 minutes (7 + 2 = 9)

> Move to passage #3 at 18 minutes

Passage 3 = 8 minutes (6 + 2 = 8)

> Move to passage #4 at 10 minutes

Passage 4 = 9 minutes (7 + 2 = 9)

Since this second example only contains 26 questions, the Plus 2 Timing Formula gives you an extra minute to check answers at the end (or to use as needed).

Remember, the LSAT is what is known as a "speeded" test. The test makers presume that the average student cannot finish each section in the allotted time (i.e., that they are "speeded" up). So performing well while increasing speed usually requires a lot of practice and subsequent scrutiny of your results. The tools we use—passage analysis, knowledge of question-generating formations and questions types, etc.—are designed to help you increase your speed once you are familiar with them. Yes, they take some time to adjust to at first, but this is true of any organized system. Keep practicing and work on becoming comfortable with the timed aspect of the test, and both your speed and your LSAT score will improve.

10

Pacing Guidelines

Every test taker must have a plan of action before they start a section. While most test takers shoot to meet the Plus 2 Timing Formula guidelines, those who read more slowly or more quickly sometimes need to make adjustments to their plans, hence the use of Pacing Guidelines. If you fall into one of those two categories, read on! If you do not, then you can use this information only if needed.

As you practice, you should strive to determine your personal Pacing Guideline. For example, how much time do you plan to spend on each passage? Approximately how much time do you expect will have elapsed when you reach question #10? Question #20? Before you sit down and take the actual test, you should be able to answer these questions.

First off, we are *not* advocating that you create a strict timeline that controls where you are every moment in the section or that dictates when you quit working on a question. Instead, you must create a loose blueprint for completing the section—one that uses your particular strengths to create an achievable set of goals. To give you a better sense of how this idea works, here are two example Pacing Guidelines for *high scorers*:

The navigation bar at the bottom of screen shows you how many questions are in the section.

Example #1:

- Complete each passage in eight minutes or less, unless a passage has eight questions.

- Last three minutes of the section: double-check my work; return to any question I noted as especially challenging.

Example #2:

- Complete each passage using a Plus 1 Timing Formula.

- Last four or five minutes of the section: double-check my work; return to any question I noted as especially challenging.

Clearly, these Guidelines are aggressive and assume that the test taker is good enough to complete all the questions accurately and still have time remaining. Your personal Guideline does not have to be the same!

10

Take a moment, however, to review the two sample Guidelines provided:

- The test taker assumes that he or she can work fast, but makes an adjustment for the number of questions.

- Despite being good enough to expect to finish all the questions, the test taker doesn't just sit back and relax for the last few minutes. Instead, he or she uses that time to re-check troublesome problems.

- The Guidelines are relatively loose and contain a minimum number of components and considerations. They're adaptable, in other words.

On the other hand, here is a sample Pacing Guideline for a test taker who struggles with regularly completing all four passages:

- Complete each passage using a Plus 3 Timing Formula.

- For the last passage attempted, use a Limited Time Strategy to complete as many questions as possible (Limited Time Strategies will be discussed in the next section).

This Guideline acknowledges that the test taker expects to go more slowly, allows more time for three passages based on question counts, and then prepares the test taker to deal with the likely end-section scenario where there is less time than needed to complete the fourth passage in its entirety.

There are numerous variations on these Guidelines, and none is universally perfect, so the exact one you create depends on your preferences and what you've learned about your abilities while practicing. Here is how to create and use your own Pacing Guideline:

1. During your practice sessions, focus on determining how fast you can do a typical Reading Comprehension passage set while retaining a high degree of accuracy. To do this, you will need to time yourself consistently.

2. Make a benchmark for where you should be after a typical passage set. If your Guideline is too complex to remember without writing down, it is too complex to use!

10

3. Try to take into account the difficulty level of a passage and the number of questions, high (8), low (5), or average (6-7).

4. Do not make your Pacing Guideline too detailed. The difficulty of the questions (and entire sections) varies, so you do not want to create a rigid Guideline that cannot be adapted to these differences. For example, do not make a Guideline that specifies where you will be at 5, 8, 12, 15 minutes, etc. That is too specific and will be unusable if you run into a hard (or very easy) passage early in the section. Try to make your Guideline broad enough to account for key points in the section. If you have more than four or five sections in your Guideline, it is getting too detailed!

5. Make sure you are comfortable with your plan by practicing, and that your goals are achievable. This is not a plan of what you hope will happen, but rather what your practice has proven you can do.

6. Use the Guideline to help monitor your performance during the test. If you end up working faster than expected and you are beating your goals, then you will know that things are going exceedingly well and that should bolster your confidence. On the other hand, if you find yourself falling behind the marking points, then you will know that you must bear down and work a bit more quickly.

You should have a different Pacing Guideline for each section.

Implementing the steps above should not be too difficult, but you would be surprised at how many people fail to prepare even the most basic plan of action for each section. In many ways, it is as if they have been asked to run a marathon but they train only sporadically and never track how fast and how far they can go without burning out. Athletes at all levels constantly measure their performance, and the LSAT is just a marathon for the mind. The important thing is that you find a Guideline that works for you and that you have confidence in. Then, follow it on test day and remember to be flexible if you face the unexpected.

A Final Note on Speed: Comfort versus the Clock

An understandable impulse exists for nearly every test taker, where they prioritize absolute confidence, even certainty, in every choice they make—reading speed, detail recall, passage notations, correct and incorrect answers, and the like—above all else, including the inescapable necessity of moving as quickly as possible. Or, as we sometimes describe it, students choose comfort over the clock.

Having made it this far in the book you can likely guess where we stand on this compromise: it is often a terrible trade-off. Simply put, the best possible outcome in every section results from a perfect marriage of speed and accuracy, but the vast majority of students fail to ever truly tap into their full-speed potential because they're stalled by that persistent, panicky inner voice saying things like, "Well are you *certain* you understood every word of that sentence?," "Wouldn't it be *safer* to write out a full paragraph summary here?," "Are you *sure* you want to keep this answer as a Contender?," and a thousand tentative things more. This degree of relentless second-guessing and self-doubt is an anchor that anyone looking to go as fast as possible must cast off.

If this chapter thus far can be summed up in a single line, a reasonable distillation might be *You need to determine what will work best for you through intensive experimentation and honest self-assessment*, and your ideal speed is no different. But with this caveat: as you practice, make it a point to occasionally push yourself to the outer boundaries, the very limits, of your pacing comfort zone. Read actively and aggressively, faster than you're used to (and certainly faster than is comfortable!), whether that means a passage set pace of 6-8 minutes, or 10-12. Be more decisive. Trust the instincts that your training has developed and refined, and *commit*.

And above all stop worrying so much about perfection in every moment as part of this exercise—aim for a pace where you'll finish the section under time no matter what, and consider what it teaches you. Did your score drop? Improve? To what extent? And is that speed potentially attainable with continued time and effort?

Yes, your accuracy can suffer somewhat as you throttle up the intensity, but if you're well-versed in the methodology we've covered, chances are good your abilities won't decline nearly as much as you might expect. And if you're struggling to get through only the second or third passage in the time allowed you may find a faster pace tips the scales in your favor: more questions attempted with only a slight dip in accuracy probably results in a better outcome than two perfect passages ever would.

The core concept is that every so often you should experience what it's like to move quickly enough that completing the section becomes possible. Will that be your target test day tempo? Perhaps. Perhaps not. Your results will determine that, as we have discussed. But by exploring a pace that may ultimately prove faster than advisable you'll be able to pinpoint exactly where on the speed-accuracy spectrum your best results lie. And you'll learn what you're truly capable of where it matters most: in the absence of comfort.

10

Limited Time Strategies ▅▅▅▅

Within each Pacing Guideline there is room to make strategic decisions during the test. With practice you will discover how to best take advantage of your strengths and mitigate your weaknesses, and you can alter your approach accordingly on test day to maximize your results. Despite all efforts, however, you might find yourself running out of time as you approach the last passage. If this occurs, there are two broad-based, special strategies you can employ to handle this problem.

Please keep in mind that **these two strategies only apply if you arrive at the last passage set and do not have time to fully read the passage and answer at least three questions**.

1. Go Global—Skim the Passage and Answer the Global Questions

    As a general rule, we strongly advise against skimming. The passages are designed in a way that easily defeats skimming as an effective strategy, and students who skim the passages are simply unable to answer all of the questions correctly. However, when time is running low, skimming might allow you to answer several questions very quickly. To employ this stratagem, skim the passage very quickly, attempting to glean the gist of what is stated and the author's overall position. Then, find all of the Global questions and attempt to answer each. Hopefully, you will encounter at least one Main Point and Global Purpose question, and you can use your very generalized knowledge of the passage to answer those quickly.

These two strategies are not mutually exclusive. If you use the first approach and still have time left, implement the second approach.

2. Go Local—Read the Questions First and do only the Specific Reference Questions.

    With this approach you employ another stratagem we normally are strongly against: you read the questions first and then attempt to find the answer to each in the passage. The key is to carefully select the questions to do. By choosing to focus on only the Specific Reference questions, you can use the line references to return to specific areas of the passage and gain the knowledge needed to answer the questions. Thus, with this stratagem you do not read or skim the passage at all; you just read small sections very closely.

10

THE POWERSCORE LSAT READING COMPREHENSION BIBLE

The choice of strategy is yours, but it is dependent on the nature of the questions. If you know you are low on time, when you arrive at the passage you should glance at the questions and attempt to determine if there are more Specific Reference questions or more Global questions. Then use that information and your personal preferences to decide which strategy to use. You cannot predetermine which strategy to choose; you must make the decision when you reach and review the passage.

Even if you are able to read through the last passage and complete (or nearly complete) all of the questions, there are still mini-strategies you can employ as the clock winds down. The following two "endpassage" strategies can save valuable time at the *end of a section*:

1. When you find an attractive answer, choose it and move on

   With time running out, you can make allowances in your approach to the questions, cutting corners as you go. For example, if you are on question #26 (of 28 total) with only one minute remaining in the section and you find that answer choice (A) is extremely attractive, you can choose it and move on to the final question. Normally you would read all the answer choices, but when time is fleeting, you can alter that approach for the sake of expediency.

2. Jump to the shortest questions

   Another example of "endpassage" management would be if you only have one minute left, but two questions to complete. In this case, choose the shorter of the two problems: with less to read there's a better chance that you can complete it more quickly. Then you can return to the other problem if time allows.

Remember, good test takers are flexible in their approach and they adapt to changing circumstances. And no matter what, they maintain focus and a positive attitude!

Note how your strategy can change depending on how much time remains. This is not inconsistency; rather, it is just an acknowledgment of the realities of testing. If slightly altering an approach as time runs out helps gain you an extra point, then by all means you should do it.

10

The Answer Choices

As you know, every LSAT question contains five answer choices. When you complete each problem, your response will be entered as soon as you select the lettered bubble to the left of your chosen answer. That question will then darken correspondingly in the navigation bar, indicating you have answered it. The navigation bar will *not* currently show which answer you selected, however, so you cannot see your exact choices when working on other questions, or whether any particular answer has appeared with an unusual frequency in the section.

As mentioned previously in this book, you can flag problems you find difficult or wish to review as you work through the section, and we strongly recommend doing so as needed. That allows you to then jump to those problems instantly using the navigation bar. This process is a significant time-saver over the old paper-and-pencil format where you had to transfer your answers to an answer sheet, and then include separate indications about which problems you found difficult and wanted to review.

Four in a row?

The test takers have many tricks to keep you psychologically off-balance.

Unlike some standardized tests, the LSAT often has three identical answer choices to consecutive questions (such as three Ds), and on multiple occasions four identical answer choices in a row have appeared. On the June 1996 LSAT, six of seven answer choices in one section were (C), and on the June 2017 LSAT, in one section every correct answer from question #7 through question #15 was A or B. That is designed to make you question yourself!

The use of multiple answer choices in a row is one of the psychological weapons employed by the test makers to unnerve test takers. Any test taker seeing four (D)s in a row on their answer sheet understandably thinks they have made some type of error, primarily because most tests avoid repetition in their answer choices. If you see three or four answer choices in a row, do not become alarmed, especially if you feel you have been performing well on the section. We are still waiting for the day that the LSAT has five identical correct answers in a row, but we will not be too surprised when it happens.

Guessing Strategy

Because the LSAT does not assess a scoring penalty for incorrect answer choices, you should always guess on every question that you cannot complete during the allotted time. However, because some answer choices have statistically been more likely to occur than others over time, you should not guess randomly. The following tables indicate the frequency of appearance of Reading Comprehension answer choices over the years.

Never leave an answer blank on the LSAT! There is no penalty for wrong answers and so it is in your best interest to guess on any problem you cannot complete.

All Reading Comprehension Answer Choices June 1991 – November 2022*					
% appearance of each answer choice throughout the entire section	A%	B%	C%	D%	E%
	19.3	21.0	19.6	**21.5**	18.6

*These statistics do not include nondisclosed LSAT administrations.

The table above documents the frequency with which each answer choice appeared as a percentage of all Reading Comprehension answer choices between June 1991 and June 2021 inclusive. If history holds, when guessing on the LSAT Reading Comprehension section, you would be best served by always choosing answer choice (D). Do *not* choose random answer choices, and do *not* put in a pattern such as A-B-C-D-E etcetera. Although guessing answer choice (D) does not guarantee you will get the questions correct, if history is an indicator then choosing answer choice (D) gives you a better chance than guessing randomly. Consider the following comparison of students guessing on five consecutive answer choices:

We discuss guessing strategy and many other LSAT concepts on the PowerScore LSAT PodCast and in the Free LSAT Help Section of powerscore.com.

Correct Answer Choice	Student #1 Answer Choices (Pattern)	Student #2 Answer Choices (Random)	Student #3 Answer Choices (All Ds)
B	A	D	D
D	B	C	D
E	C	A	D
A	D	E	D
C	E	B	D
# Correct	0	0	1

Guessing randomly reduces each question to an independent event with a 1 in 5 chance of success.

10

Although one question may not seem significant, it adds up over four sections, and depending on where you are in the scoring scale, it can increase your score several points. And every point counts! By guessing answer choice (D), you increase your chances of getting an answer correct.

The following table summarizes the historical percentage appearance of answer choices in just the last five questions of the Reading Comprehension section.

Last Five Answer Choices Per Reading Comprehension Section June 1991 – November 2022*					
% appearance of each answer choice in the last five questions of the Reading Comprehension section	A%	B%	C%	D%	E%
	16.6	**23.0**	18.0	22.2	20.2

*These statistics do not include nondisclosed LSAT administrations.

Within the last five questions, the guessing strategy dictates that you should guess answer choice (B). Notice the significant statistical deviation of answer choice (A). Answer choice (A) is not a good answer choice to guess in the last five answer choices!

Please keep in mind that the above advice holds only for pure guessing. If you are attempting to choose between two answer choices, do not choose on the basis of these statistics alone!

On a related note, if you are a strong test taker who correctly answers most questions but occasionally does not finish a section, quickly review the answer choices you have previously selected and use the answer that appears least as your guessing answer choice. For example, if you have completed twenty questions in a section, and your answers contain a majority of (A)s, (B)s, (C)s, and (E)s, guess answer choice (D) for all of the remaining questions.

10

Problem Diagnostics

Let's say that after working through this entire book you are still struggling with Reading Comprehension. Hopefully that is not the case, but it does happen on occasion, especially to non-native English speakers. If you are still encountering difficulties, then the first step is to not get discouraged and to keep practicing! A positive attitude and hard work will help carry you through most big-picture problems when it comes to the LSAT.

Score Reports and Problem Logs

The second step is to review your score reports and problem logs. While some problems are easy to identify—problems with speed, for example—other issues are more difficult to pinpoint, and only reveal themselves after careful analysis of past performance. Two basic tools you should be using to help you with this process are an analysis program when scoring your LSATs, and a tracking log of every past error and problem point.

Score reports are an invaluable tool, and every time you take an LSAT you should input your answers into our free scoring system, available at the PowerScore Self-Study Site (address at the start of this book). The feedback you receive there tells you about the types of questions you are struggling with as well as the difficulty of the questions you are missing. Use that information to better understand what you are doing well and what you need to work on.

The other tool you must use is a performance tracker to catalog everything that gives you trouble (the Study Plans available on our Self-Study Site have tracking sheets you can use). Miss a question? Mark it down and note why. Don't feel 100% comfortable? Same thing—mark it down. Then, every so often, go through those lists and look for patterns in what you are missing. There will be patterns! For example, you might miss only a single question of a certain type in each section, so it might not feel like you are having issues, but then when you look over the results of ten tests, you realize that you aren't as strong with that type as you could be.

10

Skill Tests

If, after reviewing your past performance, you find you are still uncertain of where you are having problems or of exactly what to work on, the next step is to attempt to diagnose your problems using the methods below.

Note: while each test below references a single passage, typically the results are best considered after applying each test to several passages at the least, simply to make sure that the results of any given passage are not an anomaly.

Broad versus Detail Reading Test

Broad vs Detail Reading Test:

Purpose:
To check your reading efficiency.

Timing: # of questions + 5.

Directions:
After reading the passage, do not return to the passage for confirmation of an answer, ever. Use only your memory.

Purpose:

This test is designed to see whether you are reading the passage efficiently. Good readers not only gain a strong overall picture of the passage, but also pick up enough details to quickly answer a fair selection of questions.

Timing:

To begin the test, select a single passage and question set you have not seen previously. Count the total number of questions, and add 5 to that total. This will be the number of minutes you have to complete the passage and corresponding questions. So, if a passage has 6 questions, then you have 11 minutes to complete the passage and questions (6 + 5 = 11). If a passage has 8 questions, then you have 13 minutes total (8 + 5 = 13), and so on.

Directions:

With your timer or watch set for the appropriate time, read through the passage and complete the questions. The catch? Once you finish reading the passage, *you cannot look back at the text of the passage*. You must use only your recall of the text to complete each question.

The reason for the extra time is to allow you to thoroughly read each question and search your memory. This is a test of how you acquired and absorbed information, not a speed test.

10

Analysis:

After you complete all of the questions, check the answer key and look for patterns in your answers. Did you miss all the Global Reference (GR) questions? Then you are missing the broad strokes of the passage, and you can adjust your approach to look for the bigger picture items while reading. For example, you can more strongly note where the author changes course or when an opposing view is introduced. Or, did you miss a number of Concept Reference (CR) and Specific Reference (SR) questions? This could tell you that you do not have very good detail recall or are not reading for sufficient detail. Keep in mind that missing some very finely detailed questions is not necessarily an indictment of your manner of reading, so adjust your evaluation if you see you missed a CR or SR question that you could have easily answered had you been allowed to look back at the passage. Perhaps you missed questions related to different viewpoints, both the author's and some of the subject's. That often indicates that you are not paying enough attention to who says what during the passage, which would allow you to slightly change your focus as you read.

Also, make note of the times you were caught between two attractive answers. Did that occur because the answers were legitimately attractive, or did it occur because you need to read in a more consistent and focused fashion?

Adjustments:

If you are relatively strong in Reading Comprehension and are shooting for a top score, reduce the number of minutes you add from 5 to a lower number. But, make sure you allow for enough time to completely read each question and contemplate the answers thoroughly.

Diagramming
Test:

Purpose: To test
the quality of
your passage
diagramming.

Timing: # of
questions + 2.

Directions: Read
and diagram
the passage
as usual. Use
only your marks
and notations
to answer the
questions.

Diagramming Test

Purpose:

This test is designed to check whether you diagram (as in, mark the passage and make scratch paper notes) too much, too little, or just enough.

Timing:

In this case, use your standard "number of questions plus two" timing approach, meaning a passage with 6 questions allows you 8 minutes (6 + 2 = 8), and a passage with 7 questions allows you 9 minutes (7 + 2 = 9), and so on.

Directions:

Read the passage in its entirety, making your normal marks and notes. Then, move on as you would normally. When answering the questions, you are allowed to return to the passage, but you can only refer to areas of the passage you marked. So, if you underlined a section that is mentioned in a question, you can refer to that section and consider it. Or if you wrote a note on your scratch paper about that section, you can refer to that. If you did not note that section in any way (underlining, highlighting, or with notes), then you cannot return to it and you must use your memory to answer the question.

Note: Do not cheat! Attempt to mark and notate as you would normally; do not suddenly decide you will write an entire summary or mark every paragraph extensively when you normally wouldn't.

Analysis:

The point of the drill is to test your passage diagramming skills, and to see how well they match up with the questions. Did you mark many of the relevant points? Good, you are on the right track! Or, did you mark and note a bunch of portions that were never tested? If so, you need to go back and improve your passage diagramming skills (likely by diagramming less). Similarly, if you failed to either note or recall the majority of tested text you should consider diagramming with greater frequency.

10

If you believe you might be overutilizing a certain tool (such as underlining too much, or writing out summaries too frequently), you can adjust the test by using just the marks within the passage text, or alternately use just the side notes and comments you made to answer questions. This can help reveal if your approach is too one-sided, although expect to miss more questions than you would otherwise due to using only part of your work.

Comprehension Test

Purpose:

This is an examination of how well you understand what you read. If you struggle with understanding individual sections or the passage as a whole, this will reveal that problem.

Timing:

There is no time limitation for this drill, although use common sense.

Directions:

Read the passage at your normal speed, and make any marks or notations as you would normally. At the conclusion of each paragraph, write out a short but specific description of the contents of the paragraph. However, do *not* refer to the text as you do this! It must be from memory.

After you complete the final paragraph, summarize the passage as a whole, and identify the main point and the major players within the passage. Then move on to the questions, and attempt to answer all of them using only your written summarizations.

Analysis:

The point of this test is clear: how well are you able to summarize what was said, and how well do you identify the relevant points within the passage? While some misses are expected on SR questions, you should be able to dominate all big picture questions such as Main Point and Primary Purpose, as well as any questions about Perspective and Tone.

Comprehension Test:

Purpose: To check your understanding of what you have read.

Timing: No limit.

Directions: After reading each paragraph, write out a summary of its contents. Then do the same at the end of the passage. Use only your summaries to answer the questions.

10

Note that this is also a short-term memory test, and your short-term memory is like a muscle in that you can make it stronger with exercise. Thus, the mere act of practicing in this fashion will improve recall.

Adjustments:

If you want to further examine your process, reduce the amount of time available to complete your summaries down to one minute per paragraph (in other words, you have 1 minute following the end of each paragraph to write out a complete synopsis). This forces you to identify just the most important points presented.

Speed Test:

Purpose: To see how fast you can read while maintaining reasonable accuracy.

Timing: # of questions equals number of minutes.

Directions: Read and diagram the passage as quickly as possible, attempt to maximize accuracy on the questions.

Speed Test

Purpose:

To check how fast you can read while still maintaining comprehension, and to establish that your basic approach is sound.

Timing:

In this case, use your standard "number of questions" as your total time. Meaning, a passage with 6 questions allows you 6 minutes, and a passage with 7 questions allows you 7 minutes, and so on.

Directions:

Read the passage in its entirety, making your normal marks and notations, but attempt to finish it as quickly as possible. You will be under time pressure so move fast!

Analysis:

The Speed Test tends to automatically produce some misses since most students cannot complete every question in the given time, but do not worry too much about those. Instead, focus on the questions you did complete; how was your performance on those attempts?

Underneath it all, this is a pressure test exercise that can reveal some problems with your approach (if there are any). You will not have extra time to return to the passage frequently, and you will be forced to rely on your basic VIEWSTAMP analysis and mental map of the passage.

One side benefit of performing this test: you get an excellent idea of the pace you can set while still performing reasonably well, and you can learn what speed works for you and what speed is too fast. You can also discover the question types you tend to successfully answer following a fast-paced read through of the passage text, which is very helpful in end-of-section situations where time is low and you must rush to complete the remaining content.

For further clarification of the Speed Test ideas, re-read the section on Comfort versus the Clock (at the end of our Pacing Guidelines discussion earlier in this chapter)!

Adjustments:

Depending on your performance, adjust your timing to reduce or add more time to the process. For example, if you perform very well using just the total questions as your time limit, next try to do some passage sets using "total questions minus 1" as the guideline, and then "total questions minus 2" if you continue to perform well.

Prediction Test

Purpose:

To check your ability to predict what the test makers will ask you.

Timing:

This test is often applied in combination with one or more of the prior tests, although it can also be done on its own. When done alone, use the standard "number of questions plus two" timing approach, where a passage with 6 questions allows you 8 minutes (6 + 2 = 8), and a passage with 7 questions allows you 9 minutes (7 + 2 = 9), and so on.

Directions:

Read the passage in its entirety, making your normal marks and notations. Then, before moving to the questions, pause the clock, and attempt to predict with some specificity what the test makers will ask you, both in terms of question types and specific parts of the passages.

Next, immediately after noting the questions you think will be asked, compare what you predicted to what the test makers actually did (this requires you to preview each question stem, which is fine for our purposes here). You may find you are close in some cases and way off in others. That's okay: you want to be as accurate as possible, but the real point here is to see how you value and prioritize pieces of the passage as compared to what the test makers actually do. If your RC Radar is poorly calibrated, this drill tends to show it immediately.

Prediction Test:

Purpose: To see how well you can predict what you will be asked.

Timing: # of questions + 2.

Directions: Read and diagram the passage as usual, but stop prior to the questions and attempt to predict exactly what will be tested.

10

Analysis:

In all likelihood your accuracy will be extremely variable, with a wide range of successes and failures in your predictions. Again, that's okay: the purpose here is not to be perfect, but rather to better understand how the test makers choose information from the passage to serve as the basis for questions, and how you can develop a sharper eye for it as you read.

Keep in mind too that not all questions can be predicted, so there's really no such thing as 100% accuracy in this drill. It's the process that is important, more so than a perfect result.

Adjustments:

If needed when combining this with one of the other tests, save the comparison of predicted questions and actual questions until after the questions have been completed. Then consider your expected questions relative to those that appeared and see how you did.

If you are still struggling with the Prediction Test, review the Passage Elements That Generate Questions section in Chapter Four.

Prephrasing Test:

Purpose: To see how well you can predict what correct answers will say or do.

Timing: No limit.

Directions: Read and diagram the passage as usual, but stop prior to the questions and attempt to predict exactly what will be tested.

Prephrasing Test

Purpose:

To determine how well you prephrase answer choices, both in terms of your expectations' accuracy and effectiveness.

Timing:

This test is often applied in combination with one or more of the prior tests, although it is most often done on its own. When performed alone, read the passage at your regular pace, but do not worry about the time it takes to complete the questions.

Directions:

Before you begin a passage set, take Post-it Notes (or something similar) and cover the answer choices for each question so that they are no longer visible. Leave the questions exposed.

Then approach the passage as you normally would—same pace, notations, and analysis—and immediately after reading move to the questions. At this point, you can see each question but not the answers, so instead of finding the correct answers your goal is to predict them by writing prephrases on the Post-its still covering the answers. Try to make your predictions as powerful and precise as possible, without ever going beyond what you know to be true. Do this for each question in the set without removing any Post-its.

Once you've written a prephrase for each question, go back to the first question, remove the Post-it, and, without re-examining the passage or question, use your prephrase notes to evaluate the answer choices and choose the one you believe is correct.

Analysis:

What you will likely find is that for some questions your prediction is spot on and the correct answer stands out, while for a number of others you'll be able to eliminate a few answers but remain a bit uncertain as to which choice is correct. That is, at times you'll predict the correct answer almost verbatim (such as Main Point or Specific Reference questions); other times your prephrase will only be about the nature of the correct choice or what you know it will represent or reflect (like Tone, or Weaken and Strengthen).

The key is that for every question you need to consider what you wrote and what you could/should have done to make it more powerful: deconstruct the correct answer choice and ask yourself how your prephrase could be improved to better capture the essence of that choice. How could you have been more accurate? How could you have better anticipated the test makers' actions? As your prephrasing abilities improve, so too will your speed and accuracy.

Adjustments:

If you are still struggling despite continued practice, make the process more explicit: Write down your improved prephrase next to your original and compare the two, considering how far off you were and how you could have been closer. Go through entire Reading Comprehension sections analyzing your prephrases and comparing them to the credited answer choices, and then adjusting them to form a better lens through which the correct choice can be seen more clearly.

10

Practice and Skill Building Solutions

If the prior Tests revealed problems that you need to fix, then the solution is fairly straightforward: practice the skills that are subpar until you master them. This, however, is easier said than done when it comes to Reading Comprehension. Simply doing passage after passage can become tedious to the point of exhaustion, and at that stage it becomes difficult to draw inspiration or elucidation from the work you are doing.

To combat that problem, vary your practice routines when working with RC:

1. Use the Diagnostic Tests in the Prior Section as Drills

   Any of the Tests in the last section can be used as the basis for a drill. Simply select three or four passages for each drill and work through them. Or, select several passages and then work through each of the Diagnostic Tests successively. This provides a unique and informative set of challenges, with the important element that you vary your timing as you move from drill to drill, which helps better attune you to the ticking clock in RC, a side bonus of using this approach.

2. Individual Section Challenges

   Individual, full-section challenges taken under regular time are an important part of practicing Reading Comp. While doing individual passages is also important, you must practice your entire section strategy, including such choices as which passage to do first, how to handle running low on time, etc. The more sections you take as full challenges the more often you will encounter the various problems that can crop up in RC, and the better you will become at resolving them.

The Teaching Test

The suggestions on the prior pages provide different tools you can use to identify problems and ways to keep practice and review fresh. But what if none of these approaches fully resolves your difficulties, or helps you reach what you know is your Reading Comprehension potential?

The highest-level litmus test for reviewing LSAT questions is what we call the Teaching Test: ask yourself if you could effectively teach the passage and each question to someone else. If the answer is no, then review it again until you can! If the answer is yes, then for the harder and more confusing questions, try to find someone (a friend, parent, study partner) that will let you teach the question to them. This will force you to organize your thoughts about how the problem works, to know the nuances of the passage structure, and to recognize the way in which the answers were constructed in order to entice or repel you.

The beauty of this approach is that it forces you to fundamentally understand what you read and how that information relates to each question. Can you identify passage structure and viewpoints without thinking? Do you know the main point and why the author wrote the passage? Did you catch the subtleties (and possible flaws) of arguments made in the passage? And so on. Instant execution with no delays or hesitation is your goal as you review each question.

Because a teaching-level comprehension is the standard of mastery you are attempting to meet, it is preferable that you spend more time with fewer questions as opposed to simply doing as many questions as possible. For example, it's better to take one LSAT Reading Comprehension section and review it deeply for perfect clarity, as opposed to working through two sections and only giving them a superficial review.

10

Section Triage Strategies ▮

If you are still struggling with Reading Comprehension after trying all the prior strategies, this section is for you. If this is *not* a problem for you, then ignore the following section.

Note: the following strategies are different from the "Limited Time Strategies" presented earlier in this chapter. The Limited Time Strategies are meant to be applied when you have only a few minutes left to complete the last passage of the section. The strategies below are for use from the outset of the section, and *are intended for those having serious difficulties with Reading Comprehension in general.*

Alternate Passage Selection Strategies

The usual approach to the Reading section is to do the passages either in order of presentation or to select passages by the most attractive topic. While topic at least allows you to choose passages that you find the most interesting, the following two wrinkles can help improve the return on your time:

1. Attack the Comparative Reading passage first

    For many students, the two shorter passages and accompanying alternate viewpoints provide greater perspective and understanding on the topic, and that can lead to a higher success rate. If this description applies to you, then start the section by seeking out the Comparative Reading passage and attacking it first. Note: this does not mean that Comparative Reading passages are inherently easier in terms of difficulty; it just means that some students prefer the Comparative Reading format. If you are one of those students, then consider using this strategy.

2. Choose the passage with the greatest number of questions

    The number of questions is not an indicator of difficulty. Passages with the fewest number of questions can be easy or hard. But, if you choose the passage with the greatest number of questions, you get more mileage from the time you spend reading. That is, if the time required to read each passage is roughly the same, you get more of a return if you can answer eight questions about the passage as opposed to five. So, if you are having trouble with the section in general, you want to maximize the return on your reading, which suggests you should seek passages that have the greatest number of accompanying questions.

Historically, the first two passages are typically easier than the last two passages. The first passage is most often the easiest passage of the section.

10

Alternate Reading Strategies

Once you have selected a passage to attack, you can decide whether to alter your reading approach as well. The following are some alternate strategies that we recommend *only if* you are having serious difficulty with Reading Comp:

1. Scan the questions first, then read the passage afterward

    We have talked previously about why this approach is generally not optimal, but if you are having extreme problems, sometimes an extreme solution is required. In this approach, you flip the normal strategy on its head and start the passage by scanning all of the questions so you get a sense of the questions you will be asked and thus what you need to look for while reading. Then you return to the passage and read through it, stopping to answer relevant questions as the answers become apparent to you.

    The goal with this strategy is not to memorize each question, but to instead get a broad sense of what you are being asked and the types of information you will need to answer the questions.

2. Focus on reading the first paragraph quite closely, but then rapidly skim the remainder of the passage, focusing on structural elements

    This alternate reading strategy relies on your ability to understand structure while reading very quickly. Because the first paragraph sets the stage for the rest of the passage, you read that at your normal speed and attempt to obtain as much information as possible. Then, as you move into the remainder of the passage, you speed up your reading so that you are mostly skimming, and you use the base of knowledge gained in the first paragraph to help you understand the general direction and structure of the rest of the passage. The overall intent of this strategy is to minimize reading time while giving you maximum time to answer the questions.

10

Here, we can use variants of the strategies discussed several pages back:

1. Go Global—Answer the Global Questions first

   Regardless of how you select the passage or read the passage, one strategy that can be employed is to answer all of the Global questions first, then the Concept questions, and finally the Local questions. This isolates the abstract questions together, then the broad idea questions, and finally the localized questions that typically require double-checking within the passage.

2. Go Local—Answer the Local Questions First

   Alternatively, you can use your knowledge of the passage to answer each Local question first, then the Concept questions, and finally the Global questions. This allows you to focus in on the questions that have specific references and are typically able to be answered directly from lines in the passage, before moving on to the broader questions. In this way, you can build your understanding of the passage, and save the broad questions for the point in the process when you should know the most about the general scope and direction of the passage.

If you are struggling, mix and match the strategies above until you find the combination that best suits your strengths and weaknesses. For example, some students don't want to spend time selecting a passage whereas for others the feeling of control that comes with selecting a passage is critical. Some test takers have a specific process they want to use with the questions but others prefer to do them in order. While we strongly advocate the method described in detail earlier in this book and we know that this is the basic method used by the majority of high-scorers, each test taker is unique and if you need to tweak the approach, do not hesitate to do so. The best approach is the one that works for you, and thus you should experiment with different approaches until you feel the most comfortable.

10

Afterword

Thank you for choosing the *PowerScore LSAT Reading Comprehension Bible* to assist you in your prep! We hope you have found this book useful and enjoyable, but most importantly we hope this book helps raise your LSAT score.

For more information relating to Reading Comprehension, please visit:

 powerscore.com/lsatprep

And check out the authors on the PowerScore LSAT PodCast at:

 powerscore.com/lsat/podcast

We talk regularly about all things LSAT, including Reading Comp concepts and methods. Also available via iTunes, Spotify, Stitcher, and YouTube.

If you wish to ask questions about items in this book, please visit our free LSAT Discussion Forum at:

 forum.powerscore.com

The forum offers thousands of responses to student questions, including many lengthy articles and conceptual discussions from the authors of this book.

Study hard, stay focused, and best of luck on the LSAT!

10

Reading Comprehension Passage ReChallenge

Reading Comprehension Passage ReChallenge

POWERSCORE

BY BARBRI

Reading Comprehension Passage ReChallenge

This chapter contains each of the full passages presented earlier in this book. The passages are mixed into three sections of four passages each, allowing you the opportunity to retake each passage without seeing any of the work you did when you first encountered the passage. If you wish to time yourself, each block of four passages should be completed in 35 minutes total. Alternatively, if you choose to do each passage one at a time, each passage should be completed in 8 minutes and 45 seconds.

A brief answer key is presented at the end of each passage set, and in addition to the answers, the page number for the complete explanation of the passage is also given.

R

Reading Comprehension Passage ReChallenge
Set #1

R

The use of computer-generated visual displays in courtrooms is growing as awareness of their ability to recreate crime scenes spreads. Displays currently in use range from still pictures in series that mimic
(5) simple movement to sophisticated simulations based on complex applications of rules of physics and mathematics. By making it possible to slow or stop action, to vary visual perspectives according to witnesses' vantage points, or to highlight or enlarge
(10) images, computer displays provide litigators with tremendous explanatory advantages. Soon, litigators may even have available graphic systems capable of simulating three dimensions, thus creating the illusion that viewers are at the scene of a crime or accident,
(15) directly experiencing its occurrence. The advantages of computer-generated displays derive from the greater psychological impact they have on juries as compared to purely verbal presentations; studies show that people generally retain about 85 percent of visual
(20) information but only 10 percent of aural information. This is especially valuable in complex or technical trials, where juror interest and comprehension are generally low. In addition, computers also allow litigators to integrate graphic aids seamlessly into
(25) their presentations.

Despite these benefits, however, some critics are urging caution in the use of these displays, pointing to a concomitant potential for abuse or unintentional misuse, such as the unfair manipulation of a juror's
(30) impression of an event. These critics argue further that the persuasive and richly communicative nature of the displays can mesmerize jurors and cause them to relax their normal critical faculties. This potential for distortion is compounded when one side in a trial
(35) does not use the technology—often because of the considerable expense involved—leaving the jury susceptible to prejudice in favor of the side employing computer displays. And aside from the risk of intentional manipulation of images or deceitful use
(40) of capacities such as stop-action and highlighting, there is also the possibility that computer displays can be inherently misleading. As an amalgamation of data collection, judgment, and speculation, the displays may in some instances constitute evidence unsuitable
(45) for use in a trial.

To avoid misuse of this technology in the courtroom, practical steps must be taken. First, counsel must be alert to the ever-present danger of its misuse: diligent analyses of the data that form the
(50) basis for computer displays should be routinely performed and disclosed. Judges, who have the discretion to disallow displays that might unfairly prejudice one side, must also be vigilant in assessing the displays they do allow. Similarly, judges should
(55) forewarn jurors of the potentially biased nature of computer-generated evidence. Finally, steps should be taken to ensure that if one side utilizes computer technology, the opposing side will also have access to it. Granting financial aid in these circumstances
(60) would help create a more equitable legal arena in this respect.

1. Which one of the following most accurately states the main point of the passage?

(A) Those involved in court trials that take advantage of computer-generated displays as evidence need to take steps to prevent the misuse of this evidence.

(B) The use of computer-generated displays has grown dramatically in recent years because computer aids allow litigators to convey complex information more clearly.

(C) The persuasive nature of computer-generated displays requires that the rules governing the use of these displays be based on the most sophisticated principles of jurisprudence.

(D) Litigators' prudent use of computer-generated displays will result in heightened jury comprehension of complex legal issues and thus fairer trials.

(E) Any disadvantages of computer-generated visual displays can be eliminated by enacting a number of practical procedures to avoid their intentional misuse.

2. Which one of the following most accurately describes the organization of the passage?

   (A) The popularity of a new technology is lamented; criticisms of the technology are voiced; corrective actions to stem its use are recommended.

   (B) A new technology is endorsed; specific examples of its advantages are offered; ways to take further advantage of the technology are presented.

   (C) A new technology is presented as problematic; specific problems associated with its use are discussed; alternative uses of the technology are proposed.

   (D) A new technology is introduced as useful; potential problems associated with its use are identified; recommendations for preventing these problems are offered.

   (E) A new technology is described in detail; arguments for and against its use are voiced; recommendations for promoting the widespread use of the technology are advanced.

3. As described in the passage, re-creating an accident with a computer-generated display is most similar to which one of the following?

   (A) using several of a crime suspect's statements together to suggest that the suspect had a motive

   (B) using an author's original manuscript to correct printing errors in the current edition of her novel

   (C) using information gathered from satellite images to predict the development of a thunderstorm

   (D) using a video camera to gather opinions of passersby for use in a candidate's political campaign advertisements

   (E) using detailed geological evidence to design a museum exhibit depicting a recent volcanic eruption

4. Based on the passage, with which one of the following statements regarding the use of computer displays in courtroom proceedings would the author be most likely to agree?

   (A) The courts should suspend the use of stop-action and highlighting techniques until an adequate financial aid program has been established.

   (B) Computer-generated evidence should be scrutinized to ensure that it does not rely on excessive speculation in depicting the details of an event.

   (C) Actual static photographs of a crime scene are generally more effective as displays than are computer displays.

   (D) Verbal accounts by eyewitnesses to crimes should play a more vital role in the presentation of evidence than should computer displays.

   (E) Computer displays based on insufficient or inaccurate input of data would not seem realistic and would generally not persuade jurors effectively.

5. The author states which one of the following about computer displays used in trial proceedings?

   (A) Despite appearances, computer displays offer few practical advantages over conventional forms of evidence.

   (B) Most critics of computer-generated evidence argue for banning such evidence in legal proceedings.

   (C) Judges should forewarn jurors of the potentially biased nature of computer-generated displays.

   (D) Computer displays are used primarily in technical trials, in which jury interest is naturally low.

   (E) Litigators who utilize computer-generated displays must ensure that the opposing side has equal access to such technology.

6. The author mentions each of the following as an advantage of using computer displays in courtroom proceedings EXCEPT:

   (A) They enable litigators to slow or stop action.

   (B) They can aid jurors in understanding complex or technical information.

   (C) They make it possible to vary visual perspectives.

   (D) They allow litigators to integrate visual materials smoothly into their presentations.

   (E) They prevent litigators from engaging in certain kinds of unjustified speculation.

One of the intriguing questions considered by anthropologists concerns the purpose our early ancestors had in first creating images of the world around them. Among these images are 25,000-year-
(5) old cave paintings made by the Aurignacians, a people who supplanted the Neanderthals in Europe and who produced the earliest known examples of representational art. Some anthropologists see these paintings as evidence that the Aurignacians had a
(10) more secure life than the Neanderthals. No one under constant threat of starvation, the reasoning goes, could afford time for luxuries such as art; moreover, the art is, in its latter stages at least, so astonishingly well-executed by almost any standard of excellence
(15) that it is highly unlikely it was produced by people who had not spent a great deal of time perfecting their skills. In other words, the high level of quality suggests that Aurignacian art was created by a distinct group of artists, who would likely have spent
(20) most of their time practicing and passing on their skills while being supported by other members of their community.

Curiously, however, the paintings were usually placed in areas accessible only with extreme effort
(25) and completely unilluminated by natural light. This makes it unlikely that these representational cave paintings arose simply out of a love of beauty or pride in artistry—had aesthetic enjoyment been the sole purpose of the paintings, they would presumably
(30) have been located where they could have been easily seen and appreciated.

Given that the Aurignacians were hunter-gatherers and had to cope with the practical problems of extracting a living from a difficult environment, many
(35) anthropologists hypothesize that the paintings were also intended to provide a means of ensuring a steady supply of food. Since it was common among pretechnological societies to believe that one can gain power over an animal by making an image of it,
(40) these anthropologists maintain that the Aurignacian paintings were meant to grant magical power over the Aurignacians' prey—typically large, dangerous animals such as mammoths and bison. The images were probably intended to make these animals
(45) vulnerable to the weapons of the hunters, an explanation supported by the fact that many of the pictures show animals with their hearts outlined in red, or with bright, arrow-shaped lines tracing paths to vital organs. Other paintings clearly show some
(50) animals as pregnant, perhaps in an effort to assure plentiful hunting grounds. There is also evidence that ceremonies of some sort were performed before these images. Well-worn footprints of dancers can still be discerned in the clay floors of some caves, and
(55) pictures of what appear to be shamans, or religious leaders, garbed in fantastic costumes, are found among the painted animals.

1. Which one of the following most accurately describes the author's position regarding the claims attributed to anthropologists in the third paragraph?

   (A) implicit acceptance
   (B) hesitant agreement
   (C) noncommittal curiosity
   (D) detached skepticism
   (E) broad disagreement

2. The passage provides information that answers which one of the following questions?

   (A) For how long a period did the Neanderthals occupy Europe?
   (B) How long did it take for the Aurignacians to supplant the Neanderthals?
   (C) Did the Aurignacians make their homes in caves?
   (D) What are some of the animals represented in Aurignacian cave paintings?
   (E) What other prehistoric groups aside from the Aurignacians produced representational art?

R

3. The author would be most likely to agree with which one of the following statements?

(A) The cave paintings indicate that the Aurignacians lived a relatively secure life compared to most other hunter-gatherer cultures.

(B) Skill in art was essential to becoming an Aurignacian shaman.

(C) Prehistoric hunter-gatherers did not create any art solely for aesthetic purposes.

(D) All art created by the Aurignacians was intended to grant magical power over other beings.

(E) The Aurignacians sought to gain magical power over their prey by means of ceremonial acts in addition to painted images.

4. The author mentions the relative inaccessibility of the Aurignacian cave paintings primarily to

(A) stress the importance of the cave paintings to the lives of the artists who painted them by indicating the difficulties they had to overcome to do so

(B) lay the groundwork for a fuller explanation of the paintings' function

(C) suggest that only a select portion of the Aurignacian community was permitted to view the paintings

(D) help explain why the paintings are still well preserved

(E) support the argument that Aurignacian artists were a distinct and highly skilled group

5. The passage suggests that the author would be most likely to agree with which one of the following claims about the Aurignacians?

(A) They were technologically no more advanced than the Neanderthals they supplanted.

(B) They were the first humans known to have worn costumes for ceremonial purposes.

(C) They had established some highly specialized social roles.

(D) They occupied a less hostile environment than the Neanderthals did.

(E) They carved images of their intended prey on their weapons to increase the weapons' efficacy.

R

The passages discuss relationships between business interests and university research.

Passage A

As university researchers working in a "gift economy" dedicated to collegial sharing of ideas, we have long been insulated from market pressures. The
(5) recent tendency to treat research findings as commodities, tradable for cash, threatens this tradition and the role of research as a public good.

The nurseries for new ideas are traditionally universities, which provide an environment uniquely
(10) suited to the painstaking testing and revision of theories. Unfortunately, the market process and values governing commodity exchange are ill suited to the cultivation and management of new ideas. With their shareholders impatient for quick returns, businesses are averse to wide-ranging experimentation. And, what
(15) is even more important, few commercial enterprises contain the range of expertise needed to handle the replacement of shattered theoretical frameworks.

Further, since entrepreneurs usually have little affinity for adventure of the intellectual sort, they can
(20) buy research and bury its products, hiding knowledge useful to society or to their competitors. The growth of industrial biotechnology, for example, has been accompanied by a reduction in the free sharing of research methods and results-a high price to pay for
(25) the undoubted benefits of new drugs and therapies.

Important new experimental results once led university scientists to rush down the hall and share their excitement with colleagues. When instead the rush is to patent lawyers and venture capitalists, I
(30) worry about the long-term future of scientific discovery.

Passage B

The fruits of pure science were once considered primarily a public good, available for society as a whole. The argument for this view was that most of
(35) these benefits were produced through government support of universities, and thus no individual was entitled to restrict access to them.

Today, however, the critical role of science in the modern "information economy" means that what was
(40) previously seen as a public good is being transformed into a market commodity. For example, by exploiting the information that basic research has accumulated about the detailed structures of cells and genes, the biotechnology industry can derive profitable
(45) pharmaceuticals or medical screening technologies. In this context, assertion of legal claims to "intellectual property"-not just in commercial products but in the underlying scientific knowledge-becomes crucial.

Previously, the distinction between a scientific
(50) "discovery" (which could not be patented) and a technical "invention" (which could) defined the limits of industry's ability to patent something. Today,

however, the speed with which scientific discoveries can be turned into products and the large profits
(55) resulting from this transformation have led to a blurring of both the legal distinction between discovery and invention and the moral distinction between what should and should not be patented.

Industry argues that if it has supported-either in
(60) its own laboratories or in a university-the makers of a scientific discovery, then it is entitled to seek a return on its investment, either by charging others for using the discovery or by keeping it for its own exclusive use.

15. Which one of the following is discussed in passage B but not in passage A?

(A) the blurring of the legal distinction between discovery and invention

(B) the general effects of the market on the exchange of scientific knowledge

(C) the role of scientific research in supplying public goods

(D) new pharmaceuticals that result from industrial research

(E) industry's practice of restricting access to research findings

16. Both passages place in opposition the members of which one of the following pairs?

(A) commercially successful research and commercially unsuccessful research

(B) research methods and research results

(C) a marketable commodity and a public good

(D) a discovery and an invention

(E) scientific research and other types of inquiry

R

17. Both passages refer to which one of the following?

 (A) theoretical frameworks
 (B) venture capitalists
 (C) physics and chemistry
 (D) industrial biotechnology
 (E) shareholders

18. It can be inferred from the passages that the authors believe that the increased constraint on access to scientific information and ideas arises from

 (A) the enormous increase in the volume of scientific knowledge that is being generated
 (B) the desire of individual researchers to receive credit for their discoveries
 (C) the striving of commercial enterprises to gain a competitive advantage in the market
 (D) moral reservations about the social impact of some scientific research
 (E) a drastic reduction in government funding for university research

19. Which one of the following statements is most strongly supported by both passages?

 (A) Many scientific researchers who previously worked in universities have begun to work in the biotechnology industry.
 (B) Private biotechnology companies have invalidly patented the basic research findings of university researchers.
 (C) Because of the nature of current scientific research, patent authorities no longer consider the distinction between discoveries and inventions to be clear-cut.
 (D) In the past, scientists working in industry had free access to the results of basic research conducted in universities.
 (E) Government-funded research in universities has traditionally been motivated by the goals of private industry.

R

Sometimes there is no more effective means of controlling an agricultural pest than giving free rein to its natural predators. A case in point is the cyclamen mite, a pest whose population can be
(5) effectively controlled by a predatory mite of the genus *Typhlodromus*. Cyclamen mites infest strawberry plants; they typically establish themselves in a strawberry field shortly after planting, but their populations do not reach significantly damaging
(10) levels until the plants' second year. *Typhlodromus* mites usually invade the strawberry fields during the second year, rapidly subdue the cyclamen mite populations, and keep them from reaching significantly damaging levels.
(15) *Typhlodromus* owes its effectiveness as a predator to several factors in addition to its voracious appetite. Its population can increase as rapidly as that of its prey. Both species reproduce by parthenogenesis-a mode of reproduction in which unfertilized eggs
(20) develop into fertile females. Cyclamen mites lay three eggs per day over the four or five days of their reproductive life span; *Typhlodromus* lay two or three eggs per day for eight to ten days. Seasonal synchrony of *Typhlodromus* reproduction with the
(25) growth of prey populations and ability to survive at low prey densities also contribute to the predatory efficiency of *Typhlodromus*. During winter, when cyclamen mite populations dwindle to a few individuals hidden in the crevices and folds of leaves
(30) in the crowns of the strawberry plants, the predatory mites subsist on the honeydew produced by aphids and white flies. They do not reproduce except when they are feeding on the cyclamen mites. These features, which make *Typhlodromus* well-suited for
(35) exploiting the seasonal rises and falls of its prey, are common among predators that control prey populations.
        Greenhouse experiments have verified the importance of *Typhlodromus* predation for keeping
(40) cyclamen mites in check. One group of strawberry plants was stocked with both predator and prey mites; a second group was kept predator-free by regular application of parathion, an insecticide that kills the predatory species but does not affect the cyclamen
(45) mite. Throughout the study, populations of cyclamen mites remained low in plots shared with *Typhlodromus,* but their infestation attained significantly damaging proportions on predator-free plants.
(50) Applying parathion in this instance is a clear case in which using a pesticide would do far more harm than good to an agricultural enterprise. The results were similar in field plantings of strawberries, where cyclamen mites also reached damaging levels when
(55) predators were eliminated by parathion, but they did not attain such levels in untreated plots. When cyclamen mite populations began to increase in an untreated planting, the predator populations quickly responded to reduce the outbreak. On average,
(60) cyclamen mites were about 25 times more abundant in the absence of predators than in their presence.

20. Which one of the following most accurately expresses the main point of the passage?

(A) Control of agricultural pests is most effectively and safely accomplished without the use of pesticides, because these pesticides can kill predators that also control the pests.
(B) Experimental verification is essential in demonstrating the effectiveness of natural controls of agricultural pests.
(C) The relationship between *Typhlodromus* and cyclamen mites demonstrates how natural predation can keep a population of agricultural pests in check.
(D) Predation by *Typhlodromus* is essential for the control of cyclamen mite populations in strawberry fields.
(E) Similarity in mode and timing of reproduction is what enables *Typhlodromus* effectively to control populations of cyclamen mites in fields of strawberry plants.

21. Based on the passage, the author would probably hold that which one of the following principles is fundamental to long-term predatory control of agricultural pests?

(A) The reproduction of the predator population should be synchronized with that of the prey population, so that the number of predators surges just prior to a surge in prey numbers.
(B) The effectiveness of the predatory relationship should be experimentally demonstrable in greenhouse as well as field applications.
(C) The prey population should be able to survive in times of low crop productivity, so that the predator population will not decrease to very low levels.
(D) The predator population's level of consumption of the prey species should be responsive to variations in the size of the prey population.
(E) The predator population should be vulnerable only to pesticides to which the prey population is also vulnerable.

22. Which one of the following is mentioned in the passage as a factor contributing to the effectiveness of *Typhlodromus* as a predator?

(A) its ability to withstand most insecticides except parathion
(B) its lack of natural predators in strawberry fields
(C) its ability to live in different climates in different geographic regions
(D) its constant food supply in cyclamen mite populations
(E) its ability to survive when few prey are available

23. Suppose that pesticide X drastically slows the reproductive rate of cyclamen mites and has no other direct effect on cyclamen mites or *Typhlodromus*. Based on the information in the passage, which one of the following would most likely have occurred if, in the experiments mentioned in the passage, pesticide X had been used instead of parathion, with all other conditions affecting the experiments remaining the same?

(A) In both treated and untreated plots inhabited by both *Typhlodromus* and cyclamen mites, the latter would have been effectively controlled.

(B) Cyclamen mite populations in all treated plots from which *Typhlodromus* was absent would have been substantially lower than in untreated plots inhabited by both kinds of mites.

(C) In the treated plots, slowed reproduction in cyclamen mites would have led to a loss of reproductive synchrony between *Typhlodromus* and cyclamen mites.

(D) In the treated plots, *Typhlodromus* populations would have decreased temporarily and would have eventually increased.

(E) In the treated plots, cyclamen mite populations would have reached significantly damaging levels more slowly, but would have remained at those levels longer, than in untreated plots.

24. It can be inferred from the passage that the author would be most likely to agree with which one of the following statements about the use of predators to control pest populations?

(A) If the use of predators to control cyclamen mite populations fails, then parathion should be used to control these populations.

(B) Until the effects of the predators on beneficial insects that live in strawberry fields are assessed, such predators should be used with caution to control cyclamen mite populations.

(C) Insecticides should be used to control certain pest populations in fields of crops only if the use of natural predators has proven inadequate.

(D) If an insecticide can effectively control pest populations as well as predator populations, then it should be used instead of predators to control pest populations.

(E) Predators generally control pest populations more effectively than pesticides because they do not harm the crops that their prey feed on.

25. The author mentions the egg-laying ability of each kind of mite (lines 20-23) primarily in order to support which one of the following claims?

(A) Mites that reproduce by parthenogenesis do so at approximately equal rates.

(B) Predatory mites typically have a longer reproductive life span than do cyclamen mites.

(C) *Typhlodromus* can lay their eggs in synchrony with cyclamen mites.

(D) *Typhlodromus* can reproduce at least as quickly as cyclamen mites.

(E) The egg-laying rate of *Typhlodromus* is slower in the presence of cyclamen mites than it is in their absence.

26. Which one of the following would, if true, most strengthen the author's position regarding the practical applicability of the information about predatory mites presented in the passage?

(A) The individual *Typhlodromus* mites that have the longest reproductive life spans typically also lay the greatest number of eggs per day.

(B) The insecticides that are typically used for mite control on strawberry plants kill both predatory and nonpredatory species of mites.

(C) In areas in which strawberry plants become infested by cyclamen mites, winters tend to be short and relatively mild.

(D) *Typhlodromus* are sometimes preyed upon by another species of mites that is highly susceptible to parathion.

(E) *Typhlodromus* easily tolerate the same range of climatic conditions that strawberry plants do.

27. Information in the passage most strongly supports which one of the following statements?

(A) Strawberry crops can support populations of both cyclamen mites and *Typhlodromus* mites without significant damage to those crops.

(B) For control of cyclamen mites by another mite species to be effective, it is crucial that the two species have the same mode of reproduction.

(C) Factors that make *Typhlodromus* effective against cyclamen mites also make it effective against certain other pests of strawberry plants.

(D) When *Typhlodromus* is relied on to control cyclamen mites in strawberry crops, pesticides may be necessary to prevent significant damage during the first year.

(E) Strawberry growers have unintentionally caused cyclamen mites to become a serious crop pest by the indiscriminate use of parathion.

R

Reading Comprehension Passage ReChallenge Set #1 Answer Key

Passage #1: June 2006 Questions 1-6   *1. A 2. D 3. E 4. B 5. C 6. E*

Explanations begin on page 276

Passage #2: December 2005 Questions 1-5   *1. A 2. D 3. E 4. B 5. C*

Explanations begin on page 282

Passage #3: December 2007 Questions 15-19   *15. A 16. C 17. D 18. C 19. D*

Explanations begin on page 298

Passage #4: December 2007 Questions 20-27   *20. C 21. D 22. E 23. A 24. C 25. D 26. E 27. A*

Explanations begin on page 398

Reading Comprehension Passage ReChallenge
Set #2

Passage #1: September 2007 Questions 7-12

Passage A

Readers, like writers, need to search for answers. Part of the joy of reading is in being surprised, but academic historians leave little to the imagination. The perniciousness of the historiographic approach became
(5) fully evident to me when I started teaching. Historians require undergraduates to read scholarly monographs that sap the vitality of history; they visit on students what was visited on them in graduate school. They assign books with formulaic arguments that transform
(10) history into an abstract debate that would have been unfathomable to those who lived in the past. Aimed so squarely at the head, such books cannot stimulate students who yearn to connect to history emotionally as well as intellectually.
(15) In an effort to address this problem, some historians have begun to rediscover stories. It has even become something of a fad within the profession. This year, the American Historical Association chose as the theme for its annual conference some putative connection to
(20) storytelling: "Practices of Historical Narrative." Predictably, historians responded by adding the word "narrative" to their titles and presenting papers at sessions on "Oral History and the Narrative of Class Identity," and "Meaning and Time: The Problem of
(25) Historical Narrative." But it was still historiography, intended only for other academics. At meetings of historians, we still encounter very few historians telling stories or moving audiences to smiles, chills, or tears.

Passage B

Writing is at the heart of the lawyer's craft, and so,
(30) like it or not, we who teach the law inevitably teach aspiring lawyers how lawyers write. We do this in a few stand-alone courses and, to a greater extent, through the constraints that we impose on their writing throughout the curriculum. Legal writing, because of the purposes
(35) it serves, is necessarily ruled by linear logic, creating a path without diversions, surprises, or reversals. Conformity is a virtue, creativity suspect, humor forbidden, and voice mute.
Lawyers write as they see other lawyers write, and,
(40) influenced by education, profession, economic constraints, and perceived self-interest, they too often write badly. Perhaps the currently fashionable call for attention to narrative in legal education could have an effect on this. It is not yet exactly clear what role
(45) narrative should play in the law, but it is nonetheless true that every case has at its heart a story—of real events and people, of concerns, misfortunes, conflicts, feelings. But because legal analysis strips the human narrative content from the abstract, canonical legal
(50) form of the case, law students learn to act as if there is no such story.
It may well turn out that some of the terminology and public rhetoric of this potentially subversive movement toward attention to narrative will find its
(55) way into the law curriculum, but without producing corresponding changes in how legal writing is actually taught or in how our future colleagues will write. Still, even mere awareness of the value of narrative could perhaps serve as an important corrective.

7. Which one of the following does each of the passages display?

    (A) a concern with the question of what teaching methods are most effective in developing writing skills
    (B) a concern with how a particular discipline tends to represent points of view it does not typically deal with
    (C) a conviction that writing in specialized professional disciplines cannot be creatively crafted
    (D) a belief that the writing in a particular profession could benefit from more attention to storytelling
    (E) a desire to see writing in a particular field purged of elements from other disciplines

8. The passages most strongly support which one of the following inferences regarding the authors' relationships to the professions they discuss?

    (A) Neither author is an active member of the profession that he or she discusses.
    (B) Each author is an active member of the profession he or she discusses.
    (C) The author of passage A is a member of the profession discussed in that passage, but the author of passage B is not a member of either of the professions discussed in the passages.
    (D) Both authors are active members of the profession discussed in passage B.
    (E) The author of passage B, but not the author of passage A, is an active member of both of the professions discussed in the passages.

9. Which one of the following does each passage
indicate is typical of writing in the respective
professions discussed in the passages?

   (A)   abstraction
   (B)   hyperbole
   (C)   subversion
   (D)   narrative
   (E)   imagination

10. In which one of the following ways are the
passages NOT parallel?

   (A)   Passage A presents and rejects arguments
         for an opposing position, whereas passage
         B does not.
   (B)   Passage A makes evaluative claims, whereas
         passage B does not.
   (C)   Passage A describes specific examples of a
         phenomenon it criticizes, whereas passage
         B does not.
   (D)   Passage B offers criticism, whereas passage
         A does not.
   (E)   Passage B outlines a theory, whereas
         passage A does not.

11. The phrase "scholarly monographs that sap the
vitality of history" in passage A (lines 6-7) plays a
role in that passage's overall argument that is most
analogous to the role played in passage B by which
one of the following phrases?

   (A)   "Writing is at the heart of the lawyer's craft"
         (line 29)
   (B)   "Conformity is a virtue, creativity suspect,
         humor forbidden, and voice mute" (lines
         37-38)
   (C)   "Lawyers write as they see other lawyers
         write" (line 39)
   (D)   "every case has at its heart a story" (line 46)
   (E)   "Still, even mere awareness of the value
         of narrative could perhaps serve as an
         important corrective" (lines 57-59)

12. Suppose that a lawyer is writing a legal document
describing the facts that are at issue in a case.
The author of passage B would be most likely to
expect which one of the following to be true of the
document?

   (A)   It will be poorly written because the lawyer
         who is writing it was not given explicit
         advice by law professors on how lawyers
         should write.
   (B)   It will be crafted to function like a piece of
         fiction in its description of the characters
         and motivations of the people involved in
         the case.
   (C)   It will be a concise, well-crafted piece of
         writing that summarizes most, if not all, of
         the facts that are important in the case.
   (D)   It will not genuinely convey the human
         dimension of the case, regardless of how
         accurate the document may be in its details.
   (E)   It will neglect to make appropriate
         connections between the details of the case
         and relevant legal doctrines.

R

Asian American poetry from Hawaii, the Pacific island state of the United States, is generally characterizable in one of two ways: either as portraying a model multicultural paradise, or as
(5) exemplifying familiar Asian American literary themes such as generational conflict. In this light, the recent work of Wing Tek Lum in *Expounding the Doubtful Points* is striking for its demand to be understood on its own terms. Lum offers no romanticized notions of
(10) multicultural life in Hawaii, and while he does explore themes of family, identity, history, and literary tradition, he does not do so at the expense of attempting to discover and retain a local sensibility. For Lum such a sensibility is informed by the fact
(15) that Hawaii's population, unlike that of the continental U.S., has historically consisted predominantly of people of Asian and Pacific island descent, making the experience of its Asian Americans somewhat different than that of mainland
(20) Asian Americans.

In one poem, Lum meditates on the ways in which a traditional Chinese lunar celebration he is attending at a local beach both connects him to and separates him from the past. In the company of new
(25) Chinese immigrants, the speaker realizes that while ties to the homeland are comforting and necessary, it is equally important to have "a sense of new family" in this new land of Hawaii, and hence a new identity-one that is sensitive to its new environment.

(30) The role of immigrants in this poem is significant in that, through their presence, Lum is able to refer both to the traditional culture of his ancestral homeland as well as to the flux within Hawaiian society that has been integral to its heterogeneity. Even in a laudatory
(35) poem to famous Chinese poet Li Po (701-762 A.D.), which partly serves to place Lum's work within a distinguished literary tradition, Lum refuses to offer a stereotypical nostalgia for the past, instead pointing out the often elitist tendencies inherent in the work of
(40) some traditionally acclaimed Chinese poets.

Lum closes his volume with a poem that further points to the complex relationships between heritage and local culture in determining one's identity. Pulling together images and figures as vastly
(45) disparate as a famous Chinese American literary character and an old woman selling bread, Lum avoids an excessively romantic vision of U.S. culture, while simultaneously acknowledging the dream of this culture held by many newly arrived immigrants.
(50) The central image of a communal pot where each person chooses what she or he wishes to eat but shares with others the "sweet soup / spooned out at the end of the meal" is a hopeful one; however, it also appears to caution that the strong cultural
(55) emphasis in the U.S. on individual drive and success that makes retaining a sense of homeland tradition difficult should be identified and responded to in

ways that allow for a healthy new sense of identity to be formed.

1. Which one of the following most accurately expresses the main point of the passage?

    (A) The poetry of Lum departs from other Asian American poetry from Hawaii in that it acknowledges its author's heritage but also expresses the poet's search for a new local identity.

    (B) Lum's poetry is in part an expression of the conflict between a desire to participate in a community with shared traditions and values and a desire for individual success.

    (C) Lum writes poetry that not only rejects features of the older literary tradition in which he participates but also rejects the popular literary traditions of Hawaiian writers.

    (D) The poetry of Lum illustrates the extent to which Asian American writers living in Hawaii have a different cultural perspective than those living in the continental U.S.

    (E) Lum's poetry is an unsuccessful attempt to manage the psychological burdens of reconciling a sense of tradition with a healthy sense of individual identity.

2. Given the information in the passage, which one of the following is Lum most likely to believe?

    (A) Images in a poem should be explained in that poem so that their meaning will be widely understood.

    (B) The experience of living away from one's homeland is necessary for developing a healthy perspective on one's cultural traditions.

    (C) It is important to reconcile the values of individual achievement and enterprise with the desire to retain one's cultural traditions.

    (D) One's identity is continually in transition and poetry is a way of developing a static identity.

    (E) One cannot both seek a new identity and remain connected to one's cultural traditions.

R

3. The author of the passage uses the phrase "the flux within Hawaiian society" (line 33) primarily in order to

(A) describe the social tension created by the mix of attitudes exhibited by citizens of Hawaii
(B) deny that Hawaiian society is culturally distinct from that of the continental U.S.
(C) identify the process by which immigrants learn to adapt to their new communities
(D) refer to the constant change to which the culture in Hawaii is subject due to its diverse population
(E) emphasize the changing attitudes of many immigrants to Hawaii toward their traditional cultural norms

4. According to the passage, some Asian American literature from Hawaii has been characterized as which one of the following?

(A) inimical to the process of developing a local sensibility
(B) centered on the individual's drive to succeed
(C) concerned with conflicts between different age groups
(D) focused primarily on retaining ties to one's homeland
(E) tied to a search for a new sense of family in a new land

5. The author of the passage describes *Expounding the Doubtful Points* as "striking" (lines 7-8) primarily in order to

(A) underscore the forceful and contentious tone of the work
(B) indicate that the work has not been properly analyzed by literary critics
(C) stress the radical difference between this work and Lum's earlier work
(D) emphasize the differences between this work and that of other Asian American poets from Hawaii
(E) highlight the innovative nature of Lum's experiments with poetic form

6. With which one of the following statements regarding Lum's poetry would the author of the passage be most likely to agree?

(A) It cannot be used to support any specific political ideology.
(B) It is an elegant demonstration of the poet's appreciation of the stylistic contributions of his literary forebears.
(C) It is most fruitfully understood as a meditation on the choice between new and old that confronts any human being in any culture.
(D) It conveys thoughtful assessments of both his ancestral homeland tradition and the culture in which he is attempting to build a new identity.
(E) It conveys Lum's antipathy toward tradition by juxtaposing traditional and nontraditional images.

R

The pronghorn, an antelope-like mammal that lives on the western plains of North America, is the continent's fastest land animal, capable of running 90 kilometers per hour and of doing so for several
(5) kilometers. Because no North American predator is nearly fast enough to chase it down, biologists have had difficulty explaining why the pronghorn developed its running prowess. One biologist, however, has recently claimed that pronghorns run as
(10) fast as they do because of adaptation to predators known from fossil records to have been extinct for 10,000 years, such as American cheetahs and long-legged hyenas, either of which, it is believed, were fast enough to run down the pronghorn.
(15) Like all explanations that posit what is called a relict behavior—a behavior that persists though its only evolutionary impetus comes from long-extinct environmental conditions—this one is likely to meet with skepticism. Most biologists distrust explanations positing relict
(20) behaviors, in part because testing these hypotheses is so difficult due to the extinction of a principal component. They typically consider such historical explanations only when a lack of alternatives forces them to do so. But present-day observations sometimes yield
(25) evidence that supports relict behavior hypotheses.
In the case of the pronghorn, researchers have identified much supporting evidence, as several aspects of pronghorn behavior appear to have been shaped by enemies that no longer exist. For example,
(30) pronghorns—like many other grazing animals—roam in herds, which allows more eyes to watch for predators and diminishes the chances of any particular animal being attacked but can also result in overcrowding and increased competition for food. But, since
(35) pronghorns have nothing to fear from present-day carnivores and thus have nothing to gain from herding, their herding behavior appears to be another adaptation to extinct threats. Similarly, if speed and endurance were once essential to survival, researchers would
(40) expect pronghorns to choose mates based on these athletic abilities, which they do—with female pronghorns, for example, choosing the victor after male pronghorns challenge each other in sprints and chases.
Relict behaviors appear to occur in other animals
(45) as well, increasing the general plausibility of such a theory. For example, one study reports relict behavior in stickleback fish belonging to populations that have long been free of a dangerous predator, the sculpin. In the study, when presented with sculpin, these
(50) stickleback fish immediately engaged in stereotypical antisculpin behavior, avoiding its mouth and swimming behind to bite it. Another study found that ground squirrels from populations that have been free from snakes for 70,000 to 300,000 years still clearly recognize
(55) rattlesnakes, displaying stereotypical antirattlesnake behavior in the presence of the snake. Such fear, however, apparently does not persist interminably. Arctic ground squirrels, free of snakes for about 3 million years, appear to be unable to recognize the
(60) threat of a rattlesnake, exhibiting only disorganized caution even after being bitten repeatedly.

16. Which one of the following most accurately states the main point of the passage?

(A) Evidence from present-day animal behaviors, together with the fossil record, supports the hypothesis that the pronghorn's ability to far outrun any predator currently on the North American continent is an adaptation to predators long extinct.

(B) Although some biologists believe that certain animal characteristics, such as the speed of the pronghorn, are explained by environmental conditions that have not existed for many years, recent data concerning arctic ground squirrels make this hypothesis doubtful.

(C) Research into animal behavior, particularly into that of the pronghorn, provides strong evidence that most present-day characteristics of animals are explained by environmental conditions that have not existed for many years.

(D) Even in those cases in which an animal species displays characteristics clearly explained by long-vanished environmental conditions, evidence concerning arctic ground squirrels suggests that those characteristics will eventually disappear.

(E) Although biologists are suspicious of hypotheses that are difficult to test, there is now widespread agreement among biologists that many types of animal characteristics are best explained as adaptations to long-extinct predators.

17. Based on the passage, the term "principal component" (line 21) most clearly refers to which one of the following?

(A) behavior that persists even though the conditions that provided its evolutionary impetus are extinct

(B) the original organism whose descendants' behavior is being investigated as relict behavior

(C) the pronghorn's ability to run 90 kilometers per hour over long distances

(D) the environmental conditions in response to which relict behaviors are thought to have developed

(E) an original behavior of an animal of which certain present-day behaviors are thought to be modifications

18. The last paragraph most strongly supports which one of the following statements?

   (A) An absence of predators in an animal's environment can constitute just as much of a threat to the well-being of that animal as the presence of predators.
   (B) Relict behaviors are found in most wild animals living today.
   (C) If a behavior is an adaptation to environmental conditions, it may eventually disappear in the absence of those or similar conditions.
   (D) Behavior patterns that originated as a way of protecting an organism against predators will persist interminably if they are periodically reinforced.
   (E) Behavior patterns invariably take longer to develop than they do to disappear.

19. Which one of the following describes a benefit mentioned in the passage that grazing animals derive from roaming in herds?

   (A) The greater density of animals tends to intimidate potential predators.
   (B) The larger number of adults in a herd makes protection of the younger animals from predators much easier.
   (C) With many animals searching it is easier for the herd to find food and water.
   (D) The likelihood that any given individual will be attacked by a predator decreases.
   (E) The most defenseless animals can achieve greater safety by remaining in the center of the herd.

20. The passage mentions each of the following as support for the explanation of the pronghorn's speed proposed by the biologist referred to in line 8 EXCEPT:

   (A) fossils of extinct animals believed to have been able to run down a pronghorn
   (B) the absence of carnivores in the pronghorn's present-day environment
   (C) the present-day preference of pronghorns for athletic mates
   (D) the apparent need for a similar explanation to account for the herding behavior pronghorns now display
   (E) the occurrence of relict behavior in other species

21. The third paragraph of the passage provides the most support for which one of the following inferences?

   (A) Predators do not attack grazing animals that are assembled into herds.
   (B) Pronghorns tend to graze in herds only when they sense a threat from predators close by.
   (C) If animals do not graze for their food, they do not roam in herds.
   (D) Female pronghorns mate only with the fastest male pronghorn in the herd.
   (E) If pronghorns did not herd, they would not face significantly greater danger from present-day carnivores.

R

Passage #4: September 2006 Questions 6-13

In many Western societies, modern bankruptcy laws have undergone a shift away from a focus on punishment and toward a focus on bankruptcy as a remedy for individuals and corporations in financial
(5) trouble—and, perhaps unexpectedly, for their creditors. This shift has coincided with an ever-increasing reliance on declarations of bankruptcy by individuals and corporations with excessive debt, a trend that has drawn widespread criticism. However,
(10) any measure seeking to make bankruptcy protection less available would run the risk of preventing continued economic activity of financially troubled individuals and institutions. It is for this reason that the temptation to return to a focus on punishment of
(15) individuals or corporations that become insolvent must be resisted. Modern bankruptcy laws, in serving the needs of an interdependent society, serve the varied interests of the greatest number of citizens.
    The harsh punishment for insolvency in centuries
(20) past included imprisonment of individuals and dissolution of enterprises, and reflected societies' beliefs that the accumulation of excessive debt resulted either from debtors' unwillingness to meet obligations or from their negligence. Insolvent debtors
(25) were thought to be breaking sacrosanct social contracts; placing debtors in prison was considered necessary in order to remove from society those who would violate such contracts and thereby defraud creditors. But creditors derive little benefit from
(30) imprisoned debtors unable to repay even a portion of their debt. And if the entity to be punished is a large enterprise, for example, an auto manufacturer, its dissolution would cause significant unemployment and the disruption of much-needed services.
(35)   Modern bankruptcy law has attempted to address the shortcomings of the punitive approach. Two beliefs underlie this shift: that the public good ought to be paramount in considering the financial insolvency of individuals and corporations; and that
(40) the public good is better served by allowing debt-heavy corporations to continue to operate, and indebted individuals to continue to earn wages, than by disabling insolvent economic entities. The mechanism for executing these goals is usually a
(45) court-directed reorganization of debtors' obligations to creditors. Such reorganizations typically comprise debt relief and plans for court-directed transfers of certain assets from debtor to creditor. Certain strictures connected to bankruptcy—such as the fact
(50) that bankruptcies become matters of public record and are reported to credit bureaus for a number of years—may still serve a punitive function, but not by denying absolution of debts or financial reorganization. Through these mechanisms, today's
(55) bankruptcy laws are designed primarily to assure continued engagement in productive economic activity, with the ultimate goal of restoring businesses and individuals to a degree of economic health and providing creditors with the best hope of collecting.

6. Which one of the following most accurately expresses the main point of the passage?

(A)   The modern trend in bankruptcy law away from punishment and toward the maintenance of economic activity serves the best interests of society and should not be abandoned.
(B)   Bankruptcy laws have evolved in order to meet the needs of creditors, who depend on the continued productive activity of private citizens and profit-making enterprises.
(C)   Modern bankruptcy laws are justified on humanitarian grounds, even though the earlier punitive approach was more economically efficient.
(D)   Punishment for debt no longer holds deterrent value for debtors and is therefore a concept that has been largely abandoned as ineffective.
(E)   Greater economic interdependence has triggered the formation of bankruptcy laws that reflect a convergence of the interests of debtors and creditors.

7. In stating that bankruptcy laws have evolved "perhaps unexpectedly" (line 5) as a remedy for creditors, the author implies that creditors

(A)   are often surprised to receive compensation in bankruptcy courts
(B)   have unintentionally become the chief beneficiaries of bankruptcy laws
(C)   were a consideration, though not a primary one, in the formulation of bankruptcy laws
(D)   are better served than is immediately apparent by laws designed in the first instance to provide a remedy for debtors
(E)   were themselves active in the formulation of modern bankruptcy laws

8. The author's attitude toward the evolution of bankruptcy law can most accurately be described as

(A)   approval of changes that have been made to inefficient laws
(B)   confidence that further changes to today's laws will be unnecessary
(C)   neutrality toward laws that, while helpful to many, remain open to abuse
(D)   skepticism regarding the possibility of solutions to the problem of insolvency
(E)   concern that inefficient laws may have been replaced by legislation too lenient to debtors

R

9. The primary purpose of the passage is to

   (A) offer a critique of both past and present approaches to insolvency
   (B) compare the practices of bankruptcy courts of the past with those of bankruptcy courts of the present
   (C) criticize those who would change the bankruptcy laws of today
   (D) reexamine today's bankruptcy laws in an effort to point to further improvements
   (E) explain and defend contemporary bankruptcy laws

10. Which one of the following claims would a defender of the punitive theory of bankruptcy legislation be most likely to have made?

   (A) Debt that has become so great that repayment is impossible is ultimately a moral failing and thus a matter for which the law should provide punitive sanctions.
   (B) Because insolvency ultimately harms the entire economy, the law should provide a punitive deterrent to insolvency.
   (C) The insolvency of companies or individuals is tolerable if the debt is the result of risk-taking, profit-seeking ventures that might create considerable economic growth in the long run.
   (D) The dissolution of a large enterprise is costly to the economy as a whole and should not be allowed, even when that enterprise's insolvency is the result of its own fiscal irresponsibility.
   (E) The employees of a large bankrupt enterprise should be considered just as negligent as the owner of a bankrupt sole proprietorship.

11. Which one of the following sentences could most logically be appended to the end of the last paragraph of the passage?

   (A) Only when today's bankruptcy laws are ultimately seen as inadequate on a large scale will bankruptcy legislation return to its original intent.
   (B) Punishment is no longer the primary goal of bankruptcy law, even if some of its side effects still function punitively.
   (C) Since leniency serves the public interest in bankruptcy law, it is likely to do so in criminal law as well.
   (D) Future bankruptcy legislation could include punitive measures, but only if such measures ultimately benefit creditors.
   (E) Today's bankruptcy laws place the burden of insolvency squarely on the shoulders of creditors, in marked contrast to the antiquated laws that weighed heavily on debtors.

12. The information in the passage most strongly suggests which one of the following about changes in bankruptcy laws?

   (A) Bankruptcy laws always result from gradual changes in philosophy followed by sudden shifts in policy.
   (B) Changes in bankruptcy law were initiated by the courts and only grudgingly adopted by legislators.
   (C) The adjustment of bankruptcy laws away from a punitive focus was at first bitterly opposed by creditors.
   (D) Bankruptcy laws underwent change because the traditional approach proved inadequate and contrary to the needs of society.
   (E) The shift away from a punitive approach to insolvency was part of a more general trend in society toward rehabilitation and away from retribution.

13. Which one of the following, if true, would most weaken the author's argument against harsh punishment for debtors?

   (A) Extensive study of the economic and legal history of many countries has shown that most individuals who served prison time for bankruptcy subsequently exhibited greater economic responsibility.
   (B) The bankruptcy of a certain large company has had a significant negative impact on the local economy even though virtually all of the affected employees were able to obtain similar jobs within the community.
   (C) Once imprisonment was no longer a consequence of insolvency, bankruptcy filings increased dramatically, then leveled off before increasing again during the 1930s.
   (D) The court-ordered liquidation of a large and insolvent company's assets threw hundreds of people out of work, but the local economy nevertheless demonstrated robust growth in the immediate aftermath.
   (E) Countries that continue to imprison debtors enjoy greater economic health than do comparable countries that have ceased to do so.

Reading Comprehension Passage ReChallenge
Set #2 Answer Key

Passage #1: September 2007 Questions 7-12   *7. D 8. B 9. A 10. C 11. B 12. D*

Explanations begin on page 317

Passage #2: December 2007 Questions 1-6   *1. A 2. C 3. D 4. C 5. D 6. D*

Explanations begin on page 352

Passage #3: June 2005 Questions 16-21   *16. A 17. D 18. C 19. D 20. B 21. E*

Explanations begin on page 410

Passage #4: September 2006 Questions 6-13   *6. A 7. D 8. A 9. E 10. A 11. B 12. D 13. E*

Explanations begin on page 378

R

Reading Comprehension
Passage ReChallenge
Set #3

R

In the field of historiography—the writing of history based on a critical examination of authentic primary information sources—one area that has recently attracted attention focuses on the responses
(5) of explorers and settlers to new landscapes in order to provide insights into the transformations the landscape itself has undergone as a result of settlement. In this endeavor historiographers examining the history of the Pacific Coast of the
(10) United States have traditionally depended on the records left by European American explorers of the nineteenth century who, as commissioned agents of the U.S. government, were instructed to report thoroughly their findings in writing.

(15) But in furthering this investigation some historiographers have recently recognized the need to expand their definition of what a source is. They maintain that the sources traditionally accepted as documenting the history of the Pacific Coast have too
(20) often omitted the response of Asian settlers to this territory. In part this is due to the dearth of written records left by Asian settlers; in contrast to the commissioned agents, most of the people who first came to western North America from Asia during this
(25) same period did not focus on developing a self-conscious written record of their involvement with the landscape. But because a full study of a culture's historical relationship to its land cannot confine itself to a narrow record of experience, these
(30) historiographers have begun to recognize the value of other kinds of evidence, such as the actions of Asian settlers.

As a case in point, the role of Chinese settlers in expanding agriculture throughout the Pacific Coast
(35) territory is integral to the history of the region. Without access to the better land, Chinese settlers looked for agricultural potential in this generally arid region where other settlers did not. For example, where settlers of European descent looked at willows
(40) and saw only useless, untillable swamp, Chinese settlers saw fresh water, fertile soil, and the potential for bringing water to more arid areas via irrigation. Where other settlers who looked at certain weeds, such as wild mustard, generally saw a nuisance,
(45) Chinese settlers saw abundant raw material for valuable spices from a plant naturally suited to the local soil and climate.

Given their role in the labor force shaping this territory in the nineteenth century, the Chinese settlers
(50) offered more than just a new view of the land. Their vision was reinforced by specialized skills involving swamp reclamation and irrigation systems, which helped lay the foundation for the now well-known and prosperous agribusiness of the region. That
(55) 80 percent of the area's cropland is now irrigated and that the region is currently the top producer of many

specialty crops cannot be fully understood by historiographers without attention to the input of Chinese settlers as reconstructed from their
(60) interactions with that landscape.

8. Which one of the following most accurately states the main point of the passage?

(A) The history of settlement along the Pacific Coast of the U.S., as understood by most historiographers, is confirmed by evidence reconstructed from the actions of Asian settlers.

(B) Asian settlers on the Pacific Coast of the U.S. left a record of their experiences that traditional historiographers believed to be irrelevant.

(C) To understand Asian settlers' impact on the history of the Pacific Coast of the U.S., historiographers have had to recognize the value of nontraditional kinds of historiographic evidence.

(D) Spurred by new findings regarding Asian settlement on the Pacific Coast of the U.S. historiographers have begun to debate the methodological foundations of historiography.

(E) By examining only written information, historiography as it is traditionally practiced has produced inaccurate historical accounts.

9. Which one of the following most accurately describes the author's primary purpose in discussing Chinese settlers in the third paragraph?

(A) to suggest that Chinese settlers followed typical settlement patterns in this region during the nineteenth century

(B) to argue that little written evidence of Chinese settlers' practices survives

(C) to provide examples illustrating the unique view Asian settlers had of the land

(D) to demonstrate that the history of settlement in the region has become a point of contention among historiographers

(E) to claim that the historical record provided by the actions of Asian settlers is inconsistent with history as derived from traditional sources

10. The passage states that the primary traditional historiographic sources of information about the history of the Pacific Coast of the U.S. have which one of the following characteristics?

(A) They were written both before and after Asian settlers arrived in the area.

(B) They include accounts by Native Americans in the area.

(C) They are primarily concerned with potential agricultural uses of the land.

(D) They focus primarily on the presence of water sources in the region.

(E) They are accounts left by European American explorers.

R

11. The author would most likely disagree with which one of the following statements?

(A) Examining the actions not only of Asian settlers but of other cultural groups of the Pacific Coast of the U.S. is necessary to a full understanding of the impact of settlement on the landscape there.

(B) The significance of certain actions to the writing of history may be recognized by one group of historiographers but not another.

(C) Recognizing the actions of Asian settlers adds to but does not complete the writing of the history of the Pacific Coast of the U.S.

(D) By recognizing as evidence the actions of people, historiographers expand the definition of what a source is.

(E) The expanded definition of a source will probably not be relevant to studies of regions that have no significant immigration of non-Europeans.

12. According to the passage, each of the following was an aspect of Chinese settlers' initial interactions with the landscape of the Pacific Coast of the U.S. EXCEPT:

(A) new ideas for utilizing local plants
(B) a new view of the land
(C) specialized agricultural skills
(D) knowledge of agribusiness practices
(E) knowledge of irrigation systems

13. Which one of the following can most reasonably be inferred from the passage?

(A) Most Chinese settlers came to the Pacific Coast of the U.S. because the climate was similar to that with which they were familiar.

(B) Chinese agricultural methods in the nineteenth century included knowledge of swamp reclamation.

(C) Settlers of European descent used wild mustard seed as a spice.

(D) Because of the abundance of written sources available, it is not worthwhile to examine the actions of European settlers.

(E) What written records were left by Asian settlers were neglected and consequently lost to scholarly research.

14. Which one of the following, if true, would most help to strengthen the author's main claim in the last sentence of the passage?

(A) Market research of agribusinesses owned by descendants of Chinese settlers shows that the market for the region's specialty crops has grown substantially faster than the market for any other crops in the last decade.

(B) Nineteenth-century surveying records indicate that the lands now cultivated by specialty crop businesses owned by descendants of Chinese settlers were formerly swamp lands.

(C) Research by university agricultural science departments proves that the formerly arid lands now cultivated by large agribusinesses contain extremely fertile soil when they are sufficiently irrigated.

(D) A technological history tracing the development of irrigation systems in the region reveals that their efficiency has increased steadily since the nineteenth century.

(E) Weather records compiled over the previous century demonstrate that the weather patterns in the region are well-suited to growing certain specialty crops as long as they are irrigated.

R

The following passages concern a plant called purple loosestrife. Passage A is excerpted from a report issued by a prairie research council; passage B from a journal of sociology.

Passage A

Purple loosestrife *(Lythrum salicaria),* an aggressive and invasive perennial of Eurasian origin, arrived with settlers in eastern North America in the early 1800s and has spread across the continent's
(5)   midlatitude wetlands. The impact of purple loosestrife on native vegetation has been disastrous, with more than 50 percent of the biomass of some wetland communities displaced. Monospecific blocks of this weed have maintained themselves for at least 20 years.
(10)   Impacts on wildlife have not been well studied, but serious reductions in waterfowl and aquatic furbearer productivity have been observed. In addition, several endangered species of vertebrates are threatened with further degradation of their
(15)   breeding habitats. Although purple loosestrife can invade relatively undisturbed habitats, the spread and dominance of this weed have been greatly accelerated in disturbed habitats. While digging out the plants can temporarily halt their spread, there has been little
(20)   research on long-term purple loosestrife control. Glyphosate has been used successfully, but no measure of the impact of this herbicide on native plant communities has been made.

With the spread of purple loosestrife growing
(25)   exponentially, some form of integrated control is needed. At present, coping with purple loosestrife hinges on early detection of the weed's arrival in areas, which allows local eradication to be carried out with minimum damage to the native plant community.

Passage B

(30)   The war on purple loosestrife is apparently conducted on behalf of nature, an attempt to liberate the biotic community from the tyrannical influence of a life-destroying invasive weed. Indeed, purple loosestrife control is portrayed by its practitioners as
(35)   an environmental initiative intended to save nature rather than control it. Accordingly, the purple loosestrife literature, scientific and otherwise, dutifully discusses the impacts of the weed on endangered species—and on threatened biodiversity
(40)   more generally. Purple loosestrife is a pollution, according to the scientific community, and all of nature suffers under its pervasive influence.

Regardless of the perceived and actual ecological effects of the purple invader, it is apparent that
(45)   popular pollution ideologies have been extended into the wetlands of North America. Consequently, the scientific effort to liberate nature from purple loosestrife has failed to decouple itself from its philosophical origin as an instrument to control nature
(50)   to the satisfaction of human desires. Birds,

particularly game birds and waterfowl, provide the bulk of the justification for loosestrife management. However, no bird species other than the canvasback has been identified in the literature as endangered by
(55)   purple loosestrife. The impact of purple loosestrife on furbearing mammals is discussed at great length, though none of the species highlighted (muskrat, mink) can be considered threatened in North America. What is threatened by purple loosestrife is the
(60)   economics of exploiting such preferred species and the millions of dollars that will be lost to the economies of the United States and Canada from reduced hunting, trapping, and recreation revenues due to a decline in the production of the wetland
(65)   resource.

7. Both passages explicitly mention which one of the following?

    (A) furbearing animals
    (B) glyphosate
    (C) the threat purple loosestrife poses to economies
    (D) popular pollution ideologies
    (E) literature on purple loosestrife control

8. Each of the passages contains information sufficient to answer which one of the following questions?

    (A) Approximately how long ago did purple loosestrife arrive in North America?
    (B) Is there much literature discussing the potential benefit that hunters might derive from purple loosestrife management?
    (C) What is an issue regarding purple loosestrife management on which both hunters and farmers agree?
    (D) Is the canvasback threatened with extinction due to the spread of purple loosestrife?
    (E) What is a type of terrain that is affected in at least some parts of North America by the presence of purple loosestrife?

9. It can be inferred that the authors would be most likely to disagree about which one of the following?

    (A) Purple loosestrife spreads more quickly in disturbed habitats than in undisturbed habitats.
    (B) The threat posed by purple loosestrife to local aquatic furbearer populations is serious.
    (C) Most people who advocate that eradication measures be taken to control purple loosestrife are not genuine in their concern for the environment.
    (D) The size of the biomass that has been displaced by purple loosestrife is larger than is generally thought.
    (E) Measures should be taken to prevent other non-native plant species from invading North America.

R

10. Which one of the following most accurately describes the attitude expressed by the author of passage B toward the overall argument represented by passage A?

(A) enthusiastic agreement
(B) cautious agreement
(C) pure neutrality
(D) general ambivalence
(E) pointed skepticism

11. It can be inferred that both authors would be most likely to agree with which one of the following statements regarding purple loosestrife?

(A) As it increases in North America, some wildlife populations tend to decrease.
(B) Its establishment in North America has had a disastrous effect on native North American wetland vegetation in certain regions.
(C) It is very difficult to control effectively with herbicides.
(D) Its introduction into North America was a great ecological blunder.
(E) When it is eliminated from a given area, it tends to return to that area fairly quickly.

12. Which one of the following is true about the relationship between the two passages?

(A) Passage A presents evidence that directly counters claims made in passage B.
(B) Passage B assumes what passage A explicitly argues for.
(C) Passage B displays an awareness of the arguments touched on in passage A, but not vice versa.
(D) Passage B advocates a policy that passage A rejects.
(E) Passage A downplays the seriousness of claims made in passage B.

13. Which one of the following, if true, would cast doubt on the argument in passage B but bolster the argument in passage A?

(A) Localized population reduction is often a precursor to widespread endangerment of a species.
(B) Purple loosestrife was barely noticed in North America before the advent of suburban sprawl in the 1950s.
(C) The amount by which overall hunting, trapping, and recreation revenues would be reduced as a result of the extinction of one or more species threatened by purple loosestrife represents a significant portion of those revenues.
(D) Some environmentalists who advocate taking measures to eradicate purple loosestrife view such measures as a means of controlling nature.
(E) Purple loosestrife has never become a problem in its native habitat, even though no effort has been made to eradicate it there.

R

Computers have long been utilized in the sphere of law in the form of word processors, spreadsheets, legal research systems, and practice management systems. Most exciting, however, has been the
(5) prospect of using artificial intelligence techniques to create so-called legal reasoning systems—computer programs that can help to resolve legal disputes by reasoning from and applying the law. But the practical benefits of such automated reasoning
(10) systems have fallen short of optimistic early predictions and have not resulted in computer systems that can independently provide expert advice about substantive law. This is not surprising in light of the difficulty in resolving problems involving the
(15) meaning and applicability of rules set out in a legal text.

Early attempts at automated legal reasoning focused on the doctrinal nature of law. They viewed law as a set of rules, and the resulting computer
(20) systems were engineered to make legal decisions by determining the consequences that followed when its stored set of legal rules was applied to a collection of evidentiary data. Such systems underestimated the problems of interpretation that can arise at every
(25) stage of a legal argument. Examples abound of situations that are open to differing interpretations: whether a mobile home in a trailer park is a house or a motor vehicle, whether a couple can be regarded as married in the absence of a formal legal ceremony,
(30) and so on. Indeed, many notions invoked in the text of a statute may be deliberately left undefined so as to allow the law to be adapted to unforeseen circumstances. But in order to be able to apply legal rules to novel situations, systems have to be equipped
(35) with a kind of comprehensive knowledge of the world that is far beyond their capabilities at present or in the foreseeable future.

Proponents of legal reasoning systems now argue that accommodating reference to, and reasoning from,
(40) cases improves the chances of producing a successful system. By focusing on the practice of reasoning from precedents, researchers have designed systems called case-based reasoners, which store individual example cases in their knowledge bases. In contrast
(45) to a system that models legal knowledge based on a set of rules, a case-based reasoner, when given a concrete problem, manipulates the cases in its knowledge base to reach a conclusion based on a similar case. Unfortunately, in the case-based systems
(50) currently in development, the criteria for similarity among cases are system dependent and fixed by the designer, so that similarity is found only by testing for the presence or absence of predefined factors. This simply postpones the apparently intractable
(55) problem of developing a system that can discover for itself the factors that make cases similar in relevant ways.

21. Which one of the following most accurately expresses the main point of the passage?

(A)   Attempts to model legal reasoning through computer programs have not been successful because of problems of interpreting legal discourse and identifying appropriate precedents.

(B)   Despite signs of early promise, it is now apparent that computer programs have little value for legal professionals in their work.

(C)   Case-based computer systems are vastly superior to those computer systems based upon the doctrinal nature of the law.

(D)   Computers applying artificial intelligence techniques show promise for revolutionizing the process of legal interpretation in the relatively near future.

(E)   Using computers can expedite legal research, facilitate the matching of a particular case to a specific legal principle, and even provide insights into possible flaws involving legal reasoning.

22. The logical relationship of lines 8-13 of the passage to lines 23-25 and 49-53 of the passage is most accurately described as

(A)   a general assertion supported by two specific observations

(B)   a general assertion followed by two arguments, one of which supports and one of which refutes the general assertion

(C)   a general assertion that entails two more specific assertions

(D)   a theoretical assumption refuted by two specific observations

(E)   a specific observation that suggests two incompatible generalizations

23. In the passage as a whole, the author is primarily concerned with

(A)   arguing that computers can fundamentally change how the processes of legal interpretation and reasoning are conducted in the future

(B)   indicating that the law has subtle nuances that are not readily dealt with by computerized legal reasoning programs

(C)   demonstrating that computers are approaching the point where they can apply legal precedents to current cases

(D)   suggesting that, because the law is made by humans, computer programmers must also apply their human intuition when designing legal reasoning systems

(E)   defending the use of computers as essential and indispensable components of the modem legal profession

R

24. The passage suggests that the author would be most likely to agree with which one of the following statements about computerized automated legal reasoning systems?

(A) These systems have met the original expectations of computer specialists but have fallen short of the needs of legal practitioners.

(B) Progress in research on these systems has been hindered, more because not enough legal documents are accessible by computer than because theoretical problems remain unsolved.

(C) These systems will most likely be used as legal research tools rather than as aids in legal analysis.

(D) Rule systems will likely replace case-based systems over time.

(E) Developing adequate legal reasoning systems would require research breakthroughs by computer specialists.

25. It can be most reasonably inferred from the passage's discussion of requirements for developing effective automated legal reasoning systems that the author would agree with which one of the following statements?

(A) Focusing on the doctrinal nature of law is the fundamental error made by developers of automated legal systems.

(B) Contemporary computers do not have the required memory capability to store enough data to be effective legal reasoning systems.

(C) Questions of interpretation in rule-based legal reasoning systems must be settled by programming more legal rules into the systems.

(D) Legal statutes and reasoning may involve innovative applications that cannot be modeled by a fixed set of rules, cases, or criteria.

(E) As professionals continue to use computers in the sphere of law they will develop the competence to use legal reasoning systems effectively.

26. Based on the passage, which one of the following can be most reasonably inferred concerning case-based reasoners?

(A) The major problem in the development of these systems is how to store enough cases in their knowledge bases.

(B) These systems are more useful than rule systems because case-based reasoners are based on a simpler view of legal reasoning.

(C) Adding specific criteria for similarity among cases to existing systems would not overcome an important shortcoming of these systems.

(D) These systems can independently provide expert advice about legal rights and duties in a wide range of cases.

(E) These systems are being designed to attain a much more ambitious goal than had been set for rule systems.

27. Which one of the following is mentioned in the passage as an important characteristic of many statutes that frustrates the application of computerized legal reasoning systems?

(A) complexity of syntax
(B) unavailability of relevant precedents
(C) intentional vagueness and adaptability
(D) overly narrow intent
(E) incompatibility with previous statutes

28. The examples of situations that are open to differing interpretations (lines 25-30) function in the passage to

(A) substantiate the usefulness of computers in the sphere of law

(B) illustrate a vulnerability of rule systems in computerized legal reasoning

(C) isolate issues that computer systems are in principle incapable of handling

(D) explain how legal rules have been adapted to novel situations

(E) question the value of reasoning from precedents in interpreting legal rules

The survival of nerve cells, as well as their performance of some specialized functions, is regulated by chemicals known as neurotrophic factors, which are produced in the bodies of animals,
(5) including humans. Rita Levi-Montalcini's discovery in the 1950s of the first of these agents, a hormonelike substance now known as NGF, was a crucial development in the history of biochemistry, which led to Levi-Montalcini sharing the Nobel Prize
(10) for medicine in 1986.

In the mid-1940s, Levi-Montalcini had begun by hypothesizing that many of the immature nerve cells produced in the development of an organism are normally programmed to die. In order to confirm this
(15) theory, she conducted research that in 1949 found that, when embryos are in the process of forming their nervous systems, they produce many more nerve cells than are finally required, the number that survives eventually adjusting itself to the volume of
(20) tissue to be supplied with nerves. A further phase of the experimentation, which led to Levi-Montalcini's identification of the substance that controls this process, began with her observation that the development of nerves in chick embryos could be
(25) stimulated by implanting a certain variety of mouse tumor in the embryos. She theorized that a chemical produced by the tumors was responsible for the observed nerve growth. To investigate this hypothesis, she used the then new technique of tissue culture, by
(30) which specific types of body cells can be made to grow outside the organism from which they are derived. Within twenty-four hours, her tissue cultures of chick embryo extracts developed dense halos of nerve tissue near the places in the culture where she
(35) had added the mouse tumor. Further research identified a specific substance contributed by the mouse tumors that was responsible for the effects Levi-Montalcini had observed: a protein that she named "nerve growth factor" (NGF).
(40) NGF was the first of many cell-growth factors to be found in the bodies of animals. Through Levi-Montalcini's work and other subsequent research, it has been determined that this substance is present in many tissues and biological fluids, and that it is
(45) especially concentrated in some organs. In developing organisms, nerve cells apparently receive this growth factor locally from the cells of muscles or other organs to which they will form connections for transmission of nerve impulses, and sometimes from
(50) supporting cells intermingled with the nerve tissue. NGF seems to play two roles, serving initially to direct the developing nerve processes toward the correct, specific "target" cells with which they must connect, and later being necessary for the continued
(55) survival of those nerve cells. During some periods of their development, the types of nerve cells that are affected by NGF—primarily cells outside the brain and spinal cord—die if the factor is not present or if they encounter anti-NGF antibodies.

15. Which one of the following most accurately expresses the main point of the passage?

(A) Levi-Montalcini's discovery of neurotrophic factors as a result of research carried out in the 1940s was a major contribution to our understanding of the role of naturally occurring chemicals, especially NGF, in the development of chick embryos.

(B) Levi-Montalcini's discovery of NGF, a neurotrophic factor that stimulates the development of some types of nerve tissue and whose presence or absence in surrounding cells helps determine whether particular nerve cells will survive, was a pivotal development in biochemistry.

(C) NGF, which is necessary for the survival and proper functioning of nerve cells, was discovered by Levi-Montalcini in a series of experiments using the technique of tissue culture, which she devised in the 1940s.

(D) Partly as a result of Levi-Montalcini's research, it has been found that NGF and other neurotrophic factors are produced only by tissues to which nerves are already connected and that the presence of these factors is necessary for the health and proper functioning of nervous systems.

(E) NGF, a chemical that was discovered by Levi-Montalcini, directs the growth of nerve cells toward the cells with which they must connect and ensures the survival of those nerve cells throughout the life of the organism except when the organism produces anti-NGF antibodies.

16. Based on the passage, the author would be most likely to believe that Levi-Montalcini's discovery of NGF is noteworthy primarily because it

(A) paved the way for more specific knowledge of the processes governing the development of the nervous system

(B) demonstrated that a then new laboratory technique could yield important and unanticipated experimental results

(C) confirmed the hypothesis that many of a developing organism's immature nerve cells are normally programmed to die

(D) indicated that this substance stimulates observable biochemical reactions in the tissues of different species

(E) identified a specific substance, produced by mouse tumors, that can be used to stimulate nerve cell growth

17. The primary function of the third paragraph of the passage in relation to the second paragraph is to

(A) indicate that conclusions referred to in the second paragraph, though essentially correct, require further verification

(B) indicate that conclusions referred to in the second paragraph have been undermined by subsequently obtained evidence

(C) indicate ways in which conclusions referred to in the second paragraph have been further corroborated and refined

(D) describe subsequent discoveries of substances analogous to the substance discussed in the second paragraph

(E) indicate that experimental procedures discussed in the second paragraph have been supplanted by more precise techniques described in the third paragraph

18. Information in the passage most strongly supports which one of the following?

(A) Nerve cells in excess of those that are needed by the organism in which they develop eventually produce anti-NGF antibodies to suppress the effects of NGF.

(B) Nerve cells that grow in the absence of NGF are less numerous than, but qualitatively identical to, those that grow in the presence of NGF.

(C) Few of the nerve cells that connect with target cells toward which NGF directs them are needed by the organism in which they develop.

(D) Some of the nerve cells that grow in the presence of NGF are eventually converted to other types of living tissue by neurotrophic factors.

(E) Some of the nerve cells that grow in an embryo do not connect with any particular target cells.

19. The passage describes a specific experiment that tested which one of the following hypotheses?

(A) A certain kind of mouse tumor produces a chemical that stimulates the growth of nerve cells.

(B) Developing embryos initially grow many more nerve cells than they will eventually require.

(C) In addition to NGF, there are several other important neurotrophic factors regulating cell survival and function.

(D) Certain organs contain NGF in concentrations much higher than in the surrounding tissue.

(E) Certain nerve cells are supplied with NGF by the muscle cells to which they are connected.

20. Which one of the following is most strongly supported by the information in the passage?

(A) Some of the effects that the author describes as occurring in Levi-Montalcini's culture of chick embryo extract were due to neurotrophic factors other than NGF.

(B) Although NGF was the first neurotrophic factor to be identified, some other such factors are now more thoroughly understood.

(C) In her research in the 1940s and 1950s, Levi-Montalcini identified other neurotrophic factors in addition to NGF.

(D) Some neurotrophic factors other than NGF perform functions that are not specifically identified in the passage.

(E) The effects of NGF that Levi-Montalcini noted in her chick embryo experiment are also caused by other neurotrophic factors not discussed in the passage.

R

Reading Comprehension Passage ReChallenge
Set #3 Answer Key

Passage #1: October 2004 Questions 8-14 *8. C 9. C 10. E 11. E 12. D 13. B 14. B*

Explanations begin on page 358

Passage #2: October 2008 Questions 7-13 *7. A 8. E 9. B 10. E 11. A 12. C 13. A*

Explanations begin on page 310

Passage #3: December 2006 Questions 21-28 *21. A 22. A 23. B 24. E 25. D 26. C 27. C 28. B*

Explanations begin on page 385

Passage #4: October 2004 Questions 15-20 *15. B 16. A 17. C 18. E 19. A 20. D*

Explanations begin on page 415

R

Appendix

Consolidated Answer Key

The *PowerScore LSAT Reading Comprehension Bible* contains many passages that have appeared on previously released LSATs, and the answers to every LSAT question used in this book are found in the passage explanations. The consolidated answer key in this section contains two parts: the first part provides a quick chapter-by-chapter answer key for students who need to find the answers quickly, and the second part provides a comprehensive listing of the source of all the complete LSAT passages used in this book. The second part is especially helpful for students who are taking practice LSATs and want to know ahead of time which passages we have used in this book. They can then skip those passages ahead of taking the test, or avoid taking certain tests until later.

Chapter-by-Chapter Answer Key

The chapter-by-chapter answer key lists every passage in this book in the presented order and provides the correct answer for each question used from each passage. You can use this answer key as a quick reference when you are solving problems. Each problem is explained in more detail in the text of the chapter.

Chapter Three: What to Read For—VIEWSTAMP

Page 96, PrepTest 44, October 2004, Passage #1, Question 5 (Passage Structure)
5. C

Page 117, A Sample Passage Analyzed: PrepTest 46, June 2005 Passage #1, Question 1
1. B

Chapter Seven: Putting It All Together

Page 272, Practice Passage I: PrepTest 49, June 2006 Passage #1, Questions 1-6
1. A 2. D 3. E 4. B 5. C 6. E

Page 274, Practice Passage II: PrepTest 48, December 2005 Passage #1, Questions 1-5
1. A 2. D 3. E 4. B 5. C

Chapter Eight: Comparative Reading Passages

Page 302, Passage Analysis: PrepTest 53, December 2007 Passage #3, Questions 15-19
15. A 16. C 17. D 18. C 19. D

Chapter-by-Chapter Answer Key

Page 312, Practice Passage I: PrepTest 55, October 2008 Passage #2, Questions 7-13
    7. A 8. E 9. B 10. E 11. A 12. C 13. A

Page 314, Practice Passage II: PrepTest 52, September 2007 Passage #2, Questions 7-12
    7. D 8. B 9. A 10. C 11. B 12. D

Chapter Nine: Common Passage Themes

Page 335, Affirming Underrepresented Groups Passage: PrepTest 20, October 1996 Passage #1
    4. E

Page 340, Undermining Overrepresented Groups Passage: PrepTest 39, December 2002 Passage #2, Question 9
    9. D

Page 345, Mixed Group Passage: PrepTest 21, December 1996 Passage #4, Question 24
    24. B

Page 348, Diversity Practice Passage I: PrepTest 53, December 2007 Passage #1, Questions 1-6
    1. A 2. C 3. D 4. C 5. D 6. D

Page 350, Diversity Practice Passage II: PrepTest 44, October 2004 Passage #2, Questions 8-14
    8. C 9. C 10. E 11. E 12. D 13. B 14. B

Page 371, Law-Related Passage Analysis: PrepTest 47, October 2005 Passage #3, Question 17
    17. C

Page 374, Law-Related Practice Passage I: PrepTest 50, September 2006 Passage #2, Questions 6-13
    6. A 7. D 8. A 9. E 10. A 11. B 12. D 13. E

Page 376, Law-Related Practice Passage II: PrepTest 51, December 2006 Passage #4, Questions 21-28
    21. A 22. A 23. B 24. E 25. D 26. C 27. C 28. B

Page 396, Science Passage Analysis: PrepTest 53, December 2007 Passage #4, Questions 20-27
    20. C 21. D 22. E 23. A 24. C 25. D 26. E 27. A

Page 406, Science Practice Passage I: PrepTest 46, June 2005 Passage #3, Questions 16-21
    16. A 17. D 18. C 19. D 20. B 21. E

Page 408, Science Practice Passage II: PrepTest 44, October 2004 Passage #3, Questions 15-20
    15. B 16. A 17. C 18. E 19. A 20. D

Test-by-Test Passage Use Tracker

This section contains a reverse lookup that cross references each passage according to the source LSAT. The tests are listed in order of the PrepTest number (if any). The date of administration is also listed to make the process easier. If a test is not listed, then no questions from that exam were used in this book.

Passages listed under each test begin by listing the *Reading Comprehension Bible* chapter the passage appears in, the page number, the passage date, and then the question numbers.

For information on obtaining the publications that contain the LSATs listed below, please visit the *PowerScore Free LSAT Help area* at powerscore.com/lsat/help.

PrepTest 20—October 1996 LSAT

Chapter 9, Page 334, October 1996, Passage #1, Question 4 (Affirming Underrepresented Groups)

PrepTest 21—December 1996 LSAT

Chapter 9, Page 345, December 1996, Passage #4, Question 24 (Mixed Group Passages)

PrepTest 39—December 2002 LSAT

Chapter 9, Page 340, December 2002, Passage #2, Question 9 (Undermining Overrepresented Groups)

PrepTest 44—October 2004 LSAT

Chapter 3, Page 96, October 2004, Passage #1, Question 5 (Passage Structure)
Chapter 9, Page 350, October 2004, Passage #2, Questions 8-14 (Diversity Practice Passage II)
Chapter 9, Page 408, October 2004, Passage #3, Questions 15-20 (Science Practice Passage II)

PrepTest 46—June 2005 LSAT

Chapter 3, Page 117, June 2005, Passage #1, Question 1 (A Sample Passage Analyzed)
Chapter 9, Page 406, June 2005, Passage #3, Questions 16-21 (Science Practice Passage I)

PrepTest 47—October 2005 LSAT

Chapter 9, Page 371, October 2005, Passage #3, Question 17 (Law-Related Passage Analysis)

PrepTest 48—December 2005 LSAT

Chapter 7, Page 274, December 2005, Passage #1, Questions 1-5 (Practice Passage II)

Test-by-Test Passage Use Tracker

PrepTest 49—June 2006 LSAT

Chapter 7, Page 272, June 2006, Passage #1, Questions 1-6 (Practice Passage I)

PrepTest 50—September 2006 LSAT

Chapter 9, Page 374, September 2006, Passage #2, Questions 6-13 (Law-Related Practice Passage I)

PrepTest 51—December 2006 LSAT

Chapter 9, Page 376, December 2006, Passage #4, Questions 21-28 (Law-Related Practice Passage II)

PrepTest 52—September 2007 LSAT

Chapter 8, Page 314, September 2007, Passage #2, Questions 7-12 (Practice Passage II)

PrepTest 53—December 2007 LSAT

Chapter 9, Page 348, December 2007, Passage #1, Questions 1-6 (Diversity Practice Passage I)
Chapter 8, Page 302, December 2007, Passage #3, Questions 15-19 (Passage Analysis)
Chapter 9, Page 396, December 2007, Passage #4, Questions 20-27 (Science Passage Analysis)

PrepTest 55—October 2008 LSAT

Chapter 8, Page 312, October 2008, Passage #2, Questions 7-13 (Practice Passage I)